The Dark Web:

Breakthroughs in Research and Practice

Information Resources Management Association
USA

Published in the United States of America by
IGI Global
Information Science Reference (an imprint of IGI Global)
701 E. Chocolate Avenue
Hershey PA, USA 17033
Tel: 717-533-8845
Fax: 717-533-8661
E-mail: cust@igi-global.com
Web site: http://www.igi-global.com

Library of Congress Cataloging-in-Publication Data

Names: Information Resources Management Association, editor.
Title: The dark web: breakthroughs in research and practice / Information
  Resources Management Association, editor.
Description: Hershey, PA : Information Science Reference, [2018]
Identifiers: LCCN 2017015184| ISBN 9781522531630 (hardcover) | ISBN
  9781522531647 (ebook)
Subjects: LCSH: Computer crimes. | Internet. | World Wide Web.
Classification: LCC HV6773 .D37 2018 | DDC 364.16/8--dc23 LC record available at https://lccn.loc.gov/2017015184

British Cataloguing in Publication Data
A Cataloguing in Publication record for this book is available from the British Library.

All work contributed to this book is new, previously-unpublished material. The views expressed in this book are those of the authors, but not necessarily of the publisher.

For electronic access to this publication, please contact: eresources@igi-global.com.

List of Contributors

Álvarez, Víctor Manuel Prieto / *University of A Coruña, Spain* 84

Antunes, Adelaide Maria de Souza / *National Institute of Industrial Property (INPI), Brazil &*
   Federal University of Rio de Janeiro (UFRJ), Brazil 138

Bhatia, Komal Kumar / *YMCA University of Science & Technology, India* 65,319

Cambre, Maria-Carolina / *King's University College at Western University Ontario, Canada* 290

Díaz, Manuel Álvarez / *University of A Coruña, Spain* 84

El Azab, Ahmed / *Institute of Statistical Studies and Research, Egypt* 227

El-Aziz, Abd / *Institute of Statistical Studies and Research, Egypt* 227

Flor, Alexander G. / *University of the Philippines (Open University), Philippines* 37

Gonzalez-Flor, Benjamina / *University of the Philippines – Los Baños, Philippines* 37

Gupta, Sonali / *YMCA University of Science & Technology, India* 65

Hai-Jew, Shalin / *Kansas State University, USA* 255

Holland, James / *University of Kent, UK* 1

James, Mark / *University of Kent, UK* 1

Kaczmarek, Tomasz / *Poznań University of Economics, Poland* 175

Kalpana, R. / *Pondicherry Engineering College, India* 199

Lima de Magalhães, Jorge / *Ministry of Health, Brazil & Aix-Marseille Université, France* 138

Mahmood, Mahmood A. / *Institute of Statistical Studies and Research, Egypt* 227

Mendes, Flavia Maria Lins / *Federal University of Rio de Janeiro, Brazil* 138

Pina, Afroditi / *University of Kent, UK* 1

Quoniam, Luc / *Aix-Marseille Université, France* 138

Ranjan, Sudhakar / *Apeejay Stya University, India* 319

Richet, Jean-Loup / *University of Nantes, France* 51

Schumacher, Suzanne de Oliveira Rodrigues / *Federal University of Rio de Janeiro, Brazil* 138

Seijo, Fidel Cacheda / *University of A Coruña, Spain* 84

Sharma, A. K. / *YMCA University of Science and Technology, Faridabad, India* 114,334,359

Sharma, Dilip Kumar / *G.L.A. Institute of Technology and Management, Mathura,*
   India 114,334,359

Stacey, Emily / *Swansea University, UK* 18

Umamageswari, B. / *New Prince Shri Bhavani College of Engineering and Technology, India* 199

Węckowski, Dawid Grzegorz / *Poznań University of Economics, Poland* 175

Table of Contents

Preface.. viii

Section 1
Cyber Crime and Security

Chapter 1
The Malevolent Side of Revenge Porn Proclivity: Dark Personality Traits and Sexist Ideology........... 1
Afroditi Pina, University of Kent, UK
James Holland, University of Kent, UK
Mark James, University of Kent, UK

Chapter 2
Contemporary Terror on the Net... 18
Emily Stacey, Swansea University, UK

Chapter 3
Dysfunctional Digital Demeanors: Tales From (and Policy Implications of) eLearning's
Dark Side 37
Alexander G. Flor, University of the Philippines (Open University), Philippines
Benjamina Gonzalez-Flor, University of the Philippines – Los Baños, Philippines

Chapter 4
How to Become a Cybercriminal? An Explanation of Cybercrime Diffusion 51
Jean-Loup Richet, University of Nantes, France

Section 2
Data Mining and Analysis

Chapter 5
Optimal Query Generation for Hidden Web Extraction Through Response Analysis 65
Sonali Gupta, YMCA University of Science & Technology, India
Komal Kumar Bhatia, YMCA University of Science & Technology, India

Chapter 6
The Evolution of the (Hidden) Web and Its Hidden Data 84
    Manuel Álvarez Díaz, University of A Coruña, Spain
    Víctor Manuel Prieto Álvarez, University of A Coruña, Spain
    Fidel Cacheda Seijo, University of A Coruña, Spain

Chapter 7
Deep Web Information Retrieval Process: A Technical Survey 114
    Dilip Kumar Sharma, G.L.A. Institute of Technology and Management, Mathura, India
    A. K. Sharma, YMCA University of Science and Technology, Faridabad, India

Chapter 8
The Contribution of Information Science Through Intellectual Property to Innovation in the
Brazilian Health Sector 138
    Adelaide Maria de Souza Antunes, National Institute of Industrial Property (INPI), Brazil &
        Federal University of Rio de Janeiro (UFRJ), Brazil
    Flavia Maria Lins Mendes, Federal University of Rio de Janeiro, Brazil
    Suzanne de Oliveira Rodrigues Schumacher, Federal University of Rio de Janeiro, Brazil
    Luc Quoniam, Aix-Marseille Université, France
    Jorge Lima de Magalhães, Ministry of Health, Brazil & Aix-Marseille Université, France

Chapter 9
Harvesting Deep Web Data Through Produser Involvement 175
    Tomasz Kaczmarek, Poznań University of Economics, Poland
    Dawid Grzegorz Węckowski, Poznań University of Economics, Poland

Chapter 10
Web Harvesting: Web Data Extraction Techniques for Deep Web Pages 199
    B. Umamageswari, New Prince Shri Bhavani College of Engineering and Technology, India
    R. Kalpana, Pondicherry Engineering College, India

Chapter 11
Effectiveness of Web Usage Mining Techniques in Business Application 227
    Ahmed El Azab, Institute of Statistical Studies and Research, Egypt
    Mahmood A. Mahmood, Institute of Statistical Studies and Research, Egypt
    Abd El-Aziz, Institute of Statistical Studies and Research, Egypt

Section 3
Online Identity

Chapter 12
In Plaintext: Electronic Profiling in Public Online Spaces 255
    Shalin Hai-Jew, Kansas State University, USA

Chapter 13
Becoming Anonymous: A Politics of Masking 290
Maria-Carolina Cambre, King's University College at Western University Ontario, Canada

Section 4
Web Crawling

Chapter 14
Design of a Least Cost (LC) Vertical Search Engine Based on Domain Specific Hidden Web
Crawler 319
Sudhakar Ranjan, Apeejay Stya University, India
Komal Kumar Bhatia, YMCA University of Science & Technology, India

Chapter 15
A Novel Architecture for Deep Web Crawler 334
Dilip Kumar Sharma, Shobhit University, India
A. K. Sharma, YMCA University of Science and Technology, India

Chapter 16
Search Engine: A Backbone for Information Extraction in ICT Scenario 359
Dilip Kumar Sharma, Shobhit University, India
A. K. Sharma, YMCA University of Science and Technology, India

Index 375

Preface

The constantly changing landscape surrounding the Dark Web makes it challenging for experts and practitioners to stay informed of the field's most up-to-date research. That is why IGI Global is pleased to offer this one-volume comprehensive reference collection that will empower students, researchers, and academicians with a strong understanding of these critical issues by providing both broad and detailed perspectives on cutting-edge theories and developments. This compilation is designed to act as a single reference source on conceptual, methodological, and technical aspects, as well as to provide insight into emerging trends and future opportunities within the discipline.

The Dark Web: Breakthroughs in Research and Practice is organized into four sections that provide comprehensive coverage of important topics. The sections are:

1. Cyber Crime and Security
2. Data Mining and Analysis
3. Online Identity
4. Web Crawling

The following paragraphs provide a summary of what to expect from this invaluable reference source:

Section 1, "Cyber Crime and Security," opens this extensive reference source by highlighting the latest developments in criminal activity in the cyber sphere. Through perspectives on online terrorism, cyberbullying, and policy implementation, this section demonstrates emerging trends in cybercrime. The presented research facilitates a better understanding of criminal activity in digital settings.

Section 2, "Data Mining and Analysis," includes chapters on strategies for extracting digital data and information. Including discussions on the Hidden Web, information retrieval, and the Deep Web, this section presents research on emerging trends in harvesting digital information. This inclusive information assists in advancing current practices in data mining and analysis techniques.

Section 3, "Online Identity," presents coverage on the creation and protection of digital identities in modern society. Through innovative discussions on electronic profiling, anonymity, and online communities, this section highlights the changing landscape of identity in digital environments. These inclusive perspectives contribute to the available knowledge on virtual settings and personal identification.

Section 4, "Web Crawling," discusses coverage and research perspectives on Internet browsers. Through analyses on search engines, information extraction, and Deep Web crawling, this section contains pivotal information on the latest developments in web crawlers. The presented research facilitates a comprehensive understanding of how emerging innovations are optimizing search engine architectures.

Although the primary organization of the contents in this work is based on its four sections, offering a progression of coverage of the important concepts, methodologies, technologies, applications, social issues, and emerging trends, the reader can also identify specific contents by utilizing the extensive indexing system listed at the end.

As a comprehensive collection of research on the latest findings related to *The Dark Web: Breakthroughs in Research and Practice,* this publication provides researchers, practitioners, and all audiences with a complete understanding of the development of applications and concepts surrounding these critical issues.

Section 1
Cyber Crime and Security

Chapter 1
The Malevolent Side of Revenge Porn Proclivity:
Dark Personality Traits and Sexist Ideology

Afroditi Pina
University of Kent, UK

James Holland
University of Kent, UK

Mark James
University of Kent, UK

ABSTRACT

This paper presents a novel study, exploring a form of technology facilitated sexual violence (TFSV) known as revenge porn. Despite its emerging prevalence, little is known about the characteristics of revenge porn perpetrators. In the current study, a revenge porn proclivity scale was devised to examine participants' behavioural propensity to engage in revenge porn. One hundred adults, aged 18-54, were recruited online from a community sample. The correlational relationship between revenge porn proclivity and the self-reported endorsement of the Dark Triad, sadism, and ambivalent sexism was examined. Additional proclivity subscales of revenge porn enjoyment and revenge porn approval were also created. The study's main findings revealed a positive correlation between a greater behavioural propensity to engage in revenge porn and higher levels of the Dark Triad and ambivalent sexism. Moreover, endorsement of psychopathy was found to be the only Dark Triad trait that independently predicted revenge porn proclivity. The results suggest that perpetrators of revenge porn may have distinct personality profiles. Limitations and directions for future research are discussed.

DOI: 10.4018/978-1-5225-3163-0.ch001

INTRODUCTION

Advancements in modern technology have enabled public access to a breadth of knowledge, facilitated by widespread communication that can reach both national and international audiences (Taylor, Fritsch, & Liederbach, 2015). However, the integration of communication technologies in our daily lives and intimate relationships (Klettke, Hallford, & Mellor, 2014) also provides additional opportunities for sexual exploitation and criminal victimization (Roberts, 2008). This is an emerging phenomenon of societal concern that has sparked research interest with a focus on the ethical dimension of technological advancement. The multidisciplinary domain of Technoethics is concerned with the study of moral, legal and social issues involving technology (Luppicini & Adell, 2008). One of these social and legal phenomena involving technology is that of 'revenge porn,' otherwise known as non-consensual pornography, currently sparking increasing media interest (BBC, 2016; Guardian, 2015). Whilst there exists a wealth of literature on perpetrators of traditional acts of sexual violence (Greathouse, Saunders, Matthews, Keller, & Miller, 2015), little is known of the characteristics of those who endorse and display revenge porn behaviour. An in-depth understanding of the psychological profiles of these individuals could benefit preventative and rehabilitative methods for reducing the prevalence of this crime (Gerhart, Ronan, Russ, & Seymour, 2013; Voller & Long, 2010). This paper examines the relationship between aversive personality traits and the behavioural propensity to engage in revenge porn behaviours.

THE GROWING PROBLEM OF REVENGE PORN: ETHICAL AND LEGAL ISSUES

Revenge porn is the act of sharing intimate, sexually graphic images and/or videos of another person onto public online platforms (e.g. Facebook) without their consent (Burris, 2014; Citron & Franks, 2014). These images are often either produced non-consensually (e.g. by means of surveillance or hacking) or consensually (e.g. by the victim in the context of either a private relationship or courtship) (Citron & Franks, 2014; Stroud & Henson, 2016). This is largely motivated by the malicious intent to harm and humiliate the victim, who is often the perpetrator's previous romantic partner (Burris, 2014; Citron & Franks, 2014). Not all acts are perpetrated for revenge, and can instead be committed as a means of blackmail, coercion, or for the enjoyment of causing torment upon others (Henry & Powell, 2016). For the purposes of this paper we will name all these acts revenge porn due to the intent behind the instigation of such events. However, the term non-consensual pornography is also frequently used in the literature to encompass all different facets of these behaviours (Citron & Franks, 2014).

Although revenge porn can affect individuals of all ages, sexuality and gender, it is predominantly perpetrated against, and severely negatively affects women (Citron & Franks, 2014; Poole, 2015; Salter & Crofts, 2015). Researchers have acknowledged that revenge porn reflects larger issues over women's social and interpersonal status, and can be seen as a form of hostility towards female autonomy (Citron & Franks, 2014; Poole, 2015) and policing women's sexuality, with large online communities (of males in their majority) enforcing the "bounds of appropriate femininity" by means of ridicule and harassment (Salter & Crofts, 2015, p.1). As Noah Berlatsky states: "the web has made it possible to crowdsource misogyny [...] and stalking" (2013, www.digitalethics.org).

While most people would consider sharing intimate images of themselves or other people online, without their consent, unethical, there are certain processes at play that make the perpetrators rationalize the act. These processes make the act seem more acceptable, and in some cases justified; such as the culpability of the victim in creating the images in the first place, or the victim's alleged infidelity against the perpetrator (Poole, 2015). Although these issues can, and do, affect men as well, it is female infidelity and display of sexuality that is punished and regulated to such a cruel degree (Poole, 2015).

The permanence and dissemination speed afforded by the internet can cause victims of revenge porn to endure great distress. This is often due to the difficultly in removing material published online, and also in preventing its re-distribution, due to legislation protecting free speech (Berlatsky, 2013; Dick et al., 2014). Furthermore, there are lucrative websites devoted to publishing revenge porn and displaying the victim's personal information linking them to their social media accounts (Stroud, 2014), profiting from victims' distress (Salter & Crofts, 2015). While these sites are protected under the Federal Communications Decency Act (1996; Berlatsky, 2013; Poole, 2015), where they cannot be prosecuted or held accountable for user-submitted content, the onus lies with the victim to sue websites requesting the names of the users in order to bring about lawsuits against them. Victims can seek (and have successfully sought) justice through tort law, suing for intentional infliction of emotional suffering (Citron & Franks, 2014). However, it is important to note that not all victims have the knowledge or financial resources to instigate civil suits against their perpetrators, and often, the confusion surrounding online harassment laws and lack of anonymity can act as a deterrent for both litigators and victims (Citron & Franks, 2014).

This severe lack of victim anonymity enables further harassment from others, both offline and online (Henry & Powell, 2015a). It is unsurprising that victims of revenge porn experience an array of negative effects, including the dissolution of relationships, problems with employment, and decreased self-esteem (Henry & Powell, 2015a). Some cases of revenge porn have even resulted in the victim committing suicide (Guardian, 2012; Independent, 2014).

Revenge porn has recently been acknowledged in legislation passed in England and Wales. As of April 2015, courts can prosecute individuals who non-consensually share sexual images or videos of another person (Criminal Justice and Courts Bill, 2015). Furthermore, those found guilty can be imprisoned for up to two years (Ministry of Justice, 2015). Within the first eight months since its criminalisation, police in England and Wales received 1,160 reports of revenge porn (BBC, 2016). Of additional concern is that a large proportion (61%) of these reports were not followed up due to victims no longer wanting to pursue an investigation (BBC, 2016). The lack of anonymity afforded to victims of revenge porn is seen as one of the reasons for these high attrition rates (Citron & Franks, 2014; Thom, 2015).

The aforementioned legal issues surrounding the legislation of the phenomenon, when linked with the ethical issues interwoven in this phenomenon, highlight the importance of further exploring this concerning societal issue to provide a more informed understanding of revenge porn and the motives of its perpetrators.

REVENGE PORN AS A FORM OF TECHNOLOGY FACILITATED SEXUAL VIOLENCE

Whilst there is an absence of research devoted to revenge porn perpetration, there are aspects of revenge porn behaviour that can be found in research examining other forms of Technology Facilitated Sexual Violence (TFSV; Henry & Powell, 2016). These include cyber-dating abuse (Henry & Powell, 2015b; Martinez-Pecino & Duran, 2016), cyber-harassment (Woodlock, 2016), and the non-consensual sharing of sexual texts (Morelli, Bianchi, Baiocco, Pezzuti, & Chirumbolo, 2016). For example, sharing (or threatening to share) intimate images onto social media has been identified as a behaviour engaged in by perpetrators of cyber-dating abuse and harassment (Henry & Powell, 2015b; Woodlock, 2016).

Despite being in its infancy, research on TFSV has found support for the association between psychological characteristics and the perpetration of these acts. For example, Tang and Fox (2016) found that male participants who reported perpetrating sexual harassment online (e.g. issuing threats of rape) endorsed hostile sexism more than non-harassing participants. Furthermore, sexist beliefs have also been associated with greater levels of cyber-dating abuse, such as spreading false rumours about a partner online and sharing sexual texts received from a partner (Martinez-Pecino & Duran, 2016; Morelli et al., 2016). In addition, research has demonstrated a relationship between aversive personality traits and perpetrating forms of TFSV. For instance, endorsement of psychopathy, Machiavellianism, and narcissism have been associated with a greater propensity to sexually harass others (Zeigler-Hill, Besser, Morag, & Campbell, 2016), and greater enjoyment in doing so (Buckels, Trapnell, & Paulhus, 2014). Moreover, a higher endorsement of these traits has been found to predict a greater likelihood to commit 'romantic revenge' after experiencing infidelity (Brewer, Hunt, James, & Abell, 2015). This is a particularly pertinent finding considering that revenge porn is largely perpetrated as an act of revenge. Furthermore, traits of psychopathy, such as high levels of impulsivity and irresponsibility, have been found to predict cyber-bullying behaviours, such as spreading private images online of another person (Kokkinos, Antoniadou, & Markos, 2014). Lastly, perpetrating online harassment was reported as most enjoyable by participants endorsing greater levels of sadism (Buckels et al., 2014). In summary, these findings present support for the association between psychological characteristics and the behavioural propensity to perpetrate an array of TFSV related to revenge porn. It would, therefore, be a reasonable assumption that research should examine the influence of the aforementioned factors in relation to revenge porn as well.

Potential Factors Influencing Revenge Porn Proclivity

Sexist Beliefs

TFSV is largely considered a form of gendered violence. It is argued that females are more likely to be victimised and they will experience greater negative impact, due to gender expectations rooted in societal norms (Henry & Powell, 2016). Sexist ideologies held towards gender roles, behaviours, and relationships in society are deemed an important factor in sexual violence, especially towards women (Glick & Fiske, 1996, 2011). Furthermore, measures of sexist ideology, such as the Ambivalent Sexism Inventory (Glick & Fiske, 1996), have recently been used to demonstrate the relationship between sexism and the perpetration of online sexual violence (Martinez-Pecino & Duran, 2016; Morelli et al., 2016; Tang & Fox, 2016). Therefore, it appears necessary that research also examines the relationship between sexism and revenge porn proclivity.

The Dark Triad

The socially aversive traits of Machiavellianism, psychopathy, and narcissism are commonly studied in unison, and are referred to as the '*Dark Triad*' of personality (Paulhus & Williams, 2002). The Dark Triad traits have been comprehensively reviewed (Furnham, Richards, & Paulhus, 2013) and are characterised by high levels of callousness, egocentrism, low empathy, and a readiness to exploit others (Jones & Paulhus, 2011b, 2014). Despite their general overlap, the Dark Triad traits each have distinct properties. Psychopathy is most indicative of a severe lack of empathy for others and impulsivity, which may result in the abandonment of relationships with no concern for self-reputation (Hare & Neumann, 2008). Furthermore, psychopathic callousness is exercised with short-term action for immediate gratification (Jones & Paulhus, 2011a). This deficit in self-control is notably present in both criminal (Hare & Neumann, 2008) and non-criminal expressions of psychopathy (Hall & Benning, 2006). Both Machiavellianism and narcissism are also characterised by a callous affect which facilitates social manipulation, in addition to their unique factors (Jones & Paulhus, 2011b). Specific to Machiavellianism is a strategic orientation in which alliances may be built as part of ruthless manipulation (Jones & Paulhus, 2014). Instead, narcissists are identified by their self-perceived entitlement and grandiosity in which a driving motive behind callous behaviour is ego reinforcement (Bushman, Bonacci, van Dijk, & Baumeister, 2003). As stated previously, endorsement of the Dark Triad traits was found to predict a greater propensity to commit romantic revenge (Buckels et al., 2014), and greater enjoyment of tormenting others online (Brewer et al., 2015).

Sadistic Tendencies

Sadism is often found to predict the infliction of suffering upon others, and is commonly associated with psychopathy and Machiavellianism (Buckels, Jones, & Paulhus, 2013). A sadistic personality denotes a person who purposely incites physical, psychological, or sexual harm upon others to demean and humiliate them, whilst motivated by their desire for enjoyment and power assertion (O'Meara, Davies, & Hammond, 2011). However, O'Meara et al. (2011) acknowledged that this definition rests on a continuum upon which levels of sadism can range from that considered 'everyday sadism' to 'pathological'. Nevertheless, everyday sadism has recently been found to predict sexual violence (Russell & King, 2016) and the enjoyment of online trolling (Buckels et al., 2014). It is also recommended that everyday sadism is measured in conjunction with the Dark Triad (Paulhus, 2014).

THE CURRENT STUDY

Whilst progress has been made with regards to legislation and policy, the topic of revenge porn remains understudied. The current study is presented as the first to examine revenge porn proclivity and its association with particular psychological characteristics. Specifically, the objectives of this study were to: 1) assess the correlational relationship between the propensity to engage in revenge porn and the endorsement of the Dark Triad, sadistic tendencies, and ambivalent sexism; and 2) provide a preliminary understanding of this phenomenon to eventually aid and benefit prevention, treatment, educational, and research efforts. In light of the current literature, it was hypothesised that revenge porn proclivity would be significantly related to: 1) higher levels of the Dark Triad; 2) everyday sadism; and 3) a greater endorsement of ambivalent sexism.

METHOD

Participants

Participants were recruited through advertising the study on social media (e.g. Facebook). The total sample consisted of 100 participants, comprising of 16 males and 82 females (two undisclosed). Due to the sensitive nature of the study's content, all participants were required to be aged 18 years and over. Participant ages ranged from 18-54 years ($M = 25.81$, $SD = 7.11$) and the majority of participants were British (87%).

Measures

The Short Version of the Ambivalent Sexism Inventory (ASI)

The short version of the Ambivalent Sexism Inventory (ASI) is a 12-item scale devised by Glick and Whitehead (2010). It is a reconstruction of the original 22-item ASI (Glick & Fiske, 1996), consisting of the items found to have the greatest factor loadings onto hostile sexism (six items) and benevolent sexism (six items). The items are presented as a series of statements regarding relationships between men and woman in society (e.g. 'women seek to gain power by getting control over men'). Participants were required to rate their agreement with each statement using a 6-point Likert scale ranging from disagree strongly (0) to agree strongly (5). An overall score was calculated by averaging the sum of all responses given by a participant. A higher ASI score is indicative of a greater endorsement of sexism. Extensive assessment of the short version of the ASI revealed good psychometric properties consistent with the full-length scale (Rollero, Glick, & Tartaglia, 2014). In the current study, the Cronbach's alpha of reliability for the short-ASI was $\alpha = .70$.

The Short Dark Triad (SD3)

The Short Dark Triad scale (SD3; Jones & Paulhus, 2014) contains 27 items and was implemented as an assessment of Machiavellianism (e.g. 'make sure your plans benefit yourself, not others'; $\alpha = .77$), narcissism (e.g. 'people see me as a natural leader'; $\alpha = .67$), and subclinical psychopathy (e.g. 'people who mess with me always regret it'; $\alpha = .71$). Each subscale contains nine items to which participants rated their agreement to using a 5-point Likert scale, ranging from 1 (disagree strongly) to 5 (agree strongly). After relevant items were reverse coded, participants' average scores were computed for each subscale. Higher scores are representative of possessing greater levels of the trait. Extensive psychometric testing has been conducted on the utility of the SD3. Maples, Lamkin, and Miller (2014) found the SD3 to have adequate discriminant and criterion validity, as well as stronger convergent and incremental validity, than comparative measures available (e.g. The Dirty Dozen; Jonason & Webster, 2010).

Comprehensive Assessment of Sadistic Tendencies (CAST)

The Comprehensive Assessment of Sadistic Tendencies (CAST; Buckels & Paulhus, 2014) was used as a measure of everyday sadistic disposition to inflict harm upon others. The scale contains 18 items which measure three discrete types of sadistic tendencies: direct verbal sadism (e.g. 'I have purposely tricked someone and laughed when they looked foolish'; six items, $\alpha =.75$); direct physical sadism (e.g. 'I enjoy tormenting people', five items, $\alpha =.54$); and vicarious sadism (e.g. 'In video games, I like the realistic blood spurts', seven items, $\alpha =.76$). Filler items were also intermixed in an attempt to offset the negativity of the scale's items, as advised by Buckels and Paulhus (2014). Participants rated their agreement to these items using a 7-point Likert scale, with responses ranging from 1 (strongly disagree) to 7 (strongly agree). After relevant items were reverse scored, a composite variable of overall sadism was computed as an average of the three sadistic tendency scores. The overall CAST measure achieved adequate reliability ($\alpha =.77$).

The Revenge Porn Proclivity Scale

A proclivity scale[1] was created to assess the behavioural propensity to perpetrate an act of revenge porn. Proclivity scales have been effectively implemented among non-offender samples in research examining rape (Bohner et al., 1998; Bohner, Pina, Viki, & Siebler, 2010), sexual harassment (Zeigler-Hill et al., 2016), child molestation (Gannon & O'Connor, 2011), and animal abuse (Alleyne, Tilston, Parfitt, & Butcher, 2015; Parfitt & Alleyne, 2016). The use of these scales arguably provides an opportunity to detect offending behaviours among community samples that would otherwise remain unknown.

Consistent with other proclivity scales used within the literature (e.g. Alleyne, Gannon, Ó Ciardha, & Wood, 2014; Parfitt & Alleyne, 2016), participants in the current study were instructed to read scenarios in which they were the central character. In this study, participants read five scenarios, which each concluded with an intimate image of another person being shared onto the internet without consent. An example of the scenarios presented includes:

'You and your partner have been together for a few years, but recently they have become distant with you. You try to do things to make them happy but they respond with little interest. A few days later, your partner arranges to meet up with you. Here they explain that they no longer want to be in a relationship, saying that they no longer love you. Afterwards you begin to think about all the lost time and effort you have invested into this ended relationship. Whilst going through photos on your phone, you come across a naked photo that your now ex-partner sent to you during the relationship. You then decide to upload this photo onto the Internet[1].

After each scenario, participants responded to a proclivity question (i.e. 'In this situation, would you do the same?') using a 5-point Likert scale. Response options ranged from 1 (definitely would not do the same) to 5 (definitely would do the same). This was followed by additional questions which gauged emotions of excitement, control, blame, amusement, anger, and regret towards the behaviours committed in the scenario (e.g. 'In this situation, how amused would you be?'). Again, participants rated their agreement to these items using a 5-point Likert scale (e.g. 1 = not at all amused to 5 = very amused).

A participant's proclivity score was computed by summing their ratings across all five scenarios to the question 'In this situation, would you do the same?'. Reliability for this proclivity scale was $\alpha =.76$. In addition, two further subscales were devised as exploratory components. A sum score for the responses to the questions on excitement, control, and amusement was computed to create a scale of revenge porn enjoyment. Secondly, the responses to the questions on blame, anger, and regret (reverse scored) were summed to form a scale of revenge porn approval. These subscales of revenge porn enjoyment ($\alpha =.87$) and revenge porn approval ($\alpha =.80$) also yielded high internal consistency.

Procedure

The research was given ethical approval by the authors' university research ethics panel. The study was completed by participants online using Qualtrics and advertisements for the study were placed online, which included a link to the study's information sheet. Those who chose to participate were asked to provide their consent.

Participants were first asked to provide basic demographic questions (e.g. gender and nationality). Following this, they were presented with each questionnaire measure to complete, in the order of: the ASI,; the CAST; the SD3; and lastly the series of five revenge porn proclivity scenarios. Participants were later debriefed and thanked.

RESULTS

Preliminary Analysis

Firstly, positive skewness was attended to by computing square root transformations for CAST, psychopathy and revenge porn enjoyment, and a log10 transformation was computed for revenge porn proclivity. All other assumptions of normality were met.

Consistent with previous research utilising proclivity measures (Alleyne et al., 2015, Gannon & O'Connor, 2011), only participants who emphatically stated their disagreement with the questions were regarded as presenting no endorsement of revenge porn. In using this method, it was found that 28.6% of participants presented at least some proclivity to perpetrating revenge porn (i.e. scored > 5 on the proclivity scale overall). In addition, 87% of participants reported some endorsement of revenge porn enjoyment (i.e. scored >15 on the enjoyment subscale overall), and 99% of participants expressed at least some approval of the revenge porn being committed in the scenarios (i.e. scored >15 on the approval subscale overall).

Correlations

A Pearson's correlation analysis was computed including all variables to identify significant relationships (see Table 1). These findings were then used to inform the variables' input for a regression analysis, in order to further explain the prediction of revenge porn proclivity, approval and enjoyment.

As shown in Table 1, the CAST measure had a strong positive correlation with the SD3 measures of Machiavellianism, narcissism and psychopathy, yet no significant correlation with revenge porn proclivity, approval or enjoyment. Endorsement of everyday sadism was, therefore, not related to greater revenge porn proclivity and so this hypothesis (2) was not supported.

However, higher levels of the SD3 and ASI were found to have a positive relationship with greater revenge porn proclivity, supporting the hypotheses made (1&3). In addition, the ASI and Machiavellianism each yielded a positive correlation with revenge porn approval. Lastly, higher levels of narcissism and Machiavellianism (although Machiavellianism is marginal, $p = .06$) were both positively correlated with greater revenge porn enjoyment.

Table 1. Pearson's correlation analysis of all variables

	Correlations							
	1	**2**	**3**	**4**	**5**	**6**	**7**	**8**
1. ASI	–							
2. Machiavellianism	.43***	–						
3. Narcissism	.15	.32**	–					
4. Psychopathy	.09	.43***	.44***	–				
5. CAST	.14	.48***	.34***	.45***	–			
6. RP Proclivity	.21*	.32	.29*	.36***	.16	–		
7. RP Approval	.28**	.34**	.09	.13	.02	.48***	–	
8. RP Enjoyment	.18	.19	.26**	.16	.06	.43***	.51***	–

Note: *p<.05; **p<.01; ***p<.001

Predicting Proclivity

The SD3 personality traits were entered together in a multiple regression as predictors of revenge porn proclivity. These variables significantly explained 18% of the variance in revenge porn proclivity, $F(3,87) = 6.17$, $p = .001$, in support of the hypothesis (1). However, only psychopathy remained an independently significant predictor of greater revenge porn proclivity ($\beta = .23$, $p = 05$). In response to their strong correlation, ASI and Machiavellianism were also entered together as predictors of revenge porn proclivity. Together they explained 11% of the variance in revenge porn proclivity. Whilst significant, $F(2,88) = 5.34$, $p = .006$, only Machiavellianism remained an independently significant predictor ($\beta = .28$, $p = .01$).

As this was an exploratory analysis, ASI and Machiavellianism were input as predictors of revenge porn approval. Together they significantly explained 14% of the variance in revenge porn approval, $F(2,97) = 7.69$, $p = .001$, however, only Machiavellianism remained an independently significant predictor ($\beta = .27$, $p = .01$). In addition, Machiavellianism and narcissism were entered together as predictors of revenge porn enjoyment. Together they significantly explained 7.9% of the variance in revenge porn enjoyment, $F(2,97) = 4.17$, $p = .02$, although only narcissism remained an independently significant predictor of greater revenge porn enjoyment ($\beta = .22$, $p = .03$).

DISCUSSION

The current study is presented as the first to examine the behavioural propensity to engage in revenge porn and associated perpetrator characteristics. This study utilised a proclivity scale to measure a person's likelihood to perpetrate an act of revenge porn among an adult community sample. Additional subscales of revenge porn approval and enjoyment were subsequently devised and implemented with adequate reliability ($\alpha > .75$). Secondly, the study examined whether a relationship exists between the endorsement of aversive traits and a greater propensity to engage in revenge porn. Informed by prevalent characteristics found in the reviewed TFSV literature, the traits included were the Dark Triad, sadism, and ambivalent sexism.

Interpreting the Results

The magnitude of the revenge porn proclivity finding is difficult to comment on due to there being no previously published findings to compare to. Nevertheless, a greater likelihood to commit an act of revenge porn was found in some participants (28.6%). A more staggering finding was that a majority of participants presented endorsement of both revenge porn enjoyment (87%) and revenge porn approval (99%). This disparity suggests that whilst participants may be unlikely to commit an act of revenge porn themselves, they present an acceptance of this behaviour we now know is frequently occurring online. This can have significant implications, especially if one considers the facilitating role of online "bystanders" in the rapid dissemination of these materials.

It is plausible to suggest that revenge porn victims may be vulnerable to the same stereotypical myths held towards victims of rape (Bohner, Eyssel, Pina, Siebler & Viki, 2009), such that individuals are blamed and considered responsible for their victimisation occurring (Maier, 2014). It is known that these attitudes give leniency towards the perpetrator whilst attributing greater blame upon the victim (Bohner et al., 2009; Sleath & Bull, 2009). This finding is supported by recent research by Hatcher (2016) who found that rape myth acceptance and victim infidelity were predictive of revenge porn victim blaming. Moreover, endorsement of gender norms was found to be a mediator of revenge porn acceptance, whilst a bad relationship breakup was found to directly predict the acceptance of behaviours associated with revenge porn, such as spreading lies (Knieps & Hatcher, 2016).

The paper's second aim, and subsequent hypotheses, were partially supported by the current findings. Firstly, higher levels of ambivalent sexism, Machiavellianism, narcissism and psychopathy were all correlated with a greater likelihood to perpetrate revenge porn. However, surprisingly, sadistic tendencies yielded no significant relationship with revenge porn proclivity. This finding is not consistent with recent research that implicates sadism alongside the Dark Triad in the perpetration of sexual assault (Russell & King, 2016) and online sexual violence (Buckels et al., 2014). This inconsistency may be due to the current study using a sample that largely comprised of female participants. Buckels (2012) found that sadistic tendencies were endorsed more highly by males than females. The unanticipated skewness in the gender ratio in the current study could, therefore, explain the low levels of sadism observed. However, each of the Dark Triad traits were found to have a positive correlation with revenge porn proclivity, a finding consistent with literature on sexual harassment proclivity (Zeigler-Hill et al., 2016). This firstly suggests that the trait of interpersonal manipulation motivated by a general callous affect, which is characteristic of the Dark Triad (Jones & Paulhus, 2014), is important in the perpetration of revenge porn. Conversely, only psychopathy retained independent significance in the prediction of revenge porn proclivity. This suggests that the endorsement of psychopathic traits, such as a deficit in empathy (Hare & Neumann, 2008), are of greater influence upon revenge porn proclivity than the unique traits of narcissism and Machiavellianism. This finding is consistent with research by Brewer et al. (2015) who found that, aside from the Dark Triad, only psychopathy was an independent predictor of committing romantic revenge. The strong positive correlation between ambivalent sexism and Machiavellianism indicates that these share a common factor, such that both increase in a relatively parallel manner. However, only Machiavellianism was found to retain significant independent prediction of revenge porn proclivity. This suggests that Machiavellian traits, such as a strategic orientation and ruthless manipulation, were of greater influence upon predicting revenge porn proclivity, than endorsement of sexism alone.

In the current study, proclivity subscales of revenge porn approval and enjoyment were also devised. Whilst specific hypotheses were not made about these scales, their inclusion allowed greater exploration of the psychological characteristics pertaining to those endorsing revenge porn behaviour. Unexpectedly, psychopathy retained no significant relationship with either revenge porn approval or enjoyment. This was somewhat surprising as the measures of revenge porn approval and enjoyment were positively correlated with revenge porn proclivity, with which psychopathy demonstrated a positive correlation. Instead, it was found that both Machiavellianism and ambivalent sexism held a positive correlation with revenge porn approval, such that higher endorsement of these traits was correlated with a greater approval of revenge porn being committed. However, only Machiavellianism was found to retain independent prediction of revenge porn approval. It could be surmised that the deceitful and strategic orientation found in both Machiavellian behaviour and revenge porn explains this relationship. The relationship between ambivalent sexism and Machiavellianism found here is in need of greater clarification in future research.

In contrast, whilst both narcissism and Machiavellianism yielded positive correlations with revenge porn enjoyment, only narcissism was an independent predictor. This suggests that narcissistic traits hold greater unique influence upon the likelihood of enjoying revenge porn (i.e. experiencing greater control, excitement, and amusement), compared to traits unique to Machiavellianism. Perhaps engaging in revenge porn fulfils a narcissistic individual's notion of entitlement, grandiosity, and need for ego reinforcement (Jones & Paulhus, 2014), which are all needs that are potentially prevalent after a relationship breakup.

Limitations of the Current Study

Despite providing a novel insight into the relationships between psychological characteristics and revenge porn proclivity, the current study is not without its limitations. Firstly, the scale of revenge porn proclivity and the measures of sadism, sexism and the Dark Triad required participants to provide responses to personal and sensitive topics. Due to this, the findings could be vulnerable to social desirability bias. Whilst this effect may have been minimised by using online self-report, participants could either withhold or exaggerate their responses. Although, the use of online self-report did allow participation to occur in a less time-consuming and less invasive manner, it is still encouraged that future research should implement a measure of social desirability to control for this confound (e.g. Social Desirability Scale, Crowne & Marlowe, 1960). Secondly, it is imperative to acknowledge that the study's design does not allow for the conclusion that participants who endorse revenge porn will engage in these behaviours. In addition, as a community sample was recruited for this study, the self-reported likelihood to perpetrate an act of revenge porn was relatively low. This may differ when using a forensic or clinical sample, hence future studies should consider these populations.

Moreover, the cross-sectional design of this study means that caution should be made when inferring causality among significant relationships. To the researchers' knowledge, this is the first empirical study examining the psychological correlates of individuals presenting endorsement of revenge porn behaviour. Consequently, the current findings stand alone as support for these relationships, but in doing so, form a much-needed understanding of this emerging phenomenon. Lastly, but equally importantly, the sample acquired comprised of an unanticipated skewness in gender ratio, with a majority of female participants. Due to this, the influence of gender upon revenge porn proclivity could not formally be assessed. Findings were instead reported and discussed across the sample. It is important to note that since previous research (e.g. Citron & Franks, 2014; Poole, 2015; Salter & Crofts, 2015) has shown that the majority of perpetrators and disseminators of revenge porn are men, future research should replicate these findings using the proclivity scale with male samples or equal samples of males and females.

FUTURE RESEARCH AND CONCLUSION

Whilst the current study has its limitations, it shows promise in exploring an emerging research interest. The findings highlight characteristics pertaining to the psychological profiles of people with a greater likelihood to perpetrate revenge porn. Nevertheless, it remains clear that additional research is required to increase our understanding of this phenomenon. For example, research could explore a greater array of psychological and social factors that may both enhance and inhibit the likelihood that an individual will commit this form of sexual violence.

Future research could use both community samples and apprehended offenders of revenge porn to further validate the scale. This valuable comparison could be used to examine whether the characteristics of community participants with a greater revenge porn proclivity reflect the characteristics of actual revenge porn perpetrators. This would allow well-versed prevention to take place among individuals considered most at risk of perpetrating revenge porn. Moreover, this highlights the need for education on respectful relationships, digital citizenship and online safeguarding in schools and workplaces as it would both reduce the acceptance as well as the occurrence of revenge porn, and provide people with an informed awareness on how to help protect themselves from being victimised.

Importantly, future research should also focus on victim impact so that support services, practitioners, police, and legal professionals alike are well informed on how to appropriately respond to victims. In summary, it is evident that revenge porn is a concerning, yet understudied, form of sexual violence, and thus warrants further research attention. Through increasing our knowledge of revenge porn, the characteristics of offenders, and victim impact, we can generate well-informed theory, education, prevention, and treatment.

REFERENCES

Alleyne, E., Gannon, T., Ó Ciardha, C., & Wood, J. L. (2014). Community males show multiple-perpetrator rape proclivity: Development and preliminary validation of an interest scale. *Sexual Abuse: A Journal of Research and Treatment, 26*(1), 82-104. doi:10.1177/1079063213480819

Alleyne, E., Tilston, L., Parfitt, C., & Butcher, R. (2015). Adult-perpetrated animal abuse: Development of a proclivity scale. *Psychology, Crime & Law, 21*(6), 570–588. doi:10.1080/1068316X.2014.999064

BBC. (2016). *Revenge pornography victims as young as 11, investigation finds.* Retrieved from http://www.bbc.co.uk/news/uk-england36054273

Berlatsky, N. (2013). *Ethics of Revenge Porn.* Retrieved from http://digitalethics.org/essays/ethics-of-revenge-porn/

Bohner, G., Eyssel, F., Pina, A., Siebler, F., & Viki, G. T. (2009). Rape myth acceptance: Cognitive, affective, and behavioural effects of beliefs that blame the victim and exonerate the perpetrator. In M. Horvath & J. Brown (Eds.), *Rape: Challenging contemporary thinking* (pp. 17–45). Devon, UK: Willan Publishing.

Bohner, G., Pina, A., Viki, G. T., & Siebler, F. (2010). Using social norms to reduce men's rape proclivity: Perceived rape myth acceptance of out-groups may be more influential than that of in-groups. *Psychology, Crime & Law, 16*(8), 671 693. doi:10.1080/1068316X.2010.492349

Bohner, G., Reinhard, M.-A., Rutz, S., Sturm, S., Kerschbaum, B., & Effler, D. (1998). Rape myths as neutralizing cognitions: Evidence for a causal impact of anti-victim attitudes on men's self-reported likelihood of raping. *European Journal of Social Psychology, 28*(2), 257–268. doi: 0992(199803/04)28:2<257::aid ejsp871>3.0.co;2-110.1002/(sici)1099

Brewer, G., Hunt, D., James, G., & Abell, L. (2015). Dark Triad traits, infidelity and romantic revenge. *Personality and Individual Differences, 83*, 122–127. doi:10.1016/j.paid.2015.04.007

Buckels, E. E., Jones, D. N., & Paulhus, D. L. (2013). Behavioral confirmation of everyday sadism. *Psychological Science, 24*(11), 2201–2209. doi:10.1177/0956797613490749 PMID:24022650

Buckels, E., & Paulhus, D. L. (2014). *Comprehensive assessment of sadistic tendencies (CAST) (Unpublished measure)*. Canada: University of British Columbia.

Buckels, E. E., Trapnell, P. D., & Paulhus, D. L. (2014). Trolls just want to have fun. *Personality and Individual Differences, 67*, 97–102. doi:10.1016/j.paid.2014.01.016

Buckels, E.E. (2012). The pleasures of hurting others: Behavioral evidence for everday sadism. [Unpublished master's dissertation]. University of British Columbia, Canada

Burris, A. (2014). *Hell Hath No Fury Like a Woman Porned: Revenge Porn and The Need for a Federal Nonconsensual Pornography Statute*. Retrieved from http://www.floridalawreview.com/wp-content/uploads/11-Burris.pdf

Bushman, B. J., Bonacci, A. M., van Dijk, M., & Baumeister, R. F. (2003). Narcissism, sexual refusal, and aggression: Testing a narcissistic reactance model of sexual coercion. *Journal of Personality and Social Psychology, 84*(5), 1027–1040. doi:10.1037/0022-3514.84.5.1027 PMID:12757146

Citron, D. K., & Franks, M. A. (2014). Criminalizing revenge porn. *Wake Forest Law Review, 49*, 345–391.

UK Criminal Justice and Courts. (2015). *Criminal Justice and Courts Bill (HL Bill 49)* Retrieved from http://www.publications.parliament.uk/pa/bills/lbill/2014-2015/0049/lbill_201420150049_en_5.htm

Crowne, D. P. & Marlowe, D. (1960). A new scale of social desirability independent of psychopathology. *Journal of Consulting Psychology, 24*(4), 349 354. doi:10.1037/h0047358

Dick, R., McCauley, H. L., Jones, K. A., Tancredi, D. J., Goldstein, S., … Miller, E. (2014). Cyberdating abuse among teens using school-based health centers. *Pediatrics, 134*, 1560 1567. doi:10.1542/peds.2014-053

Furnham, A., Richards, S. C., & Paulhus, D. L. (2013). The Dark Triad of Personality: A 10 Year Review. *Social and Personality Psychology Compass, 3*(3), 199–216. doi:10.1111/spc3.12018

Gannon, T. A., & O'Connor, A. (2011). The development of the interest in child molestation scale. *Sexual Abuse*, *23*(4), 474–493. doi:10.1177/1079063211412390 PMID:22031298

Gerhart, J. I., Ronan, G. F., Russ, E., & Seymour, B. (2013). The moderating effects of cluster B personality traits on violence reduction training: A mixed-model analysis. *Journal of Interpersonal Violence*, *28*(1), 45–61. doi:10.1177/0886260512448849 PMID:22829213

Glick, P., & Fiske, S. T. (1996). The Ambivalent Sexism Inventory: Differentiating hostile and benevolent sexism. *Journal of Personality and Social Psychology*, *70*(3), 491–512. doi:10.1037/0022-3514.70.3.491

Glick, P., & Fiske, S. T. (2011). Ambivalent sexism revisited. *Psychology of Women Quarterly*, *35*(3), 530–535. doi:10.1177/0361684311414832 PMID:24453402

Glick, P., & Whitehead, J. (2010). Hostility toward men and the perceived stability of male dominance. *Social Psychology*, *41*(3), 177–185. doi:10.1027/1864-9335/a000025

Greathouse, S., Saunders, J., Matthews, M., Keller, K., & Miller, L. (2015). A review of the literature on sexual assault perpetrator characteristics and behaviors. RAND Corporation, Santa Monica, CA. Retrieved from 10.7249/rr1082

The Guardian. (2012). *Amanda Todd's suicide and social media's sexualisation of youth culture.* Retrieved from https://www.theguardian.com/commentisfree/2012/oct/26/amanda-todd-suicide-social-media-sexualisation

The Guardian. (2015). *Revenge porn cases increase considerably, police figures reveal.* Retrieved from https://www.theguardian.com/technology/2015/jul/15/revenge-porncases-increase-police-figures-reveal

Hall, J., & Benning, S. (2006). The "successful" psychopath: Adaptive and subclinical manifestations of psychopathy in the general population. In C. J. Patrick (Eds.), Handbook of Psychopathy (pp. 459-480). Guilford, NY: Guilford Press.

Hare, R. D, & Neumann, C. S. (2008). Psychopathy as a clinical and empirical construct. *Annual Review of Clinical Psychology*, *4*(1), 217–246. doi:10.1146/annurev.clinpsy.3.022806.091452 PMID:18370617

Hatcher, R. (2016, June). Who is to blame for 'revenge pornography'? The contribution of relationship duration, nature of media capture and victim behaviour on public perceptions. *Paper presented at the Division of Forensic Psychology annual conference for The British Psychological Society*, Brighton, England

Henry, N. & Powell, A. (2015a). *Digital harassment and abuse of adult Australians: A summary report.* Retrieved from https://research.techandme.com.au/wp-content/uploads/REPORT_AustraliansExperiencesofDigitalHarassmentandAbuse.pdf

Henry, N., & Powell, A. (2015b). Beyond the sext: Technology-facilitated sexual violence and harassment against adult women. *Australian and New Zealand Journal of Criminology*, *48*(1), 104–118. doi:10.1177/0004865814524218

Henry, N., & Powell, A. (2016). Sexual violence in the digital age: The Scope and Limits of Criminal Law. *Social & Legal Studies*, *25*(4), 397–418. doi:10.1177/0964663915624273

Jonason, P. K., & Webster, G. D. (2010). The Dirty Dozen: A concise measure of the dark triad. *Psychological Assessment*, *22*(2), 420–432. doi:10.1037/a0019265 PMID:20528068

Jones, D. N., & Paulhus, D. L. (2011a). The role of impulsivity in the Dark Triad of personality. *Personality and Individual Differences*, *51*(5), 67 682. doi:10.1016/j.paid.2011.04.011

Jones, D. N., & Paulhus, D. L. (2011b). Differentiating the dark triad within the interpersonal circumplex. In L. M. Horowitz & S. Strack (Eds.), *Handbook of Interpersonal Psychology: Theory, research, assessment, and therapeutic interventions* (pp. 249–269). New York, US: Wiley.

Jones, D. N., & Paulhus, D. L. (2014). Introducing the Short Dark Triad (SD3): A brief measure of dark personality traits. *Assessment*, *21*(1), 28–41. doi:10.1177/1073191113514105 PMID:24322012

Klettke, B., Hallford, D. J., & Mellor, D. J. (2014). Sexting prevalence and correlates: A systematic literature review. *Clinical Psychology Review*, *34*(1), 44–53. doi:10.1016/j.cpr.2013.10.007 PMID:24370714

Knieps, M. & Hatcher, R. (2016, June). Revenge porn is never okay: The effect of a 'good/bad' breakup on perceptions of acceptability. *Paper presented at the Division of Forensic Psychology annual conference for The British Psychological Society*, Brighton, England.

Kokkinos, C., Antoniadou, N., & Markos, A. (2014). Cyber-bullying: An investigation of the psychological profile of university student participant. *Journal of Applied Developmental Psychology*, *35*(3), 204–214. doi:10.1016/j.appdev.2014.04.001

Luppicini, R, & Adell, R. (2008). *Handbook of Research on Technoethics*. Hershey, PA: IGI Publishing. Doi:10.4018/978-1-60566- 022-6

Maier, S. (2014). *Rape, Victims, and Investigations: Experiences and perceptions of law enforcement officers responding to reported rapes*. Abingdon Oxon, UK: Routledge.

Maples, J. L., Lamkin, J., & Miller, J. D. (2014). A test of two brief measures of the dark triad: The dirty dozen and short dark triad. *Psychological Assessment*, *26*(1), 326–31. doi:org/10.1037/a0035084

Martinez-Pecino, R., & Duran, M. (2016). I love you but I cyberbully you: The role of hostile sexism. *Journal of Interpersonal Violence*. [online first] doi:10.1177/0886260516645817 PMID:27118344

Ministry of Justice. (2015). *Revenge Porn: the facts*. Retrieved from https://www.gov.uk/government/publications/revenge-porn

Morelli, M., Bianchi, D., Baiocco, R., Pezzuti, L., & Chirumbolo, A. (2016). Not allowed sharing of sexts and dating violence from the perpetrators perspective: The moderation role of sexism. *Computers in Human Behavior*, *56*, 163–169. doi:10.1016/j.chb.2015.11.047

O'Meara, A., Davies, J., & Hammond, S. (2011). The psychometric properties and utility of the Short Sadistic Impulse Scale (SSIS). *Psychological Assessment, 23*(2), 523–531. doi:10.1037/a0022400 PMID:21319907

Parfitt, C. & Alleyne, E. (2016). Taking it out on the dog: Psychological and behavioural correlates of animal abuse proclivity. *Society and Animals, 24*(1), 1-16. doi:10.1163/15685306-12341387

Paulhus, D. L. (2014). Toward a taxonomy of dark personalities. *Current Directions in Psychological Science, 23*(6), 421–426. doi:10.1177/0963721414547737

Paulhus, D. L., & Williams, K. M. (2002). The Dark Triad of Personality: Narcissism, Machiavellianism, and Psychopathy. *Journal of Research in Personality, 36*(6), 556–563. doi:10.1016/S0092-6566(02)00505-6

Poole, E. (2015). Fighting back against non-consensual pornography. *University of San Francisco Law Review. University of San Francisco. School of Law, 49*, 181–214.

Roberts, L. D. (2008). Cyber-Victimization. In R. Luppicini & R. Adell (Eds.), *Handbook of Research on Technoethics*. Hershey, PA: IGI Publishing; doi:10.4018/978-1-60566-022-6.ch037

Rollero, C., Glick, P., & Tartaglia, S. (2014). Psychometric properties of short versions of the Ambivalent Sexism Inventory and Ambivalence Toward Men Inventory. *TPM: Testing, Psychometrics, Methodology in Applied Psychology, 21*(2), 149–159. doi:10.4473/TPM21.2.3

Russell, T. D., & King, A. R. (2016). Anxious, hostile, and sadistic: Maternal attachment and everyday sadism predict hostile masculine beliefs and male sexual violence. *Personality and Individual Differences, 99*, 340–345. doi:10.1016/j.paid.2016.05.029

Salter, M. & Crofts, T. (2015). Responding to revenge porn: Challenging online legal impunity. In L. Comella & S. Tarrant (Eds.), *New Views on Pornography: Sexuality, Politics, and the Law*. Retrieved from http://UWSAU.eblib.com.au/patron/FullRecord.aspx?p = 1930115

Sleath, E., & Bull, R. (2009). Male rape victim and perpetrator blaming. *Journal of Interpersonal Violence, 25*(6), 969–988. doi:10.1177/0886260509340534 PMID:19738198

Stroud, S. (2014). The dark side of the online self: A pragmatist critique of the growing plague of revenge porn. *Journal of Mass Media Ethics, 29*(3), 168–183. doi:10.1080/08900523.2014.917976

Stroud, S. R. & Henson, J. (2016). What exactly is revenge porn or nonconsensual pornography? In A.C. Scheinbaum (Ed.), *Online Consumer Behavior: The Dark Side of Social Media*. Routledge. Retrieved from https://papers.ssrn.com/sol3/papers.cfm?abstract_id = 2828740

Tang, W. Y., & Fox, J. (2016). Men's harassment behavior in online video games: Personality traits and game factors. *Aggressive Behavior, 42(6), 513-21.* doi:10.1002/ab.21646 PMID:26880037

Taylor, R., Fritsch, E., & Liederbach, J. (2015). *Digital crime and digital terrorism (3rd Edition)*. New Jersey, US: Pearson, Inc.

The Independent. (2014). *Ex-rated: The total scandal of revenge porn.* Retrieved from http://www. independent.ie/life/exrated-the-total-scandal-of-revenge -porn30430621.html

Thom, C. (2015). Ethical dilemma for editors as revenge porn law does not give victims anonymity. Retrieved from http://www.pressgazette.co.uk/ethical-dilemma-for-editors-as-revenge-porn-law-does-not-give-victims-anonymity/

Voller, E. K., & Long, P. J. (2010). Sexual Assault and rape perpetration by college men: The role of the big five personality traits. *Journal of Interpersonal Violence, 25*(3), 457–480. doi:10.1177/0886260509334390 PMID:19443734

Woodlock, D. (2016). The abuse of technology in domestic violence and stalking. *Violence Against Women.* [online first] doi:10.1177/1077801216646277 PMID:27178564

Zeigler-Hill, V., Besser, A., Morag, J., & Keith Campbell, W. (2016). The Dark Triad and sexual harassment proclivity. *Personality and Individual Differences, 89*, 47–54. doi:10.1016/j.paid.2015.09.048

ENDNOTE

[1]   Full scale is available from lead author upon request.

This research was previously published in the International Journal of Technoethics (IJT), 8(1); edited by Rocci Luppicini, pages 30-43, copyright year 2017 by IGI Publishing (an imprint of IGI Global).

Chapter 2
Contemporary Terror on the Net

Emily Stacey
Swansea University, UK

INTRODUCTION

The networked global society that has been enabled by the internet and accompanying digital technologies and social media platforms has created an affordable, geographically and temporally unbounded, and semi-anonymous space where the exchange of dialogue, ideas, and calls to action have become increasingly more frequent. This networked space provides for both egalitarian democratic efforts as witnessed in the Arab Spring (2009-2013) as well as Hong Kong (2014) and the Black Lives Matter movement in the United States (2013-present). Yet many theorists dating back to the late 1990s have pontificated on the availability of this unbounded network to *bad actors*, including hacktivists, international criminal cartels, as well as terrorist groups (Conway, 2006; Hinnen, 2004; Soriano, 2008; Teich, 2013), which will be the focus of this book.

While research on the use of the internet by terrorist organizations is available in abundance, the correlation of social media platforms, more advanced technology, the dark web, and their exploitation by much demographically younger and savvier terrorist networks has provided a new landscape for research into not only the organization of these groups in the contemporary digital age, but also their goals, intentions, and their affective persuasion online in order to accomplish their mission. This has been particularly true for the Islamic State (also known as the Islamic State of Iraq and Syria (ISIS), the Islamic State of Syria and the Levant (ISIL), and more globally, as Daesh). The foundation for the Islamic State were established in the period after the U.S.-led invasion of Iraq in 2003, the group was formed out of Al Qaeda in Iraq, and is an unprecedented organization that combines terrorism with military capabilities. IS began its true rise in 2011 after the United States removed troops from Iraq, the moment was heralded as a celebration of seemingly, the beginning of the end of the War on Terror and notably, the government of Iraq being stable enough for the U.S. to dislodge from the puppet government.

Prime Minister al-Maliki began a crusade against Sunnis, including in the government, military and law enforcement within the Iraqi society after the U.S. removed itself from the situation, inflaming centuries old religious and sectarian tension in the region (Frontline, 2014). Although Al Qaeda in Iraq

DOI: 10.4018/978-1-5225-3163-0.ch002

was essentially decimated after the American invasion, the militants that remained (becoming the foundation of the Islamic State) were Baathists from Saddam Hussein's military, battle-hardened terrorists who managed to escape death at the hands of an international coalition in Iraq, and were able to form an organization through the opportunity of the Syrian civil war. The Islamic State used the violence and anti-Assad sentiment in Syria to their advantage, marketing their message to a rebel groups fighting the government, this enabled the meager group that crossed the border into the Syrian conflict to grow its numbers and influence into the formidable group that exists today. IS has obtained advanced weapons from the Iraqi and Syrian militaries, including tanks, artillery, and chemical weapons that it has seized in successful combat engagements (Kam, 2015). This arsenal now reportedly includes armed drones, which were confirmed to have been used in an attack in Northern Iraq in early October 2016 that killed two Kurdish peshmerga fighters and wounded two French Special Operations troops (Gibbons-Neff, 2016). The group is also in possession of chemical weapons, which prompted the U.S. to target chemical weapons plants in September 2016, blaming IS for using chlorine and mustard gas (Starr, 2016).

IS distinguished itself from Al Qaeda as early as 2007 by using violence against civilians (Vitale & Keagle, 2014). Yet the formal announcement of the formation of the Islamic State from Baghdadi would not come until 2014. The division among the groups was clear and generational. While Al Qaeda, led by al-Zawahiri born in 1951, prefers more methodical, slow-developing plans to engage with the community to gain trust and support for their government, and targets were entities or officials of the state; IS uses violence against all, including women and children in extremely violent, and often public (whether executions are preformed as theatre for locals in ancient ruins, or recorded for mass consumption online).

In terms of leadership, Islamic State leader, Abu-Bakr al-Baghdadi, born in 1971 proved a strong influence on the global jihadist community by using a combination of physical and spiritual (ideological) power on the ground and in the hearts and minds of many, much of this strategy relied on available technologies to broadcast the message.

Framing the message is crucial to the ability of terror groups to elicit support that turns into active membership. IS focuses much of its messaging on the plight of Muslims, particularly those living in the West with the enemy, and how that enemy tears apart the foundation of the Islamic culture, religion, and identity. This, IS claims, can only be counterbalanced by the establishment of a caliphate for all Muslims. The recruitment of foreign fighters was

part and parcel of its leader's vision to restore the Islamic caliphate, a vision directly threatening the future of local regimes and representing the magnet attracting the thousands of young people streaming to Syria and Iraq to enlist" in the jihad (Kam, 2015, Pg. 22).

The ideological is combined, as Zelin (2015) explains, with the daily reinforcement that the IS military is continuing to gain ground and make achievements that attempt to legitimize and stabilize the caliphate. Terrorist groups today still have not started utilizing social media to the extent that IS has in the last two years to spur recruitment and inspire attacks around the world (Vitale & Keagle, 2014, Pg. 6).

DIGITAL TERRORISM AND THE OTHER

Brian Jenkins identifies emerging trends in terrorism, although he does not provide correlations between the new trends and the availability of the internet, many of the trends he notes can be amplified via use of the internet. In the interest of this work three of Jenkins' six concepts will be examined: 1) terrorism has become bloodier; 2) terrorists can now wage global campaigns; and 3) some terrorists have moved beyond tactics to strategy. Terrorism research notes the increase of not only lone wolf attacks but also the rise of more violent "bloodier" attacks (Jenkins, 2006, Pg. 118).

Terrorists are using more sophisticated weaponry and communications technologies to coordinate their attacks; where in the 1980s fatalities were in the hundreds, by the 2000s fatalities had reached the thousands with large-scale, high impact, soft target attacks. The Islamic State through its effective use of political communication via the internet, notably direct communication with potential recruits has inspired an increased surge in lone wolf and small cell attacks, those not coordinated at a organizational level, but encouraged by online tactics, communication or calls to action. Research in lone wolf terrorism notes that lone wolf attackers are more prone to display "some form of psychopathology as well as degrees of social ineptitude" (Teich, 2013, Pg. 2). One prominent study into lone wolf terrorism indicated that a majority of individuals (six out of 14 studied) suffered from mental illnesses ranging from bipolar disorder to schizophrenia to depression (Jasparro, 2010). Yet Bakker and de Graaf (2011) note that researchers should not generalize about the mental states of lone wolf terrorists, terrorists' backgrounds are all different, and some are psychologically disturbed while others are mentally healthy.

The psychological and emotional aspects related to communicating ideology and the foment of enduring attitudes of political change are important to consider when looking at digital protest movements. Hegel's concept of the "constitutive Other" (1977) should factor into current analyses of global terrorism and the use of digital technologies to recruit or create awareness of their cause. This concept emphasizes the relation of one's essential nature to an outward manifestation, or a point-of-view of binary nature of the essential and superficial, where each is the inversion of each other.

Social networking sites allow for the manipulation of the Other and collective action networks, particularly those that are mobilizing for a sustained engagement of dissent (IS) are using this 'Otherness' against citizens to persuade them into joining their ranks. IS has proven quite adept at seeping into mainly younger Middle Eastern women that have grown up in the Western world and preying on their feeling of isolation within a society that does not always accept or understand who they are fundamentally. So the lure of an Islamic State that is solely for them, where everyone will understand their plight and struggles, and there is a built-in family unit based around religious beliefs appeals to many youth living in the West, who fear for their futures after September 11, 2001 and a global War on Terror being waged for decades.

This shared emotional state is crucial to contemporary social movements as well as global jihad that are relying at least partially on social networking sites and digital technologies to assist in the spread of ideology and tactics. Where once having a solid, singular leader of a movement to espouse ideology and calls for change were enough, in the digital age of protest, having an engaged large network of loose, weak ties is much more important than having a small, extremely active network of strong ties.

The ability for IS to recruit, coordinate and execute as well as inspire global attacks using digital technologies and an adept message of confusion, alienation and understanding to be found by joining their movement has aided the group in its nearly three-year development, and takeover of large swathes of Syria and Iraq. As Stern states (2003, Pg. 283),

Unless we understand the appeal of participating in extremist groups and the seduction of finding one's identity in oppositions to Other, we will not get far in our attempts to stop terrorism.

So the anger and hate that groups like the Islamic State are honing in on and cultivating among Western Muslims or disaffected citizens becomes effective in recruiting individuals actors, but also in sowing seeds of discontent and distrust of the Other in Western society, which keeps the cycle of hate, attacks and fear churning.

As previously stated, lone wolf attacks are on the rise in the West, Spaaij (2010) noted that the United States has experienced more lone wolf terrorism than the other fourteen countries studied (all Western). Teich (2013, Pg. 9) studied lone wolf terrorist attacks between 1990 and 2013, there were a total of 73 attacks: 27 lone wolf attacks and 46 attempted attacks by Islamic extremists, with 29 out of 73 attacks occurring within the span of three years, between 2010 and 2013. The United States was the nation targeted most often, accounting for 63 percent of all attacks (46 total attacks). When political scientists examine the factors that may contribute to this uptick in lone wolf attacks in the United States, it must be noted that it is much easier for self-radicalization online and to coordinate an attack in a place where you live, than to send hordes of fighters to attempt to infiltrate the U.S. and plot a large-scale attack.

In 2003, Stern recognized the growing threat of lone wolf terrorism and showed through research that there was a correlation between the increase of individual attacks and the proliferation of more powerful weapons. Although Stern is referencing a quote from Ayman al-Zawahiri's autobiography, in which he encourages the youth of Islam to arm themselves to defend their religion and themselves with pride, this sentiment is particularly chilling in the contemporary United States where self-radicalization and the availability of high capacity firearms makes a tumultuous combination. Stern notes, "As increasingly powerful weapons become more and more available, lone wolves, who face few political constraints, will become more of a threat, whatever their primary motivation" (2003, Pg. 34). Lone wolves, to reiterate, tend to mix ideological motivation with personal grievances as the world witnessed most recently with the Orlando night club shooting, the perpetrator swore allegiance to the Islamic State in the hours before the attack on the LGBTQ night club, which he had allegedly frequented, concealing a side of himself that directly conflicted with his religious inclinations and likely resulted in psychological issues regarding identity.

According to Koerner (2016),

…When Americans perpetrate violence in the name of the Islamic State, they tend not to be strict adherents of the organization's ideology, but rather disturbed individuals who hope to layer a political façade atop their personal grievances – grievances sometimes known only to themselves,

reiterating the description of lone wolves as often half-heartedly supporting the terror organization, while harboring personally felt injustices that manifest in the form of an attack.

Going back further to the 2009 mass shooting at Fort Hood, Texas perpetrated by Major Nidal Malik Hasan, who was working as an Army psychiatrist at the time of the attack that killed 13 people. Hasan had a life history of devout Sunni religious practice but was not radicalized until after the death of his parents, and subjection to deployment in the Iraq War, which Hasan resisted (Teich, 2013). Hasan was inspired by the teachings of Al-Awlaki, a radical American-born Yemenite preacher, which further enraged Hasan about the killing of Muslims in the War on Terror in both Iraq and Afghanistan. Although Hasan showed signs of self-radicalization stemming from a lifetime of devout religious practice that eventually coincided with the global War on Terror and his personal feelings regarding the ethics and politics of the engagement. The combination of religious devotion along with political obligations (military) manifested conflicting feelings for Hasan, there were no links to terrorist organizations found on Hasan's computers during the investigation and his court martial. Teich (2013, Pg. 5) emphasizes that "terrorists' organizational narratives assist in the externalizing of these individuals' [lone wolves] personal grievances as part of the Islamic radicalization process", so while lone wolves may act in accordance with shared tactics and ideologies of a well-known terrorist organization, their mission is often mixed with their own personal vendettas simultaneously.

The contemporary iteration of terrorism has become not only adept at utilizing the resources available to them via the internet, but also not to over-reach in terms of strategy, coordination, and execution of attacks. Terrorist attacks have digressed in the number of fatalities, no longer in the thousands with a single attack, as the world witnessed during September 11, 2001. Yet the frequency of attacks by lone wolf inspired actors combines fatalities into the thousands. According to Jenkins (2006, Pg. 127),

Terrorist strategy is based not on achieving military superiority but rather on making the enemy's life unbearable by attacking incessantly; by inflicting endless casualties; by destroying tourism and discouraging investment, and thus inflicting economic pain; and by carrying out spectacular operations like 9/11; terrorism at its core is about the disturbance of the norm, causing such fear and anxiety that entire societies must adapt their behavior in order to have the perception of safety.

It is this author's opinion that more frequent lone wolf style attacks have outpaced large-scale events such as September 11th due to the amount of planning, coordination, and transference of resources overseas. It is much less risky for autonomous actors carrying out attacks in the name of, and in allegiance to the larger terrorist organization. For example, over the month of Ramadan 2016, in just one week from June 28-July 4, there were three major attacks: the first occurred June 28 at Istanbul's Ataturk airport that killed 36 and injured an additional 147 people (Tuysuz & Almasy, 2016); the next on July 1 was an attack on an international fine dining restaurant in Dhaka, Bangladesh that killed 28 people, 20 of whom were hostages (Hammadi et al., 2016); and finally, detonation of a truck bomb in a predominately Shia neighborhood of Baghdad killed nearly 300 people on July 3. The Islamic State has claimed responsibility for two of the three aforementioned attacks, while not publicly noting their involvement in the Istanbul plot, the pattern of the attack closely resembles that of the Brussels airport and metro attack.

USE OF AVAILABLE MEDIA IN THE PROMOTION OF JIHAD

Arguably, the 21st century internet with its ever-increasing multimodal platforms, levels of encryption, and lack of regulation has made the internet a place of golden opportunity for groups like the Islamic State or Boko Haram. Not only to share their jihad through videos, audio, and photographs, but also to prey on disaffected Western Muslims living on the outside of their society and enabling them to take action within their own countries. Koerner notes,

Unlike Al Qaeda, which has generally been methodical about organizing and controlling its terror cells, the more opportunistic Islamic State is content to crowd source its social media activity – and its violence – out to individuals with whom it has no concrete ties (2016).

The necessity for fighters and supporters to cross borders to training in the Middle East has become obsolete. In the digital age, radicalization is as simple as clicking on the correct website, connecting to the right communications network, and conducting a Google search for the recommended content. This book will emphasize the growing number of lone wolf style attacks in the West and the ability of modern terrorist organizations to affect citizens living in nations outside the Middle East to the point of action. Unlike terrorist groups of the pre-internet (1980s) and development/proliferation period of the internet (1990s-2004), the groups that exist today are utilizing social media platforms to directly communicate ideology to potential followers, and inflict horror in (or upon) the West (as was the case in the most recent attacks outside a U.S. consulate building in Saudi Arabia as well as the fine dining restaurant in Bangladesh) without having to send en masse fighters to U.S. or European borders.

As former White House Cyber Security Chief Richard Clarke (2004) notes, "Terrorists use the internet just like everybody else", and the ways in which terrorist groups are using the internet has adapted to new platforms, capabilities, and available technologies as well as the adaptation of strategies for jihad. Conway (2006, Pg. 11) provides a categorization of terrorist uses of the internet, noting five standard applications of the net in promulgating the organization's mission, including: 1) information provision; 2) financing; 3) networking; 4) recruitment; and 5) information gathering. The five categories remain highly relevant in contemporary internet use by terrorist organizations. This work will focus on provision of information, or the spreading of ideology and propaganda, as well as networking, which this author argues encompasses recruitment through involved, personal and direct communications with potential members or actors, this was something the traditional media was unable to accomplish.

While early terrorist organizations had to rely on coordinating attacks so large as to attract the attention of television producers, print publishers and radio broadcasters, contemporary groups have a constant connection to their own websites, social media networks, and YouTube channels to broadcast their message in an unadulterated or edited fashion. The traditional media apparatus was able to define the terrorist groups and their intentions before the internet, and now global citizens are able to consume their message without the filter of decency or foreign policy explanations to decide for themselves if the cause is righteous. Conway notes that although the intended audience for consumption of terrorist propaganda might be small, a "well-designed and well-maintained website gives a group an aura of legitimacy" (2006, Pg. 12).

This is clearly amplified in 2016, where terrorist groups are not only expected to maintain a constant online presence but to keep the content fresh (i.e.: the Islamic State's monthly *Dabiq*). In a report released in October 2015 entitled *Documenting the Virtual Caliphate*, IS releases 38 new items per day, including extended videos, documentaries, audio, and instructional documents in numerous languages. In April 2016, an Islamic State published online magazine, *Dar Al-Islam*, put out an issue devoted to online safety and privacy, which gave explicit instruction on using various applications and platforms to access IS content safely (Frenkel, 2016). It is interesting to note that *Dar Al-Islam* is published in French, and writing in July 2016, France thus far has experienced the most deadly lone wolf attacks in the Western world at the hands of IS.

Most recently, on July 14, where a celebration was marred by a Tunisian-born French citizen who plowed a commercial refrigerated truck through a large crowd assembled in Nice to watch a fireworks display commemorating the French holiday of Bastille Day, leaving 84 people dead. This comes after the French government released a mobile application in June 2016 to alert and transmit information to citizens during a terrorist attack, known as the Systeme d'Alerte et d'Information aux populations, or the Population Alert and Information System (Newman, 2016). The app is able to track users' locations to send timely updates as to the dangers in their immediate environment, and enables users to set up alerts for eight different postal codes. While it is a step by the French government to provide security and information to their citizenry, the application begins sending alerts within 15 minutes of the government declaring there has been an attack or event, making social media a much more efficient, but not always accurate news source.

Al Qaeda and other contemporary terrorist organizations have moved their online presence to YouTube, Twitter, Facebook, Instagram, and other social media outlets. Abu Mohammed al-Golani, the head of an Al Qaeda branch that operates in Syria known as the al-Nusra Front, utilizes Facebook and various other social media sites frequently. In August 2013, al-Golani vowed

unrestrained rocket attacks on Alawite communities, alongside attacks on President Bashar Assad's government in revenge for an alleged chemical strike – a message that was posted on Facebook and Twitter, as well as on a militant website that often broadcasts the views of Al Qaeda and other extremist groups (Weimann, 2014, Pg. 2).

Networking emphasizes the ability in the digital age for terrorist (and other NGOs, social movements, etc.) to become less centralized and non-hierarchical. Networking allows for the dissemination and coordination of attacks that are independent of the small, symbolic leadership but still connected to the terrorist organization through inspiration, ideology, or allegiance pledged by the perpetrators. The internet has allowed for the dispersion of tactics, coordinated attacks, and ideology well beyond the nations or even the region that the terror groups occupy. Many theorists note the rise of *global jihad* where the ideology of extreme Islamists has permeated through the world in reaction to recent political events such as the War on Terror (Conway, 2006; Torok, 2013, etc.). So while there may be stated leaders in these terror organizations that handle certain aspects of the mission (such as fundraising, weapons coordination, public relations), "there is no specific heart or head that can be targeted" (Conway, 2006, Pg. 14).

The world is witnessing how true this statement is with the death of top members of IS being replaced overnight. Torok (2013, Pg. 9) notes, "Although key leaders may be influential, power is not possessed by an individual; it is a circular relation that flows through many networks and individuals that make up that network" - making the internet and social media platforms a great environment to coordinate global jihad. Although the largest attacks recently in Brussels and Paris have been communicated through older technologies such as burner or temporary cell phones, the adoption of Islamic State tactics and ideology has been a coordinated digital effort on behalf of their organization. This digital dissemination has increased the network of terrorists or radicalized individuals to global reach. As Arquilla, Ronfeldt, and Zanini (2000, Pg. 41) articulate,

Terrorists will continue to move from hierarchical toward information-age network designs. More effort will go into building arrays of transnationally internetted groups than into building stand alone groups.

Hierarchies are more vulnerable than the network model that emphasizes strength and coordination among levels rather than a top-down structure.

Jenkins (2006) notes that Al Qaeda was one of the first groups to model its organization on international business models, featuring "hierarchical but not pyramidal, loosely run, decentralized but linked [operations…that are] able to assemble and allocate resources and coordinate operations, but hard to depict organizationally or penetrate" (Pg. 123). This organizational structure was adopted by the fringe wing of Al Qaeda that became the Islamic State that boasts a strong presence of physical occupation in Syria and Iraq, but occupy the hearts and minds of disaffected Muslims globally via the internet, social networking, and deft propaganda marketing.

The use of a monthly magazine to keep would-be terrorists and supporters aware about the global fight, tactics that can be used to conduct their own personal jihad, and ideology to keep the legions motivated are published in the Islamic State's *Dabiq*. The magazine was first published in 2014 and continues to put out fresh content monthly via the dark web. Weimann (2014) notes the potential of the dark web to provide a relatively cloaked space for the dissemination of jihadist and terrorist propaganda. The dark web has been linked to numerous controversial developments in the digital age, including WikiLeaks, Bitcon (the currency of the dark web), and criminal enterprise The Silk Road, which existed for two years. The lure of the dark web's decentralized and anonymous networks allow for criminals and terrorists alike to conduct business on a level that is difficult for government officials to control, monitor, or stop. The Islamic State increasingly has turned toward the dark web in the aftermath of the attacks on Paris in November 2015, after which the hacktivist organization Anonymous declared war on the group's digital communication apparatus. Hussain and Saltman (2014) conclude that while "Islamist forums and chat rooms in English and French are still widely available, a large portion of more extremist Islamic discourse now takes place within the dark web."

The Islamic State has responded tactically to increased government and non-government surveillance and disruption of mainstream communication channels, such as Twitter. They have instead migrated their socialization onto encrypted cell phone applications such as Telegram, which unveiled the ability to create channels, enabling the Islamic State to create their own known as *Nashir* (distributor in English), allowing for the free and wide distribution of jihadist ideologies. Pavel Durov, CEO of *Telegram* noted in an 2015 interview with the *Washington Post,* "Privacy, ultimately, and our right to privacy is more important than our fear of bad things happening, like terrorism" (Dewey, 2015). This sentiment is one that corporate officials are having to balance in the realm of free speech and national security.

However, the Islamic State harnessed the tools and tactics that Al Qaeda initiated, according to Jenkins (2006), the group used online monthly manuals to provide instruction to their followers around the world, led by shared ideology the periodical encouraged believers to wage their personal jihads autonomously of the central organization, or leadership. Stern (2003) articulates the terror world's shift from jihad on central governing organizations and entities of the State, to a more egalitarian style of attack on Western civilians beyond the coordinated attacks planned by the organizational structure. Stern (2003) notes that Osama Bin Laden's calls to jihad began in 1992 when he urged believers to kill American and Western soldiers stationed in Saudi Arabia; the second call came in 1996 via a 40-page manifesto that listed cruel acts committed on the Muslim world, predominately by Western nations (militaries); and the third, which was released in February 1998, called on his followers to target and attack Western civilians rather than the military-state complex.

Bin Laden still had to rely on the traditional media apparatus to promulgate his ideologies and calls for jihad. However, new communication technologies create interactive platforms through which individuals and communities share, co-create, discuss, and modify content (Weimann, 2014). Weimann also notes the increased time spent on social media sites in the United States as a veritable pool of recruits for terrorist organizations, with an increase from 88 billion minutes in July 2011 to 121 billion minutes in July 2012, an increase of 37 percent in a single year.

Wieviorka (2004, Pg. 43-45) was one of the first theorists to characterize the varying relationships that terrorist and the media may have, including complete indifference (this is uncommon), relative indifference (terrorists are not concerned with being on the news but are aware of the power that they provide), media-oriented strategies (many terror groups operate under this characterization, which note terrorists want to manipulate the media in order maximize coverage of an attack, event or promulgating ideology), and complete breakaway (this occurs when terrorists view the media as enemy combatants that must be destroyed along with other infidels. The world is witnessing a surge in the breakaway, as groups like the Islamic State are purposefully capturing Western journalists for public, or recorded executions.

Arguably, the traditional media including television and print outlets are still integral aspects to the contemporary landscape of global jihad. Yet the internet has altered the structural element of communication and organization, moving away from the hierarchy of the broadcast media, and allowing citizens and terrorists to dictate the news from the bottom-up and in a multidirectional fashion allowing for instant diffusion of ideology and calls for action. The infusion of the internet in Al Qaeda and other terrorist organizations' strategies allows for their message to be spread unperverted of the editorial framing of the mainstream outlets. This has become increasingly important as modern terror groups dislike the traditional media as their targeted audience (Soriano, 2008). Soriano notes, "From Al Qaeda's point of view, the news media are principally responsible for the liberating message of the Salafist Islam being ignored or distorted. This makes it impossible for the Jihad to penetrate in large sectors of the Muslim community, which finds itself immersed in the most pure ignorance and error" (2008, Pg. 7).

According to Soriano (2008, Pg. 7-11), jihadists perceive the media in various negative connotations including their role as a pacifier to the global Muslim population, keeping the population blind to the motivations of the West; constructing a straw man of strength on behalf of Western governments in response to global jihad; and contributing to the use of violence against Muslims as a way to reinforce Western democratic principles over the forces of evil. This understanding about the role of the media in perception of the terrorist organization by global audiences has understandably led to an increased role for the internet in becoming the main vehicle of communication among and between global jihadists and the organizational structures in the Middle East. Soriano highlights,

Al Qaeda understands that the type of relationship that it has with the mass media in recent years highly threatens the organization's and its members' security. Its desire to eliminate these vulnerabilities has led the terrorist organization to put new technology to even more use (2008, Pg. 15).

It is crucial to note here that the new media (digital technologies and the internet) has not replaced traditional mechanisms of political communication of jihad, but has enhanced and supplemented those traditional networks. Because the traditional media use the internet to find trending stories in order to build a broadcast or the next day's paper, the online presence and public relations machine of terror organizations have become crucial in dissemination of ideology. This cyclical relationship between the traditional and digital media has made simply the existence of jihadi websites, content, forums, etc. more likely to receive some sort of mainstream attention, and if not, it is still spreading the message via the internet. The relationship has also blurred the responsibility of morality and decency in reporting the news. Television stations that were once reluctant to broadcast scenes from war or brutality have become less concerned when it comes to the consumption of terrorist content, most notably the IS beheading videos, making the mainstream media accomplices of terrorists by normalizing their behavior.

SOCIAL MEDIA, THE INTERNET, AND TERRORISM

Terrorists use the internet and social media as propaganda channels, radicalization avenues, and recruitment tools. Due to the amount of freely available information found on social media platforms such as Facebook, where the default is to show all published information besides one's birthday and contact information, terror organizations have a much easier time recognizing and accumulating lists of potential recruits or followers to assist in the cause. Weimann notes that social media outlets allow terrorists to use traditional media strategies such as narrowcasting, which aims messages at specific segments of the public "defined by values, preferences, demographic attributes, or subscription" (2014, Pg. 4). The nature of social media sites is that they allow for customization or individualization of the message, which makes the sites a great tool for recruiting younger membership into terrorist organizations. Anthony Bergin highlights this point, saying that terrorists perceive and use youth-heavy websites as recruitment tools "in the same way a pedophile might look at those sites to potentially groom would-be victims" (Bergin, 2008).

The proliferation of the internet and social media platforms among terrorist organizations culminated into a formal call for "electronic jihad" from Al Qaeda in May 2012 (CNN Wire, 2012). Internet platforms that are used to promote electronic jihad are also used in an organizational manner to provide tactics and training, collecting information about potential recruits and/or followers, and coordination. This includes the introduction of virtual training camps that teach would-be jihadists how to make bombs and weapons, hacking skills, and other instructional materials (Weimann, 2014). The perpetrators of the 2008 terrorist attack in Mumbai used digital technologies, including mobile GPS devices to plan and execute the attack, Google Earth satellite images, and cell phones to keep them up-to-date regarding hostages.

Facebook is a medium of choice among terror organizations, due to its high level of penetration in the Middle East, reaching 67 percent in 2010 (Weimann, 2014). Through Facebook, terrorists look for and target disaffected Westerners and marginalized Muslims. The U.S. Department of Homeland Security (2010) noted various uses of the internet by terror organizations, including: a gateway to extremist sites and radical online content by linking on Facebook group pages, and as a media outlet for terrorist propaganda and extremist ideological messaging. Twitter has more recently emerged as *the* platform of choice by terrorist organizations, becoming more popular than Facebook to disseminate propaganda as well as to communicate among leadership and the extended network. The Islamic State has effectively co-opted extremely popular and globally pervasive hashtags during large events, notably during the 2014 World Cup, the group flooded #Brazil2014 and #WC2014 with gruesome photos and horrifying messages of violence. One such message spread through World Cup trending hashtags was a video entitled *There is No Life without Jihad,* which features British members of IS fighting on the battlefields. Weimann states that terrorists' use of Twitter takes

advantage of a recent trend in news coverage that often sacrifices validation and in-depth analysis for the sake of almost real-time coverage....under these conditions, mainstream media may take tweets as a legitimate news source (2014, Pg. 8).

Twitter has proven to be a stronghold for the Islamic State's decentralized communication strategy, and enables the group's influencers to gain the trust and support of potential recruits around the world using clever marketing and personal contact (i.e.: direct messaging). Islamic State fighters have also capitalized on the glossy Hollywood video production and understand the pervasiveness of gruesome photos as a marketing tool, but the group has more than any other terror organization grasped the necessity to make their jihad personal to recruits. The near intimacy that IS operatives use while luring disaffected global citizens into the web has been a cornerstone of their success in receiving an estimated 30,000 foreign fighters since 2014 (Brooking & Singer, 2016). The authors note a Dutch IS member fighting in the caliphate maintained an active Tumblr presence, with photos ranging from "his fellow fighters at rest; his newborn baby; even his cat, stretched alongside a suicide belt" (ibid., 2016).

It is important to again distinguish the Islamic State's use of social media as opposed to more traditional media to disseminate ideology and propaganda. Where terror organizations that are more insular and traditional rely on spreading messages through proper channels from the leadership to the masses, the Islamic State has advantageously co-opted the democratic character of the internet and social media to allow anyone and everyone (including those who oppose them) to join and promulgate the conversation. Terror organizations based in Africa such as The Mujahideen Youth Movement, Al Qaeda in the Lands of the Islamic Maghreb, the Oromo Liberation Front, the Movement for the Emancipation of the Niger Delta, as well as Boko Haram all maintain a Twitter presence and will provide content in English to target Western audiences. Although Twitter and various other social media platforms leave the potential for corrupting the message or feed by flooding it with memes such as IS Chan, an anime girl meant to shame IS members by depicting her in various real footage scenes, the benefit for recruitment obviously outweighs the negatives as IS has only increased its use of Twitter (Vitale & Keagle, 2014). As 2016 U.S. presidential candidate, Donald Trump says, "There is no such thing as bad publicity."

Contemporary terrorist organizations such as the militant group Al-Shabab use Twitter in increasingly advanced manners. During the 2013 rampage on Westgate Mall in Nairobi, Al-Shabab militants used Twitter to provide live commentary on the attack. Directly following the attack, a Somali-based Al Qaeda affiliate tweeted the rationale for the attack on the mall and provided operational details in real-time. The attack that killed 72 people was the first time a terrorist group claimed responsibility via Twitter (Weimann, 2014). Twitter has become an important tool for communication and coordination during movements and terrorist attacks alike, due to its real-time updates as well as photo, audio, and visual capabilities. This skillful adoption of not only the internet, but also social media platforms that allow for personal communication and consumption of extremist ideology has given global terrorist organizations an upper hand in waging electronic jihad. Weimann states,

Terrorist followers, sympathizers, converts, and newcomers find in the new media a much lower threshold to access terrorist-produced and terrorism-related content than they faced in discovering and signing up for access to the hardcore forums (2014, Pg. 20).

The average citizen is now aware when a new video message is posted or published from the Islamic State. Traditional media outlets are redistributing the content in neatly-packed current events stories that are widely available across the world through *The Guardian, The New York Times,* and BBC to be consumed by global citizens, young and old. This may be contributing to the mainstream normalization of the horrific acts committed by terrorist organizations and a propaganda machine that is constantly churning out content, reminding marginalized Western Muslims of the inequities in the societies in which they live. The Counter Terrorism Internet Referral Unit in the United Kingdom, which was established in 2010, removed 49,000 pieces of extremist content between 2010 and October 2014. This does not seem like much until the unit reported that 30,000 pieces of content alone had been removed between December 2013 and October 2014, of which, the majority referred to Syria and Iraq.

In terms of the Islamic State, while a majority of their members are located within Iraq and Syria, through using the internet to craft a global network of what U.S. intelligence officials deem as a

small unit within IS [that] is leading the group's cyber ambitions, which range from working with hackers to launch cyber attacks against their enemies, to publishing manuals that help their supporters mask their online communication and defend themselves from those hunting them (Frenkel, 2016).

The issues with IS and their use of the internet for terroristic purposes become more complicated because the group, like the web itself, is ever-evolving and becoming more sophisticated users of tools like encryption, malware to take down sites that are attempting to expose the atrocities of IS to Muslims, and a standard favorite of hacktivists and terrorists alike, denial-of-service (DDoS) attacks. Not only are terrorist groups becoming more technologically savvy, the younger demographic allows for the swift adoption of new platforms from across the globe that aid in the communication.

A recent study found that the median age of the world's 1.6 billion Muslims is 23-years old (Talbot, 2015), making them within the first "digital generation" (Alder, 2013), a generation that has never not known what it was like without the internet or digital technologies. The dominance of IS by younger members does help the group take advantage of newer applications or platforms before governments catch on. For example, the Berlin-based messaging application known as Telegram has become a popular tool for Islamic State followers. In October 2015, use of Telegram spiked among IS supporters with nearly 9,000 users following the IS channel in less than a week (Russon, 2016), and the founders Nikolai and Pavel Durov noted at a TechCrunch panel that privacy is more crucial than fear of terrorism (Frenkel, 2016). However, Telegram did eventually suspend "78 public Islamic State-related channels in 12 languages" (Russon, 2016).

Terror groups are using photo-sharing services such as Instagram as a means to relate with younger recruits and sympathizers, most of whom are within the digital generation and consume information visually just as much as they do textually. Instagram allows IS members to showcase their battles, their conception of the utopian caliphate and provide details into the daily life of an IS member, helping to normalize their actions to new recruits (Vitale & Keagle, 2014). Applications such as Ask.fm and KIK are both aimed at teenage-use and are used by IS to assist in answering questions anonymously. The anonymity is crucial to Western users who may be interested in joining the jihadist movement but do not know how to begin the process. These applications assist by linking the possible recruit to a member who can provide them with answers to lure them into participation.

IS supporters are also in the business of creating applications and platforms, such as Alwari, which operates on an Android system. Alwari was created to ensure that communications between IS supporters would remain secure, as reported by Ghost Security Group (GhostSec), a counterterrorism hacktivist organization (Russon, 2016). This is not the first application that was IS-devised either. Kingsley reports (2014), the Palestinian affiliate of the Islamic State created the Dawn of Glad Tidings application with assistance and approval from leaders in Iraq and Syria. At the peak of its popularity Dawn of Glad Tidings "posted 40,000 tweets in a single day from the battlefield using countless users' accounts" (Vitale & Kegale, 2014, Pg. 7). The application

allows IS to use their accounts to send out centrally written updates....the messages swamp social media, giving IS a far larger online reach than their own accounts would otherwise allow (Kingsley, 2014).

Hackers with numerous pro-Islamic State groups, including the United Cyber Caliphate (UCC) have made the work of Western governments working to dismantle the communication structure of jihadism to a new level. The UCC has published a 'kill list' that contained the names and personal identification of more than 40 U.S. government employees whose jobs encompass national security and counterterrorism. The Cyber Caliphate Army is another hacker group that has pledged allegiance to the Islamic State who also released a 'kill list' of American officials, and threatened "Electronic War" on the U.S. and Europe (Masi, 2015). The Islamic State Hacking Division has leaked personal information of nearly 100 members of the U.S. military and invited IS supporters to find and kill them (Dunham & Beech, 2015). Mikko Hypponen, cyber security expert noted in 2015 that the Islamic State has the technological capabilities to conduct a major infrastructural attack on the West (Yadron, 2015). This is coming at a particularly vulnerable time for U.S. digital infrastructure as international actors such as China and Russia have exposed not only civilian data and information, but also government officials and employees. If the Islamic State is paying attention to the U.S. presidential campaign during Summer 2016, and the hacks of party apparatus servers or state voter registration databases, the U.S. cyber landscape can be compromised, leaving the door open for more than just theft of data.

Beyond social media platforms and mobile applications, major technological actors like Google are weighing free speech and content on their search engine. The company noted in May 2016 that more than 50,000 people search for the phrase 'join IS' every month (Frenkel, 2016), and when one completes the search, one can find most of the information necessary to join the organization, as well as their ideological content that inspires attacks globally. Zelin (2015) emphasizes the breadth of the Islamic State's media apparatus in his study of one week's (April 18-24, 2015) media releases from the group, the group indeed conducts much of their communication via the internet and social media. However, they have established numerous media "wings" that include its news agency, A'maq and radio station al-Bayan (Pg. 88). According to Zelin's analysis, al-Bayan Radio Station characterizes IS military fronts, advances, and achievements daily (2015, Pg. 90). While the radio station's broadcast area remains secluded to Iraq, Syria and Libya, the news/talk radio format is broadcast in Kurdish, Arabic, English, French, and Russian languages (Sharma, 2015). The Islamic State releases segments of broadcasts featuring military advances on Twitter in various languages for mass consumption, adding yet another level to their ability to influence.

OUTSOURCING TERRORISM

Transference of tactics to other established terror organizations that are not (or initially were not) affiliated with the Islamic State have attempted to mimic their social media and digital campaign to increase membership. Groups such as Boko Haram, a Nigerian-based terrorist organization began borrowing from the Islamic State tactics in 2014, taking their strategy of conquering lands and made claims of establishing a caliphate (Youssef, 2015). Boko Haram was established in 2002 but did not begin military operations until 2009 in northern Nigeria. The group came into international awareness when it abducted at least 200 schoolgirls in April 2014, which led to the #BringBackOurGirls campaign via social media whose participants included United States First Lady Michelle Obama (Ross, 2016). In January 2015, the group established their online presence with a media channel, The *Indissoluble Link* that appeared similar to the Islamic State's *Furqan* channel. The Indissoluble Link also created a Twitter profile that was immediately publicized by IS supporters (Youssef, 2015). The adoption and streamlining of Boko

Haram's social media and propaganda campaign suggested to many in the international community that the group was receiving assistance from the Islamic State or wanted to legitimize themselves with the Islamic State in order for cooperation to take place.

According to Zellin (Youssef, 2015), "For Boko Haram, working with the Islamic State bolsters its legitimacy and could potentially help it gain recruits and funding." According to a *New York Times* article from April 2016, Boko Haram and IS are cooperating more since the former pledged allegiance to the latter in March 2015, citing a convoy of seized weapons on route to the Lake Chad region believed to have originated with the Islamic State in Libya, which provides evidence that the organizations are cooperating (Cooper, 2016). The intercontinental coordination of terrorism is as much of a consequence of the internet and digital media as increased transparency and democracy in the West.

Although terrorism beyond IS, particularly when discussing Al Qaeda, has become more localized in recent years (Berger, 2015) – the digital precedent set by IS has led to significant alliances for the group in their spread of not only ideology, but in physical space. The United States, launched in August 2016, an airstrike campaign against IS in Libya in the stronghold of Sirte (Ackerman et al., 2016); it is widely known that Tunisia is a major exporter of terrorists who are sympathetic to the IS cause (Trofimov, 2016); and Egypt has been fighting the group in the Sinai Peninsula since 2014 (Cunningham, 2014). The advancement of IS in the Middle East and Northern Africa (MENA) region, which includes the physical occupation of land, utilities, and geopolitical resources as well as the effective spread of the ideological mission has resulted in a multi-continental conflict. This conflict includes Western countries that seek to destroy the Islamic State at its roots without considering their language and message that continues to resonate. This global resonance that has manifested into inspired or coordinated attacks is possible thanks to the leveling of the communications structure on the part of the Islamic State. It is through "direct, real-time, and independently targeted engagements [that IS] formulate and solidify group loyalties around jihadist messages that enact moral and religious responsibilities" (Bjelopera, 2013, Pg. 18).

As of 2016, there are more than 50 international organizations that have pledged allegiance or *bay'at* to the Islamic State, making an extension of the group in their region, which now includes Egypt, Libya, Tunisia, Chechnya, Uzbekistan, and Tajikistan (Day, 2016). This expansion of IS ideology to the MENA region has presented numerous challenges to Western governments who would like to militarily quell the spread of IS ideology and political theatre, but also threatens the stability of fragile Arab Spring nations who have yet to rebuild stable governments. Many of the groups pledging allegiance are focused on local or regional issues as opposed to the global jihadist movement. This is particularly interesting if the Islamic State is going to sustain those international alliances when they are predicated on localized issues. Although the future of the stratified Islamic State structure is to be determined, the short-term gains and projection of strength in numbers does aid in the perception of their organization's resiliency.

IS has taken advantage of the digital media environment's lack of structure when it comes to communication, offering a non-hierarchical, horizontal, and decentralized means to share content. While it is critical to not overstate the importance of digital media, that is to say, traditional networks of communication, namely the family and other foundational aspects of a community (media, churches/mosques, etc.) remain crucial pieces of radicalization, the internet and accompanying tools have supplemented and enhanced traditional networks as well as opening the jihadist network to millions who would have not had access to it as readily in the pre-digital era. Michael Steinbach, Assistant Director of the Federal Bureau of Investigation, noted in testimony before the U.S. House Committee on Homeland Security that the Islamic State's use of horizontal media distribution "allows direct access to spot, assess, recruit, and radicalize" via the internet, something that no other terror organization before had attempted to do (Steinbach, 2015).

The IS media strategy provides for personalization and a recruiter being able to customize the message in order to appeal to individuals using various types of content, from the vicious beheading and killing videos to memes featuring kittens to attract young women theoretically. The Islamic State has mastered using both *hard power* (military fronts and inspired and/or coordinated attacks) as well as *soft power* (communication of religious and political utopianism in the creation of the Caliphate), which has been quite effective thus far not only in recruitment but confusing oppositional tactics for fighting back. For example, as Twitter account suspensions for users dedicated to the Islamic State began to destabilize the group's network, which hit 235,000 suspensions in August 2016 (Flores & Brennan, 2016), IS methodically shifted their social media use from user-centric (profiles associated with or belonging to known IS members) content dissemination to a hashtag-driven model, which further decentralizes their messages making it hard to pin down to a single individual user profile (Glavin, 2015).

The threat of IS is occurring at a peculiar time for global relations, as we are seeing a trend in many Western societies turning away from the globalism and integration that defined the post-modern era toward nationalism, or rebuilding of a strong national identity while eschewing international brands, values, and norms. This move inward could be a very dangerous detriment to the collective international response to the Islamic State, as more nations are taking disparate measures to counter terrorism within their borders (i.e.: immigration and/or refugee policies), yet there is not an evident coordinated global effort to combat the spread of extremist ideology via digital tools.

REFERENCES

Ackerman, S., Stephen, C., & MacAskill, E. (2016, Aug. 1). US launches airstrikes against ISIS in Libya. *The Guardian*. Retrieved from https://www.theguardian.com/world/2016/aug/01/us-airstrikes-against-isis-libya-pentagon

Alder, J. (2013, April 16). Meet the First Digital Generation. Now Get Ready to Play by Their Rules. *Wired*. Retrieved from https://www.wired.com/2013/04/genwired/

Arquilla, J., & Ronfeldt, D., & Zanini, M. (2000, April). Information-Age Terrorism. *Current History (New York, N.Y.)*, *99*(636), 179–185.

Bakker, E., & de Graaf, B. (2011). Preventing Lone Wolf Terrorism: some CT Approaches Addressed. *Perspectives on Terrorism, 5*(5-6).

Berger, J. M. (2015, March 6). *The ISIS Twitter census: Making sense of ISIS's use of Twitter*. Brookings Institute. Retrieved from https://www.brookings.edu/blog/order-from-chaos/2015/03/06/the-isis-twitter-census-making-sense-of-isiss-use-of-twitter/

Bergin. (2008, April 5). Facebook terrorism investigation. *The Advertiser*.

Bjelopera, J. P. (2013). American Jihadist Terrorism: Combating a Complex Threat. *Congressional Research Service*. Retrieved from https://www.fas.org/sgp/crs/terror/R41416.pdf

Brooking, E., & Singer, P. W. (2016, Nov.). War goes Viral. *The Atlantic*. Retrieved from http://www.theatlantic.com/magazine/archive/2016/11/war-goes-viral/501125/

Conway, M. (2006). Terrorism and the Internet: New Media- New Threat? *Parliamentary Affairs*, *59*(2), 283–298. doi:10.1093/pa/gsl009

Cooper, H. (2016, April 20). Boko Haram and ISIS are collaborating more, U.S. military says. *New York Times*. Retrieved from http://www.nytimes.com/2016/04/21/world/africa/boko-haram-and-isis-are-collaborating-more-us-military-says.html

Cunningham, E. (2014, Oct. 24). Bomb blast in Egypt's Sinai Peninsula is deadliest attack on army in decades. *Washington Post*. Retrieve from https://www.washingtonpost.com/world/bomb-attack-in-egypts-sinai-peninsula-is-deadliest-attack-on-its-army-in-years/2014/10/24/98d14ad7-91c0-4acd-835f-e61b8f18a434_story.html

Day, J. (2016, March). *The ISIS Bandwagon: Under What Conditions Do Groups Pledge Support?* Boston University Institute on Culture, Religion, and World Affairs. Retrieved from https://www.bu.edu/cura/files/2016/03/The-ISIS-Bandwagon-V3.pdf

Dewey, C. (2015, Nov. 23). The secret American origins of Telegram, the encrypted messaging app favored by the Islamic State. *The Washington Post*. Retrieved from https://www.washingtonpost.com/news/the-intersect/wp/2015/11/23/the-secret-american-origins-of-telegram-the-encrypted-messaging-app-favored-by-the-islamic-state/

Dunham, W., & Beech, E. (2015, March 21). Islamic State calls on backers to kill 100 U.S. military personnel. *Reuters*. Retrieved from http://www.reuters.com/article/us-mideast-crisis-threat-idUSKBN-0MH0QQ20150321

Flores, R., & Brennan, M. (2016, Aug. 18). Twitter announces it has suspended 235,000 terror-linked accounts. *CBS News*. Retrieved from http://www.cbsnews.com/news/twitter-announces-it-has-suspended-235000-terror-linked-accounts/

Frenkel, S. (2016, May 12). This is How ISIS uses the Internet. *Buzzfeed News*. Retrieved from https://www.buzzfeed.com/sheerafrenkel/everything-you-ever-wanted-to-know-about-how-isis-uses-the-i?utm_term=.jr0AjwPE5#.vseo9gxq2

Frontline. (2014). *The Rise of ISIS*. Retrieved from http://www.pbs.org/wgbh/frontline/film/rise-of-isis/

Gibbons-Neff, T. (2016, Oct. 11). ISIS used an armed drone to kill two Kurdish fighters and wound French troops, report says. *The Washington Post*. Retrieved from https://www.washingtonpost.com/news/checkpoint/wp/2016/10/11/isis-used-an-armed-drone-to-kill-two-kurdish-fighters-and-wound-french-troops-report-says/

Glavin, N. (2015, Dec. 7). Counter ISIS' Narratives on Social Media. *The New York Times*. Retrieved from http://www.nytimes.com/roomfordebate/2015/12/06/how-can-america-counter-the-appeal-of-isis/counter-isis-narratives-on-social-media

Hammadi, S., Scammell, R., & Yuhas, A. (2016, July 3). Dhaka cafe attack ends with 20 hostages among dead. *The Guardian*. Retrieved from https://www.theguardian.com/world/2016/jul/01/dhaka-bangladesh-restaurant-attack-hostages

Hegel, G. W. F., & Miller, A. V. (1977). Force and the Understanding: Appearance and the Supersensible World: Phenomenology of Spirit (5th ed.). New York: Oxford University Press.

Hussain, G., & Saltman, E. (2014). Jihad Trending: A Comprehensive Analysis of Online Extremism and How to Counter It. *Quilliam*. Retrieved from https://www.quilliamfoundation.org/wp/wp-content/uploads/publications/free/jihad-trending-quilliam-report.pdf

Jasparro, C. (2010). *Lone Wolf – The Threat from Independent Jihadists*. Retrieved from https://wikileaks.org/gifiles/attach/168/168290_Osac-jir1209.pdf

Jenkins, B. M. (2006). *The New Age of Terrorism*. RAND Corporation. Retrieved from http://www.rand.org/content/dam/rand/pubs/reprints/2006/RAND_RP1215.pdf

Kam, E. (2015). The Islamic State Surprise: The Intelligence Perspective. *Strategic Assessment*, *18*(3), 21–31.

Kingsley, P. (2014, June 23). Who is behind ISIS's terrifying online propaganda operation? *The Guardian*. Retrieved from https://www.theguardian.com/world/2014/jun/23/who-behind-isis-propaganda-operation-iraq

Koerner, B. (2016, June 12). The Orlando Nightclub Shooting could have been an ISIS plan with ISIS knowing nothing about it. *Wired*. Retrieved from https://www.wired.com/2016/06/orlando-massacre-shows-isis-outsources-terror/

Masi, A. (2015, May 11). ISIS-Affiliated Hackers Threaten Cyberattacks, 'Electronic War' on US, Europe. *International Business Times*. Retrieved from http://www.ibtimes.com/isis-affiliated-hackers-threaten-cyberattacks-electronic-war-us-europe-1917320

Newman, L. (2016, June 8). France releases terror alert app. *Slate*. Retrieved from http://www.slate.com/blogs/future_tense/2016/06/08/france_releases_terror_alert_app.html

Ross, W. (2016, May 18). Chibok girls: Kidnapped schoolgirl found in Nigeria. *BBC News*. Retrieved from http://www.bbc.com/news/world-africa-36321249

Russon, M. (2016, Jan. 14). Alrawi: ISIS has built secure Android messaging app to replace Telegram, says Anonymous affiliate GhostSec. *International Business Times*. Retrieved from http://www.ibtimes.co.uk/alrawi-isis-builds-secure-android-messaging-app-replace-telegram-says-anonymous-affiliate-ghostsec-1537948

Sharma, S. (2015, June 4). Islamic State has an English-language radio broadcast that sounds eerily like NPR. *The Washington Post*. Retrieved from https://www.washingtonpost.com/news/worldviews/wp/2015/06/04/islamic-state-has-a-daily-english-language-radio-broadcast-that-sounds-eerily-like-it-could-be-on-npr/

Soriano, M. (2008). Terrorism and the Mass Media after Al Qaeda: A Change of Course? *Athena Intelligence Journal, 3*(1), 1–20.

Spaaij, R. (2010). The Enigma of Lone Wolf Terrorism: An Assessment. *Studies in Conflict and Terrorism, 33*(9), 854–870. doi:10.1080/1057610X.2010.501426

Starr, B. (2016, Sept. 13). US bombs ISIS chemical weapons plant. *CNN News*. Retrieved from http://www.cnn.com/2016/09/13/politics/isis-chemical-weapons-plant/

Steinbach, M. (2015, June 3). *Terrorism Gone Viral: The Attack in Garland, Texas and Beyond*. Federal Bureau of Investigations. Statement before the House Homeland Security Committee. Retrieved from https://www.fbi.gov/news/testimony/terrorism-gone-viral-the-attack-in-garland-texas-and-beyond

Stern, J. (2003). *Terror in the Name of God: Why Religious Militants Kill*. New York: HarperCollins.

Talbot, D. (2015, Sept. 30). Fighting ISIS Online. *MIT Technology Review*. Retrieved from https://www.technologyreview.com/s/541801/fighting-isis-online/

Teich, S. (2013, Oct.). Trends and Developments in Lone Wolf Terrorism in the Western World. *International Institute for Counter-Terrorism*. Retrieved from http://www.ctcitraining.org/docs/LoneWolf_SarahTeich2013.pdf

Torok, R. (2013). Developing an explanatory model for the process of online radicalization and terrorism. Perth, Australia: Springer. Retrieved from http://www.security-informatics.com/content/2/1/6

Trofimov, Y. (2016, Sept. 9). What Happens After ISIS Falls? *The Wall Street Journal*. Retrieved from http://www.wsj.com/articles/what-happens-after-isis-falls-1473435007

Trofimov, Y. (2016, Feb. 25). How Tunisia Became a Top Source of ISIS Recruits. *The Wall Street Journal*. Retrieved from http://www.wsj.com/articles/how-tunisia-became-a-top-source-of-isis-recruits-1456396203

Tuysuz, G., & Almasy, S. (2016, July 6). Istanbul airport explosions: 36 dead, 147 injured, Turkish officials say. *CNN News*. Retrieved from http://www.cnn.com/2016/06/28/europe/turkey-istanbul-airport-attacks/

Vitale, H. M., & Keagle, J. M. (2014). A time to tweet, as well as a time to kill: ISIS's projection of power in Iraq and Syria. *Defense Horizons,* (77). Retrieved from http://search.proquest.com/docview/1618549256?accountid=8289

Weimann, G. (2014). New Terrorism and New Media. Washington, DC: Commons Lab of the Woodrow Wilson International Center for Scholars. Retrieved from https://www.wilsoncenter.org/sites/default/files/STIP_140501_new_terrorism_F.pdf

Wieviorka, M. (2004). *The making of Terrorism*. Chicago: The University of Chicago Press.

Wire Staff, C. N. N. (2012, May 23). U.S. senators: Al Qaeda calls for 'electronic jihad'. *CNN*. Retrieved from http://www.cnn.com/2012/05/23/politics/al-qaeda-electronic-jihad/

Yadron, D. (2015, Oct. 20). Free Services Make the Internet a Privacy Nightmare, Security Researcher Says. *Wall Street Journal.* Retrieved from http://www.wsj.com/articles/free-services-make-the-internet-a-privacy-nightmare-security-researcher-says-1445370168

Youssef, N. (2015, Jan. 29). ISIS and Boko Haram's Unholy Online Alliance. *The Daily Beast.* Retrieved from http://www.thedailybeast.com/articles/2015/01/29/isis-and-boko-haram-s-unholy-online-alliance.html

Zelin, A. (2015). Picture Or It Didn't Happen: A Snapshot of the Islamic State's Official Media Output. *Perspectives on Terrorism, 9*(4). Retrieved from http://www.terrorismanalysts.com/pt/index.php/pot/article/view/445/html

This research was previously published in Combating Internet-Enabled Terrorism edited by Emily Stacey, pages 16-44, copyright year 2017 by Information Science Reference (an imprint of IGI Global).

Chapter 3
Dysfunctional Digital Demeanors:
Tales From (and Policy Implications of) eLearning's Dark Side

Alexander G. Flor
University of the Philippines (Open University), Philippines

Benjamina Gonzalez-Flor
University of the Philippines – Los Baños, Philippines

ABSTRACT

eLearning has been associated with a number of behaviors that are considered dysfunctional. Among these behaviors that form part of the Dark Web are cyber-bullying, plagiarism, hacking and other forms of cheating. This chapter describes, illustrates and typologizes these behaviors with cases observed by the authors among their online students or culled from student disciplinary boards in the past ten years. The elaboration of tales from eLearning's dark side is followed by an exploration of policy implications. Employing the problematique method, the authors attempt to trace the root causes (psychological, sociological and technological) and offer policy options to address these roots.

INTRODUCTION

Background: The Elephant in the Online Classroom

Figure 1, an image of smiling multi-racial faces and "Like" handsigns is the stuff that nightmares of eLearning champions are made of.

It is the frontpage screenshot of *We Take Your Class*, a site that would allow anyone, anywhere in the world, to complete a formal eLearning course without even visiting the course site. It is a paid, indiscreet classwork-by-proxy service. For a "reasonable" fee, this globally available Web service offers to perform

DOI: 10.4018/978-1-5225-3163-0.ch003

Figure 1. Online classwork-by-proxy service
www.wetakeyourclass.com Retrieved 23 March 2014.

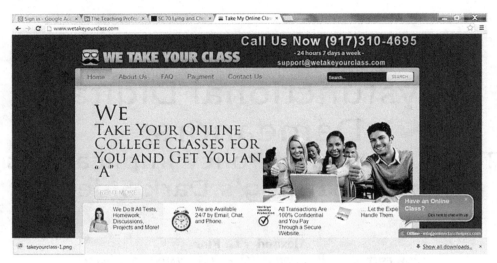

all tests, homework, discussions and projects. On top of that, it promises the client, who may very well be your past, present or future student, a grade of A.

In almost every forum where eLearning is discussed, questions on the means of validating student identities have been raised. Answers range from employing fraud-detecting software to conducting identity authentication measures such as Web on-camera examinations. Some of us have resorted to skirting the issue by replying that students who cheat online actually cheat themselves, not the system.

We Take Your Class confirms the doubts raised by eLearning detractors and jolts us from our state of denial. More alarming is the fact that fraud is not the only dysfunctional behavior encountered in on-line classes. Throughout its short and rapidly paced history, eLearning has been associated with learner behaviors considered dysfunctional not only in the higher educational arena. At times, these behaviors - including cyberbullying, plagiarism, hacking and the active search for shortcuts - are not explicitly manifested but assume the nature of a reality, an accepted conduct, or a matter-of-course attitude. It is a bearing that one assumes consciously or unconsciously upon logging into the course site, which could be more appropriately referred to as a *demeanor*, one that allows Web services such as the above to thrive. Sadly, many of us too familiar with these demeanors have been sweeping them under the rug for too long. Whenever these cases pop out in discussions among eLearning advocates they tend to be summarily dismissed as insignificant. Collective cognitive dissonance that result in selective exposure, perception and retention prevail.

There is an elephant in the eLearning classroom. It cheats, it bullies, and it loves to cut corners. But we act as if it is not there. This animal needs to be dissected, its anatomy examined and its invisibility explained.

Purpose of the Chapter

Open, distance and eLearning or ODeL is fast becoming the educational system of the future. The Open Educational Resources (OER) initiative of the Massachusetts Institute of Technology and Massive Open

Online Courses (MOOCs) of major Ivy League universities demonstrate the promise. A meta-analysis conducted by the US Department of Education that synthesized the findings of over one thousand empirical studies found that online students performed better than those receiving face-to-face instruction because of: increased learning time; innovative curriculum and pedagogy; opportunities for collaboration and reflection; and learner control over interactions with the media (Means et al, 2010).

Quality education can be made accessible to all through ODeL. However, part of ODeL resides in the Dark Web. It is encumbered by a problematique shaped by questions of fraud, security and propriety: "Are we sure that our students are the ones taking our exams? Are their submissions plagiarized? Why do discussion forums become venues for insolent exchanges? Why do students act as if the eLearning course is an online game with their instructor as an opponent who they must outsmart?"

This chapter comes to grips with this problematique, which has not been comprehensively addressed and at times ignored in the current ODeL discourse. It attempts to explain the problematique by tracing the subordinate influential factors and superordinate influential factors of this corner of the Dark Web and explores their policy implications. Moreover, it enables us to rethink and re-examine our basic assumptions regarding the relationships between delivery systems, content, pedagogy and assessment that may be impinging upon this problematique.

Based on current literature and cases observed or culled from student disciplinary boards in the past ten years, the chapter describes, illustrates and provides a typology of dysfunctional digital demeanors among online students. The elaboration of tales from eLearning's dark side is followed by an exploration of policy implications on eLearning, in particular, and higher education, in general. Employing the problematique method, the chapter traces the causes of this cluster of problems and offers policy options to be considered, if indeed the global educational sector will embark earnestly upon ODeL.

THEORETICAL FRAMEWORK

Basic Constructs

A *problematique* refers to a cluster of interrelated problems and sub-problems having multiple causes. Molenda and Di Paolo (1979) introduced the term in educational systems research using overpopulation as an illustration, which is "...better thought of as a problematique -- a force which shows itself in many forms and which has many roots, social, cultural, economic, etc." Molenda and Di Paolo also developed *problematique analysis*, a method founded on general systems theory that traces root causes and symptoms of complex problem situations within educational systems.

General systems theory identifies interrelatedness as an attribute of all subsystems or system components (Von Bertalanfly and Rapoport, 1967). This inquiry begins with the proposition that open, distance and eLearning is an educational system, specifically a curricular system, made up of the following components: the content subsystem; the pedagogic subsystem; the delivery subsystem; and the assessment subsystem. These subsystems are likened to four posts that hold a curricular program together. Any change in one subsystem requires equivalent degrees of changes in the others. Otherwise, system stability is lost.

Open, distance and eLearning presents drastic changes in the delivery system of the conventional educational program. To some degree, content has adjusted to these changes. However, the pedagogic and assessment subsystems have generally maintained their traditional face-to-face instruction models. The maintenance of traditional pedagogic and assessment models in ODeL is resulting in instabilities within the curricular system, which now manifest as dysfunctional behaviors and demeanors of online students.

Three Cs: A Typology of Dysfunctional Digital Demeanors

The initial step in dissecting the ODeL Dark Web problematique is determining the types of dysfunctional behaviors. Based on a decade long practice and observation of teacher-learner online interactions supplemented by current literature, dysfunctional eLearning behaviors may be classified under three types: cheating; cyberbullying; and cutting corners.

Type 1: Cheating

Case Number 1: Student A represents a composite picture of plagiarism respondents in student disciplinary board transcripts and instructor's journals at the University of the Philippines - Open University.

Student A, enrolled in an online graduate program, is charged with plagiarism. He is based in Europe working for an international development agency. The deadline for a term paper in one of his elective courses coincided with the submission date of an important report that he has to prepare for the agency. Faced with conflicting priorities, he focused his efforts on the agency report rather than on his paper. Having very little time to prepare the class requirement he cut and pasted substantive sections of his main reference into the paper thus attributing them as his own.

What was going on in his mind at the time? The following thoughts are indicative:

It felt easy since my instructor was thousands of miles away. Cutting and pasting is so convenient and time saving. It can be done in three mouse clicks.

My main reference is already written perfectly and there was no other way to rewrite the paragraphs without losing the thought. This is not really plagiarism because I already wrote half the paper anyway. Moreover, I am not a bad person. I just need the extra time for my report.

Description: Under cheating is a variety of behaviors that demonstrate dishonesty such as classwork-by-proxy, ghostwriter engagement, and plagiarism. Students plagiarize in spite of detection services such as Turnitin.com, IntegriGuard, EduTie, and PlagiServ. In fact, plagiarism can also be detected through search engines such as Google, Bing, Yahoo, and others.

Engaging the services of ghostwriters is also getting prevalent. Heberling (2002) identified services that sell readily available term papers or thesis for a fee or customized ones with more expensive price tags. These include A1 Term Papers, The Cheat Factory, SchoolSucks.com, Cheater.com, Genius Papers, Evil House of Cheat, Superior Term Papers, 12000 Papers.com and Accepted.com, among others. At times, these services are offered with waived fees since profits can be generated through advertisements posted on ghostwriting sites. More disturbing is the finding that engaging the services of ghostwriters is an accepted practice among many undergraduate students (Caballero, 2012).

Classwork by proxy, engaging ghostwriters, and plagiarism are identity-related cheating. However, cases of dishonesty among online students go beyond identity-related fraud. They come in various forms. Rowe (2004) enumerates a number of "technical tactics" used by students:

1. A student who has taken an examination in advance may take screen shots of online tests or memorize test items. They he/she leaks or even sells the test questions.
2. A student may hack course sites or crack software codes allowing him/her to log in as the instructor. He will access test answer keys especially if questions are taken from a pool or item bank.
3. A student may use spyware to view the answers of others during the test.
4. A student may use "sniffers" that decipher the message packets of a local area network that have been used by fellow students or the instructor to obtain answers and passwords.
5. A student may use a variety of hacker attack methods to gain server administrator privileges on the course server.
6. A student may use computer-forensics tools that access the cache after a fellow student or the instructor logs out.
7. A student may pretend that there was a power failure while taking the online exam and thus be given the opportunity to retake the test after getting familiar with the items.
8. A student may change the system clock making the grading server assign an earlier date to a new assessment.
9. A student may steal the password of instructors to change the grades.

In summary, the online cheating type comes in two forms: identity-related cheating (e.g., plagiarism, engaging ghostwriters, credit-by-proxy); and technology-augmented cheating (e.g., hacking, sniffing, employing spyware, doctoring, etc.)

Type 2: Cyberbullying

Case Number 2: In online discussion forums, teachers are often confronted with a situation similar to the following.

Students B and C are enrolled in an undergraduate social science course. Student B posts a response to a discussion thread started by the teacher. In an unguarded moment, Student C emboldened by the lack of physical presence loses her sense of propriety and throws in an unkind remark of Student B's post without giving it a second thought. Student B is offended and responds with a venomous reply to Student C's comment, calling her an "Idiot." After an embarrassing silence, the instructor steps in to diffuse the situation. However, from then on, Student B would insolently pick on any item posted by Student C discouraging her from actively participating in the online discussion forum for the rest of the semester.

Then there is Student D, enrolled in a post baccalaureate pre-master's computer science program. Student D has been a software developer for several years. In the class discussion forum, he questions the reasons behind the use of the C++ language given in the course module written by the faculty-incharge. The FIC does not respond but his tutor does implying that the instructor knows best. Student D goes ballistic with the tutor's explanation arguing that he (Student D) "knows his stuff." He "flames" his tutor with invectives. Other students come to the aid of the tutor. Consequently, they find themselves at the receiving end of Student D's abusive tirades.

Description: Cyberbullying is a manifestation of what is known as the *online disinhibition effect*, the decline of social reservation during online interactions. In the past ten years, we have personally observed several forms of cyberbullying in our online discussion forums. At times, it is done by an individual, a class bully who dominates the discussion and would always have the last word. It may be done by a group who would collective pick or *gang up* on individuals at a time.

Bullying in our online classes takes the form of the following: imposing one's ideas in an online discussion; responding to a post with a humiliating remark; taking credit for a classmate's idea; belittling somebody else's work or opinion; revealing embarrassing facts about a classmate; and others that revolve around abuse, humiliation, intimidation, and domination. Bullies in online classrooms are as threatening as bullies in traditional classrooms. Even if those who engage in it are relatively few, bullying is disruptive. We have noted that a bullying episode changes the atmosphere of the class and it does not end there. The exchanges between the bully and the victim become a spectator sport that spreads in other social media platforms.

Type 3: Cutting Corners - The Path of Least Resistance

Case Number 3: Student E is an undergraduate under the multimedia studies program. She has occupied herself with computer games for the greater part of her life. Subconsciously, she assumes the gamer mode when engaged in online learning and would, as gamers do, cut corners and look for hidden "cheats" even within the MOODLE course site.

Student E considers her online course as a game to win. She sees herself and her online instructors (and even the learning management system) as protagonists. Upon successfully passing a course, she would announce in her social network that it was time to celebrate because she has outsmarted her instructor.

Description: Among online students, the tendency to cut corners and look for shortcuts is influenced by the "gamer's agenda," the intent to win by outsmarting the system. This factor prompts students to produce what Hebertling (2002) describes as sloppy output from cut and paste technology to beat course calendars. Furthermore, students rationalize their online behavior through their game identities. The person who cuts corners in the online classroom is not really him/her but an avatar, which is on a quest and would do what it takes to succeed.

Suler explains, "… some people see their online life as a kind of game with rules and norms that don't apply to everyday living. Once they turn off the computer and return to their daily routine, they believe they can leave behind that game and their game identity. They relinquish their responsibility for what happens in a make-believe play world that has nothing to do with reality (p.323)." That make-believe play world just happens to be a formal online course.

What factors cause these attitudes and behaviors? The following section will trace these factors and will endeavor to differentiate the root causes from their symptoms.

PROBLEMATIQUE ANALYSIS

Problem structure analysis or *problematique* analysis is a systems research procedure that has been used almost exclusively in identifying and analyzing subordinate and superordinate influential factors of complex problems within educational systems (Tiffin, 1978; Molenda and DiPaolo, 1979; Flor, 1982). Subordinate influential factors are the immediate or primary order causes of individual conditions in the complex web of glitches and snags within the problematique. More often than not, these immediate causes are merely symptomatic of deeply embedded roots known as superordinate influential factors. The significance of differentiating subordinate influential factors from superordinate influential factors come into play when one attempts to solve the problematique. Addressing the subordinate factors become ineffectual since the problem situation will most certainly recur or reappear. Addressing the comparatively few root causes or superordinate influential factors on the other hand would disentangle the entire problematique. Thus, problematique analysis enables us to focus our time, energy and resources on resolving the factors that matter.

Subordinate Influential Factors

Of Cheating: Lincoln (2002) pointed out the following reasons for online cheating. It enables one to maintain high Grade Point Averages. Online cheaters are unlikely to get caught. It is no longer socially unacceptable and everyone does it. Cutting and pasting material is quick, easy, and very tempting. Everything on the Internet is in the public domain. Some faculty members prefer to ignore the problem.

The perception that online cheating is no longer socially unacceptable and that everyone does it is indicative of the scale at which cheating is practiced. The act of cheating feeds on itself, specifically the awareness that similar acts have been done without consequences. This perception coupled with the apathy displayed by some faculty members are higher order causes. On the other hand, maintaining high GPAs; the unlikeliness of getting caught; and the speed and ease of cutting and pasting are direct causes of cheating.

- **Inappropriate Assessment Models:** Maintaining high GPAs is indicative of a defective evaluation and assessment system adopted by many ODeL programs, which by definition should be guided by open education philosophies. Applying the conventional grading system in ODeL is unwise given the distance between the teacher and the learner as well as its attendant technologies. Measures of cognitive gain may no longer be appropriate nor accurate given these factors. Instilling GPA primacy among online learners is clearly out-of-place within the ODeL environment, particularly in higher education. Additionally, inappropriate assessment models give rise to oppositional relationship between teachers and students, which in-turn influence students to see the online classroom as an arena for a game. It encourages the student to adopt the very same gamer's agenda that has been discussed above and will be elaborated further below. Engaging in this cat and mouse game has been the preoccupation of both students and teachers perennially sacrificing the primacy of learning and instruction.

- **Technology:** While cheating is found in both traditional and online settings, it occurs more often in the online mode (Heberling, 2002; Watson and Sottile, 2010). The technical tactics enumerated in the previous section imply that technology enhances online cheating. Heberling (2002) noted that there is a greater propensity to cheat during online tests or assessments. Technology augments cheating. It is a double-edged sword. The very technology that one employs to enhance learning is the same technology that augments cheating.

- **Distance:** Another factor that influences cheating is distance. Cizek (1999) observed the increase of cheating incidents in the second half of the twentieth century among older students through age 25. He found that cheating increases as the bandwidth (information per second) of the communications channel between teacher and student decreases. Thus, cheating is inversely related to teacher-student interaction. Cheating now becomes a function of distance. The farther the distance between the learner and the teacher, the greater is the tendency for cheating (George and Carlson, 1999; Cizek, 1999). This was recently validated by Ravasco (2012) in a study conducted among online graduate students. However, distance may likewise be a factor in the unsuitability of assessment models used.

- **Remedial Measures:** Ravasco believes that distance could be bridged through frequency of interaction, "Frequent interaction, no matter how informal, creates good teacher-student relations. Frequent teacher feedback and timely suggestions make the students feel attended to. Frequency of course board discussion and participation of students increase personal knowledge and styles of each other's writing and thinking capabilities thus preventing dishonesty in the process."

In summary, the subordinate influential factors of online cheating are: inappropriate assessment models; technology; and distance. It can also be said that these factors influence one another. Specifically, technology and distance make traditional assessment models inappropriate.

Of Cyberbullying: It has already been explained that cyberbullying's immediate cause is *online disinhibition*, which we describe as the decline, loss or absence of proper social reservation or restraint during online interactions.

- **Factors Creating Online Disinhibition:** Suler (2004) names six factors that interact with each other in creating the online disinhibition effect. These are: dissociative anonymity, invisibility, asynchronicity, solipsistic introjection, dissociative imagination, and minimization of authority.

Dissociative anonymity is an attribute of one's online persona wherein the online and offline identities are not integrated. Hence, one may not own up to one's online behavior. Suler explains, "Whatever they say or do can't be directly linked to the rest of their lives... The online self becomes a compartmentalized self in the case of expressed hostilities or other deviant actions (p.322)..." such as cyber-bullying. Invisibility, on the other hand, relates to the lack of physical presence during online interactions. Thus, online students do not have to worry about how they look or sound or how others look or sound in response to what they post (p.322). Asynchronicity refers to the online attribute of controlled feedback. Ordinarily, feedback inhibits us from engaging in outrageous behavior. Conversely, not having to cope with someone's immediate reaction disinhibits people (p.322-323). Solipsistic introjections or talking with oneself, which encourages disinhibition because talking with oneself, feels safer than talking with others (p 323). Dissociative imagination is the tendency to relinquish responsibility for what happens in the online world (p323) and the distinction between online fantasy environments and online social environments blur (p324). Lastly, minimization of authority refers to the unwritten tenet of equality within the Internet environment. Everyone - regardless of gender, race, wealth, designation or status - has an equal voice and starts off on a level playing field (p.324). A related concept to this is that of entitlement, i.e. everyone is entitled to express his or her own opinion.

- **Remedial Measures:** Race and Pickford (2007) believe that it is more challenging to manage cyberbullies because of the difficulty in interpreting emotions. They outline the following measures for dealing with disruptive students online:
    ◦ Delete any inappropriate postings on the discussion board.
    ◦ Phone or email the disruptive student and objectively inform the student of the problem and how they were disruptive.
    ◦ Explain what the possible consequences will be if they continue.
    ◦ For a persistent offender consider blocking the student from posting in a forum or removing that student from the group.
    ◦ Save any postings for future reference.

These remedial measures, however, would not guarantee that students no longer engage in cyberbullying. They may be discouraging the act but they do not address the causes of the act. Given the opportunity, the cyber-bully's attitude and behavior will resurface and recur, as elements of a problematique do, if the root causes are not addressed.

Of Cutting Corners: Online students cut corners because they think and act like gamers. It is in the nature of gamers to look for short-cuts or "cheats" (Maligalig, 2012). Apart from satisfying the gamer's agenda, online students cut corners because most of them are engaged in full-time employment and/or encumbered by domestic responsibilities. They have limited time to do their online coursework and, thus, see their salvation in short-cuts.

These are further exacerbated by other socio-cultural factors such as: peer pressure of having their classmates complete the requirements way before they do; and the need for an advanced degree in order to succeed in their career. For students who are prompted to cut-corners because of the latter, their main objective in enrolling is not to learn but to move up in their careers. They do not feel the need to engage in the learning activities afforded to them. The less time it takes for them to complete a requirement, the better. Additionally, they feel no qualms about their behavior because of the same cyber-psychological factors that create the online disinhibition effect. In our experience, remedial measures to curb cutting-corners are yet to be instituted and documented.

In summary, the subordinate influential factors of cutting corners are: the adoption of the gamer's agenda; socio-cultural factors such as peer pressure, domestic responsibilities and career demands; and cyber-psychological factors that create online disinhibition. The superordinate influential factors or root causes of cheating, cyber-bullying and cutting-corners will now be traced.

Superordinate Influential Factors

The subordinate influential factors that bear primarily upon cheating, cyberbullying and cutting-corners are: inappropriate assessment models; online disinhibition; and the adoption of the gamer's agenda. These, in turn, are caused by: the distance factor that makes conventional assessment models inappropriate; the technological factor that bears upon assessment and online disinhibition; cyber-psychological factors that influence both online disinhibition and the adoption of the gamer's agenda; and socio-cultural factors that result in the adoption of the gamer's agenda and cutting corners. Inappropriate assessment models likewise cause adversarial relationships between online teachers and students, which in turn contributes to the gamer's agenda that lead to cutting corners. It is a complex web of causes and effects of the primary and secondary order.

Can we now refer to the secondary order causes – distance, technology, cyber-psychological factors, socio-cultural factors - as superordinate influential factors? Note that these factors are attributes of open, distance and eLearning. In other words, they are *givens* and ordinarily should not lead to dysfunction. But they do. Hence, there may still be causes of a higher order.

What then are these causes? Based on our theoretical framework, the clusters of problems have only one superordinate influential factor. Contradictions between the delivery system, the pedagogical system and the assessment system cause the subordinate influential factors and are responsible for the entire problematique. Employing lower order cognitive instead of meta-cognitive learning objectives; adopting highly structured course outlines; enforcing strict course calendars; necessitating inflexible course requirements; and implementing non-authentic assessment methods - all pose contradictions to an open and distance delivery system. These contradictions make up the superordinate influential factor or the root cause of the ODeL problematique.

We revisit our theoretical framework, which submits that open, distance and eLearning is a curricular system. Curricular systems are made up of the following subsystems: the content system; the pedagogic system; the delivery system; and the assessment system. These subsystems are likened to four posts that hold a curricular program together. Changes in one subsystem require equivalent degrees of changes in the others. With the dramatic changes in the ODeL delivery system, equally profound adjustments in content, pedagogy and assessment need to be instituted as well, without which contradictions emerge that now manifest as dysfunctional student behaviors and attitudes.

The Problematique Map

The preceding analysis can be visually represented with the problematique map shown in Figure 2.

The open, distance and eLearning problematique presents itself with three faces: online cheating, cyber-bullying and cutting corners. Distance and inappropriate assessment models cause cheating. Online disinhibition result in cyberbullying. The gamer's agenda influence students to cut corners. The technological factor makes conventional assessment models inappropriate for ODeL, which in turn result in a perceived adversarial relationship between the teacher and the online student. The latter coupled with cyber-psychological and socio-cultural factors contribute to the gamer's agenda. Technology, cyber-psychological and socio-cultural factors result in online disinhibition. Distance, technology, cyber-psychological factors and socio-cultural factors are not superordinate influential factors but simultaneously occurring givens within an ODeL delivery system. Contradictions among delivery, pedagogy and assessment bear upon these four to weave the ODeL problematique.

Figure 2. Subordinate and superordinate influential factors

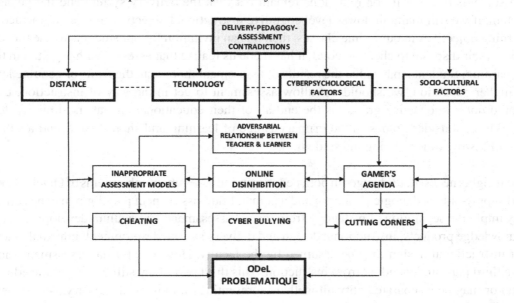

POLICY IMPLICATIONS

How do we disentangle this problematique?

Theoretically, if we try to solve the subordinate influential factors individually they may disappear for a while. But the problems will soon recur because we are merely addressing the symptoms instead of the root cause. Suppose we shift to on-camera or face-to-face assessment procedures, impose sanctions on disruptive students who display online disinhibition, and enforce rules on cutting corners. We may be able to control these dysfunctional digital demeanors for the semester. But there is no guarantee that in succeeding semesters, our courses will not have their share of cheats, bullies and gamers. Not unless we address the superordinate influential factor and resolve the contradictions between our online delivery, pedagogy and assessment models through policy.

- **ODeL Policy for TVET, NFE, and Higher Ed:** One policy option that may be considered is to use ODeL exclusively for higher education, technical-vocational education and training, and non-formal education. It should discourage the use of open, distance and eLearning to basic education levels in the formal mode. Blended learning may be employed with the appropriate congruencies among delivery, pedagogy and assessment. But it is inadvisable to apply a purely self-regulated, autonomous learning system on basic education.
- **Authentic Assessment Policy for ODeL:** Another option is to rethink our assessment approach and adopting authentic modes instead. However, there should be several levels of assessment: assessment for feedback on learning design; assessment to pass or fail; assessment for scholastic achievement; and portfolio assessment. The level of assessment is inversely proportional to the degree of learning autonomy.
- **Divorcing Instruction From Assessment:** The preceding analysis offers several insights. First, it reveals that the circumstances of eLearning such as distance and technology enable and encour-

age students to cheat if contradictions remain between the delivery system and the pedagogical system. If we still maintain lower level cognitive instructional objectives instead of metacognitive learning objectives in our online classes, then it is an invitation for our students to use the technology at their disposal to cheat. Second, it has made us realize that assessment has gotten in the way of learning. Students may value the results of assessment more than the fruits of genuine learning. In higher education, we should not allow assessment to get in the way of instruction. Learners should not acknowledge grades as the end-all of their educational endeavor. Similarly, teachers should not consider grades as the primary gauge of learning and should not spend a substantial part of his/her time policing the student.

These insights necessitate changes in both pedagogic and assessment subsystems of ODeL. A research informed supply-side pedagogic paradigm and a demand side-assessment paradigm may be considered. This may imply the separation of pedagogy from formal assessment. Curriculum development, production of knowledge products, instructional design and delivery system development, informal assessment in aid of instructional design may be assumed by the faculty. However, formal assessment should be done by a third party independent from instruction. This third party may still be part of the educational institution or may be a separate entity altogether representing employers or industry. Assessment may be linked directly to accreditation, whether the University's or the employer's.

- **Educational Policy Consistent With Openness:** Open, distance and eLearning is founded upon educational philosophies of openness, learner-centeredness, connectivism and constructivism. ODeL is not merely employing the Internet as an educational platform. It is enabling the student to learn for him/herself on his/her own terms. It means allowing networking synergies to bear upon the learning process unhindered by rules and boundaries typical of conventional face-to-face instruction. One may argue that this type of independent, self-regulated learning cannot be applied effectively on basic education, which requires dependencies and control. However, open universities have never claimed nor have recommended that ODeL be used for any level in the formal mode other than higher education.

This is how we untangle the problematique, by addressing the root cause. An educational policy consistent with openness, independence and constructivism should guide our open, distance and eLearning undertakings.

REFERENCES

Caballero, A. (2012). *Outsource Writers Or Intellectual Prostitutes? Views Of University of the Philippines Los Baños Writers And Journalism Students On Internet Ghostwriters*. (Unpublished BS Development Communication Thesis). UPLB College of Development Communication, Los Baños.

Cizek, G. J. (1999). *Cheating on tests: how to do it, detect it, and prevent it*. Mahwah, NJ: Lawrence Erlbaum.

Gayol, Y. (1998). Technological Transparency: A Myth of Virtual Education. *Bulletin of Science, Technology & Society, 18*(3), 180–186. doi:10.1177/027046769801800305

George, J., & Carlson, J. (1999). *Group support systems and deceptive communication*. Paper presented at the 32nd Hawaii International Conference on Systems Sciences.

Heberling, M. (2002). *Maintaining Academic Integrity in Online Education*. Retrieved April 7, 2014 from http://www.westga.edu/distance/ojdla/spring51/html

Lincoln, M. (2002). *Cheating. An insiders guide to cheating at Lakeview High School*. Retrieved on 7 April 2014 from www.infotoday.com/mmschools/jan02/Cheating.pdf

Maligalig, J. P. (2012). *Employing games in development communication instruction. Professorial Chair Lecture*. Los Baños: UPLB College of Development Communication.

McKinnon, R. (1996). Searching the leviathan in usenet. In S. Jones (Ed.), *Cybersociety: Computer mediated communication and community*. Baltimore, MD: Johns Hopkins University Press.

Means, B., Toyama, Y., Murphy, R., Bakia, M., & Jones, K. (2010). *Evaluation of Evidence-Based Practices in Online Learning: A Meta-Analysis and Review of Online Learning Studies*. Washington, DC: US Department of Education.

Moore, J. L., Dickson-Deane, C., & Galyen, K. (2010). eLearning, online learning, and distance learning environments: Are they the same? *The Internet and Higher Education*, *14*(2), 129–135. doi:10.1016/j.iheduc.2010.10.001

Race, P., & Pickford, R. (2007). Dealing with disruptive students. In Making Teaching Work: 'Teaching Smarter' in Post-Compulsory Education. London: SAGE Publications Ltd.

Ravasco, G. (2012). Technology Aided Cheating in Open and Distance eLearning. *Asian Journal of Distance Education, 10*(2), 71-77.

Rowe, N. C. (2004). *Cheating Online Student Assessment: Beyond Plagiarism*. Retrieved April 7, 2014 from www.westga.edu/~distance/ojdla/summer72/rowe72.html

Suler, J. (2004). The Online Disinhibition Effect. *Cyberpsychology & Behavior*, *7*(3), 321–326. doi:10.1089/1094931041291295 PMID:15257832

Turkle, S. (1996). Constructions and reconstructions of the self in virtual reality. In T. Druckery (Ed.), *Electronic culture: Technology and visual representation*. New York, NY: Aperture Foundation Books.

Watson, G., & Sottile, J. (2010). *Cheating in the Digital Age: Do Students Cheat More in Online Course*s. Retrieved 8/4/2014 from www.westga.edu/~distance/ojdla/spring131/watson131.html

KEY TERMS AND DEFINITIONS

Assessment: In the educational sense, reviewing and measuring the learning outcomes of an educational activity.

Cyberbullying: Abusive, domination and intimidating behavior during online interactions.

Cyberpsychological: Of or pertaining to states of mind associated with online activities.

Dark Web: That part of the World Wide Web where illegal, illicit and illegitimate activities are conducted clandestinely.

Demeanor: Conduct or behavior arising from a character, a bearing or an attitude.

ODeL: Acronym for Open, Distance, and eLearning.

Online Disinhibition: The lack or decline of social decorum or reserved behavior during online interactions.

Problematique: A complex cluster of simultaneously occurring interrelated problems.

Subordinate Influential Factors: Immediate causes of a problem situation.

Superordinate Influential Factors: Root causes of a problem situation.

This research was previously published in Developing Successful Strategies for Global Policies and Cyber Transparency in E-Learning edited by Gulsun Eby, T. Volkan Yuzer, and Simber Atay, pages 46-59, copyright year 2016 by Information Science Reference (an imprint of IGI Global).

Chapter 4
How to Become a Cybercriminal?
An Explanation of Cybercrime Diffusion

Jean-Loup Richet
University of Nantes, France

ABSTRACT

The main purpose of this chapter is to illustrate a landscape of current literature in cybercrime taking into consideration diffusion of innovation theories and economic theory of competition. In this chapter, a narrative review of the literature was carried out, facilitators leading to cybercrime were explored and explained the diffusion of Cybercriminals' best practices. Cybercrime is compatible with young adults lifestyle (familiarity) and requires little knowledge. Moreover, barriers to entry related to costs (psychological, financial), risks and investments are low. This review provides a snapshot and reference base for academics and practitioners with an interest in cybercrime while contributing to a cumulative culture which is desired in the field. This chapter provides insights into barriers to entry into cybercrime and the facilitators of cybercrime.

INTRODUCTION

Cyberspace has created a new dimension of social interaction. It has transcended time and space, and, as such, physical context is no longer linked with social situation. A virtual presence need not be true to the actual persona of its creator in the physical world. This simple fact has had an alarming effect on the negative cyber behaviors of today's youth, who have used the anonymity of the web to indulge in cybercrime or hacking. It has become critical to inquire into and understand the growing criminal cyber-behavior of teenagers. This requires a detailed study of the meanings of and differences between hacking and cybercrime and the visualization and use of these terms by the youth alongside their attitudes towards both.

Further, a growing number of scholars state that the Internet presents "some unique opportunities for deviant behavior" (Rogers et al., 2006). Technology has given people the unprecedented ability to

DOI: 10.4018/978-1-5225-3163-0.ch004

hide their identities under cover of anonymity, and they can avoid the penalty for embarrassing or illegitimate activity. Whereas few people (of any age) would be able to walk into a room full of complete strangers and share nude photos of themselves, talk about sex, or discuss illegal use of drugs, they can do it online behind the "protection" of the magically anonymous keyboard. This ability profoundly affects the online behavior of teenagers.

Nevertheless, although some researchers have studied this issue, the factors leading young adults to adopt a web-deviant behavior have received less attention. From this background, the present article sets out to explore the facilitators of hacking and cybercrime. This paper will explain the diffusion of web-deviant behavior amongst young people through an analysis of the literature study while taking into consideration the conceptual model of diffusion of innovation by Greenhalgh et al. (2004).

CYBERCRIME VS. HACKING

Cyberspace transforms the scale and scope of offense; has its own limits, interactional forms, roles, and rules; and it has its own forms of criminal endeavor (Capeller, 2001). According to Yar (2005), the "novel socio-interactional features of the cyberspace environment (primarily the collapse of spatial-temporal barriers, many-to-many connectivity, and the anonymity and plasticity of online identity) [...] make possible new forms and patterns of illicit activity." Anyone who is computer literate can become a cybercriminal.

There is still no clear definition of "cybercrime" (Fafinski et al., 2010). In some cases, cybercrime can encompass the use of computers to assist "traditional" offending but it can also be a crime mediated through technology (Wall, 2007) or an exclusive technological crime, such as a denial-of-service attack). Many criminal law scholars focus on the legalistic framework. For instance, Wall (2001) uses the categories of criminal law to create categories of cybercrime. Others categorize cybercrime as an offense "related to computers, related to content or against the confidentiality, integrity and availability of computer data and systems" (Council of Europe Convention on Cybercrime, 2001).

The use of the term "hacker" has changed over the years from a positive and complimentary definition — the enthusiastic computer programmer who is particularly brilliant — to a negative and pejorative one: the cybercriminal. Nowadays, "cybercriminal" is a term synonymous with "hacker." Hacker, as a term, is commonly used by the mass media to refer to an intruder breaking into computer systems to steal or destroy data. Police describe almost any crime committed through, with, by, or against a computer as "hacking." "For many people, the hacker is an ominous figure, a smart-aleck sociopath ready to burst out of his basement wilderness and savage other people's lives for his own anarchical convenience" (Sterling, 1993).

This concept of "hackers" is still the subject of heated controversy. In response to the common demonization of the term hacker, *The New Hacker's Dictionary* (Raymond & Steele, 1991) has coined the term "cracker." Crackers use their computer-security-related skills to author viruses, trojans, etc., and illegally infiltrate secure systems with the intention of doing harm to the system or criminal intent and to differentiate them from the original and non-criminal hacker. This article will use the term hacker in its original positive meaning and the term cracker for those committing cybercrime.

CONCEPTUAL MODEL AND METHODOLOGY

Originally, hacking was seen as innovative behavior; even the original term "hack" was a slang word used by MIT students in the 1950s to refer to an improvement. According to Rogers (1983), an innovation is "an idea, practice, or object that is perceived as new by an individual or other unit of adoption." Further, the central meaning of innovation relates to improvement or renewal, with novelty being a consequence of this improvement. However, eventually hacking led to many teenagers deviating from using their skills to improve or push the limits of their expertise to using those same skills for cybercrimes, such as Internet extortion and fraud. Our hypothesis is that hacking is an innovation compared to cybercrime and is different from either cyber or traditional criminal behavior. Computer hacking can lead to constructive technological developments; for example, former hackers Dennis Ritchie and Ken Thompson went on to create the UNIX operating system in the 1970s, and hacker Shawn Fanning created Napster. An analysis of literature through a model of diffusion of innovation highlights the facilitators of hacking.

We used the conceptual model of diffusion of innovation by Greenhalgh et al. (2004). The authors conducted a systematic review of empirical literature and theory pertaining to the diffusion of innovation. They studied 6,000 papers, books, and abstracts, focusing on 495 sources for the final report. They formulated a conceptual model from the synthesis of these theoretical and empirical findings; this model categorizes the critical success factors for innovation.

The key attributes of successful innovation indicated in their model involve multiple elements:

1. Compatibility — Must be consistent with the adopter's values and perceived needs.
2. Risk — Zero risk is highly unlikely, so we have modified this need to an acceptable level of risk, where the possibility and value of loss is inferior to the expected positive outcome.
3. Relative advantage — Better than the previous model in terms of effectiveness or cost-effectiveness.
4. Ability to solve user issues — Improving users' performance.
5. Observability — Must have visible benefits.
6. Accessibility — Must be easy to use and require only a little knowledge.
7. Adaptability — Must be modifiable to fit users' needs.
8. Support — Should be open to experiment and have a supporting community providing training and customization.

This research used this framework to analyze the present literature on cybercrime and hacking. An extensive narrative literature review (King & He, 2005) was conducted, synthesizing prior research and analyzing it with regard to the hypothesis. Traditionally, literature reviews target prominent journals and conferences. This approach is relevant to mature research topics but is not pertinent for a literature review on cybercrime, as it is a contemporary phenomenon; therefore, focusing on limited outlets cannot be justified. In light of this, this effort mainly focused on online databases and targeted Business Source Complete, ProQuest, ScienceDirect, Scirus, Scopus, and Web of Science. We conducted keyword and abstract searches across these six databases for all available years. Articles were filtered by scanning titles, abstracts, and excluding duplicates and articles only mentioning hacking or cybercrime that were not focused on these topics. After a full text review, irrelevant articles were discarded and we classified the remaining articles under each of the critical success factors described by Greenhalgh et al.

VALIDITY THREATS

This paper has several limitations. First, although the procedure followed includes searching, filtering, and classifying processes, our approach is vulnerable to subjectivity because it is based on a qualitative interpretation of the literature. Second, the sample was largely based on grey and professional literature. Although the search was oriented towards peer-reviewed and scholarly articles, the literature on hackers is recent, and because it is industry-driven — from the information systems security industry to national agencies — very few research articles were found that also embrace this phenomenon, compared to more mature literature like electronic commerce. Even if untrustworthy studies and non-rigorous articles are excluded from this review, the research method — a narrative literature review — might hinder the ability of the present paper to draw a complete picture of the current development in this field. Finally, the search criteria may be incomplete, as some papers that do not have the term cybercrime in the keywords or abstract may not have been included.

FROM YOUNG HACKERS TO CRACKERS

In this first part, we will study those two critical success factors: risk and observability.

Hacking is a normal part of the lives of most youngsters. Multiple surveys have been carried out on teenagers and hacking (Panda Security, 2009; Trend Micro, 2009; Tufin Technologies, 2010). Although there is suspicion about industry bias, these studies generally come to the same conclusion: casual hacking is almost as established a part of teenage life as downloading music to an iPod. The most common reasons cited for hacking were "for fun," (50%) followed by "curiosity" (30%). Over four out of ten teens have hacked into another person's account to read e-mails, looked at another's bank account details, or logged into another person's social networking profile. The majority of these young hackers are pranksters making fun of their friends, but one in three teens have admitted to being tempted to try hacking or spying on the Internet to make money (with eventual transition to cybercrime). The history of hacking is replete with juvenile hackers. Jonathan James was a fifteen-year-old American hacker arrested in 1999 for a series of intrusions into various systems from NASA to the Department of Defense. Michael Calce was a Canadian high school student who shut down Yahoo, Amazon, eBay, and other websites in 2000.

However, many youngsters have also turned into crackers committing serious criminal offenses. In 2005, eighteen-year-old Phillip Shortman from South Wales was sentenced for having fraudulently stolen £102,000 from eBay users (Griffith, 2005). In 2009, young Australian cracker Anthony Scott Harrison infected more than 3,000 computers to steal credit card and other bank account details with his malware in Australia and abroad (Fewster, 2010). In 2010, twenty-one-year-old Alistair Peckover was jailed for scamming, ID theft, and online fraud of around £110,000 (Blincoe, 2010).

In his economic approach to crime, G. Becker (1968) states that people decide whether to commit a crime through a cost-benefit analysis. According to this perspective, people choose illegal over legal alternatives in the same way they make consumption and economic choices in the marketplace. The decision to commit a crime involves calculations based on an assessment of the availability, risks, and costs of the opportunity and one's ability to reach a desired end. Low earnings or the lack of sufficient opportunities to obtain income are factors behind committing crime. Teenagers have lower earnings, fewer opportunities to obtain income, and may easily discount the future in assessing the opportunity costs of crime (Becker, 1976). Hacking is perceived as riskless and highly compatible to the lifestyles of the computer-savvy teenage population.

Cracking, too, is perceived as low risk or riskless — teenagers discount the future — and its benefits are apparent: how else could a teenager earn nearly £100,000 a year? The mass media indirectly promotes crackers' earnings, and even academic studies show that spam is highly profitable and that botmasters (individuals who are responsible for or maintain a herd of compromised computers) can earn roughly $3,500,000 a year (Kanich et al., 2009; TrendMicro, 2011). Although cybercrime is under-recorded and under-reported (Fafinski et al., 2010), studies highlight crackers' "huge profits" (Bizeul, 2007; Shah & Cole, 2005) For instance, Esthost botnet owner generated at least $14 million in fraudulent advertising fees (FBI, 2011). The aim of this paper is not to give statistical evidence but to point out media emphasis on crackers' revenue — Greenhalgh's observability factor, i.e., visible benefits of online crime compared to traditional crime. In fact, the reality of cybercrimes is under documented, and some researchers criticize statistical abuse and misuse in information security (Ryan & Jefferson, 2003; Florencio & Herley, 2011).

LOW BARRIERS TO ENTRY

In economic theories of competition, barriers to entry are obstacles that make it difficult to enter a given market (Fisher, 1984); technical expertise and accessibility could act as barriers to entry. However, in this case, it is observed that the barriers to entry into the "world of hacking" through technical expertise are low; hence, we could say that Greenhalgh's compatibility factor is present. Young people find hacking an easily accessible activity because hacking is compatible with their lifestyle (Richet, 2012). Computers are in everyone's lives, and the "digital natives" were born with Internet and a keyboard (Prensky, 2001). These digital natives make little distinction between the online and offline realms, the virtual and the real (Palfrey & Gasser, 2008). They may not even know that they behaved illegally (Kallman & Grillo, 1996); for example, searching on the web and downloading a movie from a hacking forum board may seem like a casual and insignificant activity. This is an unfamiliar mindset for many "digital immigrants" born before the 1980s who perceive hacking as being foreign and elusive because they are less familiar with contemporary perceptions of cyberspace. "Hackers are generally teenagers and college kids not engaged in earning a living. They often come from fairly well-to-do middle class backgrounds, and are markedly anti-materialistic" (Sterling, 1993).

KNOWLEDGE DIFFUSION AND INNOVATION

Furthermore, hacking is much less complex than it was a few years ago, as hacking communities have greatly diffused their knowledge through the Internet (Kshetri, 2006; Richet, 2013). The web has, therefore, progressively reduced the complexity of becoming a hacker. With a simple search on Google, anybody can find a large amount of documentation, including hacking how-tos, toolkits, and tips (Long, 2005). For instance, a Google search with the keywords "hacker toolkit" could lead one to a website where he or she could find all of the tools needed for hacking. With the query "how to hack," this researcher found easy entry to a website with a vast number of hacking guides. "By using Google, [one] can gain access to information that may otherwise be hidden" (Billig et al., 2008). The main problem is that the majority of tools used by information systems security auditors can be used by hackers, too, whether it be network protocol packet sniffers, network vulnerability scanners, password recovery tools, web server scanners, or packet crafters. Consequently, hackers disguise themselves with a disclaimer such as "this site is devoted to internet security, and we help people in the security field investigate tools they are unfamiliar with." Similarly, numerous books on hacking were published during the 2000s; there was even a *Hacking for Dummies*. Several hacking tools are available online and require very little knowledge (Krebs, 2006).

Blogs and communities have hugely contributed to information sharing: beginners could benefit from older hackers' knowledge and advice (Imperva, 2011). Teenagers could also easily adopt deviant behavior through experimentation. It is simple to try a network sniffer tool on a private network and then just use it on a public network out of sheer curiosity. A great number of hacking tools are very easy to use or completely user friendly (Krebs, 2006). For instance, with port scanners, the user only has to input the IP address of the computer to scan in order to get detailed descriptions for common ports.

Thus, we could say that cybercrime is accessible, i.e., according to Greenhalgh's definition, cybercrime is easy to do and requires little knowledge. Moreover, online communities not only provide support and training, but also offer customizations and opportunities for innovations (Imperva, 2011).

FITTING USERS' NEEDS

The last factor that contributes to lower barriers is that hacking is now cheaper than ever, and that could easily fit criminals' needs. For instance, cloud computing is a way to easily increase capacity or add capabilities without even investing in infrastructure. Hosted services are delivered over the Internet; they are sold on demand, are "elastic," and are fully managed by the provider. One needs nothing but a personal computer and Internet access. Infrastructure as a Service (IaaS) provides a virtual server with the ability to create, access, and configure virtual servers and storage. Cloud computing allows a student to pay for only as much capacity as is needed and bring more functionalities online as soon as they are required. Cloud computing could be helpful for a cracker as a way to leverage his attack (Subashini & Kavitha, 2011).

In other words, a cracker could use the IaaS massive computing power to brute-force a password (Meer et al., 2009). Brute force software can generate millions of passphrases, encrypt them, and see if they allow access to the network. Thus, cracking a wireless network could be done cheaply and easily (Roth, 2011). Because there are no bandwidth agreements — or detection of servers taking malicious actions — in order to set up an account on an IaaS, an amateur hacker can easily conduct a denial-of-service attack, sending a flood of packets toward the target company's network at low cost and on a large scale, using the high capabilities of the service provider (Ristanpart et al., 2009). In addition, scamming and spamming are facilitated. Indeed, before cloud computing, in order to spam one needed a dedicated server, skills in server management, network configuration and maintenance, knowledge of Internet service provider standards, etc. By comparison, a mail software as a service is a scalable, inexpensive, bulk, and transactional e-mail-sending service for marketing purposes and could be easily set up for spam (Krebs, 2008; Armbrust et al., 2010). On-demand e-mail service providers don't deserve to be blamed for the capabilities they are making accessible to potential criminals, but one should be aware that these services could easily be manipulated to send cheap spam and malware.

As mentioned above, teenagers are digital natives and are accustomed to using computers and the Internet. Cybercrime is thus compatible with their environment. Furthermore, hacking/cracking has become easier than ever nowadays through the diffusion of toolkits, advice, and support from the hacking community. Thanks to the ease of cloud computing, attempting to perform hacking is cheaper and requires fewer skills than ever before.

RELATIVE ADVANTAGES OVER TRADITIONAL CRIME

The psychological cost of committing a crime through the web is low for two main reasons. The first one is that victims of cybercrime are frequently difficult to identify (Phukan, 2002). This means that in massive scamming campaigns, for instance, hackers send an overwhelming amount of e-mails and do not face the victims (they effectively just press "send"). Alternatively, when a hacker creates and distributes malware through the web to steal credit card numbers, he catches "someone" (i.e., numbers) but never sees the victims' faces or physically interacts with them. The second reason is that hackers do not see their behavior as unethical. Scholars report that many students do not consider software piracy as unethical behavior (Im & Van Epps, 1991; Reid et al., 1992). On the contrary, some believe that unethical behavior could help them be successful in life (Davis & Vitell, 1991).

The main advantage of cybercrime over traditional crime is that "such crimes are less likely to be caught and prosecuted [...] only about 5% of cyber-criminals are caught" (Kshetri, 2009). Cybercrimes could be large-scale and highly profitable crimes; even a minuscule response rate to spam is enough to reward spammers with a large profit (Kanich et al., 2009). Moreover, cybercrimes are committed from home. For instance, instead of sifting through rubbish for personal information and searching in the target victim's residential trash (dumpster diving), an identity thief could browse social networking websites for personal details published by his or her target or could search online databases (Delaney, 2005).

Teenage crackers are aware of their victims' weak points, the first one being ignorance. In fact, a majority of computer users are still ignorant of computer security. A survey of home computers and their owners revealed a gap between user perception and the increasing prevalence of threats on the Internet (McAfee, 2010). The National Cyber Security Alliance (NCSA) is a non-profit group that seeks to raise public awareness of cyber security issues. This organization pointed out in 2004 that users thought they were safe from online threat despite the fact that a virus or worm infected 20% of home computers and that snooping programs such as spyware and adware were on an overwhelming 80% of systems (following the interview, technical experts examined home computers, looking for viruses and spyware).

The second weakness of most victims is fear. Businesses are frequently the victims of ransomware (Tsiklis, 2010), computer malware that holds a computer system or data hostage and then demands a ransom for its restoration. Ransomware is like a virus, but instead of destroying a file, it encrypts it, leaving the author of the malware as the only person with the knowledge of the "private decryption key" needed to release the system or data. The author of this crypto-viral extortion attack then offers to recover the key for a fee; businesses prefer to pay instead of being publicized or losing key data (Luo & Liao, 2009). Web extortions are increasing. In 2006, two teenagers attempted to extort $150,000 from MySpace (Evers, 2006). Recently, teens are being extorted in online schemes and both federal prosecutors and child safety experts have seen a rise in online sexual extortion, now called "sextortion." In 2010, Anthony Stancl, an eighteen-year-old student from Wisconsin, was sentenced to fifteen years in prison after prosecutors said he posed as a girl on Facebook to trick male high school classmates into sending him nude cell phone photos, which he then used to extort them (Ellis, 2010).

CONCLUSION

It was established that anonymity of cyberspace has several advantages. A hacker or cracker is less likely to be caught, feels no guilt or remorse after cracking or spamming, profits from his or her victims' ignorance, and inspires fear. Further, in *The Rites of Passage* (1960), Van Gennep states that there are rituals marking transitional phases between childhood and the full inclusion into a social group. Theses rites have three stages: separation, transition, and reincorporation.

Hacking is seen as a rite of passage from childhood to adulthood, as the teenager will come to consider hacking as a childish activity — just for pranks — and enter into the legal economy. This phase would be the departure from the status of teenager, during which the young adult is formally accepted into his or her new role. A great number of hackers are self-taught prodigies and some organizations actually employ hackers as part of their information technology staff. These hackers use their skills to find vulnerabilities in the company's information system(s) so that they can be fixed quickly. This type of hacker activity actually prevents serious cybercrimes. On the other hand, it could be seen that hacking has become a rite of aggregation, the detachment from childish cyber activities to the assumption of a new criminal cyber identity. Similarly, cracking is perceived as a rite of passage from the age of pranks, such as logging into a friend's Facebook profile, to the age of crimes – using another person's ID in on-line fraud. By learning the hacking subculture and language (Holt, 2010), hackers integrate themselves into the hacker social subculture, which is not necessarily criminal. By leaving the legal market, they become part of the cybercriminal underground.

The intention of this paper is to illustrate a landscape of current literature in cybercrime, taking into consideration Greenhalgh et al.'s conceptual model of diffusion of innovation. A narrative review of the literature was carried out, facilitators leading to cybercrime were explored and explained, and how hacking expertise is disseminated was discovered. Beginning with innocent hacking, teenagers could be tempted to crack and spy on the Internet to make money. The shift from non-criminal to criminal activity is facilitated by various factors: hacking compatibility with youth culture, relative advantage over traditional crime, ease of use, and support. This review provides a snapshot and reference base for academics and practitioners with an interest in the diffusion of cybercrime.

Webster and Watson (2002) suggested that the lack of review articles has been hindering the progress of the IS field; this article contributes to a cumulative culture that is desired in any research field, and answer a call for a greater focus on social artifact in information security research (Crossler et al., 2013; Willison and Warkentin, 2013). Although this review cannot claim to be exhaustive, it provides some insights into the diffusion of deviant behavior amongst young adults and into current literature on cybercrime.

ACKNOWLEDGEMENT

This manuscript is a summation of enhanced papers published in the International Journal of Technology and Human Interaction (IJTHI) in 2013. The original article, *From Young Hackers to Crackers*, was published in volume 9, issue 3 of the IJTHI. Anabela Mesquita & Chia-Wen Tsai, Editors-in-Chief, IJTHI, selected this article for inclusion in this summation as a chapter titled *How to Become a Cybercriminal? An Explanation of Cybercrime Diffusion*. This chapter has been enhanced in order to allow the readers to benefit from the latest findings in the area since the first publication.

REFERENCES

Armbrust, M., Fox, A., Griffith, R., Joseph, A. D., Katz, R., Konwinski, A., & Zaharia, M. (2010). A view of cloud computing. *Communications of the ACM, 53*(4), 50–58. doi:10.1145/1721654.1721672

Becker, G. (1968). Crime and punishment: An economic approach. *Journal of Political Economy, 76*(2), 169–217. doi:10.1086/259394

Becker, G. (1976). *The economic approach to human behavior*. Chicago: University of Chicago Press.

Billig, J., Danilchenko, Y., & Frank, C. (2008). Evaluation of Google hacking. In *Proc. of the 5th Conf. on Information Security Curriculum Development*, 27-32. New York: ACM.

Bizeul, D. (2007). *Russian business networks study*. Retrieved from http://www.bizeul.org/files/RBN_study.pdf

Blicoe, R. (2010). High-living hacker swaps Porsche for porridge. *The Register*. Retrieved from http://www.theregister.co.uk/2010/06/18/hacker_jailed/

Capeller, W. (2001). Not such a neat net: Some comments on virtual criminality. *Social & Legal Studies, 10*, 229–242.

Council of Europe Convention on Cybercrime. (2001). *Treaties*. Retrieved from http://conventions.coe.int/Treaty/EN/Treaties/html/185.htm

Crossler, R. E., Johnston, A. C., Lowry, P. B., Hu, Q., Warkentin, M., & Baskerville, R. (2013). Future directions for behavioral information security research. *Computers & Security, (32)*, 90–101.

Davis, D. L., & Vitell, S. J. (1991). The ethical problems, conflicts, and beliefs of small business information personnel. *Journal of Computer Information Systems, 22*(4), 53–57.

Delaney, K. (2005, March 29). Identity theft made easier. *Wall Street Journal*, p. B1.

Ellis, R. (2010, August 16). Sextortion: Are your teens being "sexploited" online? *Examiner*. Retrieved from http://www.examiner.com/cyber-safety-in-national/sextortion-are-your-teens-being-sexploited-online

Evers, J. (2006, May 2006). Teens arrested in alleged MySpace extortion scam. *Zdnet*. Retrieved from http://www.zdnet.com/news/teens-arrested-in-alleged-myspace-extortion-scam/148219

Fafinski, S., Dutton, W. H., & Margetts, H. Z. (2010). Mapping and measuring cybercrime. *OII Working Paper, 18*.

FBI. (2011). *Manhattan U.S. attorney charges seven individuals for engineering sophisticated internet fraud scheme that infected millions of computers worldwide and manipulated internet advertising business*. [Press release]. Retrieved from http://www.fbi.gov/newyork/press-releases/2011/manhattan-u.s.-attorney-charges-seven-individuals-for-engineering-sophisticated-internet-fraud-scheme-that-infected-millions-of-computers-worldwide-and-manipulated-internet-advertising-business

Fewster, S. (2010). Computer virus created by Anthony Scott Harrison sparked worldwide alert. *News*. Retrieved from http://www.news.com.au/technology/computer-virus-created-by-anthony-scott-harrison-sparked-worldwide-alert/story-e6frfrnr-1225897175334#ixzz1EiBSPNal

Fisher, F. M. (1979). Diagnosing monopoly. *The Quarterly Review of Economics and Business, 19*(2), 7–33.

Florencio, D., & Herley, C. (2011) Sex, lies and cyber-crime surveys. *Proceedings of the Tenth Workshop on the Economics of Information Security (WEIS)*, George Mason University, USA.

Greenhalgh, T., Robert, G., Macfarlane, F., Bate, P., & Kyriakidou, O. (2004). Diffusion of innovations in service organizations: Systematic review and recommendations. *The Milbank Quarterly, 82*(4), 581–629. doi:10.1111/j.0887-378X.2004.00325.x PMID:15595944

Griffith, H. (2005, June 7). eBay fraud boy con 'really easy.' *BBC News*. Retrieved from http://news.bbc.co.uk/1/hi/wales/4615117.stm

Holt, T. (2010). Examining the role of technology in the formation of deviant subcultures. *Social Science Computer Review, 28*(4), 466–481. doi:10.1177/0894439309351344

Im, J. H., & van Epps, P. D. (1991). Software piracy and software security in business schools: An ethical perspective. *Database, 22*(3), 15–21.

Imperva (2011). Monitoring hacker forums. *Research Note, 5*, 1-14.

Kallman, E. A., & Grillo, J. P. (1996). *Ethical decision making and information technology*. New York: McGraw Hill.

Kanich, C., Kreibich, C., Levchenko, K., Enright, B., Voelker, G., Paxson, V., & Savage, S. (2009). Spamalytics: An empirical analysis of spam marketing conversion. *Proceedings of the 15th ACM Conference on Computer and Communications Security*. Alexandria, Virginia: ACM doi:10.1145/1562164.1562190

King, W. R., & He, J. (2005). Understanding the role and methods of meta-analysis in IS research. *Communications of the Association for Information Systems, 16*, 1.

Krebs, B. (2006, March 16). Hacking made easy. *Washington Post*. Retrieved from http://www.washingtonpost.com/wp-dyn/content/article/2006/03/16/AR2006031600916.html

Krebs, B. (2008, July 1). Amazon: Hey spammers, get off my cloud! *Washington Post*. Retrieved fromhttp://voices.washingtonpost.com/securityfix/2008/07/amazon_hey_spammers_get_off_my.html

Kshetri, N. (2006). The simple economics of cybercrimes. *IEEE Security and Privacy, 4*(1), 33–39. doi:10.1109/MSP.2006.27

Kshetri, N. (2009). Positive externality, increasing returns, and the rise in cybercrimes. *Communications of the ACM, 52*(12), 141. doi:10.1145/1610252.1610288

Long, J. (2005). *Google hacking for penetration testers*. Rockland, MA: Syngress Publishing.

Luo, X., & Liao, Q. (2009). Ransomware: A new cyber hijacking threat to enterprises. In J. Gupta & S. Sharma (Eds.), Handbook of Research on Information Security and Assurance (1–6), Hershey, PA: IGI Global. doi:10.4018/978-1-59904-855-0.ch001

McAfee. (2010). *Threats report: Third quarter 2010*. Retrieved from http://www.mcafee.com/us/resources/reports/rp-quarterly-threat-q3-2010.pdf

Meer, H., Arvanitis, N., & Slaviero, M. (2009). *Clobbering the cloud. Black Hat USA 2009*. Las Vegas, NV: Techweb.

Palfrey, J., & Gasser, U. (2008). *Born digital: Understanding the first generation of digital natives*. New York: Basic Books.

Panda Security. (2009). *Studying or hacking? Today's adolescents could be the hackers of the future*. Retrieved from http://www.pitchengine.com/preview-release.php?id=11537

Phukan, S. (2002). *IT ethics in the internet age: New dimensions. Proc. Informing Science & IT Education Conf. (InSITE)*. Santa Rosa, CA: Informing Science Press.

Prensky, M. (2001).Digital natives, digital immigrants. On the horizon. MCB University Press, Vol. 9 No. 5.

Raymond, E. S., & Steele, G. S. (1991). *The new hacker's dictionary*. Cambridge, MA: MIT Press.

Reid, R. A., Thompson, J. K., & Logsdon, J. L. (1992). Knowledge and attitudes of management students toward software piracy. *Journal of Computer Information Systems*, *33*(1), 46–51.

Richet, J. L. (2012). Market Failure Mechanisms in Cybersecurity. *pre-ICIS workshop on Information Security and Privacy (SIGSEC)*. Paper 26. http://aisel.aisnet.org/wisp2012/26

Richet, J. L. (2013). From Young Hackers to Crackers. *International Journal of Technology and Human Interaction*, *9*(3), 53–62.

Richet, J. L. (2013). Laundering Money Online: a review of cybercriminals methods. *arXiv preprint arXiv:1310.2368*.

Ristanpart, T., Tromer, E., Sacham, H., & Savage, S. (2009) Hey, you, get off of my cloud: Exploring information leakage in third-party compute clouds. *Proceedings of the 16th ACM Conference on Computer and Communications Security*. Chicago, IL: ACM. doi:10.1145/1653662.1653687

Rogers, E. M. (1983). *Diffusion of Innovations*. New York: Free Press.

Rogers, M., Smoak, N., & Liu, J. (2006). Self-reported deviant computer behavior. *Deviant Behavior*, *27*(3), 245–268. doi:10.1080/01639620600605333

Roth, T. (2011). Breaking encryptions. *Black hat conference 2011*. Retrieved from https://media.blackhat.com/bh-dc-1/Roth/BlackHat_DC_2011_Roth_Breaking%20encryptions-Slides.pdf

Ryan, J., & Jefferson, T. I. (2003). The use, misuse, and abuse of statistics in information security research. *Proc. 23rd ASEM National Conference*. St. Louis, MO: ASEM.

Shah, S., & Cole, D. (2011). Spyware/adware. *Black hat conference 2005*. Retrieved from http://www.blackhat.com/html/bh-japan-05/bh-jp-05-en-speakers.html

Snyder, F. (2001). Sites of criminality and sites of governance. *Social & Legal Studies*, *10*, 251–256.

Sterling, B. (1993). *The hacker crackdown: Law and disorder on the electronic frontier*. New York: Bantam.

Subashini, S., & Kavitha, V. (2011). A survey on security issues in service delivery models of cloud computing. *Journal of Network and Computer Applications*, *34*(1), 1–11. doi:10.1016/j.jnca.2010.07.006

Trend Micro. (2009). Brits breeding the next-generation of computer hackers. *Global Security Mag*. Retrieved from http://www.globalsecuritymag.com/Trend-Micro-Brits-Breeding-the,20090403,8329

Trend Micro. (2011). *Big botnet busts*. Retrieved from http://blog.trendmicro.com/big-botnet-busts/

Tsiklis, T. (2010). *Avira-Ransomware threatens with official complaint of piracy*. Retrieved from http://www.virus.gr/portal/en/content/avira-ransomware-threatens-official-complaint-piracy

Tufin Technologies. (2010). *Survey of hacking habits in New York*. Retrieved from http://www.tufin.com/news_events_press_releases.php?index=2010-04-14

Van Gennep, A. (1960). *The rites of passage*. Chicago, IL: The University of Chicago Press.

Wall, D. (2001). Cybercrimes and the internet. In D. Wall (Ed.), *Crime and the internet*. London: Routledge. doi:10.4324/9780203164501_chapter_1

Wall, D. S. (2007). *Cybercrime: The transformation of technology in the networked age*. Cambridge: Polity Press.

Webster, J., & Watson, R. T. (2002). Analyzing the past to prepare for the future: Writing a literature review. *Management Information Systems Quarterly*, *26*(2), iii–xiii.

Willison, R., & Warkentin, M. (2013). Beyond deterrence: An expanded view of employee computer abuse. *Management Information Systems Quarterly*, *37*(1).

Yar, M. (2005). The novelty of cybercrime: An assessment in light of routine activity theory. *European Journal of Criminology*, *2*(4), 407–427. doi:10.1177/147737080556056

KEY TERMS AND DEFINITIONS

Botnet: The word botnet was termed by combining the words robot and network. A botnet is a network of infected computers, that will be used to participate in DDoS attacks.

Crackers: Crackers use their computer-security-related skills to author viruses, trojans, etc., and illegally infiltrate secure systems with the intention of doing harm to the system or criminal intent.

DDoS Attacks: Distributed denial-of-service (DDoS) attacks occurs when a target system or resource is overwhelmed with traffic from multiple sources.

Dumpster Diving: Activity realized by identity thieves; it is the act of sifting through rubbish for personal information and searching in the target victim's residential trash. In the cyberspace, this activity is realized through the browsing of social networking websites for personal details published by the cracker's target.

Ransomware: Computer malware that holds a computer system or data hostage and then demands a ransom for its restoration. Ransomware is like a virus, but instead of destroying a file, it encrypts it, leaving the author of the malware as the only person with the knowledge of the "private decryption key" needed to release the system or data. The author of this crypto-viral extortion attack then offers to recover the key for a fee; businesses prefer to pay instead of being publicized or losing key data.

This research was previously published in Human Behavior, Psychology, and Social Interaction in the Digital Era edited by Anabela Mesquita and Chia-Wen Tsai, pages 229-240, copyright year 2015 by Information Science Reference (an imprint of IGI Global).

Section 2
Data Mining and Analysis

Chapter 5
Optimal Query Generation for Hidden Web Extraction Through Response Analysis

Sonali Gupta
YMCA University of Science & Technology, India

Komal Kumar Bhatia
YMCA University of Science & Technology, India

ABSTRACT

A huge number of Hidden Web databases exists over the WWW forming a massive source of high quality information. Retrieval of this information for enriching the repository of the search engine is the prime target of a Hidden web crawler. Besides this, the crawler should perform this task at an affordable cost and resource utilization. This paper proposes a Random ranking mechanism whereby the queries to be raised by the hidden web crawler have been ranked. By ranking the queries according to the proposed mechanism, the Hidden Web crawler is able to make an optimal choice among the candidate queries and efficiently retrieve the Hidden web databases. The Hidden Web crawler proposed here also possesses an extensible and scalable framework to improve the efficiency of crawling. The proposed approach has also been compared with other methods of Hidden Web crawling existing in the literature.

INTRODUCTION

With the swift development of the Web, more and more web databases appear on the WWW. But the access to these databases is guarded by search forms making it inaccessible to conventional Web crawlers. This portion of the Web is commonly referred to as "hidden web" or "deep web". "In the article by Bergman (2001), the authors say hidden web content is particularly important". Not only its size is estimated as hundreds of times larger than the so-called Surface web, but also its information is considered to be of very high quality. Obtaining the content of Hidden web is challenging for which a common solution lies in designing a Hidden-Web crawler. "This topic has been covered many times in past studies (Ntoulas

DOI: 10.4018/978-1-5225-3163-0.ch005

& Zerfos & Cho, 2005; Raghavan & Garcia-Molina, 2001)." The control flow of a basic crawler for the Hidden Web is shown in Fig. 1.

A hidden Web crawler basically starts by parsing the given search form to extract the various controls and filling the search form with the help of a task-specific database. The task-specific database usually contains a list of some possible values that can be submitted to the controls on the search form. The hidden web crawler then submits the filled form to the WWW to retrieve pages from the associated database and forms a repository of the response pages called as the Hidden Web page repository.

LITERATURE REVIEW

A Hidden Web Crawler aims to harvest data records as many as possible efficiently. "This topic has been covered many times in past studies (Ntoulas & Zerfos & Cho, 2005; Barbosa & Freire, 2004)." "In the article by Barbosa and Freire (2004), the authors first introduced the idea, and presented a query selection method which generated the next query using the most frequent keywords in the previous records". However, queries with the most frequent keywords in hand do not ensure that more new records are returned from the Deep Web database. "In the article by Ntoulas and Zerfos and Cho (2005), the authors proposed a greedy query selection method where candidate query keywords have been generated from the obtained records based on the rate measure and the one with the maximum expected harvest rate will be selected for the next query".

"In the article by Kashyap and Hristidis and Petropoulos and Tavoular (2011), the authors proposed an intuitive way to categorize the results of a query using a static concept hierarchy". Their solution was meant to deal with the information overload problem and effectively navigate the results as the search queries on the web database often return a large number of results. The work focuses on the number of records retrieved rather than the size of the retrieved contents of the database.

"In the article by Cheng and Termehchy and Hristidis (2012), the authors have considered the structure and the content of both the database and the query results for identifying the queries that are likely

Figure 1. Basic crawler for the hidden web

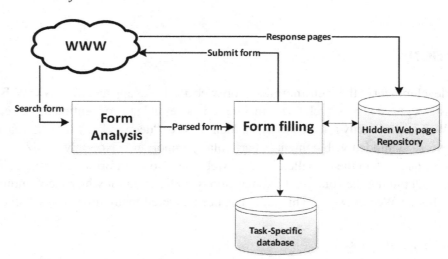

to have low ranking quality". Their system has been evaluated for keyword queries over web databases and suggests the alternative queries that can be used for substituting such low ranking or hard queries so as to improve the user's satisfaction.

A critical review of the referenced literature depicts the following shortcomings:

1. The query generation process for form filling is optimized on the basis of queries executed only during the current run of the crawler and does not takes into consideration the outcome of any queries executed during the previous runs of the crawler.
2. Some methods also consider the downloaded Hidden web pages or response pages as feedback to the crawler so as to download more and more data from the hidden web databases but none of the approaches has considered the sizes of the response pages as criteria in the feedback.
3. Most of these methods assign weights to query terms by taking into account the frequency of their occurrence, keeping view of which requires downloading and analysing all the retrieved documents. This makes the process highly inefficient.

Therefore, in this paper a novel technique for optimizing hidden web crawling based on the response pages generated during the previous runs of the crawler, has been proposed. By analysing the response pages, the proposed approach first creates a set of filling resources and then mines them to find the most promising query to be raised by the Hidden Web crawler on the search form of the Hidden Website. The following observations motivated the idea:

1. It is desirable to have a system that can automate data retrieval from these hidden web resources so as to make it rapidly available to the users of the Web and its services.
2. No single crawl can provide all the desired data that is resident in a database, therefore multiple crawls needs to be carried out in order to exhaustively retrieve all the content in the web database.
3. Some queries may not be available and return results at certain times because of database updates or network problems, the query plan should be capable of handling such situations and generating an alternative query that is still optimal.

The paper has been organized as follows: Section II describes the framework of the proposed system; section III illustrates the creation of the filling resources through the process of response analysis; section IV with the help of an example scenario presents the approach for mining the filling resources to find an optimal ordering among the queries; section V presents the metrics for evaluation and finally in the last section the paper has been concluded.

SYSTEM FRAMEWORK

A hidden web database refers to a set of records on the Web that can be accessed by issuing queries through the offered search form. "This topic has been covered many times in past studies (Barbosa & Freire, 2004; Liddle & Embley & Scott & Yau, 2002; Bergholz & Chidlovskii, 2003)." Fig. 2 presents the architecture of the proposed system that automates this process of accessing a hidden database. The

Figure 2. Architecture of the proposed hidden web crawler

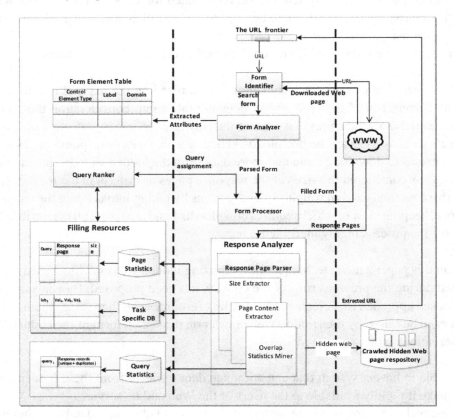

proposed hidden web crawler is based on finding relevant queries by analyzing the response pages obtained from the previous runs of the crawler and generating an optimal execution plan in an unsupervised way that improves the crawler's efficiency in terms of bandwidth & other crawler resources. Thus, the Response Analyzer and the Query Ranker form the major components of the proposed hidden web crawler.

The proposed crawler is extensible in the sense that third party components or modules can be added as per the requirements. In addition, the proposed crawler offers scalability in design as new instances executing in parallel may be incorporated in the system as per the requirements.

The proposed Hidden Web crawler has the following functional components:

Form Identifier

The crawler initially picks a URL from the URL Frontier and fetches the web page corresponding to the URL by making an HTTP request to the designated web server. The form identifier parses the Web Page, looks for any <FORM> tags to check if the webpage contains a search form. It has been observed that the search forms that are designed for the search functionality has specific type of format. The form identifier extracts such forms from the HTML source of the Web Page and passes it to the form analyser for further analysis and processing.

Form Analyzer

The form analyzer models the search forms as the set of (control_element_type, label, domain) pairs listed in the Form- Element table (FET). The control element can be of any of the standard input objects like TEXT, INPUT and SELECT. The INPUT defines areas that can be edited in the form, the Attribute TYPE of the INPUT control further describes the type as text, checkbox, radio, submit etc. The control SUBMIT of the INPUT type is generally used to submit the values filled in the form. Every control has a name attribute which is used to appoint control's label. SELECT is used to create a drop-down list box or a multi-choice list box. TEXTAREA is used to create a text box which can input multiple lines of words. The domain of a control element is the set of values that can be associated with the corresponding control on the form. Fig. 3 shows an example search form and its parsed representation structured as a form-element table FET in Table 1.

Some control elements like the ones labelled as From, To, flight trip offer a finite list of possible values such as select-option, checkboxes or radio buttons which are embedded in the webpage itself. Such elements are termed as bounded elements. Other elements like 'Search by Airline' offer free-form input, such as text boxes, have infinite domains (e.g., set of all text strings) are termed unbounded. For the research work in this paper, forms having certain bounded controls have been considered. In general, if E is any control element, then Domain (E) is the set of values that are valid as input to E. The parsed form representation is used by the Form Processor.

Form Processor

The search forms whether having bounded or unbounded controls are perceived primarily for human understanding, but they must also be tackled by the crawlers to serve applications like focused and

Figure 3. Example search form to a structured database

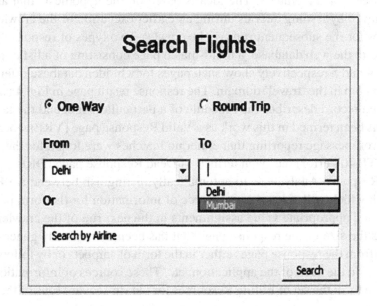

Table 1. Parsed representation as form element table (fet) for the above form

Control Element Type	Label	Domain
Select	From	Delhi, Mumbai
Select	To	Delhi, Mumbai
Radio	Flight trip	One-way, Round trip
Text	Search by airline	String of characters
Submit	Search	submit

general-purpose indexing of response pages, Web Archiving, ontology construction etc. So, for a crawler to bypass these search forms, a set of resources is typically required to fill in the search form. The form processor "fills out" the form by associating a suitable value with each control, the value being chosen from the respective control element's domain. The task specific database together with the page statistics repository form the set of such resources required by the crawler for filling forms thus have been termed as the filling resources of the crawler. Also, these resources are not static but adaptive to the behaviour of the crawler while it proceeds towards its target, thus are self-governed by the crawler. The values that define the domain of a control element comes from the task specific database which must be initialized before the launch of the crawler whereas the other two repositories are each set to null prior the crawler's launch. Having crawling as a continuous process at the search engines back-end, these repositories will be initialized before the next cycle of the crawler begins but only after the completion of execution of the first cycle of the crawler. After the first run of the crawler is over, the obtained set of response pages is analysed to collect data for these repositories.

Response Analyzer

The major component of the proposed crawling system is the Response Analyser that helps in generating the filling resources for the crawler. The idea is based on the hypothesis that analyzing the set of response pages retrieved by issuing queries during an earlier execution of the crawler, can help in generating better queries for the subsequent runs of the crawler. Two types of response pages are typically retrieved for a search in the web database: a multi-match page consisting of a list of result records and a no match page; Fig. 4 and 5 respectively show such pages for a hidden database offered by querying the website makemytrip.com in the 'travel' domain. The response result page in Fig. 4 has multiple records. Herein, each retrieved record describes the schedule of a particular flight and the fare incurred. Such a multi-match page has been termed in this work as a Valid Response page (VRP) whereas a page in Fig.5 which contain an error message reporting that either no matches were found for the submitted query or page not found (HTTP 404 error) has been termed as Dead Response page (DRP).

The aim of the Response Analyzer is to automatically distinguish between a VRP and a DRP and provide the feedback which will act as a huge source of information for the form processor to tune the crawler for suitable and appropriate value assignments in the next run of the crawler. The feedback includes items such as the size of the response page that has been dynamically generated; the content or data items extracted from the response pages either in the form of snippets or by following any embedded hyperlinks depending on the need of the application; etc. These sources of information together with the task specific database form the set of Filling Resources for the subsequent runs of the crawler. However,

Figure 4. A valid response page or a multi-match page from a hidden database in 'travel' domain

Figure 5. A dead Response page or a no-match page from the same hidden database of 'travel' domain

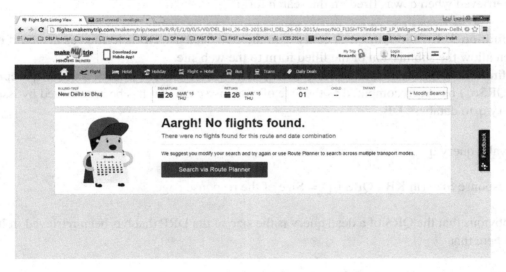

for the ease of implementation of the response analyser, we have not chosen immediate navigation of the response pages further. The response analyser has the following functional components.

Size Extractor

The dynamically generated response pages are usually structured in a similar fashion, be it an answer page with a single record or a long list of matching records. In usual, a response page containing a long list of matching records is of a bigger size as compared to the one that contains fewer number of matching records which in turn is bigger in size to a dead response page. It has been assumed here that the size of a no match page lies in the range 1-3KB. The Size extractor calculates the size of the data retrieved by a query in terms of the size of the response pages, based on which it later guides the path of the crawler through the wise suggestion of better valid queries in future. Such queries are hereafter termed as 'wise' queries. The size of the data retrieved by a query or in short, the size of a query is assumed to be the size of its retrieved response pages for that query submission. We define a few terms that are used for the purpose:

- **Definition 1: Valid Query:** A query q_i submitted to the web database DB, is a valid query if it returns m search result records that are forked into n response pages with each page accommodating at most M result records. In other words, a valid query is one that returns a valid response page.
- **Definition 2: Dead Query:** A query q_i submitted to the web database DB, is a dead query if it retrieves a dead response page.

For a valid query, q_i: $m> =1, n> =1$

For any dead query, q_i: $m=0, n =1$

where n is the number of response pages retrieved in response to q_i & m is the total number of records that are retrieved when q_i.was fired on the search form.

- **Definition 3: Invalid Query:** A query q_i to the web database DB is termed as invalid if does not even allow the submission of the filled form to the web site.
- **Definition 4: Query response Size, QRS():** The query response size of a query q_i, represented as $QRS(q_i)$ has been computed as the size of response page that has been retrieved by issuing the query q_i to database DB.

For any valid query q_i:

Query Response Size (in KB), QRS (q_i) = Size of the response page

It is obvious that the QRS of a dead query is the size of the DRP that has been retrieved. It has been assumed here that

For any dead query q_i: 1KB <= QRS (q_i) <=3 KB

Calculation of the size of the query will not only help the crawler to distinguish between the valid, invalid and dead queries in its future runs but also in estimating the cost of issuing the specified query which depends directly on the huge cost of downloading from the Web. The queries that have once been marked invalid remains in the same status always but the queries which might have been marked as Dead in a particular run of the crawler may not necessarily behave the same always. Thus, elimination of invalid queries from the query space will reduce both the time of execution of un-meaningful queries and the space required by these queries but elimination of dead queries may debar certain promising queries from consideration in the subsequent runs. Thus, in this work, the dead queries have not been eliminated from the consideration of being wise queries. Thus, among all queries- valid or dead, the crawler wisely predicts the 'optimal' or 'promising' query by ranking them based on the query response sizes.

Page Content Extractor

The content extractor basically creates and populates a repository called as task-Specific database. Initially, this database is manually equipped with instances provided by the domain experts based on their knowledge to formulate relevant queries. The proposed approach organizes the task specific database in terms of labels and an associated set of values. Also, this task-specific database is updated from time-to time and populated with the entries that have been extracted from the result pages returned in response to the queries. Whenever the crawler encounters a finite domain form element, it extracts the label and domain values of that element and adds the information to the task-specific database. This will improve the crawler's ability to more effectively fill the forms during its subsequent runs. The various alternatives that have been used to generate such a repository are:

- The repository is initialized with the help of domain experts with values for the controls and labels that the crawler is likely to encounter. For example: when configuring the crawler for 'Air travel domain ', the domain experts initialized the repository with a list of possible airports that can be associated with the labels like 'From', 'To', 'Leaving from', 'Going To' and certain built-in entries for some commonly used categories as day, dates, times, etc., which are likely to be useful across applications.
- When a form is parsed, the crawler can gather (label, value) pairs for form elements with finite domains and add them to the task-specific database. These gathered values can be helpful in filling the search forms for the future runs of the crawler.

The Query Ranker

This component of the proposed work generates the rank of the candidate queries listed in the task-specific database based on the various statistics collected during the process. For ranking the queries, consider **domain(E_i)** to indicate the set of values in the domain of control element E_i for each $i \in [1, d]$ where d is the number of controls on the form; then, the Cartesian product of domain(E_1), domain(E_2), domain(E_3),..., domain(E_d) form the query space for the Hidden Web crawler.

We refer to each element of the Cartesian product as a query q_i in the query space i.e. **Q= {q_{Q1}, q_2, q_3,......q_m}** i.e. a query is one of the possible combinations from the values of all the elements. Alternatively, each q_i is a list of (label, value)pair where label of the control element is an attribute of the form and value is one of the instances from the domain of the associated control element.

Let **CD$_i$** denote the number of choices for each control field, thus

$$CDi = |domain(Ei)| \text{ for each } i \in [1,d] \tag{1}$$

Then the query space **Q**, comprises of a maximum of **m** queries that can be sent correctly for filling a form where

$$m = CD_1 * CD_2 * CD_3 .... * CD_d$$

OR

$$m = \prod_{i=1}^{d} CDi = \prod_{i=1}^{d} \left| \text{domain}\left(Ei \right) \right| \qquad (2)$$

Thus, m is the total number of possible query combinations for a search form.

Consider the multi-attribute search form as in Fig. 3 and a sample of the task specific database for the same in table 2(a) that will be used as running example to explain the working of the query ranker while filling out the designated search form. The first column of the task-specific database contains the labels of the various control attributes of the referred search form and the second column contains the possible values for the corresponding attribute.

For the referred case, the control element say 'FROM' can have either 'DELHI' or 'MUMBAI' as a valid value, 'To' can take either 'DELHI' or 'MUMBAI' & the control 'SEARCH FLIGHTS' can take one-way or round-trip as its possible values, thus each control element offers a choice of two values giving the values of m=2*2*2=8. This value of m specifies the number of queries that can be possibly raised for the form. The possible set of queries has been listed in table 2(b).

When the proposed crawler starts initially, its working is based on the contents of the task-specific database where all the query combinations have equal probabilities of selection. But, practically, dependencies exist among the attributes of the hidden database, because of which the query ranker excludes certain combination of values from forming a candidate query. In the above example, with proper external knowledge of the dependency between the Source of departure and the Destination of arrival many combinations of queries can be chopped out, so as to form the query space Q as in table 3. Thus, the crawler need not explore queries having values for FROM= Delhi and TO= Delhi. Such excluded queries (at s. no. 3, 4, 5, 6in table 2 (b)) form the set of invalid queries which should also be debarred

Table 2. Running example used throughout the paper. (a) Sample task-specific database showing the 3 attributes or controls of the search form and the domain of each such attribute. (b) the set of 8 possibLe query combination

Control Element (Ei)	Domain(Ei)		
From	Delhi, Mumbai		
To	Delhi, Mumbai		
Search flights	One-Way, Round-trip		
S.No.	**From**	**To**	**Search Flights**
1	Mumbai	Delhi	One-way
2	Mumbai	Delhi	Round-trip
3	Mumbai	Mumbai	One-way
4	Mumbai	Mumbai	Round-trip
5	Delhi	Delhi	One-way
6	Delhi	Delhi	Round-trip
7	Delhi	Mumbai	One-way
8	Delhi	Mumbai	Round-trip

Table 3. The query space q and the assigned query id's

Query ID	Source of Departure	Destination of Arrival	Search Flights
Q1	Mumbai	Delhi	One-Way
Q2	Mumbai	Delhi	Round-trip
Q3	Delhi	Mumbai	One-Way
Q4	Delhi	Mumbai	Round-trip

from all the future runs of the crawler. The query Space Q thus formed consists of 4 queries which have been shown in table 3. The Query Ranker now assigns a query ID to each query in Q so as to uniquely identify them during the ranking process.

But as soon as the queries are issued according to the rank as predicted by the Query Ranker, the retrieved set of response pages has to be analysed for updating the task-specific database and initializing the page statistics repository.

For the example under consideration, the page statistics repository has been initialized as in Table 4 which contains the URL & sizes of the response pages retrieved by issuing the queries in table 3:

The query Ranker performs a random ranking of the queries in the task specific database based on the size of pages in the page statistics repository. Also, the proposed random ranking mechanism considers the following:

1. Not all the candidate queries from the Query space Q that are listed in the task-specific database can retrieve valid response pages from the hidden database. Certain queries appear to be valid but when fired on the search form does not retrieve valid response page. The reason might be because the hidden web database does not offer search for the criteria that has been stated in the query.
2. A query that once retrieved dead response pages and thus was termed as 'dead' may not necessarily be 'dead' always when raised in the next crawls. The possible reason being that the organization which hosts the hidden database follow a regular process of updating and maintaining the database contents so as to include the information which is highly relevant and authentic.

Intuitively, the proposed ranking approach defines a random ranking function, random_rank () based on two factors: a static and a dynamic factor. The static factor considers the behaviour the query exhibited

Table 4. The contents of the page statistics repository for the queries

Query ID	Response page	Query Response Size (KB)
Q1	http://flights.makemytrip.com/search/O/O/E/1/0/0/S/V0/BOM_DEL_18-03-2014	**100**
Q2	http://flights.makemytrip.com/search/R/R/E/1/0/0/S/V0/BOM_DEL_18-03-2014,DEL_BOM_18-03-2014	**96**
Q3	http://flights.makemytrip.com/search/O/O/E/1/0/0/S/V0/DEL_BOM_18-03-2014	96
Q4	http://flights.makemytrip.com/search/R/R/E/1/0/0/S/V0/DEL_BOM_18-03-2014,BOM_DEL_18-03-2014	108

in all the previous executions of the crawler whereas the dynamic factor considers the behaviour of the query in the last or immediate previous crawl. Therefore, the rank of the query q_i when the crawler runs for the kth time depends on a value of the static rank which will be computed based on the statistics from all the previous (k-2)crawls and the dynamic rank whose value is computed based on the sizes of the response pages obtained in the immediate last crawl i.e. the (k-1)th crawl. Thus, the rank of a query qi to be executed when the crawler runs for the kth time is the cumulative value of static and dynamic rank generated for the kth crawl:

$$Random\_rank(qi,k) = \alpha.static\_rank(qi, k - 1) + (1 - \alpha)dynamic\_rank(qi, k - 1) \tag{3}$$

where, for k=0

static_rank $(q_i, k)=0$

Dynamic_rank $(q_i,k) = i$

For k>=1

static_rank $(q_i, k) =$ random_ rank $(q_i, k-1)$

and

Dynamic_rank $(q_i,k) = pos(q_i, desc\_sort(QRS(Q)))$

Here, desc_sort () is a function that produces a listing in the decreasing order of the QRS (q_i) for all the queries in the query space, Q. And, Pos () gives the position of the query q_i in the sorted list.

The static ranking function has been termed so because its contribution to the value of random_rank for the kth crawl is independent of the various statistics generated during the (k-1)th execution of the crawler thereby remaining constant in that particular run of the crawler. Thus, it is a value that is assigned to the query prior to the execution in the current crawl. The value of random_rank for the for the first run of the crawler thus has been computed by using the formula stated in Equation 4.

$$Random\_rank(qi, 1) = \alpha.static\_rank(qi, 0) + (1 - \alpha)dynamic\_rank(qi, 0) \tag{4}$$

Also, the parameter α lies in the range [0, 1] and determines when random ranking should be done. If $\alpha=1$, the initial static rank of the query is returned even after the execution ; which means no statistics need to be collected and no re-ranking is performed. But this always issues the queries in the same order repeatedly which may always project the same response from the server, and might not help to obtain the other records present in the hidden database DB.

If $\alpha=0$, the initial static rank is excluded from consideration and only the effect of collected statistics is examined to predict the 'wise' query i.e. only the dynamic factor is taken into consideration.

As an example we have considered the value of $\alpha =0.25$. This assigns a higher weight to the dynamic_rank so as to give more importance to the behaviour of the query in the most recently executed crawl. The size needs consideration as some queries may bring a detailed description of certain records and thus more of the data that is resident in the hidden database. Thus, by taking the value of α as 0.25

$$\text{Random\_rank } (qi, 1) = 0.25*\text{static\_rank } (qi, 0) + 0.75 * \text{dynamic\_rank } (qi,0) \qquad (5)$$

The values of static_rank $(q_i, 0) = 0$ for all q_i and the value of dynamic_rank $(q_i,0) =i$ when the queries were arranged randomly in any order by the crawler for its initial start.

Table 5 shows the computation of random rank values used in the first run of the crawler.

As depicted by the values of random_rank(qi,1) in table 5, when the queries were raised in the order $_{Q1}$, Q_2, Q_3, Q_4 for the first run, different response pages with varying sizes were retrieve. The retrieved response pages and their sizes have been shown in table 4. The ranking of the queries for the next run of the crawler depends on the output or the size of response pages obtained in the previous run.

Thus, the static rank for the queries for the second run is obtained from the order of random rank values computed using equation 3 for the first run. This has been shown in table 6. This way the first query gets a rank static_rank$(_{Q1},1)=1$, while the last is assigned static_rank$(q_n)=N$

The dynamic rank for the queries for the second run have been obtained by ranking the queries in the decreasing order of their Query Response Sizes (QRS) values obtained for each query in the first run. The QRS and the dynamic rank values have been shown in table 7.

By considering the values of $\alpha=0.25$ which gives more weight age to the recent behaviour, the computation of the overall random _rank values as per the equation (A) for the second run has been shown in table 8.

As can be seen from the values of random rank in table 8, the proposed approach ranked the queries as per the order q_3, $_{Q1}$, q_2, q_4. When the queries were issued as per their rank of table 8, a total of 229 unique records were retrieved though each query independently retrieved 142, 87, 177, 150 records from the hidden database. This has been shown in table 9.

Table 5. Computation of random rank values used in the first run of the crawler

Query	Static_rank(q$_i$,0)=0	Dynamic_rank (q$_i$,0)=i	Random_rank (q$_i$,1)= 0.25 * static_rank (q$_i$,0)+ 0.75* dynamic_rank (q$_i$,0)
Q$_1$	0	1	0.75
Q$_2$	0	2	1.5
Q$_3$	0	3	2.25
Q$_4$	0	4	3.0

Table 6. The static rank of the queries for the second run of the crawler

Query ID	Static_rank (q$_i$, 1)
Q$_1$	1
Q$_2$	2
Q$_3$	3
Q$_4$	4

Table 7. Dynamic rank values for the second run

Queries	Response Page Size	Dynamic_rank (q_i,2)
Q_1	100	2
Q_2	96	3
Q_3	108	1
Q_4	96	3

Table 8. Computation of random_rank for the queries

Queries	Static-rank (q_i,1)	Dynamic_rank (q_i,1)	Random_rank (q_i,2)
Q_1	1	2	2.5
Q_2	2	3	2.75
Q_3	3	1	1.5
Q_4	4	3	3.25

Table 9. Number of records retrieved by each query

Queries	Number of Records Retrieved
Q_3	142
Q_1	87
Q_2	177
Q_4	150

The proposed random ranking approach ensures that by issuing the queries as per their random_rank values, some minimum number of queries will be required to exhaustively retrieve the contents of the target database. Thus, the component, Overlap Statistics Miner has been used to analyze the obtained records retrieved by each query. When the Miner extracted the duplicates and unique records retrieved by each query, it was found that just Q3 and $_{Q1}$ would suffice to retrieve all the 229 records as the two queries Q2 and Q4 retrieved only duplicates. The Query Q2 retrieved a total of 177 records of which 39 records have already been retrieved by $_{Q1}$ and 138 records have already been retrieved by Q3. Similarly, the query Q4 fetched 150 records of which 23 records overlapped with $_{Q1}$ and another 127 were duplicates with Q3. Thus, the proposed approach leads to an optimal solution as per which only two queries have been issued for retrieving the same amount of data from the hidden database.

EXPERIMENTAL EVALUATION

Conventional crawlers deal with only the publicly indexable Web that is reachable by following the hyperlink structure. "This topic has been covered many times in past studies (Gravano & Ipeirotis & Sahami, 2003; Gupta & Bhatia, 2012)." And so certain metrics like crawling speed, scalability, page importance, freshness etc. can be used to measure the effectiveness of their crawling activity. "This topic has been covered many times in past studies (Bergholz & Chidlovskii, 2003; Madhavan & Ko & Kot & Ganapathy & Rasmussen & Halevy, 2008)." However, none of these crawling metrics capture the fundamental challenge in dealing with the Hidden Web –processing and submitting forms. In practice, a crawler for the Hidden Web must be able to retrieve the records from the hidden database in a progressive manner. It must surely though slowly, churn out new records from the database during its execution rather than providing all the records together in the end. This allows the crawler to terminate its execution at any moment depending on the proportion between the number of obtained records and the duration involved in collecting those records. Also, most systems have a restriction on the number of queries that can be submitted by a user within a period of time (called the search session). So the crawler must also be polite in issuing request to the server and thus minimize the number of queries required to get the task done.

The proposed crawler has been implemented in JAVA which fires queries on the search form offered by *makemytrip.com*. The search form under consideration allows users to search the various flights that are available between two cities and book the one as per his choice. The proposed crawler first fires the queries based on any arbitrary ordering among them but the crawler simultaneously keeps a record of the percentage content that has been retrieved by issuing each query. The crawler stops issuing queries as soon as this percentage reaches approximately hundred. The crawler next fires the queries according to the random rank predicted by the proposed mechanism. Table 10 presents the results for evaluating the proposed approach in terms of a comparison between the number of queries required in each approach i.e. the arbitrary and the proposed approach when a fixed percentage of the contents of the hidden database has been retrieved.

The proposed system measures the progress of the crawler based on the metric *Reduction Efficiency, R*. The metric has been defined as the ratio of the number of queries that has been cut off to the number of queries required when any arbitrary ordering among the queries was specified..

Thus,

$$R = \frac{Reduction\ in\ the\ number\ of\ queries}{the\ number\ of\ queries\ required\ in\ the\ arbitrary\ approach} \qquad (6)$$

The numerator can be computed by finding the difference between the number of queries required for arbitrary ordering and the proposed random ranking mechanism. For example when 40% of the database content has been retrieved, the value of R can be calculated as:

Table 10. Experimental evaluation

%age of Database Contents Fetched	Number of Queries Required		%age Reduction of Queries
	Arbitrary Ordering	**Proposed Random Ranking**	
20	4	2	50
40	20	8	60
60	40	18	55
80	50	22	56
100	60	28	53.3

$$R = \frac{20-8}{20} * 100 = \frac{12}{20} * 100 = 60 \tag{7}$$

As can be depicted from the last column of table 10, our proposed approach cut shorts the number of queries to approximately 50% of the total queries that were needed when the queries have been raised in any arbitrary order. This nearly stable 50% ratio has been possibly achieved by including the factor of dynamic rank which is a query-dependent factor that predicts the behaviour of the query for the next run according to the query size statistics generated in the immediate previous run of the crawler.

Figure 6 presents the percentage of the obtained records (the x-axis) against the number of queries issued (the y-axis). The crawler initially progresses rapidly with the increase in the number of queries justifying the target of the proposed approach which was to choose the wise queries (based on the analysis of the response pages) in such a way that most of the data from the database can be retrieved as early as possible rather than retrieving the entire contents in the end.

For example, for the proposed approach a point (60, 18) in this figure means that the crawler was able to discover 60% records from the database when it had issued just 18 queries. The same amount of data has been extracted by issuing 40 queries using the arbitrary approach earlier. Thus, the proposed algorithm is asymptotically optimal (in terms of number of queries and database coverage) in the sense that it retrieves the same size of Hidden web database by issuing less number of queries as compared to any arbitrary approach for firing the queries.

Table 11 compares our proposed crawler over certain parameters with some of the existing crawlers for the Hidden Web.

CONCLUSION

The explosive growth of the databases on the Web has posed challenges in front of crawlers to efficiently retrieve the contents in these databases for the purpose of indexing. The proposed framework addresses

Figure 6. Comparison of different query ranking approaches

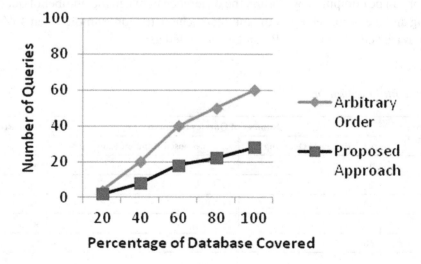

Table 11. Comparison of the proposed optimal hidden web crawler with existing hidden web crawlers

Characteristics	Deep Web Crawler [3]	Hidden Web Crawler[6]	DSHWC[12]	AKSHR[18]	Proposed Crawling Approach
Description	Processes the form and fills it by using LVS table	Analyze the form, classify it and fills the form	Downloads the forms, merges them into USI and fills it automatically	Downloads the form and fills them automatically	Downloads forms from the WWW & then processes them using the Query Ranker
Search Form Collection	Doesn't downloads forms	Doesn't downloads forms	Downloads the forms automatically using Search Interface Crawler	Downloads the forms automatically using Search Interface Crawler	Uses Form Identifier module to download forms
Selection of Candidate Forms	No	No	No	No	Yes Uses Form Analyzer module for the purpose
Form Filling	Not Fully Automatic	Not Fully Automatic	Fully Automatic using Domain-specific Data Repository	Fully Automatic using Domain-specific Data Repository	Fully automatic using the *Filling Resources* comprising of a *Task-Specific Database and Page Statistics Repository*
Query Optimization	No	No	No	No	Yes
Reduction Efficiency	No	No	No	No	Yes, $R = \dfrac{\#\,of\,queries\,eliminated\,or\,reduced}{\#\,of\,queries\,required\,in\,the\,arbitrary\,approach}$
Extensible	*	*	Yes	Yes	Yes
Scalable	*	*	Yes	Yes	Yes
Network Load	Uses Large Band Width	Uses Large Band Width	Uses optimal Band Width (due to Batch Mode)	Uses optimal Band Width (due to Batch Mode)	Due to optimal number of queries, optimal Bandwidth is used

* not claimed.

this problem by designing an optimized hidden web crawler. As the invalid queries are filtered at an early stage, the query search space significantly reduces for the initial and any subsequent runs of the crawler. The approach further ranks the valid queries in a manner that guarantees early and continuous retrieval of the database contents rather than retrieving all records together in the end.

The proposed approach suggests the following advantages:

1. **Query Elimination:** The Hidden Web crawler must automatically come up with meaningful queries to be issued at the interface. The proposed crawler significantly eliminates a large number of queries that seems invalid or redundant thereby improving the efficiency of the crawler.
2. **Reduction Efficiency:** The approach proposes a new metric of *Reduction Efficiency* to measure the progress of the crawler through the calculation of the total and eliminated number of queries.
3. **Extensible:** The proposed crawler is a self-dependent system but is open to extensibility by the addition of third party modules like indexer.
4. **Scalable:** As the size of the Hidden Web expands, the proposed crawler is easier to scale by increasing the number of instances that execute in parallel.

REFERENCES

Barbosa, L., & Freire, J. (2004). Siphoning hidden-web data through keyword-based interfaces. In *In* (pp. 309–321). Brasilia, Brazil: SBBD.

Bergholz, A., & Chidlovskii, B. (2003). Crawling for domain-specific Hidden Web resources. In Proceedings of *the Fourth International Conference on Web Information Systems Engineering (WISE'03).* IEEE Press (pp.125-133). doi:10.1109/WISE.2003.1254476

Bergman, M. (2001). The Deep Web: Surfacing Hidden Value. *Journal of Electronic Publishing*, *7*(1). doi:10.3998/3336451.0007.104

Cheng, S., Termehchy, A., & Hristidis, V. (2012). Predicting the Effectiveness of Keyword queries on Databses in *ACM Conference on Information and knowledge Management CIKM.* doi:10.1145/2396761.2398422

Gravano, L., Ipeirotis, P. G., & Sahami, M. (2003). QProber: A System for Automatic Classification of Hidden-Web Databases [TOIS]. *ACM Transactions on Information Systems*, *15*(1).

Gupta, S., & Bhatia, K. K. (2012). Exploring Hidden parts of the Web: The Hidden Web. *In Springer-Verlag LNEE, Proceedings of the International Conference ArtCom,* (pp 508-515).

Gupta, S., & Bhatia, K. K. (2013). HiCrawl: A Hidden Web crawler for Medical Domain in proceedings of *IEEE International Symposium on Computing and Business Intelligence,* Delhi, India(pp 152-157).

Kashyap, A., Hristidis, V., Petropoulos, M., & Tavoular, S. (2011). Effective navigation of Query results based on Concept Hierarchies *IEEE Trans. Knowl. Data Engg.*, *23*(4), 540–553. doi:10.1109/TKDE.2010.135

Liddle, S. W., Embley, D. W., Scott, D. T., & Yau, S. H. (2002). Extracting Data Behind Web Forms. In proceedings of *the 28th International Conference on Very Large Databases,* HongKong, China. doi:10.1007/978-3-540-45275-1_35

Liu, J., Wu, Z., Jiang, L., Zheng, Q. H., & Liu, X. (2009). "Crawling Deep Web Content Through Query Forms", In Proceedings of the *Interantional Conference of WEBIST,* Lisbon Portugal, (pp. 634-642).

Madhavan, J., Ko, D., Kot, L., Ganapathy, V., Rasmussen, A., & Halevy, A. (2008). Google's Deep-Web Crawl. In proceedings of *International Conference on Very Large Databases VLDB endowment,* Auckland, New Zealand, (pp. 1241-1252).

Ntoulas, A., Zerfos, P., & Cho, J. (2005). Downloading Textual Hidden Web Content Through Keyword Queries. *In Proceedings of the 5th ACM/IEEE Joint Conference on Digital Libraries,* Denver, USA, (pp. 100-109). doi:10.1145/1065385.1065407

Peisu, X., Ke, T., & Qinzhen, H. (2008). A Framework of Deep Web Crawler, *In Proceedings of the 27th Chinese Control Conference,* Kunming,Yunnan, China.

Raghavan, S., & Garcia-Molina, H. (2001). Crawling the Hidden Web. In Proceedings of the 27th *International Conference on Very large databases* Rome, Italy,Morgan Kaufmann Publishers Inc., San Francisco, CA, (129-138).

Sharma, A. K., & Bhatia, Komal Kumar. (2008). A Framework for Domain-Specific Interface Mapper (DSIM). *International Journal of Computer Science and Network Security, 8*(12).

Sharma, A. K., & Bhatia, Komal Kumar (2009). "AKSHR: A Novel Framework of a Domain-specific Hidden Web Crawler", *IEEE International Conference of Advanced Computing*.

Wang, Y., Lu, J., Liang, J., Chen, J., & Liu, J. (2010). *Selecting queries from sample to crawl deep web data sources. Web Intelligence and Agent Systems, an International Journal*. IOS press.

Wang, & Lochovsky, F. H. (2003). Data extraction and label assignment for web databases. In *Proceedings of the International Conference WWW*, Budapest, Hungary.

This research was previously published in the International Journal of Information Retrieval Research (IJIRR), 4(2); edited by Zhongyu (Joan) Lu, pages 1-18, copyright year 2014 by IGI Publishing (an imprint of IGI Global).

Chapter 6
The Evolution of the (Hidden) Web and Its Hidden Data

Manuel Álvarez Díaz
University of A Coruña, Spain

Víctor Manuel Prieto Álvarez
University of A Coruña, Spain

Fidel Cacheda Seijo
University of A Coruña, Spain

ABSTRACT

This paper presents an analysis of the most important features of the Web and its evolution and implications on the tools that traverse it to index its content to be searched later. It is important to remark that some of these features of the Web make a quite large subset to remain "hidden". The analysis of the Web focuses on a snapshot of the Global Web for six different years: 2009 to 2014. The results for each year are analyzed independently and together to facilitate the analysis of both the features at any given time and the changes between the different analyzed years. The objective of the analysis are twofold: to characterize the Web and more importantly, its evolution along the time.

INTRODUCTION

Since its origins, the WWW has been the subject of numerous studies. However, one constant has been and continues to be the analysis of its size. Although it is nearly impossible to compute the exact size of the Web, because it is in constant change, everyone agrees that his size is in the order of billions of documents or pages (Gulli & Signorini, 2005). In this way, the WWW could be considered the largest repository of documents ever built.

Due to the large size of the Web, search engines are essential tools for users who want to access relevant information for a specific topic. Search engines are complex systems that allow, among other things: gathering, storing, managing and granting access to the information. Crawling systems are those which perform the task of gathering information. These programs are capable of traversing and analysing the Web in a certain order, by following the links between different pages.

DOI: 10.4018/978-1-5225-3163-0.ch006

The task of a crawling system presents numerous challenges due to the quantity, variability and quality of the information that it needs to collect. Among these challenges, specific aspects can be highlighted, such as the technologies used in web pages to access to data, both in the server-side (Raghavan & Garcia-Molina, 2001) or in the client-side (Bergman, 2001); or problems associated with web content such as Web Spam (Gyongyi & Garcia-Molina, 2005) or repeated contents (Kumar & Govindarajulu, 2009), etc. To get a detailed enumeration it is necessary to analyse the Web in more detail.

This article presents an analysis of the most important features of the Web and its components and also its evolution over a period of time. Particular emphasis is placed on the use of client/server side technologies. It is very important to remark that the Hidden Web is "hidden" just for the existence of some technologies used in web documents that difficult the task of crawler systems for accessing to it.

The analysis focuses on a snapshot of the Global Web for six different years: from 2009 to 2014. The results for each year are analysed independently and together to simplify the evaluation of the features at any given time and the changes between the different analysed years. The objectives of the analysis are twofold: to characterize the Web and more importantly, its evolution along the time, and also to analyze how its changes affect tools such as crawlers and search engines. So, changing trends are presented and explained.

The structure of this paper is as follows. Background section introduces works related with the study and characterization of the Web. Methodology section shows the methodology followed to characterize the Web. Dataset section explains the dataset used. The analysis section discusses the results obtained for each year, and their evolution through the time. Finally, the future research directions section includes possible future works and the conclusions section summarises the results of the paper.

BACKGROUND

The characterization of the Web is a topic widely studied in the supported literature. Baeza-Yates et al. (Baeza-Yates, Castillo & Efthimiadis, 2007) performed a study which analyses various features of the Web at several levels: web page, web site and national domains. On the other hand, there are several studies that are focused on the Web of a particular country. In 2000, Sanguanpong et al. (Sanguanpong, Piamsa-nga, Keretho, Poovarawan & Warangrit, 2000) presented an analysis of various issues related to web servers and web documents in Thailand. Baeza-Yates et al. presented two articles (Baeza-Yates, Castillo, & Lopez, 2005; Baeza-Yates & Castillo, 2000), which were focused more specifically on the characteristics of the Spanish and Chilean Web, respectively. The Spanish Web was also studied by Prieto et al. (Prieto, Álvarez, & Cacheda, 2013), by comparing the analysis of the Spanish Web with the Global Web in a tree-years period. In 2002, Boldi et al. (Boldi, Codenotti, Santini, & Vigna, 2002) presented an interesting article, where the authors have studied different features (content and structure analysis, web graph, etc.) of the African Web. Gomes et al. (Gomes & Silva, 2005), carried out a study to characterise the community Web of the people of Portugal. The authors studied different features such as: the number and domain distribution of sites, the number and size distribution of text documents, the structure of this Web, etc. Years later, Miranda and Gomes (Miranda & Gomes, 2009) performed a study which presented trends on the evolution of the Portuguese Web, derived from the comparison of two characterizations of a web portion performed within a 5 year interval. This study analyses several metrics regarding content and site characteristics. Modesto et al. (Modesto, Pereira, Ziviani, Castillo, & Baeza-Yates, 2005) presented an article, which analyses the features of approximately 2% of the.br domains. The results have been compared with the results obtained in other studies on the Chilean and Greek Web. Finally, another similar study was performed by Efthimiadis and Castillo (Efthimiadis & Castillo, 2004), where the authors did a characterization of the Greek Web.

On the other hand, there are studies that focus on studying a specific feature of the Web. It is the case of the study presented by Grefenstette and Nioche (Grefenstette & Nioche, 2000), where the authors have analysed the English and non-English language used on the Web. A relevant study was the performed by Bharat et al. (Bharat, Chang, Henzinger, & Ruhl, 2001), which discussed the links between Web sites and its meaning. Other study focused on a particular feature of the Web, was the performed by Downey (Downey, 2001), where the author has analysed models for web page sizes.

There are other studies that focus exclusively on the structure of the Web, such as that conducted by Broder et al. (Broder, Kumar, Maghoul, Raghavan, Rajagopalan, Stata, Tomkins, & Wiener, 2000). In this article they show an analysis of links between pages in the same domain, across domains within the same country and between global domains. In 1999, Huberman and Adamic (Huberman, & Adamic, 1999) carried out a study where the authors characterise the distribution of web pages per web site. According to this study the web pages are distributed among sites following to a universal power law: many sites have only a few pages, whereas very few sites have hundreds of thousands of pages. In 2007, Serrano et al. (Serrano, Maguitman, Boguñá, Fortunato, & Vespignani, 2007) reported a statistical analysis of the topological properties of four different WWW graphs obtained with different crawlers. Another relevant study was presented by Baeza-Yates et al. (Baeza-Yates, Saint-Jean, & Castillo, 2002), where they analyse the structure of the Web, its dynamics and its relationship to the quality of content. Finally, in (Baeza-Yates & Poblete, 2006), Baeza-Yates and Poblete characterise the structure of the Chilean Web.

A relevant part of the Web that has been studied by many authors is the Deep or Hidden Web. This portion of the Web contains those pages that are accessed through web forms or by means of client-side technologies such as JavaScript or Flash. Among the studies, we can highlight the one carried out by Bergman (Bergman, 2001). More recent studies are those performed by Shestakov, in 2011, (Shestakov, 2011a; Shestakov, 2011b). In these papers, the author analyses the problem of Deep Web characterization and treats to estimate the total number of online databases on the Web.

Other aspects that deserve special attention are those related to the similarity of the Web and its decline. A study of the similarity of the Web, is the one performed by Cho et al. (Cho, Shivakumar, & Garcia-Molina, 2000), which proposes a technique to detect replicated documents and collections to improve web crawlers, archivers, and ranking functions used in search engines.

There are several studies with respect to the dynamic and age of Web pages. The most notably of these is that presented by Lewandowski (Lewandowski, 2008), which discusses the evolution of the age of the pages over several years. Fetterly et al. (Fetterly, Manasse, Najork, Wiener, 2003) included a study about the degree of change of each page, and which factors are correlated with change intensity. On the other hand, there are several studies of the Web dynamic. Adar et al. (Adar, Teevan, Dumais, & Elsas, 2009) describe algorithms, analyses, and models for characterizing changes in Web content, focusing on both time (by using hourly and sub-hourly crawls) and structure (by looking at page-DOM, and term-level changes). Other interesting work about the Web dynamic is the performed by Ntoulas et al. (Ntoulas, Cho, & Olston, 2004). They seek to gain improved insight into how Web search engines should cope with the evolving Web. This study is focus on aspects of potential interest to search engine designers: the evolution of link structure over time, the rate of creation of new pages and new distinct content on the Web, and the rate of change of the content of existing pages under search-centric measures of degree of change.

At last, there are studies focused on proposing crawling strategies to improve the performance of crawlers. They are based on the age and dynamics (changes) of web pages. For instance, the work by Brewington and Cybenko (Brewington & Cybenko, 2000) or a study by Cho and Garcia-Molina (Cho & Garcia-Molina, 2003a), where the authors not only discuss the dynamics of web content, but also show methods to try to keep data collections of search engines more up to date. We can also highlight the presented by Cho and Garcia-Molina (Cho & Garcia-Molina, 2003b). This article formalizes the notion of "freshness" of copied data and propose a Poisson process as the change model of data sources. They show that a Poisson process is a good model to describe the changes of Web pages. Other similar study is the performed by Olston and Pandey (Olston & Pandey, 2008), where the authors characterize the longevity of information found on the Web, via both empirical measurements and a generative model that coincides with these measurements. They propose new recrawl scheduling policies that consider longevity.

Numerous studies have examined the Web from different points of view. However, to the best of our knowledge, only our previously presented paper (Prieto, Álvarez, & Cacheda, 2013) has studied the evolution of the main features the Web through time. This article expands the analysis previously presented in (Prieto, Álvarez, & Cacheda, 2013), by extending it to a 6-years period, but focusing on the Global Web. In addition, it puts special interest in features relevant to determine the evolution of the Hidden Web in time, such as the use of client/server side technologies.

METHODOLOGY USED FOR THE ANALYSIS

The analysis of the Web can be performed at various levels of granularity (Björneborn & Ingwersen, 2004). Below we describe the levels we have included in this article, together with the characteristics analysed in each of them, for the six-years period considered. They are also shown in Figure 1.

Figure 1. Granularity levels used to analyse the Web

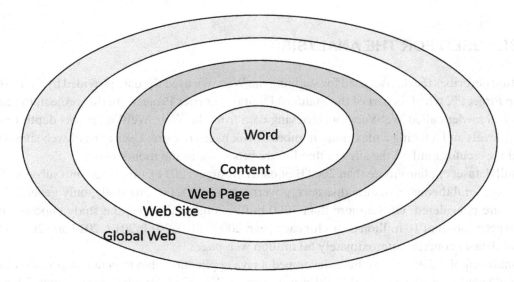

- **Word Level:** The study of this level provides information about the vocabulary used on the Web, and the most commonly used HTML tags.
- **Content Level:** The analysis of this level allows obtaining information about the evolution of the web documents size and its relationship to the useful content. It allows increasing the knowledge about the evolution of the most widely used languages on the Web, and how multimedia file formats, format styles, other types of documents or compression methods usage evolve on the Web. In addition, some meta-tags commonly used in web pages are analysed.
- **Web Page Level:** At this level, the characteristics of an entire web page are analysed: the length of the URLs/title of web pages and the age of web pages. In addition, we will pay special attention on the level of compression and the similarity of web pages.
- **Web Site Level:** The study of this level provides the main features of web sites, defined as collections of related web pages common to a domain or subdomain. We analyse the number of links (inlink, outlink, static, dynamic, relative and absolute) on the Web. This allows to know how the Web is growing and modifying its structure, and how this affects search algorithms. We also analyse the technologies used by web servers to build sites. In addition, the Hidden Web, defined as the set of web pages that are not directly accessible through links (Raghavan & Garcia-Molina, 2001) is analysed. When we talk about Hidden Web, we could differentiate two very different parts: the client-side and the server-side Hidden Web. For the client-side Hidden Web and its evolution, we study client-side technologies usage. In order to access server-side Hidden Web, it is necessary to submit a query on a web form. This part of the Web contains a large amount of data, but its treatment is more complex. The size and the quality of the Hidden Web is important for the crawlers and search engines, to decide whether they should put more resources to process it. In this study, we analyse the evolution in the number of Hidden Web entry points, which are the elements that a crawler has to be able to discover for accessing hidden web content.
- **Global Web Level:** This level allows obtaining information about the use and evolution of the software used by web servers. In addition, the mainly used configurations for the Exclusion Robots protocol are analysed.

DATASET USED FOR THE ANALYSIS

This section describes the dataset used for studying the Web. We used the data provided by "The Stanford WebBase Project[1]", which is part of the Stanford Digital Libraries Project[2]. In this project, the Stanford team uses a crawler called WebVac, for retrieving data from the Web. WebVac crawls depth first, until depth of 7 levels and fetching a maximum number of 10k pages per site. Uses a list of web sites as initial feed, and it executes until all the sites in that list are processes or the month is over.

The full dataset contains more than 260TB of data (in August 2011), organized into subsets of different topics (general thematic, natural disasters, governments, etc.). For this study, only general thematic datasets were considered. Of the more than 7000 million obtained pages, the study choose a random sample to get a subset of 10 million pages for each year, 2009, 2010, 2011, 2012, 2013 and 2014. Overall, the global dataset contains approximately 60 million web pages.

For analyzing the datasets, we have developed a java application able to generate statistics from the data downloaded from the Stanford WebBase project in WARC (Web ARChive) format. This format allows storing multiple web documents into a single, optionally compressed, file. It also includes, for each web document, its URL and the content of the HTTP headers returned by a web server when it was requested.

Our system uses the JWAT library (https://sbforge.org/display/JWAT/JWAT) for reading WARC files in streaming. For each document, we compute statistics based on the metadata of the HTTP headers associated to the document (e.g. content-type of documents, software used by the web server, etc.) and on the document content. For the second, we use the jsoup library (http://jsoup.org), a java HTML parser for modelling the document as a DOM (Document Object Model) tree. The DOM tree is queried for retrieving information about links (number of links of each type, type of linked documents, etc.), web forms, technologies used, etc.

Finally, for computing the most-used words and tags, an index built by using Apache Lucene software (http://lucene.apache.org) was used.

ANALYSIS

Taking the dataset defined in previous section as a starting point, the following subsections discuss the results obtained for the features introduced at the methodology section.

Features at Word Level

Within the scope of web pages, a word may be used mainly as a term or as an HTML tag. This section analyses the words from these two points of view.

Vocabulary

In order to study the vocabulary used on the Web, a word is any alphanumeric string with length larger or equals than one character. For computing them, we remove all the HTML tags of the pages, and used an Apache Lucene Index for the resultant content. Then, we compute the top words for each year. Table 1 shows the 25 most commonly used words in the Web in the period studied. This indicates that the top web page words remains near the same along all the years except for the token corresponding to the current year (different in each case). We can also perceive that the frequency of occurrences of the more common words is increasing. For instance, the "home" word had an occurrence frequency of 54.73% in 2009 and it grew until 63.42% in 2014. Something similar happened with "about" (from 52.74% to 63.42%) of "contact" (from 50.03% to 58.98%). Regarding the current year token, we would like to remark that in 2009, it appeared in the 32,9% of the analysed pages. I grew until 40.8% in 2010 and in the range 43%-46% between 2011 and 2014. This could be an indicator about the number of new pages created in the corresponding year, with respect to the pages that had been created in previous years, but remain in the current year.

All of these indicate a growing number of common words in web pages. From the point of view of search engines, this means an increment in the number of terms that are no so relevant to represent the content of a web page. So, selecting relevant web documents for a given set of terms, will be more difficult.

Table 1. Top web page words

2009	2010	2011	2012	2013	2014
home(54.73%)	home(56.14%)	about(59.05%)	about(61.12%)	about(61.64%)	about(63.42%)
about(52.74%)	about(56.02%)	home(57.13%)	home(57.71%)	home(57.05%)	contact(58.98%)
contact(50.03%)	contact(53.21%)	contact(55.69%)	contact(57.03%)	contact(56.9%)	home(57.41%)
from(50.02%)	from(50.75%)	us(51.08%)	us(52.74%)	us(53.5%)	us(55.65%)
all(48.23%)	all(49.8%)	from(50.99%)	all(52.69%)	all(53.03%)	all(52.5%)
us(44.95%)	us(48.74%)	all(50.97%)	from(51.9%)	from(51.02%)	from(51.53%)
search(44.44%)	search(45.92%)	search(46.97%)	search(48.44%)	**2013(46.79%)**	search(49.09%)
information(42.94%)	information(43.87%)	**2011(45.02%)**	more(45.99%)	search(46.48%)	more(48.12%)
site(41.8%)	site(42.72%)	information(44.77%)	information(45.4%)	more(46.29%)	information(46.06%)
more(40.66%)	more(42.51%)	more(44.54%)	new(44.29%)	information(45.21%)	**2014(46.01%)**
new(40.5%)	new(41.53%)	site(43.2%)	**2012(43.87%)**	new(44.36%)	new(45.06%)
1(38.89%)	**2010(40.8%)**	new(42.65%)	site(43.3%)	1(43.4%)	privacy(44.43%)
you(37.41%)	1(40.18%)	1(41.52%)	1(43.1%)	news(42.34%)	1(44.1%)
privacy(36.4%)	you(38.98%)	you(40.76%)	you(42.03%)	privacy(42.21%)	news(43.38%)
other(35.77%)	privacy(38.89%)	privacy(40.39%)	privacy(41.97%)	you(41.71%)	you(42.55%)
have(35.62%)	news(36.6%)	news(39.02%)	news(40.82%)	site(41.51%)	your(42.18%)
your(34.35%)	other(35.96%)	your(37.09%)	your(38.99%)	your(40.9%)	site(42.03%)
page(34.09%)	your(35.81%)	other(37.02%)	other(37.24%)	our(37.62%)	our(38.45%)
has(33.93%)	have(34.99%)	have(35.41%)	have(36.18%)	policy(36.59%)	policy(38.39%)
news(33.65%)	2(34.02%)	2(34.89%)	2(36.08%)	2(35.96%)	other(37.38%)
2(32.97%)	page(33.77%)	policy(34.28%)	policy(35.6%)	other(35.92%)	have(36.15%)
2009(32.9%)	policy(33.43%)	has(33.58%)	our(35.49%)	have(35.5%)	research(36.04%)
policy(32.09%)	has(33.33%)	may(33.44%)	use(33.77%)	research(34.44%)	2(35.81%)
use(31.76%)	e(31.93%)	our(33.42%)	has(33.68%)	3(33.11%)	use(34.17%)
e(30.97%)	use(31.86%)	page(33.3%)	page(33.23%)	use(33.05%)	has(34.07%)

HTML Tags

Another type of "important" words on the Web are the HTML tags, which create and shape web pages. We create an Apache Lucene Index with only the HTML tags for each document. Then, we compute the top words for each year. Table 2 shows the top 26 HTML tags for each year.

The 26 most used tags are common over the 6 years analysed, except for minimal changes. But although the top tags are essentially the same, we would like to remark the trend of the occurrence frequency for some tags:

- The use of tag "script" grew a 15% from 2009 to 2014, so the use of scripting technologies is clearly increasing, with the difficulties that it has for crawling engines.The use of lists ("li" and "ul" tags) and "div" tag grew near a 38% from 2009 to 2014 and the use of "span" tag grew a 24%.

Nevertheless, the use of tables ("table", "tr" and "td" tags) and "tbody" tags decreased a 60% in the same period (from 62% to 37%). This shows a change in the design of web documents, from a tabular representation to create the layout of pages to stylesheets. In addition, it is also interesting to remark that the use of heading tags ("h1", "h2") was increased between a 15% and 20%.The use of forms ("form" tag) grew a 21% in the last 6 years. Between a 55% and a 67% of web pages include a "form" tag. This confirms that the importance of dealing the server-side Hidden Web is growing.

All of these results show the changing trend in the way of developing web pages.

Table 2. Top web page HTML tags

2009	2010	2011	2012	2013	2014
head(100%)	head(100%)	head(100%)	head(100%)	head(100%)	head(100%)
html(100%)	html(100%)	html(100%)	html(100%)	html(100%)	html(100%)
root(100%)	root(100%)	root(100%)	root(100%)	root(100%)	root(100%)
body(99.57%)	body(99.66%)	body(99.77%)	body(99.84%)	body(99.87%)	body(99.9%)
title(93.93%)	title(93.55%)	title(93.23%)	title(92.61%)	title(92.33%)	title(91.97%)
p(82.52%)	p(82.85%)	p(83.47%)	p(83.46%)	p(83.49%)	p(83.79%)
img(81.53%)	img(81.86%)	img(81.99%)	img(81.62%)	img(81.12%)	**meta(80.96%)**
br(80.13%)	br(78.67%)	**meta(79.39%)**	**meta(79.93%)**	**meta(80.74%)**	img(80.83%)
meta(77.01%)	**meta(78.55%)**	br(77.49%)	div(77.37%)	link(78.94%)	div(78.87%)
div(70.34%)	div(74.05%)	div(75.82%)	link(76.85%)	div(78.31%)	link(78.86%)
link(69.48%)	link(72.81%)	link(75.18%)	br(75.72%)	script(76.85%)	script(78.24%)
script(68.12%)	script(71.57%)	script(73.91%)	script(75.3%)	br(74.14%)	li(72.33%)
tr(62.83%)	form(59.95%)	li(64.02%)	li(67.47%)	li(70.95%)	br(72.02%)
table(62.79%)	input(59.85%)	ul(63.25%)	ul(66.57%)	ul(70.36%)	ul(71.78%)
tbody(62.73%)	li(59.37%)	form(62.47%)	input(64.75%)	input(66.66%)	span(68.51%)
td(62.59%)	ul(58.33%)	input(62.45%)	form(64.61%)	form(66.53%)	input(67.91%)
form(55.78%)	span(58.05%)	span(61.47%)	span(64%)	span(66.23%)	form(67.76%)
input(55.11%)	tr(56.94%)	**h1(58.45%)**	**h1(60.66%)**	**h1(64.27%)**	**h1(66.56%)**
span(54.21%)	**table(56.9%)**	tr(51.6%)	h2(49.19%)	h2(52.68%)	h2(54.78%)
li(53.29%)	tbody(56.83%)	**table(51.54%)**	**table(46.74%)**	strong(43.45%)	strong(42.52%)
ul(51.98%)	td(56.7%)	tbody(51.49%)	tr(46.73%)	tr(42.55%)	h3(42.2%)
h1(47.93%)	**h1(53.12%)**	td(51.4%)	tbody(46.63%)	**table(42.48%)**	**table(37.44%)**
b(43.04%)	h2(43.67%)	h2(46.99%)	td(46.53%)	td(42.45%)	label(37.44%)
strong(37.74%)	strong(40.79%)	strong(41.73%)	strong(42.21%)	tbody(42.4%)	tr(37.43%)
h2(37.61%)	b(39.62%)	h3(36.2%)	h3(38.14%)	h3(40.37%)	td(37.34%)
style(35.54%)	style(37.13%)	b(35.78%)	style(34.34%)	style(34.45%)	tbody(37.33%)

Features at Web Content Level

This section discusses the evolution of the total/useful size of the web pages, the most commonly used languages, picture, video, music formats among others file formats and the most used styles. In addition, this section also analyses certain attributes of the "meta" tag of HTML pages, such as the content type.

Size of the Total/Useful Content

We define the useful content of a web page as its main content, where the information is really placed, without HTML tags, links, images, etc. The useful content is used by search engines to provide the correct web documents to the users. An important fact for search engines and crawlers is the size of the downloaded and stored content, and its relation to the useful content of each page.

The process of extraction of the useful content of the web pages is very complicated. This study follows the approach developed by Pan et al. in (Pan, Qiu, & Yin, 2008). It is based on that the location of the main content is very centralized and has a good hierarchical structure. Pan et al. found that the threshold values of the DOM nodes (W3C DOM IG, 2005) with useful content are obviously different from that of other DOM nodes in the same level. With these values, they have proposed an algorithm that judges the content by several parameters in the nodes (Link Text Density, Link Amount, Link Amount Density and Node Text Length).

Figure 2 shows the obtained results. It is important to note that our study has considered the full content of the pages, unlike other existing studies that truncate the pages to a certain size (Baeza-Yates & Castillo, 2000).

In the year 2009, the average content per page was 31.01 KB, but this number has been increasing in 3 KB per year, until reach 46 KB in 2014. Analysing the results taken for useful content, it is notable that in 2009 the average size of useful content was 6.7 KB, a number that was increasing in subsequent years until reach 7.9 KB in 2014. Regarding the ratio between total and useful content, it was decreasing from 21% in 2009 until 17% in 2014. So, the difference between total content and useful content is increasing.

These results continue to confirm that web documents are growing in size, mainly with common words. In addition, it is likely that these web pages use client-side technologies such as JavaScript to improve the user experience.

Language

In order to identify the language used in each web page, this study uses the "language detector" library (Shuyo, 2010), which is based on Bayesian filters. It has a precision of 0.99 to detect 53 languages.

Table 3 shows the results obtained. The predominant language is English with 88.91% in 2009, decreasing to approximately 86% in 2014. In the study presented by Grefenstette and Nioche (Grefenstette & Nioche, 2000) in the year 2000, the authors have estimated that about 70% of the web pages were written in English. According with the presented study, this figure has increased 27%, although in the last 6 years the use of English language has decreased a bit. This is due to the increment of use of other languages.

Figure 2. Evolution of the content size of a web page and relation with useful content

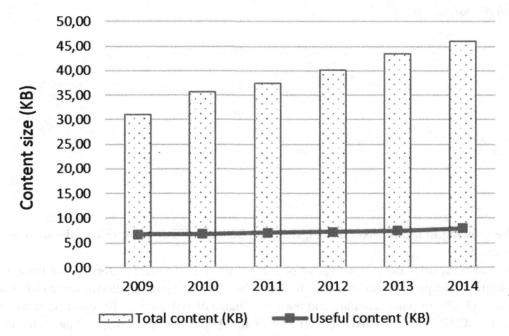

Table 3. Distribution of languages used on the Web

	2009	2010	2011	2012	2013	2014
en	88.91%	88.48%	87.92%	87.81%	87.25%	86.75%
unknown	3.19%	3.29%	3.70%	4.05%	3.91%	4.41%
fr	3.15%	3.36%	3.54%	3.34%	3.50%	3.27%
de	1.94%	2.11%	1.84%	2.02%	2.10%	2.23%
es	1.46%	1.28%	1.23%	1.11%	1.18%	1.31%
it	0.46%	0.52%	0.56%	0.54%	0.52%	0.50%
other	0.89%	0.96%	1.21%	1.12%	1.54%	1.53%

Image File Formats

Figure 3 shows the changes in the use of image file formats. Our study focused on the following formats: GIF (Graphics Interchange Format), JPEG (Joint Photographic Experts Group), PNG (*Portable* Network Graphic), Ico (Icon image file), BMP (Bitmap image format) and TIF (Tagged Image File Format).

We have observed that there is a predominance of the GIF format for images, although it has been slowly decreasing through the years. If we count all the images referenced by the analyzed documents, the 83.58% of the images were of GIF format in 2009, but only a 49.72% of the total of images in 2014. This suppose a very important decrement in the use of this format for images. This decrement has been compensated with the increment in other two relevant image file formats: JPG and PNG. The fraction of JPG images in 2009 was 13.14%, raising until 25.75% in 2014. Something similar, but more impres-

Figure 3. Distribution of image file formats on the Web: % of usage of each file format (left), % of pages using each file format (right)

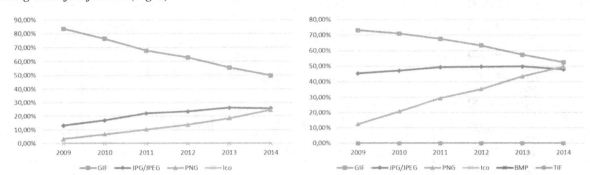

sive, is the growing in use of PNG format, from a 3.27% in 2009 to a 24.53% of the total number of images in 2014.

Figure 3 also includes the percentage of pages that use each image file format (on the right). The result is similar to the previously described. In 2009, the 73.11% of pages included some GIF image, but in 2014 only 52.42% of pages contained at least one image of GIF format. By contrast, the number of pages using PNG file format increased from 12.49% to 49.66%. The percentage of pages using at least one JPG file remained more or less the same (between 45% and 50% of pages).

These results indicate that web pages are evolving towards documents with more quality images and less size.

Video File Formats

Figure 4 shows the most used video formats. We analyzed the following video formats: WMV (Windows Media Video), MOV/QT (QuickTime), AVI (Audio Video Interleave) and MPEG (Moving *Picture* Expert Group).

The predominant video formats in 2009 were WMV and MOV/QT, with 45.39% and 44.66% respectively, followed by AVI with a 8.19%. In 2010 the usage of the MOV/QT video format grew a lot,

Figure 4. Distribution of video file formats on the Web: % of usage of each file format (left), % of pages using each file format (right)

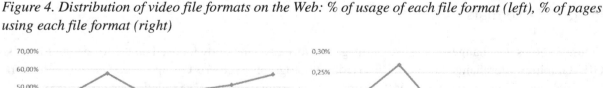

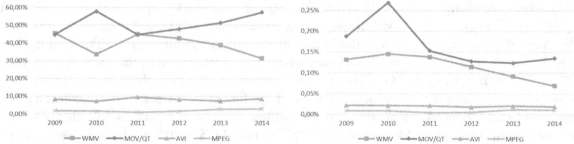

at expenses of the WMV format. In 2011 the difference between this two formats was minimal again, and from 2010 to 2014 the usage of the MOV/QT file format grew again until a 57.16%, decreasing the use of the WMV format until 31.36%. The MOV/QT file format was developed by Apple Computer, and the WMV by Microsoft. This trend could confirm the success of Apple lately. The peak observed in 2010 could be related with some of the new products of apple, the iPad. Regarding other file formats, like AVI, or MPEG, their usage do not vary greatly in the 6 studied years, remaining around 8% and 2% respectively. The AVI format was one of the oldest video formats. It has good quality but it is very heavy. In previous years, it was the most widely used format on the Internet. Today, WMV/MOV/QT has similar quality but with a smaller size. Due to this, AVI has almost disappeared with other smaller formats taking its place.

Regarding the number of pages using video resources, we conclude that videos are not too frequent in the web, except for some specialized web sites not included in this study. Figure 4 shows that WMV was the video format used by the major number of pages, followed by WMV, and there were nearly not changes in the following 6 years of the study.

Music File Formats

The music file formats used on the Web have also been analysed. We have considered the following formats: MP3 (MPEG1 - or MPEG2 - Audio Layer III), WAV (Waveform Audio File Format), WMA (Windows Media Audio), ASF (Audio Video Interleaved), MIDI (Musical Instrument Digital Interface).

During the 6 years studied, the distribution of the music file formats has not change notably. Figure 5 shows the obtained results. Focusing on the data obtained in 2014, the most widely used format is MP3 with 91.73%. The next most commonly used music format is WAV with a 5.46%. Other music formats are WMA with 1.66%, and ASF or MIDI, with very insignificant percentages. The limited evolution that has been observed is because the MP3 format has good quality with a relatively small size, and because no new formats have appeared in the recent years that have been able to replace the MP3 format.

Regarding the number of pages using music file formats, occurs something similar that the observed with video formats. Only 0.44% of web pages included a reference to a MP3 file format. We observe that the usage of music file formats in web pages increased a bit from 2009 until 2012 (0.54% to 0.60%), but from 2012 decreased until 0.44% of pages in 2014.

Figure 5. Distribution of music file formats on the Web: % of usage of each file format (left), % of pages using each file format (right)

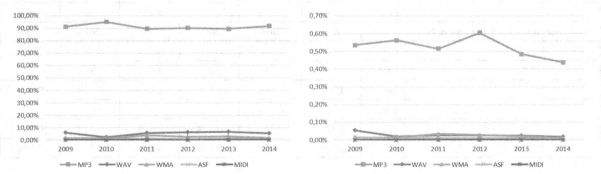

Other Document Types

One point that characterizes web pages is the different types of documents that they contain. Table 8 shows the results for the most relevant file types. For this study we considered documents of types PDF (Portable Document File), XML (eXtensible Markup Language), Txt (text files), Doc (Microsoft Word Document), Ppt (Microsoft PowerPoint presentations) and Ps (PostScript).

Table 4 shows the results obtained. The type of document which appears more often is PDF. In 2014, the 80.94% of all documents types considered were PDF. The next most common type of document is the XML, which grew from 7.46% in 2009 to 11.28% in 2014. The rest of file formats were less than 8% in 2009, and less than 4% in 2014.

Regarding the number of web pages using these document types, 12.87% of web pages used some PDF file in 2009. This percentage grow until 15.82% in 2014. XML files were referenced from 2.65% of the pages, growing until 4.68% in 2014.

In short, the obtained results are logical, since PDF documents, as its initials indicate (Portable Document Format), can be used in any operating system.

Compression File Formats

Figure 6 shows the results obtained for the compression file formats analyzed. In 2009, the most used file format was GZIP with a 55.18%, followed by ZIP with a 32.18%. Along the 6 years-period analysed, the usage of the ZIP format grew until 53.44% and GZIP usage decreased until 42.83%. This trend could justify the situation of power of Windows Operating systems, due to ZIP is a format more commonly used in this operating system.

Table 4. Distribution of other document types on the Web

% of Usage of Document Types		2009	2010	2011	2012	2013	2014
(among the following 6 types)	*Pdf*	76.14%	78.35%	84.40%	86.90%	79.40%	80.94%
	Xml	7.46%	8.54%	5.48%	5.67%	11.42%	11.28%
	Txt	8.15%	6.19%	5.18%	2.75%	3.07%	3.26%
	Doc	5.89%	4.98%	3.57%	3.47%	4.63%	3.39%
	Ppt	1.45%	1.21%	0.84%	0.73%	0.88%	0.69%
	Ps	0.91%	0.73%	0.53%	0.49%	0.60%	0.44%
% of Pages using Each Document Type		2009	2010	2011	2012	2013	2014
	Pdf	12.87%	13.87%	14.35%	14.76%	15.66%	15.82%
	Xml	2.65%	3.23%	3.10%	4.03%	4.35%	4.68%
	Doc	1.40%	1.29%	1.14%	1.08%	0.97%	0.98%
	Txt	1.10%	0.91%	0.80%	0.61%	0.61%	0.67%
	Ppt	0.42%	0.35%	0.32%	0.27%	0.24%	0.21%
	Ps	0.22%	0.20%	0.14%	0.12%	0.11%	0.10%

Figure 6. Distribution of compression file formats on the Web: % of usage of each file format (left), % of pages using each file format (right)

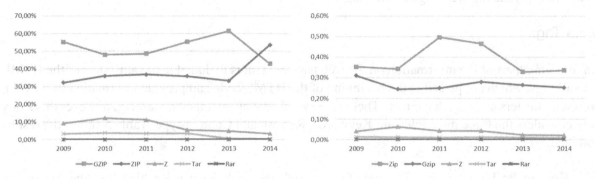

Regarding the number of web pages referencing compressed files, in 2009, only the 0.35% of pages included some file compressed using ZIP and 0.31% GZIP. This results are nearly the same along the 6-year period studied.

Styles

Search engines also consider the style in which certain terms of web page content are written. The fact that a word is highlighted (bold or italic) can indicate that it is more relevant than others. Figure 7 shows a brief survey of commonly used standard styles.

In 2009, the most widely used style is bold, with a 58.30%. But that has decreased until 41,64% in 2014. The use of italics remains around 20% in the 6-years period. The decrease in bold could be due to the increment of the styles of the title sections H2 and H3. Their use was around 7% in 2009 and it grew until around 15% in 2014.

Figure 7 also shows the number of pages in which some of the analysed styles are used. We observe a clear increment in the percentages of pages using styles of the title section. In 2009, a 47.89% of web pages used at least an H1 style, a 37.55% H2 and 27.79% H3. In 2014 the percentages grew to 66.52%,

Figure 7. Distribution of usage of styles on the Web: % of usage of each file format (left), % of pages using each file format (right)

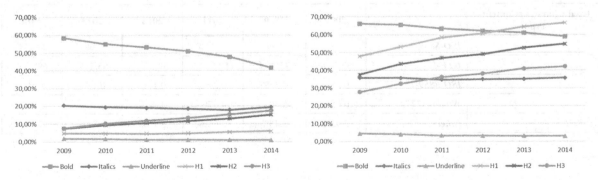

54.72% and 42.15% respectively. The increment in the use of title sections was previously observed when analysed the top web page HTML tags.

Meta Tags

An important part of the information on the web page content is included in the attributes of the HTML "meta" tags, which are placed at the beginning of the HTML code and provide information to the user, browser, crawlers and search engines. There are several attributes of the "meta" tag, however this study only considers the three most relevant: Keywords, Refresh and Content-type. Table 5 shows the results obtained.

- **Keywords:** The keywords attribute of the "meta" tag, includes words which describe the content of the page. This study analyses the average number of keywords on web documents. In 2009 the average was 9.60 keywords per web page, in 2011, 8.92 and in 2014 7.91. Over the 6 years the number of keywords has decremented in less than 2.

Attending to these results, search engines must pay special attention to the number of keywords, because as Prieto et al. (Prieto, Álvarez, & Cacheda, 2012) have demonstrated, a method to perform Web Spam includes many keywords and so improves the relevance of the web page. A logical number of words to define the topic of a web page is between 7 and 15. Search engines must use the average number of keywords and penalise those web pages that using a number of keywords bigger than this average, because it is likely that these web pages are trying to improve their ranking by illegal methods.

- **Refresh:** This attribute indicates the time when the content of the page should be updated. Table 5 shows the results obtained. Around 1% of the pages use the refresh attribute in the 6-years period analysed. Despite the increase in dynamic pages that require continuous updating of their

Table 5. Results of analysing the meta tags of web pages

Average Number of Words in the							
Keywords Meta-Tag		**2009**	**2010**	**2011**	**2012**	**2013**	**2014**
		9.60	9.21	8.92	8.35	8.27	7.91
Refresh Meta Tag		**2009**	**2010**	**2011**	**2012**	**2013**	**2014**
		1.04%	1.30%	1.63%	1.09%	0.99%	1.15%
Used Charsets (Content-Type)		**2009**	**2010**	**2011**	**2012**	**2013**	**2014**
	ISO-8859-1	55.76%	47.59%	38.61%	33.63%	28.66%	24.65%
	UTF-8	33.28%	43.26%	52.90%	59.20%	65.21%	69.44%
	ISO-8859-15	0.38%	0.36%	0.27%	0.18%	0.19%	0.21%
	Windows1252	6.65%	5.30%	4.57%	3.82%	3.12%	2.92%
	Others	3.93%	3.48%	3.66%	3.16%	2.82%	2.77%

contents, the usage of the attribute "refresh" has not grown. This may be because there are other methods of updating the page content, for the user in a transparent way, using JavaScript functions. Such methods are widely used on pages with AJAX technologies, which update their content without the user noticing.

- **Content-Type:** This attribute indicates the content type and character set used for encoding the web page. The obtained results are also shown in Table 5. We observe that in 2009 the most used charset was ISO-8859-1. In 2009, the use of ISO-8859-1 represented 55.76% of web pages. Nevertheless, in the following years its use fell until 24.65% in 2014. This decrease occurred by the increment of UTF-8, which in 2009, reached 33.28%, and it was increasing until reach a 69.44% of web documents in 2014. The increment in the use of UTF-8 and the decrement of ISO-8859-1, is due to the need for new types of encoding that allow multilingual support. The use of UTF-8 in web pages allows displaying correctly the web pages in the browsers regardless of the charset used in the computer.

Features at Web Page Level

This section focuses on analysing the characteristics of the Web at web page level. More precisely, it considers the length of the URL, the age of the pages, the compression of the content, the title length of the pages and their similarity, since these are very important characteristics from the point of view of crawlers and search engines.

URL Length

Knowing the length of the URLs is very important because it can improve the development of compression schemes for caching or indexing the Web. For that, this is an aspect very relevant for the crawlers and search engines.

Table 6 shows that the average length in bytes of the URLs on the Global Web has remained the same (between 37 and 39 bytes) during the 6-years period analysed. The most interesting change is that the percentage of URLs which length is greater than 25 bytes has incremented from a 67.83% in 2009 to reach a 76.78% in 2014, although it does not affect to the average length.

Table 6. Average length of the URLs on the Web

	2009	2010	2011	2012	2013	2014
Average length of URLs (discarding pages without URLs)	37.15	38.27	38.16	38.79	39.34	39.19
% of pages containing some URL with length > 10	98.50%	98.76%	98.81%	98.93%	99.08%	99.16%
% of pages containing some URL with length > 25	67.83%	71.79%	72.19%	74.12%	75.97%	76.78%
% of pages containing some URL with length > 50	16.50%	18.71%	18.39%	18.84%	19.50%	19.39%
% of pages containing some URL with length > 100	1.94%	2.19%	2.03%	2.07%	2.21%	2.09%
% of pages containing some URL with length > 150	0.79%	0.77%	0.79%	0.90%	0.75%	0.60%

Title Length of Web Pages

The title of a web page is one of the most important elements in a web page. The use of descriptive titles is important to the Web usability, since it allows to the web users to know the topic of the web page. To analyse web page titles, its average length was considered, to determine its real importance when describing the content of a web page.

Figure 8 shows that in 2009 the average title length was 6.61 words, in 2011 7.03 and 7.22 words in 2014. The value has remained relatively constant at about 7 words. The amount of words in the title has remained relatively constant over the years studied.

Age

It represents the time validity of a web page. To calculate this time the HTTP header "Last-Modified" was used. It can be used to know when a web page has been modified, so it determines when the content downloaded by a crawler is not valid and therefore, this web page must be gathered again.

Table 7 shows the obtained results. First, it is important to note that the number of web pages returning a "Last-Modified" header remains more or less the same in the 6 years, minimally growing from a

Figure 8. Average title length of web pages

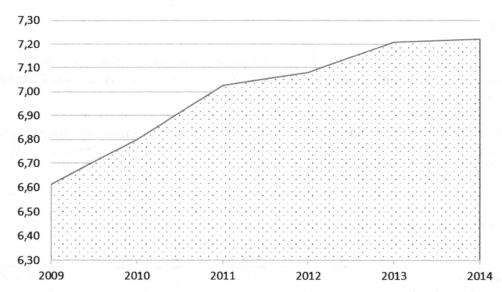

Table 7. Evolution of the Age of web pages

	2009	2010	2011	2012	2013	2014
% pages with LastModified header	33.30%	31.68%	33.37%	34.73%	36.27%	38.72%
% pages with LastModified header and age < 1 month	35.48%	42.09%	46.75%	53.35%	60.15%	66.42%
% pages with LastModified header and age < 3 months	43.83%	49.36%	53.97%	59.01%	66.18%	70.32%

33.30% of web pages in 2009 to 38.72% in 2014. So, the results obtained for the evolution of the age of web pages have only considered this percentage of web pages.

In 2009 approximately the 43% of the pages were less than 3 month old. In the next years the age of web pages increased until reach a 70% of web pages with age less than 3 month old in 2014. It is important to note that the increment was mainly for pages with less than 1 month old (35.48% in 2009 and 66.42% in 2014).

The trend of updating the contents faster means that policies of re-crawling and updating indexes have to change, as it is necessary to update contents and indexes so that the user can conduct searches on current contents. Therefore, it is necessary to create a system that allow crawlers to know in a reliable and exact way when a page has changed, improving search engine performance and user experience.

Compression of the Content

An important aspect for search engines is the compression of web pages. The compression ratio is a value that represents the relation between the size of the compressed content and the size of the content uncompressed. This information helps search engines to define appropriate storage policies, and indicates the level of similarity of the content within a web page, since repeated contents cause a higher level of compression. At a lower level of compression, the content will show more similarity and therefore will often be of lower quality.

During the 6-years period of the study, the compression ratio remained around 0.33, without changes. In summary, the results show that the compression level is quite high. This indicates that the contents of web pages on the Web are quite repetitive. Based on this fact, the search engines should take into account these results in the storage policies.

Similarity

Indicates the level of similarity, or difference, which have the content of two web pages. This study compares the useful content of each web page, using the same approach that the one described in the features at Web content level section. In order to compare the useful content of each web page, a tool implemented by Viliam Holub[3] is used. This tool divides each document in n tokens, each one of them with a weight. After this, it makes a hash of each of the tokens. Finally, with the weight and the hash of each token, the tool creates a hash for each document of each subset, which "summarizes" its contents.

In this study, a dataset per year was considered, which had 10 random subsets of 10,000 web pages. The hash of every page for each year was computed and then the Hamming distance among the document signatures. The end result, shown in Table 8, was obtained as the average of the results of each of the 10 subsets for each year.

Table 8 shows that in 2009, 30% of web pages had between 50% and 60% of similarity, 26% had between 60% and 70% and only 4.21% had a similarity between 80% and 90%. In following years, similarity for values between 40% and 70% decreased, but mainly in last two years, the similarity for values between 80% and 90% has increased from 4.21% in 2009 to 14,54% in 2014 (it reached 17.25% in 2013).

So, we can conclude that the level of similarity in the Web is growing, so search engines have to take this into account for detecting duplicate or similar content to avoid index the same content several times.

Table 8. Distribution of the similarity of the web pages

	2009	2010	2011	2012	2013	2014
0% - < 10%	0.00%	0.00%	0.00%	0.00%	0.00%	0.00%
10% - < 20%	0.00%	0.00%	0.00%	0.00%	0.00%	0.00%
20% - < 30%	0.00%	0.00%	0.00%	0.00%	0.00%	0.00%
30% - < 40%	0.23%	0.19%	0.38%	0.31%	0.13%	0.19%
40% - < 50%	13.80%	12.78%	19.84%	15.53%	13.65%	12.04%
50% - < 60%	30.12%	31.34%	32.33%	31.03%	24.49%	25.50%
60% - < 70%	26.00%	23.87%	20.41%	22.47%	21.30%	23.46%
70% - < 80%	21.05%	21.37%	17.28%	19.34%	17.66%	19.06%
80% - < 90%	4.21%	5.95%	4.79%	7.33%	17.25%	14.54%
90% - 100%	4.58%	4.49%	4.96%	3.97%	5.51%	5.20%

Features at Web Site Level

This level explains the main characteristics of a web site, such as number of links and their types (static, dynamic, inlink, outlink), and the technologies used in the client and server side. We place special emphasis on the technologies which are mainly used for the client and server side Hidden Web.

Links

Table 9 shows the results obtained for the links analysis. The number of pages having at least some anchor has remained around 87% during the 6-years period analysed. Nevertheless, the average number of links per pages has grown from 58.63 in 2009 until 107.26 links per page in 2014.

Table 9 also shows results regarding inlinks, outlinks, dynamic and static links, and the kind of path, absolute or relative.

The difference between inlinks and outlinks of a web page is that inlinks point to other pages in the same domain, and outlinks point to pages in other domains. The results obtained indicate that, in 2009, the inlinks represented 62.37% of the total number of links on the Web, and the outlinks 37.63%. The number of inlinks was growing until reach to 66.01% of the total number of links in 2014.

Analysing the type of link path, the relative links dominate the absolute address. In 2009, 61.89% of links were relative versus 38.11%, which were absolute. This result was similar in the next year, although increasing a bit the number of relative links to reach 65.55% in 2014. This result is consistent with the obtained for inlinks/outlinks. The majority of links are intra-domain.

Analysing the results for dynamic and static links, a domination of static links over dynamic links can be observed. In 2009, the static links were 76.34% as opposed to 23.66% for dynamic links, percentages which increased in 2014, reaching 84.50% for static links and 15.50% for dynamic links.

The static link against the dynamic goes slightly against the trend of use of technologies that enable dynamic access to data. This result may be due to the method of coding the URLs, which do not use ?,

Table 9. Distribution of different types of links on the Web

		2009	2010	2011	2012	2013	2014
% of Pages with Some Link		86.85%	87.94%	88.17%	88.17%	88.46%	88.17%
Average number of links per page		58.63	69.15	81.19	90.91	94.99	107.26
% of Usage of Each Type of Link		**2009**	**2010**	**2011**	**2012**	**2013**	**2014**
	Inlink	62.37%	60.39%	62.75%	62.20%	63.51%	66.01%
	Outlink	37.63%	39.61%	37.25%	37.80%	36.49%	33.99%
	Relative	61.89%	59.80%	62.10%	61.73%	63.01%	65.55%
	Absolute	38.11%	40.20%	37.90%	38.27%	36.99%	34.45%
	Static	76.34%	77.25%	79.41%	81.40%	83.12%	84.50%
	Dynamic	23.66%	22.75%	20.59%	18.60%	16.88%	15.50%
% of Pages using Each Type of Links		**2009**	**2010**	**2011**	**2012**	**2013**	**2014**
	Inlink	79.14%	80.63%	82.10%	82.43%	82.97%	82.83%
	Outlink	78.77%	80.47%	81.57%	82.21%	82.97%	83.10%
	Relative	77.86%	79.32%	80.83%	81.23%	81.72%	81.67%
	Absolute	80.19%	81.85%	82.76%	83.34%	84.09%	84.09%
	Static	83.73%	85.31%	85.91%	86.27%	86.65%	86.39%
	Dynamic	57.31%	60.77%	62.84%	63.86%	65.69%	65.94%

or that use unknown dynamic extensions. The web sites with a dynamic access to the data offer a better user experience than the static web sites, but with the disadvantage that these technologies makes the access to information by crawlers more complex.

Table 9 also shows the percentage of pages using at least one of the previously described link types. The number of pages referencing at least one link increased, for each type of link, but little. We highlight the growth experimented in the dynamic links. In 2009, the 57.31% of pages contained at least one dynamic link. In 2014, the 65.94% of web pages reference at least one dynamic link.

Server-Side Technologies

Another important information for a crawler is the technology used on the server-side. The results are shown in Table 10. In 2009, the dominant technology was PHP with 24.32% of web pages referencing at least one PHP page, followed by ASP with 22.86%. JSP/JHTML, CGI, SHTML and Perl were referenced in around a 7% of the pages. During the 6-years period analysed, the % of web pages referencing a PHP page grew until 30.94%. The use of ASP remained without changes, and JSP/JHTML, but the rest decreased its number of occurrences.

The usage of the different server-side technologies seems related to the distribution of operating systems, since ASP is a closed-source technology and only works in particular operating systems, and PHP has many open-source interpreters.

Table 10. Distribution of the server-side technologies on the Web

	2009	2010	2011	2012	2013	2014
PHP	24.32%	29.70%	31.91%	32.59%	31.73%	30.94%
ASP	22.86%	24.14%	24.30%	24.65%	24.75%	22.60%
JSP/JHTML	7.92%	8.31%	8.40%	8.57%	8.05%	7.56%
CGI	7.77%	7.57%	6.34%	5.72%	5.06%	4.63%
STHML	7.03%	8.39%	7.33%	7.12%	6.50%	5.50%
Perl	6.95%	6.49%	5.16%	5.03%	4.79%	4.28%
C#	6.83%	8.00%	6.98%	6.83%	6.27%	5.34%
Javaclass	0.03%	0.02%	0.01%	0.01%	0.01%	0.01%
C#	0.03%	0.04%	0.04%	0.04%	0.04%	0.04%
Js	0.01%	0.01%	0.01%	0.01%	0.03%	0.03%
Sh	0.01%	0.01%	0.00%	0.01%	0.01%	0.01%
C++	0.00%	0.00%	0.00%	0.00%	0.00%	0.00%

Client-Side Technologies

These are those technologies which allow the creation of dynamic web sites and improve the user experience. However, this makes the process of crawling more difficult, creating what is known as client-side Hidden Web.

Table 11 shows the obtained results. The most commonly used technologies are based on JavaScript. Its usage has increased since 2009 with a 60.97% to 75.97% rise in 2014. The second most commonly used technology is Flash, although its presence is much lower (it was present in around 2% of web pages during the period analysed).

It is also important to note that since 2009 some languages such as VBScript or Tcl have almost disappeared. These results are mainly due to the widespread use of technologies such as AJAX (Asynchronous JavaScript and XML), and the large number of problems of compatibility and security that Flash is currently experiencing. Based on these results, and on the processing cost of these technologies, a crawling system should work mainly on the processing of JavaScript, since it is the most widely used technology on the client-side for accessing data.

Table 11. Distribution of the client-side technologies on the Web

	2009	2010	2011	2012	2013	2014
JavaScript	60.97%	66.62%	69.99%	72.11%	74.43%	75.97%
Flash	2.52%	2.98%	2.90%	2.85%	2.34%	2.04%
VbScript	0.08%	0.07%	0.10%	0.08%	0.02%	0.01%
Applets	0.01%	0.01%	0.01%	0.01%	0.01%	0.01%
TclScript	0.00%	0.00%	0.00%	0.00%	0.00%	0.00%
PythonScripts	0.00%	0.00%	0.00%	0.00%	0.00%	0.00%

Table 12 shows other results related with client-side technologies that can difficult the task of a crawler:

- The number of meta-HTTP redirects has increased a bit between 2009 and 2011, but it recovered the 2009 value in 2014. Regarding the number of meta-tags used in web pages, its number has increased from 3.5 in average in 2009, to 6.5 in 2014.
- We highlight the growth in the usage of the HTML "link" element, which is used for referencing external resources, like CSS files. It was used in 69.48% of pages in 2009, and it reached 78.86% of pages in 2014.
- The usage of HTML object elements decreased, and the same occurred with framesets, but the number of iframes increased from 7.07% in 2009 to 13.46% in 2014.
- We have also analysed the usage of scripting technologies in different parts of a web page: in the body or in the header. Both in the body or in the header of web pages, the % of pages including scripts have increased: from 55.06% in 2009 to 69.40% in 2014 (in the body), and from 56.09% in 2009 to 68.64 in 2014 (out of the body).
- Inside the body, we also distinguished if the script was on a "onXX" attribute of an HTML tag, and if it was the case for "onClick", the event that is fired when a click is performed on an HTML page. The number of pages using scripts on a "onXX" attribute of a tag has decreased a bit, but the number of pages using scripts on "onClick" attributes has been increased from 30.67% in 2009 to 33,95% in 2014 (reaching peaks of 35% in 2012 and 2013).

All of this confirms that the technologies used in the construction of web sites use scripting languages for improving the accessibility/usability of the web pages.

Web Forms

As explained in the methodology section, the server-side Hidden Web is an important part of the Web. Many websites offer query forms to access the contents of an underlying database. Conventional crawlers cannot access these pages because they do not know how to execute queries on those forms.

In the analysis of the use of web forms, the Web has on average more than 1 web form per web site. This indicates that most web sites use forms to access to certain information, and have, in some cases, more than one. From 2009 to 2014, the number of web pages with more than a web form grew from 55.77% in 2009 to 67.76% in 2014.

We have also classified web forms in two types: authentication forms and data forms. The number of authentication forms grow only a bit (3.71% in 2009 to 4.72% in 2014). The number of pages with data forms, that is, forms that are not for authentication issues, but else are the entry-point to the server-side Hidden Web, have grown from 12.61% in 2009 to 16.72% in 2014.

With these data, crawlers must be prepared for accessing to this type of information, either by automatic query execution based on machine learning, or by establishing some agreement with the creators of information, which enables them to have easier access to data.

Features at Global Web Level

This section explains the software used by web servers on the Global Web.

Table 12. Client-side Hidden Web elements

	2009	2010	2011	2012	2013	2014
% Pages with Meta-Http Redirects	1.04%	1.28%	1.63%	1.09%	0.99%	1.05%
Average Number of Meta Tags used per Page	3.54	3.90	4.53	4.93	5.65	6.53
% Pages with Link Elements	69.48%	72.80%	75.18%	76.85%	78.60%	78.86%
Average Number of Link Elements per Page	2.42	3.11	3.77	4.22	4.85	5.40
% Pages with Object Elements	2.27%	2.52%	2.84%	2.51%	2.22%	1.89%
Average Number of Object Elements per Page	0.03	0.04	0.04	0.03	0.03	0.03
% Pages with Frameset Elements	0.44%	0.34%	0.23%	0.16%	0.13%	0.10%
% Pages with Iframe Elements	7.07%	7.62%	9.92%	11.20%	12.01%	13.46%
Average Number of Iframe Elements per Page	0.12	0.14	0.22	0.23	0.25	0.22
% Pages with Scripts in the Body	55.06%	60.50%	64.14%	65.64%	67.72%	69.40%
% Pages with Scripts out of the Body	56.09%	59.02%	61.92%	64.90%	67.36%	68.64%
Average Number of Scripts in the Body per Page	10.06	12.45	13.09	14.08	16.01	16.56
Average Number of Scripts out of the Body per Page	3.19	4.10	5.13	6.03	7.04	7.74
% Pages with "onXX" Elements	50.05%	52.15%	51.57%	50.10%	50.10%	47.86%
% Pages with "onXX" Elements on Anchors	32.89%	34.55%	33.09%	33.36%	32.96%	31.21%
Average Number of "onXX" Elements per Page	9.61	10.31	9.36	8.85	8.86	9.36
Average Number of "onXX" Elements on Anchors per Page	6.00	6.36	6.28	5.88	6.03	6.71
% Pages with "onClick" Element	30.67%	34.54%	34.56%	35.14%	35.83%	33.95%
% Pages with More than 1 "onClick" Element	21.11%	24.13%	24.38%	24.72%	24.79%	23.47%
Average Number of "onClick" Elements per Page	3.19	4.33	4.61	4.43	4.31	5.13

Web Server

On the Global Web the most commonly used web server in 2009 is Apache with 62.52%. The next most widely used web server is Microsoft IIS with 19.87%. Along the 6 years analysed, the Apache web server maintain its level of occurrences, but Microsoft IIS decreases until 14.36% in 2014. During these 6 years, Nginx server increased its presence in a significant way, from a 0.21% in 2009 to 7.32% in 2014. Nginx is a relatively new free, open-source web server (first version was released on 2004), and it is being more used due to its high performance, simple configuration and low resource consumption.

Figure 9 shows the obtained results.

In addition, many of the versions used were not recent. Usually, the system administrators tend to be conservative, so it is likely that they do not want update the web server version quickly, and prefer using older but more stable versions, although the probabilities of security issues is higher.

Exclusion Robots Protocol

The exclusion robots protocol is a mechanism that allows to a web page developer to specify if a web page must be indexed. A web site can define a robots.txt file for specifying a general politic for crawlers,

Table 13. Server-side Hidden Web elements

	2009	2010	2011	2012	2013	2014
% Pages with Forms	55.77%	59.95%	62.46%	64.60%	66.48%	67.76%
% Pages with More than 1 Form	24.56%	27.50%	28.04%	29.77%	31.10%	31.07%
% Pages with More than 2 Forms	10.76%	12.54%	12.25%	13.22%	13.70%	13.49%
% Pages with More than 3 Forms	5.71%	6.47%	6.02%	6.06%	6.09%	6.01%
% Pages with More than 5 Forms	1.80%	2.06%	1.96%	1.85%	1.50%	1.47%
% Pages with Get-Method Forms	33.46%	36.17%	36.71%	37.43%	38.08%	38.07%
% Pages with Post-Method Forms	24.52%	25.99%	25.96%	28.31%	30.06%	31.54%
% Pages with Password Forms	3.71%	4.21%	4.09%	4.24%	4.33%	4.72%
% Pages with More than 1 Password Forms	0.51%	0.76%	0.91%	0.84%	0.67%	0.64%
% Pages with More than 2 Password Forms	0.18%	0.16%	0.16%	0.12%	0.05%	0.02%
% Pages with Data Forms	12.61%	13.85%	14.69%	17.08%	16.99%	16.72%
% Pages with More than 1 Data Form	2.92%	3.28%	2.99%	3.13%	3.29%	3.09%
% Pages with More than 2 Data Forms	0.94%	0.86%	0.89%	0.89%	0.89%	0.78%
% Pages with More than 3 Data Forms	0.38%	0.50%	0.34%	0.26%	0.26%	0.18%
% Pages with More than 5 Data Forms	0.10%	0.18%	0.11%	0.08%	0.13%	0.10%
Average Number of Forms per Page	1.07	1.21	1.21	1.25	1.26	1.27
Average Number of GET Method Forms	0.43	0.49	0.52	0.52	0.52	0.52
Average Number of POST Method Forms	0.43	0.48	0.44	0.47	0.49	0.49
Average Number of Password Forms per Page	0.05	0.05	0.05	0.05	0.05	0.05
Average Number of Data Forms per Page	0.17	0.20	0.20	0.22	0.22	0.22

Figure 9. Web servers used on the Web

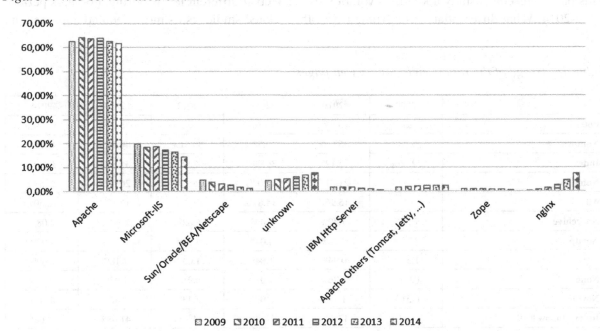

but each page can specify its own preferences by using the robots meta tag. The obtained results for the robots meta tag are shown in table 14.

The number of pages that specify to crawlers that their content must not be indexed has grown from 35% in 2009 to 40% in 2014. This result is also corroborated by the number of pages which indicate in the robots meta tag 'index+follow' or 'all'. This percentage has been reduced from 48.54% in 2009 to 40.62% in 2014. It seems that web page managers are paying more attention to the crawler's policies.

Other interesting result is that values 'noodp' and 'noydir' have grown from 2.75% and 0.51% in 2009, to 7.97% and 4.56%, respectively. 'noodp' is for not allowing to the search engines to use the oficial description of the web page in DMOZ. 'noydir' is equivalent, but only for Yahoo! (i.e., not allowing to Yahoo! to use the description of the web page in the Yahoo! Directory).

These results confirm that the robots meta tag is being more actively used for specifying to search engines how to process web pages.

FUTURE RESEARCH DIRECTIONS

Future work will focus on processing the Web and creating new datasets, allowing analysis to continue in the forthcoming years. These subsequent studies will allow to increase the knowledge on how the Web evolves, and also its users and web site creators.

In addition, other studies could allow to determine the quality of the Web, to check whether it is in decline (bad quality of contents, broken links, repeated or similar contents, etc.), or if it is improving.

CONCLUSION

This paper presents a study about the evolution of the Web at different levels during a 6-years period: 2009-2014. What differentiates this article from other related studies is its more detailed approach, its

Table 14. Usage of the robots meta tag on web pages

	2009	2010	2011	2012	2013	2014
Follow	37.31%	40.85%	41.88%	38.92%	38.25%	38.49%
Noindex	35.64%	35.60%	36.58%	39.51%	40.38%	40.76%
Index	32.66%	35.12%	36.06%	32.96%	31.89%	30.79%
Nofollow	22.23%	21.81%	22.07%	25.17%	26.00%	25.59%
All	19.32%	15.96%	14.81%	14.47%	12.80%	12.50%
Noarchive	7.52%	7.49%	7.09%	6.32%	6.62%	7.08%
Noodp	2.75%	3.56%	4.04%	5.13%	6.84%	7.97%
	1.32%	0.94%	1.04%	1.03%	1.16%	0.89%
None	0.96%	1.26%	1.07%	0.91%	1.08%	0.85%
Noydir	0.51%	1.29%	2.07%	2.43%	3.42%	4.56%
Index+follow ‖ all	48.54%	47.22%	47.69%	44.70%	41.68%	40.62%

analysis of the evolution regarding time and observations made from the point of view of search engines and crawling systems.

This study complements the results obtained for years 2009-2011 in a previously published paper (Prieto, Álvarez, & Cacheda, 2013), by considering in more detail the Hidden Web features and expanding it until year 2014.There are some minor differences in some results, mainly due to the way the datasets were built. Although in both cases "The Stanford Web Project" was used, in (Prieto, Álvarez, & Cacheda, 2013) web pages were selected randomly, but in this article we selected the first 10 million pages collected by the WebVac crawler for an specific month/year.

After analysing the features of the Web at different levels, and during several years, we can summarise the following conclusions:

- Web page sizes are growing, but not in useful content. The number of common words in web pages have increased.
- The level of similarity of the Web is growing, so search engines have to take this into account for detecting duplicate or similar content to avoid index the same content several times.
- A change in the design of web documents is observed: from a tabular representation to create the layout of pages by using stylesheets.
- Web pages are evolving towards documents with more quality images and less size, raising the usage of PNG format.
- The increment in the use of UTF-8 and the decrement of ISO-8859-1, is due to the need for new types of encoding that allow multilingual support. The use of UTF-8 in web pages allows displaying correctly the web pages in the browsers regardless of the charset used in the computer.
- Regarding the Hidden Web, the usage of scripting technologies is increasing, and the number of web forms too, although not a lot.
- Contents are updated faster. Policies of re-crawling and updating indexes have to change, as it is necessary to update contents and indexes so that the user can conduct searches on current contents.

REFERENCES

Adar, E., Teevan, J., Dumais, S. T., & Elsas, J. L. (2009). The Web Changes Everything: Understanding the Dynamics of Web Content. In *Proceedings of the 2nd ACM International Conference on Web Search and Data Mining, WSDM '09*, Barcelona, Spain. (pp. 282-291). doi:10.1145/1498759.1498837

Baeza-Yates, R., & Castillo, C. (2000). Caracterizando la Web Chilena. In Encuentro Chileno de Ciencias de la Computación. Sociedad Chilena de Ciencias de la Computación.

Baeza-Yates, R., Castillo, C., & Efthimiadis, E. N. (2007). Characterization of National Web Domains. *Journal ACM Transactions on Internet Technology*. 7(2).

Baeza-Yates, R., Castillo, C. & Lopez, V. (2005). Characteristics of the Web of Spain. *Cybermetrics*. 9(1).

Baeza-Yates, R., & Poblete, B. (2006). Dynamics of the Chilean Web Structure. *The International Journal of Computer and Telecommunications Networking*. 50(10), 1464-1473.

Baeza-Yates, R., Saint-Jean, F.,, & Castillo, C. (2002). Web Structure, Dynamics and Page Quality. *String Processing and Information Retrieval: Lecture Notes in Computer Science Series, 2476*, 453–461.

Bergman, M. K. (2001). The Deep Web: Surfacing Hidden Value. *Journal of Electronic Publishing.* 7.

Bharat, K., Chang, B., Henzinger, M. R.,, & Ruhl, M. (2001). Who Links to Whom: Mining Linkage Between Web Sites. *Proceedings of the 2001 IEEE International Conference on Data Mining, ICDM '01,* IEEE Computer Society, San José, California, USA (pp. 51-58). doi:10.1109/ICDM.2001.989500

Björneborn, L., & Ingwersen, P. (2004). Toward a Basic Framework for Webometrics. *Journal of the American Society for Information Science and Technology, 55*(14), 1216–1227. doi:10.1002/asi.20077

Boldi, P., Codenotti, B., Santini, M.,, & Vigna, S. (2002). Structural Properties of the African Web. *Proceedings of the 11st International Conference on World Wide Web, WWW'02,* Honolulu, Hawaii, USA.

Brewington, B.,, & Cybenko, G. (2000). How Dynamic is the Web? *Proceedings of the 9th Conference on the World Wide Web.* (pp. 257-276).

Broder, A., Kumar, R., Maghoul, F., Raghavan, P., Rajagopalan, S., & Stata, R. et al. (2000). Graph Structure in the Web. Computer Networks. *The International Journal of Computer and Telecommunications Networking, 33*(1-6), 309–320.

Cho, J., & Garcia-Molina, H. (2003a). Estimating Frequency of Change. *Journal ACM Transactions on Internet Technology, 3*(3), 256–290. doi:10.1145/857166.857170

Cho, J., & Garcia-Molina, H. (2003b). Effective Page Refresh Policies for Web Crawlers. *Journal ACM Transactions on Database Systems, 28*(4), 390–426. doi:10.1145/958942.958945

Cho, J., Shivakumar, N., & Garcia-Molina, H. (2000). Finding Replicated Web Collections. In *Proceedings of the ACM SIGMOD International Conference on Management of Data,* Dallas, Texas. (pp. 355-366).

Downey, A. B. (2001). The Structural Cause of File size Distributions. *Proceedings 9th International Symposium on Modeling, Analysis and Simulation of Computer and Telecommunication Systems,* Cincinnati, Ohio. (pp. 361-370).

Efthimiadis, E.,, & Castillo, C. (2004). Charting the Greek Web. *Proceedings of the Conference of the American Society for Information Science and Technology (ASIST),* Rhode Island, USA.

Fetterly, D., Manasse, M., & Najork, M. (2004). Spam, Damn Spam, and Statistics: Using Statistical Analysis to Locate Spam Web Pages. *Proceedings of the 7th International Workshop on the Web and Databases* WebDB '04, Paris, France. (pp. 1-6).

Fetterly, D., Manasse, M., Najork, M., & Wiener, J. (2003). A Large-Scale Study of the Evolution of Web Pages. *Proceedings of the 12th International Conference on World Wide Web, WWW '03,* Budapest, Hungary. (pp. 669-678). doi:10.1145/775152.775246

Gomes, D., & Silva, M. J. (2005). Characterizing a National Community Web. *Journal ACM Transactions on Internet Technology, 5*(3), 508–531. doi:10.1145/1084772.1084775

Grefenstette, G., & Nioche, J. (2000). Estimation of English and Non-English Language use on the WWW. *Proceedings of Content-Based Multimedia Information Access,* Paris, France. (pp. 237–246).

Gulli, A., & Signorini, A. (2005). The Indexable Web is more than 11.5 Billion Pages. *14th International Conference on World Wide Web, WWW '05* Chiba, Japan. (pp. 902-903).

Gyongyi, Z., & Garcia-Molina, H. (2005). Web Spam Taxonomy. *Proceedings of the First International Workshop on Adversarial Information Retrieval on the Web, AIRWeb 2005*. (pp. 39-47).

Huberman, B. A., & Adamic, L. A. (1999). Internet: Growth Dynamics of the World-Wide Web. *Nature, 401*(6749), 131–131. PMID:10490019

Kumar, J. P., & Govindarajulu, P. (2009). Duplicate and Near Duplicate Documents Detection: A Review. *European Journal of Scientific Research, 32*, 514–527.

Lewandowski, D. (2008). A Three-year Study on the Freshness of Web Search Engine Databases. *Journal of Information Science, 34*(6), 817–831. doi:10.1177/0165551508089396

Miranda, J., & Gomes, D. (2009). How Are Web Characteristics Evolving? *Proceedings of the 20th ACM Conference on Hypertext and Hypermedia, HT '09,* Torino, Italy. (pp. 369-370). doi:10.1145/1557914.1557993

Modesto, M., Pereira, A., Ziviani, N., Castillo, C., & Baeza-Yates, R. (2005). Um Novo Retrato da Web Brasileira. *Proceedings of XXXII SEMISH,* São Leopoldo, Brazil. (pp. 2005-2017).

Ntoulas, A., Cho, J., & Olston, C. (2004). What's New on the Web?: The Evolution of the Web from a Search Engine Perspective. *Proceedings of the 13th International Conference on World Wide Web, WWW '04,* New York, NY. (pp. 1-12). doi:10.1145/988672.988674

Ntoulas, A., & Manasse, M. (2006). Detecting Spam Web Pages Through Content Analysis. In *Proceedings of the World Wide Web conference, WWW'06,* Edinburgh, UK. (pp. 83-92). doi:10.1145/1135777.1135794

Olston, C., & Pandey, S. (2008). Recrawl Scheduling Based on Information Longevity. *Proceedings of the 17th International Conference on World Wide Web, WWW '08,* Beijing, China. (pp. 437-446). doi:10.1145/1367497.1367557

Page, L., Brin, S., Motwani, R., & Winograd, T. (1998). *The Pagerank Citation Ranking: Bringing Order to the Web*. Stanford Digital Library.

Pan, D., Qiu, S., & Yin, D. (2008). Web Page Content Extraction Method Based on Link Density and Statistic. *Proceedings of the 4th International Conference on Wireless Communications, Networking and Mobile Computing, WiCOM '08,* Dalian, China. (pp. 1-4). doi:10.1109/WiCom.2008.2664

Prieto, V., Álvarez, M., & Cacheda, F. (2012). Analysis and Detection of Web Spam by Means of Web Content. *Proceedings of the 5th Information Retrieval Facility Conference, IRFC '12*, Vienna, Austria. doi:10.1007/978-3-642-31274-8_4

Prieto, V., Álvarez, M., & Cacheda, F. (2013). The Evolution of the Web. *Proceedings of the 2013 International Conference on Systems, Control and Informatics, SCI 2013* Venice, Italy. (pp. 95-104).

Raghavan, S., & Garcia-Molina, H. (2001). Crawling the Hidden Web. *Proceedings of the 27th International Conference on Very Large Data Bases, VLDB '01* San Francisco, CA. (pp. 129-138).

Rubin, A. D., & Geer, D. E. Jr. (1998). A Survey of Web Security. *The Computer Journal, 31*(9), 34–41. doi:10.1109/2.708448

Sanguanpong, S., Piamsa-nga, P., Keretho, S., Poovarawan, Y., & Warangrit, S. (2000). Measuring and Analysis of the Thai World Wide Web. *Proceeding of the Asia Pacific Advance Network*. (pp. 225-230).

Serrano, M. A., Maguitman, A., Boguñá, M., Fortunato, S. & Vespignani, A. (2007). Decoding the Structure of the WWW: A Comparative Analysis of Web Crawls. *Journal ACM Transactions on the Web*, 1(2).

Shestakov, D. (2011b). Databases on the Web: National Web Domain Survey. *Proceedings of the 15th Symposium on International Database Engineering & Applications, IDEAS '11*, Lisbon, Portugal. (pp. 179-184). doi:10.1145/2076623.2076646

Shestakov, D. (2011a). Sampling the National Deep Web. *Proceedings of the 22nd International Conference on Database and Expert Systems Applications, DEXA'11*. (pp. 331-340). Toulouse, France. doi:10.1007/978-3-642-23088-2_24

Shuyo, N. (2010). Language Detection Library for Java. Retrieved from http://code.google.com/p/language-detection/

Suel, T., & Yuan, J. (2001). Compressing the Graph Structure of the Web. *Proceedings of the Data Compression Conference, DCC '01*, Snowbird, Utah. (pp. 213-213). doi:10.1109/DCC.2001.917152

Thelwall, M., & Wilkinson, D. (2003). Graph Structure in Three National Academic Webs: Power Laws with Anomalies. *Journal of the American Society for Information Science and Technology*, 54(8), 706–712. doi:10.1002/asi.10267

W3C DOM IG. (2005). The Document Object Model. Retrieved from http://www.w3.org/DOM

Wu, B., & Davison, B. D. (2005). Identifying Link Farm Spam Pages. *In 14th International Conference on World Wide Web, WWW '05*, Chiba, Japan. (pp. 820-829). doi:10.1145/1062745.1062762

KEY TERMS AND DEFINITIONS

Client Side Hidden Web: Subset of the Hidden Web that is accessible through client-side scripting languages and session maintenance mechanisms.

Crawling Systems: Programs that are capable of traversing and analyzing the Web in a certain order, by following the links between different pages.

Global Web: There only exists one Web, the so-called Global Web, formed by all web documents can be accessed through the HTTP protocol (the entire Web).

Hidden Data: Web documents contained in the Hidden Web.

Hidden Web: Subset of the Global Web that is not directly connected to the rest through conventional links. Therefore, content of this subset of the Web is out of the reach of conventional crawling systems.

Search Engines: Complex systems that allow, among other things: gathering, storing, managing and granting access to Web information.

Server Side Hidden Web: Subset of the Hidden Web that is mainly accessible through ds.

Spanish Web: Subset of the Global Web including only documents from the.es domain.

ENDNOTES

[1] http://dbpubs.stanford.edu:8091/~testbed/doc2/WebBase
[2] http://diglib.stanford.edu:8091/
[3] http://d3s.mff.cuni.cz/~holub/sw/shash/

This research was previously published in Design Strategies and Innovations in Multimedia Presentations edited by Shalin Hai-Jew, pages 1-30, copyright year 2015 by Information Science Reference (an imprint of IGI Global).

Chapter 7
Deep Web Information Retrieval Process:
A Technical Survey

Dilip Kumar Sharma
G.L.A. Institute of Technology and Management, Mathura, India

A. K. Sharma
YMCA University of Science and Technology, Faridabad, India

ABSTRACT

Web crawlers specialize in downloading web content and analyzing and indexing from surface web, consisting of interlinked HTML pages. Web crawlers have limitations if the data is behind the query interface. Response depends on the querying party's context in order to engage in dialogue and negotiate for the information. In this paper, the authors discuss deep web searching techniques. A survey of technical literature on deep web searching contributes to the development of a general framework. Existing frameworks and mechanisms of present web crawlers are taxonomically classified into four steps and analyzed to find limitations in searching the deep web.

INTRODUCTION

The versatile use of the internet has proved a remarkable revolution in the history of technological advancement. Accessibility of web pages starting from zero in 1990 has reached more than 1.6 billion during 2009. It is like a perineal stream of knowledge. The more we dig the more thirst can be quenched. Surface data is easily available on the web. Surface web pages can be easily indexed through conventional search engine. But the hidden, invisible and non-indexable contents which cannot be retrieved through conventional methods used for surface web and whose size is estimated to be thousands of times larger than the surface web is called deep web. The deep web consist of a large database of useful information such as audio, video, images, documents, presentations and various other types of media. Today people really heavily depend on internet for numerous applications such as flight and train reservations, to know

DOI: 10.4018/978-1-5225-3163-0.ch007

about new product or to find any new locations and job etc. They can evaluate the search result and decide which of the bits or scraps reached by the search engine is most promising (Galler, Chun, & An, 2008).

Unlike the surface web, the deep web information is stored in searchable databases. These databases produce results dynamically after processing the user request (BrightPlanet.com LLC, 2000). Deep web information extraction first uses the two regularities of the domain knowledge and interface similarity to assign the tasks that are proposed from users and chooses the most effective set of sites to visit by ontology inspection. The conventional search engine has limitations in indexing the deep web pages so there is a requirement of an efficient algorithm to search and index the deep web pages (Akilandeswari & Gopalan, 2008). Figure 1 shows the barrier in information extraction in the form of search form or login form.

Contributions: This paper attempts to find the limitations of the current web crawlers in searching the deep web contents. For this purpose a general framework for searching the deep web contents is developed as per existing web crawling techniques. In particular, it concentrates on survey of techniques extracting contents from the portion of the web that is hidden behind search interface in large searchable databases with the following points.

- After profound analysis of entire working of deep web crawling process, we extracted qualified steps and developed a framework of deep web searching.
- Taxonomic classification of different mechanisms of the deep web extraction as per synchronism with developed framework.
- Comparison of different algorithms web searching with their advantages and limitations.
- Discuss the limitations of existing web searching mechanisms in large scale crawling of deep web.

Figure 1. Query or credentials required for contents extraction

CURRENT DEEP WEB INFORMATION RETRIEVAL FRAMEWORK

After exhaustive analysis of existing deep web information retrieval processes, a deep web information retrieval framework is developed, in which different tasks in deep web crawling are identified, arranged and aggregated in sequential manner. This framework is useful for understanding entire working of deep web crawling mechanisms as well as it enables the researcher to find out the limitations of present web crawling mechanisms in searching the deep web. The taxonomical steps of developed framework can be classified into following four major parts.

- **Query Interface Analysis:** First of a crawler will request for any web server to fetch a page. After fetching process, it parses and process the form to build an internal representation of web page based on the model developed.
- **Values Allotment:** It provides appropriate value to each and every input element by using different combinations of keywords, which will be allocated by using some string matching algorithms by analyzing the form labels using knowledge base.
- **Response Analysis and Navigation:** Crawler analyzes the response web pages to check if the submission yielded valid search results. Crawler uses this feedback to tune the values assigned and crawl the hypertext links iteratively, received by response web page to some pre-specified depth.
- **Relevance Ranking:** Relevance ranking means the order in which search engine should return the URLs, produced in response to a user's query, to show more relevant pages on priority basis. During this step, the deep web is a completely different from traditional web. In deep web there is none of those <A href> links to content and no association of links to be followed. So in deep web retrieval process, quality of a page cannot be predicted with its reference. This need is definitely highly demanded in the future framework to be developed to increase the quality of deep web contents.

These above steps are represented in following Figure 2 which demonstrates the flow of control over the deep web contents extraction mechanism.

Exhaustive literature analysis of the above taxonomically classified steps are given below.

QUERY INTERFACE ANALYSIS

Query interface analysis can be taxonomically partitioned into the following steps.

Detection of Hidden Web Search Interfaces

Pages for search interfaces are commonly HTML forms which is filled and submitted by users and server respond appropriately according to filled forms. But every form is not search interfaces. The problem is to identify a form which is a search interface. Search interface identification can be taxonomically categorized in the following three ways:

Figure 2. Contemporary deep Web content extraction and indexing framework

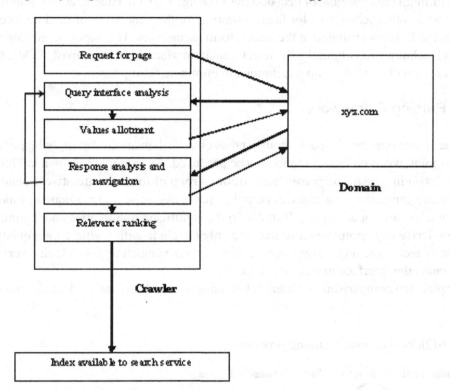

Based on Heuristic Rules

One of the simplest methods of search interface identification is done by using heuristic rules. "Heuristic" here refers to a general problem-solving rule or set of rules that do not guarantee the best solution or even any solution, but serves as a useful guide for interface matching. Automatic search interface detection was first defined by (Raghavan & Garcia-Molina, 2001), whose crawling system use heuristic rules to detect the hidden databases. The paper (Lage et al., 2004) use two heuristic rules and utilizes a pre existing data repository to identify the contents of deep web. This paper exploits the advantage of some patterns that is available in websites to find out the navigation path to be followed.

Decision Trees Classification

One of the approaches for search interface identification is based on decision trees classification models to detect search interface. One of such example is random forest algorithm. A random forest model contains a group of decision tress defined by bootstrapping the training data. An improved version of random forest algorithm (RFA) known as improved random forest algorithm (IRFA) is proposed by Deng et al. In IRFA the original RFA is extended with a weighted feature selection method to select more representative subset of features for building each decision trees. These can be vulnerable to changes in the training dataset. IRFA eliminates the problem of classification of high dimensional and sparse search interface data through the ensemble of decision trees (Deng, Ye, Li & Huang, 2008). Future work in this regard is to identify other techniques for feature waiting for the generation of random forest. Currently this paper uses the features available in the search form themselves. The paper (Jared Cope et al., 2003) defined a novel technique to automatically detect search interface from a group of HTML forms. Future work in this regard will be to develop a technique to eliminate false positives.

Best-Effort Parsing Framework

It identifies the search interface by continuously producing fresh instances by applying productions until attaining a fix-point, when no fresh instance can be produced. An example is shown in Figure 3 (Zhang, He & Chang, 2004) in which, the parser starts from a group of tokens to iteratively generate fresh instances and finally generates parse trees. A complete parse tree related to a unique instance of the start symbol QI that take cares of all tokens. But, due to the significant ambiguities and incompleteness, the parser may not derive any complete parse tree and only conclude with multiple incomplete parse trees. Best effort parser technique minimizes wrong interpretation as much as possible in a very fast manner. It also understands the interface to a large extent.

Table 1 depicts the comparison of different hidden web search interfaces detection mechanism.

Figure 3. Best-Effort (Fix point) parsing process

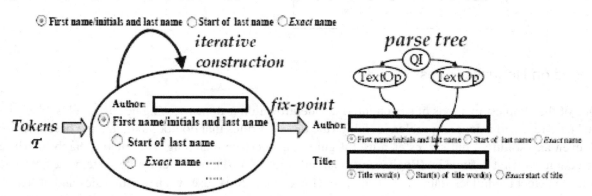

Table 1. Comparison of different hidden web search interfaces detection techniques

Search Techniques	Authors Name	Advantages	Limitations
Based on Heuristic Rules	S. Raghavan et al.	Effective label extraction technique with high submission efficiency.	No auto-leaning capability, unstable, un-scalable to diverse hidden web databases.
Decision Tree Classification Algorithm	Jared Cope et al.	Performed well when rule are generated on the same domain.	Long rules, large size of feature space in training samples, Over fitting, Classification precision is not very satisfying.
Best-Effort Parsing Framework	Zhen Zhang et al.	Very simple and consistent, No priority among preferences, Handling missing elements in form.	Critical to establish single global grammar that can be interacted to the machine globally.

Search Form Schema Mapping

After detection of hidden web search interface, the next task is to identify accurate matching for finding semantic correspondences between elements of two schemas. Schema extraction of query interface is one of the very prime research challenges for comparing and analysis of an integrated query interface for the deep web. Many algorithms are suggested in last few years which can be classified in two groups.

Heuristic

Heuristic techniques for Search form Schema Mapping are based on guessing relations which may consider similar labels or graph structures and can be further taxonomically classified in two groups.

- **Element-Level Explicit Techniques:** Explicit techniques use the semantics of labels such as used in precompiled dictionary (Cupid, COMA), Lexicons (S-Match, CTXmatch) e.g. sedan: Car is a hypernym for Four Wheeler, therefore, Car $\subseteq$ Four Wheeler.
- **Structure-Level Explicit Techniques:** These are based on taxonomic structure format (Anchor-Prompt, NOM) e.g. DEPTT and Department can be found as an appropriate match.

Formal

Formal techniques are based on model-theoretic semantics which is used to justify their results.

- **Element-Level Explicit Techniques:** It uses the OWL properties (NOM) e.g. same Class as constructor explicitly states that one class is equivalent to the other such as hybrid car = Car or CNG based car.
- **Structure-Level Explicit Techniques:** The approach is based on to translate the matching problem, namely the two graphs (trees) and mapping queries into propositional formula and then to check it for its validity.
- **Modal SAT (S-Match):** The idea is based on to enhance propositional logics with modal logic operators. Therefore, the matching problem is translated into a modal logic formula which is further checked for its validity using sound and complete search procedures.

Many automatic or semi-automatic search form schema mapping systems meticulous in a simple 1:1 matching are proposed such as Cupid method (Madhavan, Bernstein & Rahm, 2001). This method proposed a new technique by including subtential linguistic matching step and by biasing matches by leaves of a schema. Future work in this regard include intergating cupid transparently with an off-the-shelf thesaurus using schema notations for the linguistic matching and automatic tuning of control parameter.

Do and Rahm (2002), develops the COMA schema matching system to combine multiple matchers. It uses COMA as a framework to evaluate the effectiveness of different matcher and their combination for real world schemas. Future work in this regard is to add other match and combination algorithm in order to improve match quality. LSD method (Doan, Domingos & Levy, 2000), proposes a initial idea for automatic learning mappings between source schemas and mediated schemas. (Doan, Domingos & Halevy, 2001) describe LSD a system that employs and extends current machine learning techniques to semi-automatically find semantic mappings between the source schema and mediated schema.

The paper (Melnik, Garcia-Molina & Rahm, 2002) present a matching algorithm based on a fixed point computation. It uses two graphs such as schemas catalogs as input and produces as output a mapping between corresponding nodes of the graph. The paper (Kaljuvee, Buyukkokten, Molina & Paepcke, 2001) proposed a technique for automatically and dynamically summarize and organize web pages for displaying on a small devices such as PDA. This paper proposed eight algorithms for performing label-widget matches in which some algorithms based on n-gram comparisons and others based on common form layout specifications. Results can be improved by using syntactic and structural feature analysis.

For schema extraction, (He, Meng, Yu & Wu, 2005) consider the non-hierarchical structure of query interface assuming that a query interface has a flat set of attributes and the mapping of fields over the interfaces is 1:1, which neglects the grouping and hierarchical relationships of attributes. So the semantics of a query interface cannot be captured correctly.

Literature (Wu, Yu, Doan & Meng, 2004) proposed a hierarchical model and schema extraction approach which can group the attributes and improve the performance of schema extraction of query interface, but they show the poor clustering capability of pre-clustering algorithm due to the simple grouping patterns and schema extraction algorithm and possibly outputs the subsets inconsistent with those grouped by pre-clustering algorithm. Semantic matching is based on two ideas: (i) To discover an alignment by computing semantic relations (e.g., equivalence, more general); (ii) To determine semantic relations by analyzing the meaning (concepts, not labels). Although this paper provides a good accuracy but it can be improved by investigating the interaction to help break ties when the ordering based strategy does not work. Another improvement can be done by investigating the use of automatic interface model procedure into the proposed approach.

Most of the proposed search form schema mapping techniques require human involvement and not suitable for dynamic large scale data sets. Other approaches such as DCM framework (He & Chang, 2006) and MGS framework (He et al., 2003) pursues a correlation mining approach by exploiting the co-occurrence patterns of attributes and proposes a new correlation measures while other (Zhong, Fu, Liu, Lin & Cui, 2007) hypothesizes that every application field has a hidden generative model and can be viewed as instances generated from models with possible behaviors. There are certain issues in this algorithm that can be improved such as how to select the appropriate measure to filter out false matching and how to design a dynamic threshold to apply it to all domains. Table 2 depicts the comparison of different schema mapping techniques.

New schema extraction algorithm Extr (Qiang, Xi, Qiang &, Zhang, 2008), which is based on three metrics (LCA) precision, (LCA) recall, and (LCA) F1 are employed to evaluate the performance of schema extraction algorithm by pre-clustering of attributes P by using MPreCluster than all the subsets in P are clustered once again according to spatial distance. Finally all singleton clusters are merged according to n-way constrained merging operation as algorithm Ncluster. So the result is a hierarchical clustering H over the attributes of query interface on the deep web. The experimental results indicate that proposed algorithm can obviously improve the performance of schema extraction of query interfaces on the deep web and avoid resulting inconsistencies between the subsets by pre-clustering algorithm and those by schema extraction algorithm.

The last but not least correlated-clustering framework works in four phases. In first phase, it finds frequent attributes in the input attribute groups. In second phase, it discovers group where positively correlated attributes to form potential attribute groups, according to positive correlation measure and defined threshold. In third phase, it partitions the attributes into concepts, and cluster the concepts by

Table 2. Comparison of different schema mapping techniques

Name	Techniques	Advantages	Limitations
Artemis	Affinity-based analysis and hierarchical clustering	Effective label extraction technique, with high submission efficiency.	Falls into the alignments as likeness clues category.
Cupid	Structural schema matching techniques	Emphasize the name and data type similarities present at the finest level of granularity (leaf level).	Lack of integrating cupid transparently with an off-the-shelf thesaurus using schema notations for the linguistic matching and automatic tuning of control parameter.
DCM	Hybrid n:m	Identifies and clusters synonym elements by analyzing the co-occurrence of elements. DCM framework can find complex matching in many domains.	Ineffective against 'noisy' schema. DCM cannot differentiate frequent attributes from rare attributes. DCM tries to first identify all possible groups and then discover the matching between them.
GLUE	Composite n:m	It uses a composite approach, as in LSD, but does not utilize global schema.	Accuracy of the element similarity depends on training.
LSD	Corpus-based Matching	It provides a new set of machine-learning based matchers for specific types of complex mappings expressions. It provides prediction criterion for a match or mismatch.	Performance depends upon training data.

calculating the similarity of each two concepts. At last, it ranks to discover matching and then use a greedy matching selection algorithm to select the final matching results.

Komal Kumar Bhatia et al. (Bhatia & Sharma, 2008) presented in his research literature where mapping is done by using domain specific interface mapper in which search interface repository will work for matching purpose. It includes extensible domain specific matcher library. The multi-strategy interface matching is done in three steps: parsing, semantic matching and semantic mapping generation, in step one SI parser is used to extract interface schema. In second step each tuple has mapped by fuzzy matching, domain specific thesaurus and data type matching. Finally SVM generator creates matrices of mapping that are identified by the matching library. DSIM also used mapping knowledge base for avoiding repetition in map effort.

Future work may include testing the schema extraction algorithm on real world data and testing the efficiency of schema matching and schema merging over variety of query interfaces.

Domain Ontology Identification

Ontology is a formal specification of a shared conceptualization (Niepert, Buckner & Allen, 2007). This step is required for analyzing area or specialization of web page so that in further steps appropriate data set will be efficiently placed in query part of the page. This can be taxonomically classified into four different groups.

RDF Annotations Based Ontology Identification

Deitel et al. (Deitel, Faron & Dieng, 2001) present an approach for learning ontology from resource description framework (RDF) annotations of web resources. To perform the learning process, a particular approach of concept formation is adopted, considering ontology as a concept hierarchy, where each concept is defined in extension by a cluster of resources and in intension by the most specific common description of these resources. A resource description is a RDF sub graph containing all resources reachable from the considered resource through properties. This approach leads to the systematic generation of all possible clusters of descriptions from the whole RDF graph incrementing the length of the description associated to each particular concept in the source graph.

Metadata Annotations Based Ontology Identification

Stojanovic et al. (Stojanovic, Stojanovic & Volz, 2002) presents an approach for an automated migration of data-intensive web sites into the semantic web. They extract light ontologies from resources such as XML Schema or relational database schema and try to build light ontologies from conceptual database schemas using a mapping process that can form the conceptual backbone for metadata annotations that are automatically created from the database instances.

Table Analysis Based Ontology Identification

The paper (Tijerino et al., 2005) presents an approach Table Analysis for Generating Ontologies (TANGO) to generate ontology based on HTML table analysis. TANGO discovers the constraints, match and merge mini-ontology based on conceptual modeling extraction techniques. TANGO is thus a formalized technique of processing the format and content of tables that can aim to incrementally build a appropriate reusable conceptual ontology.

DOM Based Ontology Identification

Zhiming Cui et al. published his research (Cui, Zhao, Fang & Lin, 2008) which works in following steps.

- Use the query interfaces information to generate a mini-ontology model.
- To draw the instances from the intermediate result pages.
- Use of various sources to generate ontology mappings and merging ontology.

In first step it employs vision-based approach to extract query interface (Zhao et al., 2007), and in second step data region discovery is done by employing a DOM parser to generate the DOM parsed trees from the result pages. Based on parent length, adjacent and normalized edit distance, extraction of hierarchical data is done by vision-based page segmentation algorithm. In final step merging is done by label instances pairs mined from the result pages into the domain ontology. They also give an idea, of absent attribute annotation for finding absent attributes in the data records. The next generation semantic web framework is required to be able for handling knowledge level querying and searches. Main area to be focused for research is concept relations learning to increase the efficiency of the system.

VALUES ALLOTMENT

Values allotment techniques can be taxonomically classified in the following groups.

Integrating the Databases for Values Mapping

Integration of the databases with the query interfaces is done in this process. The search form interface brings together the attributes and this step will analyze appropriate data values by structure characteristics of the interface and the order of attributes in the area as much as possible. The integration of query interfaces can provide a unified access channel for users to visit the databases which belong to the same area. For integrating interfaces, the core part is dynamic query translator, which can translate the users' query into different form (Meng, Yin & Xiao, 2006) (He, Meng, Yu & Wu, 2003). There is also some scope for improvement by using open directory hierarchy to detect more hypernymy relationship.

Fuzzy Comprehensive Evaluation Methods

In this mapping is done by fuzzy comprehensive evaluation (Chen, Wen, Hu & Li, 2008) which map the attribute of the form to the data values. First it analyzes a form mapping with a view the data range mapping is the key issues and then it select the optimum matching result. Further scope of work in this area includes finding a model to detect the optimal configuration parameter to produce the results with high accuracy.

Query Translation Technique

Query translation technique is used to get query across different deep web sources to translate queries to sources without primary knowledge. The framework takes source query form and target query form as input and output a query for target query.

Some methods can be concerned such as type-based search-driven translation framework by leveraging the "regularities" across the implicit data types of query constraints.

Patterns Based

(He & Zhang et al., 2005) found that query constraints of different concepts often share similar patterns i.e. same data type (page title or author name etc.) and encode more generic translational knowledge for each data type. This indicates explicit declaration of data type that localities the translatable patterns. Therefore, getting translation knowledge for each data types are more generic rather identifying translation based on source of information. For translation purpose it uses extensible search-driven mechanism which uses type based translation.

Hierarchical Relations Based

Other approach published by Hao Liang et al (Liang, Zuo, Ren & Sun, 2008) will map on the basis of three constraints:

1. The same word in different schemas of query forms generally has the same semantics, with or without the same formalizations.

2. The words of two different forms may have same meaning. For this purpose use of thesaurus or dictionaries is required. In addition to this for dealing some special subjects like computer and electronics, some specialized dictionaries related to that subject is required.

3. There may be some hierarchical relations between the words, e.g., X is a hypernym of Y if Y is a kind of X, and on the other hand Y is hyponym of X. For example, bus is a vehicle it indicates that vehicle is hypernym of bus, vehicle is also equivalent to automobile. Thus bus is equivalent to automobile semantically.

Domain ontology is widely used in different areas. There is a scope of lot of work to be done for building ontology. One of the issues is to make automatic domain ontology inspection for some particular domain to gain information about the domain.

Type-Based Predicate Mapping

Type-based predicate mapping method (Zhang et al., 2005) proposed by Z. Zhang focusing on text type attribute with some constraint. The constraint is restricted to the query condition, for example, any, all or exactly. The minimum search space is computed but the cost of the query is not considered.

Cost Model Based

Another method of query translation is proposed by Fangjiao Jiang, Linlin Jia, Weiyi Meng, Xiaofeng Meng which is based on a cost model for range query translation (Jiang et al., 2008) in deep web data integration. This paper proposes a multiple regression cost model based on statistical analysis for global range queries that involve numeric range attributes. It works on the basis of following concepts.

1. Using a statistical-based approach for translating the range query at the global level after proposing a multiple-regression cost model (MrCoM).
2. For selecting significant independent variables into the MrCoM, a pre-processing-based stepwise algorithm is defined.
3. Global range queries are classified into three types and different models are proposed for each of the three types of global range query.
4. Experimental process is done to verify the efficiency of the proposed method.

After going through the above process conclusion is that MrCoM has good fitness and query strategy selection of MrCoM is highly accurate.

RESPONSE ANALYSIS AND NAVIGATION

Techniques for Response analysis and navigation can be taxonomically categorized in the following parts.

Data Extraction Algorithm

Data extraction is another important aspect of deep web research, which involves in extracting the information from semi-structured or unstructured web pages and saving the information as the XML document or relationship model. The paper (Crescenzi, Mecca, & Merialdo, 2001) have done a lot of work in this field. Additionally, in some papers, such as (Arlotta, Crescenzi, & Mecca et al., 2003) and (Song, Giri, & Ma, 2004), researchers have paid more attention to the influence of semantic information on deep web.

Jufeng Yang et al. (Yang, Shi, Zheng & Wang, 2007) has published his literature on data extraction in which web page is converted into a tree, in which the internal nodes represent the structure of the page and the leaf nodes preserve the information and compared with configuration tree. Moreover, structure rules are used to extract data from HTML pages and the logical and application rules are applied to correct the extraction results. The model has four layers, among which the access schedule, extraction layer and data cleaner are based on the rules of structure, logic and application. Proposed models are tested to three intelligent system i.e. scientific paper retrieval, electronic ticket ordering and resume searching. The results show that the proposed method is robust and feasible.

Iterative Deepening Search

Generally the dynamic web search interface generates some output if they are given with some input. The generation of output by some input can be visualized as a graph which is based on the keyword relationship. After getting the interface information about the targeted resource, primary query keywords are applied to generate new keywords, which can be used for further extraction. Iterative deepening search (Ibrahim, Fahmi, Hashmi & Choi, 2008) is proposed by Ahmad Ibrahim et al. His work is based on probability, iterative deepening search and graph theory. It has two phases. The first phase is about classification or identification of a resource behind search interface into some certain domain and in the second phase, each resource is queried according to its domain. Even if the deep web contains a large database but there is need of efficient technique for extracting information from deep web in relatively short time. Presently most of the techniques do not work on real time domain and a lot of time is consumed in processing to find the desired result.

Object Matching Method

Object matching process has vital role for integration of deep web sources. For integration of database information, a technique was proposed in (Hernandez et al., 1995) to identify the same object from variety of sources using well defined specific matching rules. This paper gives the solution of the merge/purge problem i.e. the problem of merging data from multiple sources in an effective manner. The sorted neighborhood method is proposed for the solution of merge/purge problem. An alternative technique based on clustering method is also proposed with the comparison with sorted neighbor method.

String Transformation Based Method

A technique to compare the same parameters of similar objects was proposed in literature (Tejada, Knoblock & Minton, 2002) through string transformation which is independent of application domain but uses application domain to gain the knowledge about attributes of weights through a very little user interaction. There are several future research areas with regard to this algorithm such as how to minimize the noise in the labels given by the user.

Training Based Method

A technique PROM was defined in (Doan, Lu, Lee & Han, 2003) to increase the accuracy of matching by using the constraint among the attributes available through training procedure or expert domain. It uses the objects from different sources having different attributes. Using the segmentation of pages into small semantic blocks defined on basis of HTML tags. The future work in this regard to implement the profilers generated in matching task to other related matching task to see the effect of transferring such knowledge.

Block Similarity Based Method

A technique proposed by (Ling, Liu, Wang, Ai & Meng, 2006),which segment pages into small semantic blocks based on html tags and change the problem of object matching into problem of block similarity. The method is based on high accuracy record and attributes extraction. Due to the limitation of existing information extraction technology, extracted object data from html pages is often incomplete.

Text Based Method

A new method of object matching is proposed by (Zhao, Lin, Fang & Cui, 2007) which is text-based standard TF/IDF cosine-similarity calculation method to calculate the object similarity, and further expended his framework to record-level object matching model, attribute-level object matching model and hybrid object matching model, which considers structured and unstructured features and multi-level errors in extraction. This paper compare the performance of the unstructured, structured and hybrid object matching models and concludes that hybrid method has the superior performance.

RELEVANCE RANKING

Surface web crawlers normally do the page-level ranking but this does not fulfill the purpose of vertical search for entity oriented. The need of entity level ranking for deep web resource has initiated a large amount of research in the area of entity-level ranking. Previously most of the approaches concentrate on the ranking the structured entities based on the global frequency of relevant documents or web pages. Method of relevance ranking can be taxonomically categorized in the following parts.

Data Warehouse Based Method

Many researchers such as (Nie, Ma, Shi, Wen & Ma, 2007) initiated the use of web data warehouse to pre-store all of entities having the capability of handling structured queries. This paper proposed various language models for web object retrieval such as an unstructured object retrieval model, structural object retrieval model and hybrid model having both structured and unstructured features. This paper concludes that hybrid model is the superior one with extraction errors at changing labels.

Global Aggregation and Local Scoring Based Method

A data integration methods based on the local uncertainties of entities is proposed in various literature. But nearly all of the method does not have the capability for local scoring of entities or aggregation of variety of web sources in a global environment. Literature survey indicates that various search engines are built for focusing on clear indication of entity type and context pattern in user request as illustrated in reference (Cheng, Yan & Chang, 2007). This paper concentrates on the ranking of entities by extracting its underline theoretical model and producing a probabilistic ranking framework that can be able to smoothly integrate both global and local information in ranking.

One of the latest techniques named as LG-ERM proposed by (Kou, Shen, Yu & Nie, 2008) for the entity-level ranking based on the global aggregation and local scoring of entities for deep web query purpose. This technique uses large number of parameters affecting the rank of entities such as relationship between the entities, style information of entities, the uncertainty involved in entity retrieval and the importance of web resources. Unlike traditional approaches, LG-ERM considers more rank influencing factors including the uncertainty of entity extraction, the style information of entities and the importance of Web sources, as well as the entity relationship. By combining local scoring and global aggregation in ranking, the query result can be more accurate and effective to meet users' needs. The experiments demonstrate the feasibility and effectiveness of the key techniques of LG-ERM.

FEW PROPOSED PROTOCOL FOR DEEP WEB CRAWLING PROCESS

Some examples of frameworks designed for extraction of deep web information are given below.

Search/Retrieval via URL

Search/Retrieval via URL (SRU) protocol is a standard XML-focused search protocol for internet search queries that uses contextual query language (CQL) for representing queries.

SRU is very flexible. It is XML-based and the most common implementation of SRU via URL, which uses the HTTP GET for message transfer. The SRU uses the representational state transfer (REST) protocol and introduces sophisticated technique for querying databases, by simply submitting URL-based queries For example URL?version=1.1&operation=retrieve &query=dilip&maxRecords=12

This protocol is only considered useful when the information about the resource is predictable i.e. the query word is already planned from any source. With reference to our previous discussion the task of SRU is comes under values allotment and data extraction.

Z39.50

Z39.50 (ANSI/NISO Z39.50, Information Retrieval: Application Service Definition and Protocol Specification, 2003) is an ANSI/NISO standard that specifies a client/server-based protocol for searching and retrieving information from remote databases. Clients using the Z39.50 protocol can locate and access data in multiple databases. The data is not centralized in any one location. When a search command is initiated, the search is normally sent simultaneously in a broadcast mode to the multiple databases. The results received back are then combined into one common set. In a Z39.50 session, the Z39.50 client software that initiates a request for the user is known as the origin. The Z39.50 server software system that responds to the origin's request is called the target. This protocol is useful for extracting data from multiple sources simultaneously but here the search phrase must also defined using any other knowledge source. The task of the protocol can be considered in our values allotment and data extraction phase.

Open Archives Initiative Protocol for Metadata Harvesting

The open archives initiative (OAI) (The Open Archives Initiative Protocol for Metadata Harvesting (Protocol Version 2.0), 2003) protocol for metadata harvesting (OAI-PMH) provides an interoperability framework based on the harvesting or retrieval of metadata from any number of widely distributed databases. Through the services of the OAI-PMH, the disparate databases are linked by a centralized index. The data provider agrees to have metadata harvested by the service provider. The metadata is then indexed by the harvesting service provider and linked via pointers to the actual data at the data provider address. This protocol has two major drawbacks. It does not make its resources accessible via dereferencable URIs, and it provides only limited means of selective access to metadata. This protocol not only provide the proper values allotment for query but also provide knowledge harvested from different source so it increases the accuracy by decreasing the unmatched query load.

ProLearn Query Language

The ProLearn Query Language (PLQL) developed (Campi, Ceri, Duvall, Guinea, Massart, & Ternier, 2008) by the PROLEARN "Network of Excellence", is query language, for repositories of learning objects. PLQL is primarily a query interchange format, used by source applications (or PLQL clients) for querying repositories or PLQL servers. PLQL has been designed with the aim of effectively supporting search over LOM, MPEG-7 and DC metadata. However, PLQL does not assume or require these metadata standards. PLQL is based on existing language paradigms like the contextual query language and aims to minimize the need for introducing new concepts.

For a given XML binding form, all relevant metadata standards for learning objects, it was decided to express exact search by using query paths on hierarchies by borrowing concepts from XPath. Thus, PLQL combines two of the most popular query paradigms, allowing its implementations to reuse existing technology from both fields i.e. approximate search (using information retrieval engines such as Lucene) and exact search (using XML-based query engines). This is simple protocol and work as a mediator for transforming data extracted from on object to other. It is applicable in the phase of querying the resource with predefined query words.

Host List Protocol

The Host-List Protocol (HLP) model (Khattab, Fouad, & Rawash, 2009) is a periodical script designed to provide a way to inform web search engines about hidden hosts or unknown hosts. The virtual hosting feature, applied in apache web server allows one Apache installation to serve different actual websites. This virtual hosts feature will be the target during the design process of this model. The algorithm of the HLP model is such that it extracts hidden hosts, in the form of virtual hosts from apache web server using one of the PHP scripting language based open source technologies which is utilizing an open standard technology in the form of XML language, building a frontier of extracted hosts then sending such hosts frontier to the web search engines that support this protocol via HTTP request in an automatic fashion through a cron job. Hosts frontier is an XML file that lists virtual hosts extracted from the configuration file of the apache web server "httpd.conf" after verifying its configuration to take a decision about from where to extract virtual hosts from "httpd.conf". This protocol is designed to reduce the task or identifying virtual host on any server. It generate host list in XML format for crawler and provide the path for data extraction.

REALLY SIMPLE SYNDICATION

RSS stands for "Really Simple Syndication" "(Grossnickle et al., 2005). It is a technique to easily distribute a list of headlines, update notices, and sometimes content to a wide number of people. It is used by computer programs that organize those headlines and notices for easy reading. Most people are interested in many websites whose content changes on an unpredictable schedule. RSS is a better technique to notify the new and changed contents. Notifications of changes to multiple websites are handled easily, and the results are presented to user are well organized and distinct from email. RSS works through the website author to maintain a list of notifications on their website in a standard way. This list of notifications is called an "RSS Feed". Producing an RSS feed is very simple and lakhs of websites like the BBC, the New York Times and Reuters, including many weblogs now providing this feature. RSS provides very basic information to do its notification. It is made up of a list of items presented in newest to oldest order. Each item usually consists of a simple title describing the item along with a more complete description and a link to a web page with the actual information being described. This mechanism of extracting contents is very effective for site updating their contents daily but the loop whole is again generating proper feed from combination of database and generated page links. It comes into the category of values allotments and data extraction.

SITEMAP PROTOCOL

The sitemaps protocol (Sitemaps, 2009) allows a webmaster to inform search engines about URLs on a website that are available for crawling. A sitemap is an XML file that lists the URLs for a website. It allows webmasters to include additional information about each URL such as when it was last updated, how often it changes and how important it is in relation to other URLs in the website. This allows search engines to crawl the site more intelligently. Sitemaps are a URL inclusion protocol and complement robots.txt, a URL exclusion protocol. Sitemaps are particularly advantageous on websites where some contents of web site is not linked with public pages and webmasters use rich Ajax or Flash contents that are not normally processed by search engines. Sitemaps helps to find out the hidden contents when submitted to crawler and it do not replace the existing crawl-based mechanisms that search engines already use to discover URLs. Sitemap protocol will come under the taxonomical categorization of values allotment and data extraction. Table 3 depicts the comparison of different protocols for deep web information extraction.

Table 3. Comparison of different protocols in the context of deep web information extraction

Name	Techniques	Advantages	Limitations
SRU	Uses the REST protocol, send encoded query words through http get request.	Simple xml based request. Independent of underlining database.	Limitation of 256 character query. Responding server must be equipped for analyzing query.
Z39.50	ANSI/NISO client/server-based protocol.	The data can be extracted from multiple locations. Access data from multiple databases. Various results combined into one result set, regardless of their original format.	Complex technique and the searching is limited to the speed of the slowest server, No updates and support.
OAI-PMH	XML response over http.	Disparate databases are linked by a centralized index, Simple http based request. Much faster and independent of database.	Evaluation on xml. limitation in object access, exchange and transfer, No technique available for the user to know when the metadata was last harvested.
ProLearn Query Language	XML XQuery and Xpath based	Best suited for approximate search and exact search, supports hierarchical metadata structures.	Complex to implement and application development model is not mature.
Host List Protocol	Apache and xml	Retrieval of url from virtual host.	Extracting hidden hosts are limited to the root.
RSS	XML	Short bunch of information, real time update, generation of RSS and reading mechanism is easy to implement.	Dependent upon site administrator to generate these feed. Because auto feed generator will read only anchor tag.
Sitemap protocol	XML based, Site administrator's protocol	Easy to generate, Simple structure and node hierarchy.	Site administrator's involvement is needed, if the pages are hidden by Ajax or flash, explicit mentioning must required.

COMPARATIVE STUDY OF DIFFERENT SEARCH ENGINES

We have conducted search on different search engines some of them are surface web search engine which crawler frontier that retrieves only anchor tag and other are deep search engines which retrieves deep web information. The results are shown below in Table 4 and Table 5. From the analysis of these results, it is clear that surface search engines show more number of results compared to deep web search engine because still at present deep web search engine are not more efficient due to the lack of technological advancement and standards. Results count for query words related to technical literature are relatively more in number deep web search engines while results count of general query words are more in surface web search engines due to the numerous public posting and search engine optimization work. Figure 4 depicts the variation of results count versus query words for different search engines. Figure 5 depicts the snap shots showing results by different surface web search engines in response to query words. Figure 6 depicts the snap shots showing results by different deep web search engines in response to query words.

CONCLUDING REMARKS

After going through the exhaustive literature survey, a general framework is developed for understanding the entire web crawling mechanisms and to find out the limitations of general web crawling mechanism

Table 4. Query words vs. Results counts for surface web search engines

Query Words	Surface Web Search Engine			
	Google.com	**Yahoo.com**	**Bing/live.com**	**Ask.com**
cloud computing	34,200,000	1,510,000	15,300,000	13,100,000
global warming	30,200,000	2,800,000	14,100,000	7,582,000
optical modulation	1,800,000	57,800	1,600,000	1,290,000
walmart	20,800,000	194,000,000	16,300,000	3,340,000
best buy	296,000,000	44,200,000	551,000,000	188,000,000
Dictionary	191,000,000	7,880,000	68,400,000	27,400,000
Astrology	25,300,000	40,400,000	22,600,000	7,790,000
Insurance	363,000,000	41,600,000	262,000,000	49,730,000

Table 5. Query words vs. results counts for deep web search engines

Query Words	Deep Web Search Engine				
	science.gov	**deepdyve.com**	**biznar.com**	**worldwide science.org**	**complete planet.com**
cloud computing	32,318,709	1,229,954	108,609	52,763	5000
global warming	14,436,593	563,694	380,240	214,452	3702
optical modulation	1,774,195	1,513,665	116,407	442,284	621
Walmart	5,960,514	87,143	234,180	244	41
best buy	315,040,211	72,574	2,613,762	111,272	2208
dictionary	56,975,239	101,835	397,173	122,385	1087
astrology	14,101,342	87,964	132,384	3,404	290
insurance	92,056,043	170,433	2,795,986	291,304	5000

in searching the deep web. The entire working of web crawling mechanisms in general is divided into four parts in the developed framework. The present web crawling mechanisms are analyzed and merged as per developed framework to understand their advantages and limitations in searching the deep web. Some existing deep web information extraction protocols are analyzed with their comparative study. We have also done a comparative study of surface web search engines and deep web search engines.

In query interface analysis, heuristic rules based techniques are the simplest one but does not guarantee even a solution. IRFA eliminates the problem of classification of high dimensional and sparse search interface data. Future work is to identify other techniques for feature waiting for generation of random forest. Various techniques of search form schema mapping are described and can be categorized as heuristic and formal techniques. In this regard an appropriate measure has to be defined to filter out false matching. In domain ontology identification the main area to be focused for research is concept relation learning to increase the efficiency of the system. In values allotment there is a scope for improvement by using hierarchy to detect more hypernymy relationship. In fuzzy comprehensive evaluation methods,

Figure 4. Variation of results count versus query words for different search engines

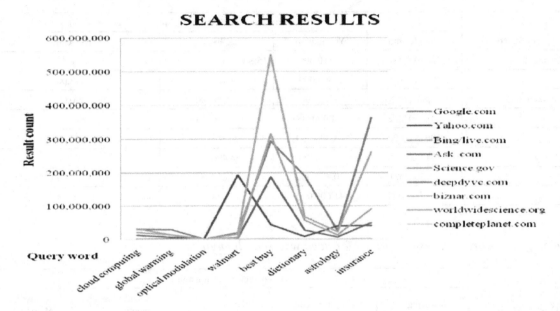

Figure 5. Snap shots showing results by different surface Web search engines in response to query words

Figure 6. Snap shots showing results by different deep Web search engines in response to query words

the future research area include to find a model to detect the optimal configuration parameter to produce the results with high accuracy but MrCOM model has good fitness with highly accurate query strategy selection. In response analysis and navigation, most of the techniques do not work on real time domain and a large time is consumed in processing to find the desired result. In relevance ranking one of the latest techniques is LG-ERM which considers a larger number of ranking influencing factors such as the uncertainty of entity extraction, the style information of entity and the importance of web sources as well as entity relationship. By combining the techniques of local scoring and global aggregation in ranking, the query result can be made more accurate and effective. There exists an improper mapping problem in the process of query interface analysis. Over traffic load problem arises from unmatched semantic query. Data integration suffers due to the lack of cost models at the global level in the process of proper values allotment. In distributed websites there is challenge for query optimization and proper identification of similar contents in the process of response analysis and navigation. The ranking of deep web contents are difficult due to the lake of reference to other sites.

On the basis of taxonomic classification and consequent analysis of different algorithms a conclusion is made that an open framework based deep web information extraction protocol is required to eliminate the limitations of present web crawling techniques in searching the deep web. Future work includes the design, analysis and implementation of open framework protocol for deep web information extraction, considering the fact that it must allow simple implementation without much modifying present architecture of web.

REFERENCES

Akilandeswari, J., & Gopalan, N. P. (2008). An Architectural Framework of a Crawler for Locating Deep Web Repositories Using Learning Multi-agent Systems. In *Proceedings of the 2008 Third International Conference on Internet and Web Applications and Services* (pp.558-562).

ANSI/NISO Z39. 50. (2003). *Information Retrieval: Application Service Definition and Protocol Specification*. Retrieved from http://www.niso.org/standards/standard_detail.cfm?std_id=465.

Arlotta, L., Crescenzi, V., Mecca, G., et al. (2003). Automatic annotation of data extracted from large Web sites. In *Proceedings of the 6th International Workshop on Web and Databases*, San Diego, CA (pp. 7-12).

Bhatia, K. K., & Sharma, A. K. (2008). A Framework for Domain Specific Interface Mapper (DSIM). *International Journal of Computer Science and Network Security*, 8, 12.

BrightPlanet.com LLC. (2000, July). *White Paper: The Deep Web: Surfacing Hidden Value*.

Campi, A., Ceri, S., Duvall, E., Guinea, S., Massart, D., & Ternier, S. (2008, January). Interoperability for searching Learning Object Repositories: The ProLearn Query Language. *D-LIB Magazine*.

Chen, S., Wen, L., Hu, J., & Li, S. (2008). Fuzzy Synthetic Evaluation on Form Mapping in Deep Web Integration. In *Proceedings of the International Conference on Computer Science and Software Engineering*. IEEE.

Cheng, T., Yan, X., & Chang, K. C. C. (2007). Entity Rank: searching entities directly and holistically. In *Proceedings of the VLDB*.

Cope, J., Craswell, N., & Hawking, D. (2003). Automated Discovery of Search Interfaces on the web. In *Proceedings of the Fourteenth Australasian Database Conference (ADC2003)*, Adelaide, Australia.

Crescenzi, V., Mecca, G., & Merialdo, P. (2001). RoadRunner: towards automatic data extraction from large Web sites. In *Proceedings of the 27th International Conference on Very Large Data Bases,* Rome, Italy (pp. 109-118).

Cui, Z., Zhao, P., Fang, W., & Lin, C. (2008). *From Wrapping to Knowledge: Domain Ontology Learning from Deep Web*. In *Proceedings of the International Symposiums on Information Processing*. IEEE.

Deitel, A., Faron, C., & Dieng, R. (2001). *Learning ontologies from rdf annotations*. Paper presented at the IJCAI Workshop in Ontology Learning.

Deng, X. B., Ye, Y. M., Li, H. B., & Huang, J. Z. (2008). An Improved Random Forest Approach For Detection Of Hidden Web Search Interfaces. In *Proceedings of the Seventh International Conference on Machine Learning and Cybernetics,* Kunming, China. IEEE.

Do, H. H., & Rahm, E. (2002, August). COMA-a System for Flexible Combination of Schema Matching Approaches. In *Proceedings of the 28th Intl. Conference on Very Large Databases (VLDB)*, Hong Kong.

Doan, A., Domingos, P., & Halevy, A. (2001). Reconciling schemas of disparate data sources: A machine-learning approach. In *Proceedings of the International Conference on Management of Data (SIGMOD)*, Santa Barbara, CA. New York: ACM Press.

Doan, A., Lu, Y., Lee, Y., & Han, J. (2003). Object matching for information integration: A profiler-based approach. *II Web*, 53-58.

Doan, A. H., Domingos, P., & Levy, A. (2000). Learning source descriptions for data integration. In *Proceedings of the WebDB Workshop* (pp. 81-92).

Galler, J., Chun, S. A., & An, Y. J. (2008, September). Toward the Semantic Deep Web. In *Proceedings of the IEEE Computer* (pp. 95-97).

Grossnickle, J., Board, T., Pickens, B., & Bellmont, M. (2005, October). *RSS—Crossing into the Mainstream*. Ipsos Insight, Yahoo.

He, B., & Chang, K. C. C. (2003). *Statistical schema matching across web query interfaces*. Paper presented at the SIGMOD Conference.

He, B., & Chang, K. C. C. (2006, March). Automatic complex schema matching across web query interfaces: A correlation mining approach. In *Proceedings of the ACM Transaction on Database Systems* (Vol. 31, pp. 1-45).

He, B., Zhang, Z., & Chang, K. C. C. (2005, June). *Meta Querier: Querying Structured Web Sources On the-fly*. Paper presented at SIGMOD, System Demonstration, Baltimore, MD.

He, H., Meng, W., Yu, C., & Wu, Z. (2005). Constructing interface schemas for search interfaces of Web databases. In *Proceedings of the 6th International Conference on Web Information Systems Engineering (WISE'05)* (pp. 29-42).

He, H., Meng, W., Yu, C. T., & Wu, Z. (2003). WISE-Integrator: An Automatic Integrator of Web search interfaces for e-commerce. In *Proceedings of the 29th International Conference on Very Large Data Bases (VLDB'03)* (pp. 357-368).

Hernandez, M., & Stolfo, S. (1995). *The merge/purge problem for large databases*. In *Proceedings of the SIGMOD Conference* (pp. 127-138).

Ibrahim, A., Fahmi, S. A., Hashmi, S. I., & Choi, H. J. (2008). Addressing Effective Hidden Web Search Using Iterative Deepening Search and Graph Theory. In *Proceedings of the 8th International Conference on Computer and Information Technology Workshops*. IEEE.

Jiang, F., Jia, L., Meng, W., Meng, X., & MrCoM. (2008). A Cost Model for Range Query Translation in Deep Web Data Integration. In *Proceedings of the Fourth International Conference on Semantics, Knowledge and Grid*. IEEE.

Kaljuvee, O., Buyukkokten, O., Molina, H. G., & Paepcke, A. (2001). Efficient Web form entry on PDAs. In *Proceedings of the 10th International Conference on World Wide Web (WWW'01)* (pp. 663- 672).

Khattab, M. A., Fouad, Y., & Rawash, O. A. (2009). Proposed Protocol to Solve Discovering Hidden Web Hosts Problem. *International Journal of Computer Science and Network Security*, *9*(8).

Kou, Y., Shen, D., Yu, G., & Nie, T. (2008). LG-ERM: An Entity-level Ranking Mechanism for Deep Web Query. Washington, DC: IEEE.

Lage, P. B. G. J. P., Silva, D., & Laender, A. H. F. (2004). Automatic generation of agents for collecting hidden web pages for data extraction. *Data & Knowledge Engineering, 49*, 177–196. doi:10.1016/j.datak.2003.10.003

Liang, H., Zuo, W., Ren, F., & Sun, C. (2008). Accessing Deep Web Using Automatic Query Translation Technique. In *Proceedings of the Fifth International Conference on Fuzzy Systems and Knowledge Discovery*. IEEE.

Ling, Y.-Y., Liu, W., Wang, Z.-Y., Ai, J., & Meng, X.-F. (2006). Entity identification for deep web data integration. *Journal of Computer Research and Development*, 46-53.

Madhavan, J., Bernstein, P. A., & Rahm, E. (2001). *Generic Schema Matching with Cupid*. Paper presented at the 27th VLBB Conference, Rome.

Melnik, S., Garcia-Molina, H., & Rahm, E. (2002) Similarity Flooding: A Versatile Graph Matching Algorithm. In *Proceedings of the l8th International Conference on Data Engineering (ICDE)*, San Jose, CA.

Meng, X., Yin, S., & Xiao, Z. (2006). A Framework of Web Data Integrated LBS Middleware. *Wuhan University Journal of Natural Sciences, 11*(5), 1187–1191. doi:10.1007/BF02829234

Nie, Z., Ma, Y., Shi, S., Wen, J., & Ma, W. (2007). Web object retrieval. In *Proceedings of the WWW Conference*.

Niepert, M., Buckner, C., & Allen, C. (2007). A Dynamic Ontology for a Dynamic Reference Work. In *Proceedings of the (JCDL'07)*, Vancouver, British Columbia, Canada.

Qiang, B., Xi, J., Qiang, B., & Zhang, L. (2008). An Effective Schema Extraction Algorithm on the Deep Web. Washington, DC: IEEE.

Raghavan, S., & Garcia-Molina, H. (2001). Crawling the hidden Web. In *Proceedings of 27th International Conference on Very Large Data Bases (VLDB'01)* (pp. 129-138).

Sitemaps. (2009). *Sitemaps Protocol*. Retrieved from http://www.sitemaps.org

Song, H., Giri, S., & Ma, F. (2004). Data Extraction and Annotation for Dynamic Web Pages. In *Proceedings of EEE* (pp. 499-502).

Stojanovic, L., Stojanovic, N., & Volz, R. (2002). Migrating data intensive web sites into the semantic web. In *Proceedings of the 17th ACM Symposium on Applied Computing* (pp. 1100-1107).

Tejada, S., Knoblock, C. A., & Minton, S. (2002). Learning domain-independent string transformation weights for high accuracy object identification. In *Proceedings of the World Wide Web conference (WWW)* (pp. 350-359).

The Open Archives Initiative Protocol for Metadata Harvesting. (2003). *Protocol Version 2.0*. Retrieved from http://www.openarchives.org/OAI/2.0/openarchivesprotocol.htm

Tijerino, Y. A., Embley, D. W., Lonsdale, D. W., Ding, Y., & Nagy, G. (2005). Towards ontology generation from tables. *World Wide Web Journal*, 261-285.

Wu, W., Yu, C., Doan, A., & Meng, W. (2004). An interactive clustering-based approach to integrating source query interfaces on the Deep Web. In *Proceedings of the ACM SIGMOD International Conference on Management of Data (SIGMOD'04)* (pp. 95-106).

Yang, J., Shi, G., Zheng, Y., & Wang, Q. (2007). Data Extraction from Deep Web Pages. In *Proceedings of the International Conference on Computational Intelligence and Security*. IEEE.

Zhang, Z., He, B., & Chang, K. (2004). Understanding Web query interfaces: Best-effort parsing with hidden syntax. In *Proceedings of the ACMSIGMOD International Conference on Management of Data (SIGMOD'04)* (pp. 107-118).

Zhang, Z., He, B., & Chang, K. C. C. (2005). Light-weight Domain-based Form Assistant: Querying Web Databases On the Fly. In *Proceedings of the VLDB Conference*, Trondheim, Norway (pp. 97-108).

Zhao, P., & Cui, Z. et al. (2007). Vision-based deep web query interfaces automatic extraction. *Journal of Computer Information Systems*, 1441–1448.

Zhao, P., Lin, C., Fang, W., & Cui, Z. (2007). A Hybrid Object Matching Method for Deep Web Information Integration. In *Proceedings of the International Conference on Convergence Information Technology*. IEEE.

Zhong, X., Fu, Y., Liu, Q., Lin, X., & Cui, Z. (2007). A Holistic Approach on Deep Web Schema Matching. In *Proceedings of the International Conference on Convergence Information Technology*. IEEE.

This work was previously published in International Journal of Information Technology and Web Engineering, Volume 5, Issue 1, edited by Ghazi I. Alkhatib, pp. 1-22, copyright 2010 by IGI Publishing (an imprint of IGI Global).

Chapter 8

The Contribution of Information Science Through Intellectual Property to Innovation in the Brazilian Health Sector

Adelaide Maria de Souza Antunes
*National Institute of Industrial Property (INPI),
Brazil & Federal University of Rio de Janeiro
(UFRJ), Brazil*

Flavia Maria Lins Mendes
Federal University of Rio de Janeiro, Brazil

Suzanne de Oliveira Rodrigues Schumacher
Federal University of Rio de Janeiro, Brazil

Luc Quoniam
Aix-Marseille Université, France

Jorge Lima de Magalhães
Ministry of Health, Brazil & Aix-Marseille Université, France

ABSTRACT

In response to the challenges of the 21st century, emerging countries have played an increasingly leading role in the global economy, and public health has been a notable feature of the government agendas in these countries. According to the IMF, Brazil is one of the countries with the greatest potential to stand out in this context. The quantity of research and development into technologies for drugs and medications is important for supporting innovation in the health sector. Information science can therefore help considerably in the analysis of patents, indicating trends, revealing opportunities for investors, and assisting the decision-taking process by private sector managers and government agents. This study is based on the extraction of valuable information contained in the hidden Web through technology foresight of products deemed strategic by the Brazilian Ministry of Heath, which are the target of public policies and investments by the state for domestic production.

DOI: 10.4018/978-1-5225-3163-0.ch008

BACKGROUND

The activities of companies, research groups, institutions and national governments are effective when they attribute value and quality to their information. These critical factors are crucial for organizations' success in their domestic and international planning, whatever their long- and short-term strategies.

Hence, identify and analyze the amount of scientific information and state of the art with respective correlations has become hard work. The world's technological per-capita capacity to store information has roughly doubled every 40 months since the 1980s. As of 2012, every day 2.5 quintillion (2.5×1018) bytes of data were created (Lynch, 2008). So, the challenge for Science and enterprises is managing Big Data for scientific visualization and transformation of these data as strategic information to decision makers.

Intellectual property capital is an important asset for businesses, and knowledge is becoming increasingly crucial for competitiveness, technology and therefore economic development. This is particularly true for technology-intensive sectors, where knowledge is regarded as a company's most valuable asset (Miller, 2000).

This is why it is so important for organizations to invest in research, development and innovation if they are to remain active and competitive. Information science has tools that can help organizations produce, treat, store and manage data on any activities or processes, resulting in more effective management for innovation. With the increasingly turbulent, complex and competitive conditions in the markets in which companies operate, the use of industrial/intellectual property has become a way of assuring the continuation of their activities into the future by protecting innovations and restricting how their competitors can act. The industrial property information contained in patents identifies the latest science and technology developments, which also makes it a powerful competitive weapon (Pierret, 2005).

It is widely known that the mechanisms for mining information have developed from "manuals" to dedicated portals or Websites (from Web 1.0 to Web 2.0)–we have progressed towards mass information that is obtainable by automated means. This new paradigm allows huge quantities of data to be downloaded in different formats, but it cannot process this data to produce indicators that can actually help decision-makers. This is why studies are required using information science, such as technology trends (Quoniam, 2011).

According to the World Economic Outlook Database maintained by the International Monetary Fund (IMF), and the official Brazilian statistics agency, Instituto Brasileiro de Geografia e Estatística (IBGE), Brazil is one of the emerging nations set to stand out most on the international stage for its development and economic growth (IBGE, 2012). Brazil's gross domestic product grew by 250 percent from 2006 to 2012, reaching around R$ 2.5 trillion. Yet despite this promising scenario, one of the many parameters of domestic consumption, or development, in the Brazilian trade balance is a "family" of health-related items, which in 2012 reached a deficit of R$ 12 billion. This group of products includes drugs, medications, equipment and diagnoses for public health (Gadelha, 2012).

The Brazilian National Policy guidelines state that all actions should strengthen innovation in the Brazilian health sector and also help to mitigate the R$ 12 billion deficit in drugs and medications in the Brazilian trade balance (Gadelha, 2012). According to the Oslo Manual published by the Organisation for Economic Cooperation and Development (OECD), there are four kinds of innovation: product innovation, process innovation, organizational innovation and marketing innovation, as well as a combination of any of the above. This means that not just knowing about, but monitoring scientific publications, patents, and networks of authors and institutions may help a country to develop its science, technology and economic development (Magalhaes, 2012). In this Brazilian case study, we will highlight product and process innovation opportunities for the list of medications used by the Unified Health System (Sistema Único de Saúde, SUS), thereby helping to reduce the trade balance, since innovation can impact even established and approved markets.

Concerns about the quality of life of the Brazilian population are on the government's agenda, with public health programs being established to foster healthy aging, linking economic development to improved sanitation conditions and therefore yielding more sustainable lifestyles. Consequently, the new applications on how to use the data adding information value to governments, companies and/or institutions so that can make the right decision are increasingly needed in everyday life.

List of Target Strategic Products for the Development of the Brazilian Health Sector

In order to help reduce the health sector trade deficit and foster technological innovation and development in Brazil, the government has over the last ten years spearheaded a number of actions and investments for different actors from universities, the business sector and government. Therefore, the quality of information has been rethought in order to improve the health of the population (Castro, 2002). One of the key actions has been the policy to harness the technological competency and drug and medication production knowhow the country boasted in the mid 1980's (Magalhães, 2012). This will encourage the development of the domestic economy, diminish the pharmaceuticals trade balance deficit, and promote national science. Directive no. 1284, issued on May 2010 by the Ministry of Health, is part of this policy and is based on several key Brazilian issues, including the following provisions:

- Whereas the provisions of art. 170 of the Federal Constitution, concerning economic order, founded on the importance of human labor and freedom of enterprise, with the purpose of guaranteeing a dignified existence for all, in accordance with the precepts of social justice;
- Whereas the provisions of art. 197 of the Federal Constitution concerning the regulation of health actions and services;
- The fragility and dependency of the Brazilian health industry trade balance, which lacks significant international competitiveness, contributing to the vulnerability of social policies and with a serious impact on sanitation and the SUS budget;
- Observing that any pharmaceutical welfare, immunization programs and healthcare activities, including diagnoses, amongst others, should have their supply guaranteed irrespective of international market oscillations;
- Whereas the health sector plays a key role in orienting policies with an impact on Brazilian social and economic development;
- Whereas the Brazilian health sector has great potential for development, for which reason it is benefitted as a strategic sector in the Brazilian policy for industry, technology and foreign trade; and
- Whereas the cooperation and technical assistance agreement signed by the Ministry of Health and the Brazilian Development Bank (Banco Nacional de Desenvolvimento Econômico e Social, BNDES) on December 5th, 2007, with the aim of introducing actions, programs and studies designed to develop the Brazilian health sector in Brazilian territory, by which the Ministry of Health is responsible for compiling a list of strategic products to subsidize BNDES in the support of profit-share operations, as set forth in its Health Sector Development Support Program (Profarma).

This directive establishes a list of strategic products for the Unified Health System (SUS) with the purpose of contributing to the development of the health sector. In the same document, it states that this list will be reviewed every two years in order to keep at the forefront and guide the country towards the most innovative and strategic solutions for the good of the nation. All the actions pertaining to this matter are managed by the Secretariat for Science, Health and Strategic Inputs, which is directly answerable to the Minister of Health.

The aim of the list is not just to divulge the strategic products for the Ministry of Health, but to indicate to the country's main agents which products should be the subject of specific initiatives for boosting local production, for innovation and technology transfer, and mechanisms for their regulation, thereby providing strategic support for the Brazilian health sector. Examples of these agents are public[1] and private producers, regulatory and funding agencies, e.g. the public health regulatory agency (National Agência Nacional de Vigilância Sanitária, ANVISA), BNDES, and the science, technology and innovation funding agency, FINEP.

The list is split into two sections, as shown below:

- **Section 1:** Pharmaceuticals industry, made up of six groups. The criteria for selecting the products were: they should be of great importance to society (e.g. neglected diseases[2]); they should be of high technological and economic value (e.g. biotechnological products); products should be included that the government spends over R$ 10 million on (listed in directive no. 2.981 GM/MS of November 26th, 2009) or which have recently started being used by the SUS and have new clinical protocols. Medications and inputs with consolidated production in Brazil have been excluded from the list, and fixed-dose drug combinations have been included. These products are divided into to six large groups, with those that fit into more than one group being included in the group in which they are most representative. These are:
  - **Group 1–Antivirals (Including Antiretrovirals):** Encompasses the strategic products used in the treatment of viral diseases, sexually transmitted diseases and HIV/AIDS;
  - **Group 2–Neglected Diseases:** Includes products for widespread diseases, such as: Chagas disease, leprosy, malaria, leishmaniasis, tuberculosis, dengue fever and schistosomiasis;
  - **Group 3–Chronic Non-Communicable Diseases:** Products for degenerative diseases, mental diseases, oncology products and others.
  - **Group 4–Biological Pathways:** Inclusion of technology-intensive products, such as products of recombinant DNA encoding and monoclonal antibody pathways, among others.
  - **Group 5–Vaccines and Hemoderivatives:** This covers vaccines and hemoderivatives because of their importance for public health and technological development.
  - **Group 6:** Medications and inputs for the treatment of medical issues resulting from nuclear accidents.
- **Section 2:** Medical devices and healthcare devices in general.

This chapter only discusses the products from section 1, groups 1 to 4, which are medications per se. We will quantify and identify the assignees of the patents filed around the world for innovations in the synthesis, formulation, and synthesis and formulation of the medications on the SUS list.

The information contained in a patent document is recognized worldwide as an important source of data for innovation purposes, even though it is existing Web hidden, you can use tools to add value and quality of the data extracted (Carpineto, Osiński, Romano, & Weiss, 2009). By making use of information science tools, such as technology foresight, it was possible to observe all the patent applications filed for the section in question up to 2010 (because of pendency).

The database used to access the patent documents was SciFinder Scholar[3], from the Chemical Abstracts Service (a division of the American Chemical Society), while data on public universities was obtained from the CAPES portal, run by the Brazilian Ministry of Education. This database is very broad, containing patent applications filed since 1907 by the leading patent offices in the world, and it can be accessed using filters to obtain only the information of interest. The main advantage of SciFinder® is that substances can be searched for just using the CAS RN (Chemical Abstracts Service Registry Number)[4]. These rules out the need to make repeated searches using the different synonyms a given substance may be known by. The database can also retrieve complete patent documents that can then be processed using specialized software, such as VantagePoint®[5], which serves to group information into sets and draw correlations between the data.

The methodology was based on a search for each drug from the SUS list of strategic medications, using the CAS Registry Number of the substance. Next, the patent documents were filtered and exported from the database. Having obtained the patent documents, VantagePoint® was used to organize the data and subsequently analyze it to identify trends and make correlations.

Based on the survey of the patent applications/documents, five foresight indicators were analyzed and are presented for each drug:

- Patents relating to processes (synthesis and/or formulation);
- **Main Assignees:** i.e. The companies that have filed the most patent applications, since these are the ones that protect their R&D most in the sector;
- **Top Countries:** i.e. The countries in which the greatest number of priority patent applications have been filed, which, in the vast majority of cases, are also the countries where the technology is being developed;
- **Information About the First Patent for the Drug:** Date and respective assignee;
- **Patents Filed in Brazil:** Number of patents filed in the country, and the main assignees;
- **Trends Over Time of Patenting:** Since this indicates the rise or decline in companies' interest in investing in certain technologies.

It is important to note that Brazil is a signatory of the Patent Cooperation Treaty (PCT), which enables a single patent application to be filed in one language that is valid for all the countries that are signatories to this treaty. Having made this single application, the applicant has up to 12 months to choose the country/ies where it will file its application. After this period the application enters the national phase, i.e. the patent application must be filed in the country of interest and studied against its national intellectual property laws, and may be granted or declined. As such, the assessment of patent applications filed in Brazil includes those that are still filed under the PCT and which, upon entering the national phase, may be filed and protected in the country.

The knowledge acquired over time and its use by companies, scientists and/or institutions has led to incremental innovations in formulations or syntheses, in turn resulting in the more flexible use of raw materials and intermediates and/or inputs. This attitude gives owners of patents a potential competitive advantage in a given market and also a sustainable advantage when they enter a market after the expiration of the patent due to new practical applications of the techniques of Information Science.

Group 1: Antivirals (Including Antiretrovirals)

Figure 1 shows a rise in the global interest in "antiviral" can be seen by using one of the tool search information, such as the Google Trends. In the graph and map below, the numbers of searches for this term per country since 2004 are presented. The darker the color of the country, the more this term has been searched for. Beside the map is a list of the related terms searched for in the period.

Antivirals belong to the first group in the list of strategic products for SUS and antiretrovirals are the drugs that form the backbone of HIV/AIDS treatment in Brazil. The country's HIV/AIDS program includes the free distribution of these medications and has received international recognition, serving as a model for programs in other countries.

In the following, we set forth information within of the hidden Web on intellectual property related to health (Huberman, 2012). Thus, it was possible prepare better information management, quality and value attributed to the establishment of new public policies for SUS. About each antiretroviral in the searched group concerning:

- Patent applications filed for synthesis and formulation;
- Countries with the most patents filed;
- Main assignees;
- Date of first patent and respective assignee;
- Patents in Brazil vs. worldwide trends.

Figure 1. Global interest in antiviral in the world

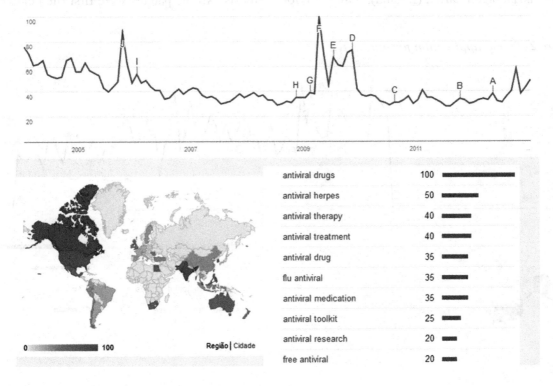

Atazanavir (CAS RN: 198904-31-3)

Of all the patents filed for atazanavir, 18 refer to process patents (eight for the synthesis of the active ingredient, five for the formulation of the medication, and five for synthesis and formulation). The first patent for the synthesis of atazanavir is from 1996 and was filed by Novartis A.G. (Switzerland). The leading process patent holder is Bristol-Myers Squibb (USA) with four patents: three for formulation and one for synthesis and formulation. In Brazil, three patents have been filed, all related to the synthesis and formulation of atazanavir: one by Bristol-Myers Squibb, one by Gilead Sciences (USA) and the first patent by Novartis. Additionally, there are ten patent applications filed under the PCT, which could potentially be filed in Brazil.

The country with the most patenting of atazanavir is the United States, with nine patents, four by Bristol-Myers Squibb, one by Gilead Sciences, two by Nektar Therapeutics, one by Oxyrane and one by Roche Diagnostics Operations. Switzerland and Italy have two patents filed for the synthesis of the drug at the European Patent Office, filed by Solmag S.p.A. and Esteve Quimica. India has two patents for synthesis (one by Aptuit Private Limited and one by Lupin Ltd.) and China has one for synthesis and formulation. The pattern of the patenting of processes for atazanavir can be seen in the Figure 2.

Darunavir (CAS RN: 206361-99-1)

There are 15 process patents for darunavir, of which 11 are for its synthesis, two for its formulation, and two for its synthesis and formulation, with a total of 12 different assignees. The first patent was filed in 1998 by the United States Department of Health and Human Services. The company with the most patents is Tibotec Pharma (Ireland), with three for synthesis. All the patents were first filed under the

Figure 2. Patent application for atazanavir

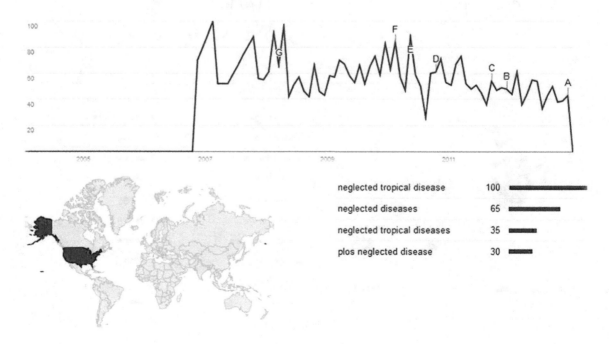

100 neglected tropical disease

65 neglected diseases

35 neglected tropical diseases

30 plos neglected disease

PCT. At the time of writing, only one patent had been filed in Brazil, for synthesis, by the leading assignee, Tibotec, in 2004, and there are a further nine PCT applications. Progress of the patents numbers over the years may be known such as: year (patents number)–1998 (1); 2002 (1); 2003 (1); 2005 (1); 2006 (1); 2007 (2); 2008 (2); 2009 (4); and 2010 (2).

Efavirenz (CAS RN: 154598-52-4)

There are 30 process patents filed for efavirenz by 20 institutions: 22 for its synthesis, six for its formulation and two for a combination of synthesis and formulation. Most are from the United States. The top assignee, Merck & Co. (USA), holds eight, as well as the first patent, filed in 1992. Analyzing patents filed over the last 18 years: there are nine patents filed in Brazil, all relating to the synthesis of efavirenz, of which five belong to the leader, Merck & Co., two to DuPont Pharmaceuticals (USA), one to Bristol-Myers Squibb (USA) and one to Gilead Sciences (USA). Eight international applications have been filed under the PCT. Progress of the patents numbers over the years may be known such as: year (patents number)–1992 (1); 1994 (1); 1995 (2); 1996 (3); 1997 (4); 1998 (3); 2000 (1); 2002 (1); 2004 (2); 2006 (1); 2007 (1); 2008 (3); 2009 (6); 2010 (1).

Enfuvirtide (CAS RN: 159519-65-0)

A total of 32 process patents have been filed for enfuvirtide, 26 for its synthesis and six for its formulation. The first was filed in 1993 by Duke University (USA) and the most recent was filed in 2010 by Matrix Laboratories (India). Most of the 26 assignees have just one patent. The leader, Hoffmann La-Roche (Switzerland), has five patents for the synthesis of enfuvirtide, followed by Trimeris (USA), with two for its formulation and one for its synthesis.

To date, seven patents have been filed for enfuvirtide in Brazil. Three are for its formulation (two by Trimeris [USA] and one by an individual American) and four are for its synthesis: one by the leader, Hoffmann La-Roche, one by Rohm and Haas (USA), one by Ambrx (USA) and one by Lonza (Switzerland). There are currently eight PCT applications filed. Progress of the patents numbers over the years may be known such as: year (patents number)–1993 (1); 1998 (2); 1999 (1); 2002 (2); 2003 (10); 2004 (4); 2005 (1); 2006 (2); 2007 (2); 2008 (3); 2009 (3); 2010 (1).

Entecavir (CAS RN: 142217-69-4)

28 process patents have been filed for entecavir, of which 21 are for its synthesis, two for its formulation and five for its synthesis and formulation. The first patent was filed in 1990 by US Company, Bristol-Myers Squibb. From 1990 to 2005 only seven patents were filed, one a year, but from 2006 on there was a considerable increase in patenting activity. The main country is China, with 19 patents filed, 17 by companies, one by a university and one by an individual researcher. The second country is the United States, with six patents, followed by South Korea with two, and Sweden and the European Patent Office with one each. Two patents have been filed in Brazil by Bristol-Myers Squibb (USA), one for synthesis and one for formulation. Four patent applications are filed under the PCT. Progress of the patents numbers over the years may be known such as: year (patents number)–1990 (1); 1996 (1); 1997 (1); 2002 (1); 2003 (1); 2004 (1); 2005 (1); 2006 (4); 2007 (6); 2008 (3); 2009 (4); 2010 (4).

Lopinavir (CAS RN: 192725-17-0)

There are 14 process patents for lopinavir, all filed by companies: 12 for its synthesis, one for its formulation, and one for its synthesis and formulation. The first patent was granted to Abbott Laboratories in 1995 (USA) and the latest went to an Indian organization, Hetero Research Foundation, in 2009 and was filed under the PCT. The priority applications for eight of the ten patents granted until 2004 were filed in the US, with one in Australia and one in Italy. From 2005, all the patent applications have come from India. So far, only three patents have been filed in Brazil, all from the US: two for the synthesis of the drug (Abbott) and one for its formulation (Gilead Sciences). There are a further two applications filed under the PCT. Progress of the patents numbers over the years may be known such as: year (patents number)–1995 (1); 1999 (1); 2000 (2); 2001 (2); 2002 (2); 2004 (1); 2005 (2); 2007 (2); 2009 (1).

Raltegravir (CAS RN: 518048-05-0)

Raltegravir is an antiretroviral that has been the object of seven process patent applications (one for synthesis, four for formulation and two for synthesis and formulation). Five of these were filed by Merck & Co (USA) in partnership with Instituto di Ricerche di Biotecnologia Molecolare (Italy). One patent was filed in 2009 by Ratiopharm (Germany), and one in 2001 by Instituto di Ricerche di Biotecnologia Molecolare, this latter being the first patent application for the synthesis of the drug. All the patent applications were filed under the PCT, with four having been filed in Brazil, all for the formulation: three by the aforementioned US/Italy partnership and one by the Italian institute on its own. There are two more applications filed under the PCT. Progress of the patents numbers over the years may be known such as: year (patents number)–2001 (1); 2004 (3); 2006 (1); 2008 (1); 2009 (1).

Ritonavir (CAS RN: 155213-67-5)

A total of 18 process patents have been filed for ritonavir, 11 for its synthesis, five for its formulation and two for its synthesis and formulation. The first patent was filed in the United States in 1992 by Abbott Laboratories. This is the leading assignee (nine patents), making the United States the leading country for ritonavir patents, with 11. There are four patents filed in Brazil. One (synthesis) was filed by a Brazilian company, Cristália Produtos Químicos Farmacêuticos, in 2004; two were filed by the leading assignee, Abbott Laboratories (one each for synthesis and formulation) and one by another US firm, Gilead Sciences (formulation). Progress of the patents numbers over the years may be known such as: year (patents number)–1992 (1); 1993 (2); 1994 (2); 1995 (1); 1998 (1); 1999 (1); 2001 (1); 2002 (1); 2003 (1); 2004 (2); 2005 (2); 2006 (1); 2007 (1); 2008 (1).

Tenofovir (CAS RN: 147127-20-6)

We identified 29 process patents for tenofovir using SciFinder®: 12 for its synthesis, six for its formulation, and 11 for its formulation and synthesis. Half of these patents come from China, 33% from the United States, and the others are from India and the European Patent Office. 21 of the patents have been filed since 2005, most by China (15) and India (four). The Chinese patent holders are a mix of companies and government research institutions, while three of the four Indian patents are held by Matrix Laboratories

Ltd, and the other by Emcure Pharmaceuticals Ltd. The first patent for the synthesis of tenofovir, filed in 1992, was the outcome of a partnership between the Institute of Organic Chemistry and Biochemistry (Czech Republic) and Gilead Sciences (USA). Until 2004, there was only one application filed a year, but since 2005 the pace of patenting of the synthesis of tenofovir has quickened. Matrix Laboratories holds the most patents (three), followed by Gilead Sciences and Academy of Sciences of the Czech Republic (two each). Of the total 29 process patents filed, only one is protected in Brazil, held by Gilead Sciences, for the synthesis of the drug. There are currently four patent applications filed under the PCT. Progress of the patents over the years and assignee numbers in parentheses may be known such as: year (patents number)–1992 (1); 1996 (1); 1997 (1); 1999 (1); 2000 (1); 2003 (1); 2004 (1); 2005 (5); 2006 (2); 2007 (2); 2008 (6); 2009 (3); 2010 (4).

Group 2: Neglected Diseases

This group contains the medications from the SUS list for the treatment of priority neglected diseases in Brazil: malaria, Chagas disease, schistosomiasis and leishmaniasis, tuberculosis and leprosy.

The following active ingredients are used to treat these diseases:

- **Malaria:** artesunate, cloroquine, mefloquine and primaquine;
- **Chagas Disease:** benznidazolee and nifurtimox;
- **Schistosomiasis:** praziquantel;
- **Leishmaniasis:** amphotericin B, meglumine antimoniate and amphotericin B deoxycholate;
- **Tuberculosis and Leprosy:** chlofazimine, dapsone, ethambutol, ethionamide, isoniazid, pyrazin-amide, rifabutin and rifampicin.

Figure 3 shows how much the term "neglected disease" has been searched on Google since 2004. The darker the color of the country, the more searches have derived from there. Beside the map is a list of the main related terms searched in the same period.

In the following, we set forth information about the patent applications filed for the synthesis and formulation of each product in this group, the countries with the most patents, the main assignees, the year of the patent and its respective assignee. We also present the patents filed in Brazil and worldwide trends.

Drugs for Malaria Treatment

Artesunate (CAS RN: 88495-63-0)

There are 11 process patents for artesunate (four for its synthesis, six for its formulation and one for its synthesis and formulation) filed by nine different entities. The first patent was filed by Swiss firm Mepha in 1995. China is the country with the most patents (four), the earliest of which was filed in 1998 and the most recent in 2010, followed by Germany with two, both filed in 2005. There is one patent for the synthesis of the drug filed in Brazil by the Shanghai Institute of Materia Medica (China) and there is one filed under the PCT. Progress of the patents numbers over the years may be known such as: year (patents number)–1995 (1); 1998 (1); 2002 (1); 2005 (3); 2007 (3); 2009 (1); 2010 (1).

Figure 3. Global interest in neglected disease in the world

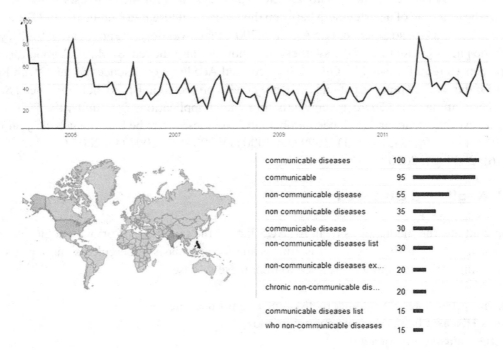

Cloroquine (CAS RN: 54-05-7)

The first patent for the synthesis of cloroquine was filed in Germany in 1937 by I. G. Farbenindustrie AG. The top country is the USA, with 11 of the total of 24 process patents for the drug (ten each for its synthesis and formulation and four for its synthesis and formulation). 19 are held by research institutes and five by individuals. There are no patents filed in Brazil, but there are two that have been filed under the PCT. Progress of the patents numbers over the years may be known such as: year (patents number)–1937 (1); 1941 (1); 1949 (1); 1951 (1); 1960 (1); 1963 (1); 1974 (1); 1981 (1); 1983 (1); 1990 (1); 1991 (2); 1992 (1); 1995 (1); 2004 (1); 2005 (6); 2007 (2); 2008 (1).

Mefloquine (CAS RN: 53230-10-7)

The first patent for mefloquine, according to the search using SciFinder®, was filed in 1976 by the U.S. Army Medical Research and Material Command. We identified a total of 17 process patents in this database (ten for synthesis, six for formulation, and one for synthesis and formulation) filed by companies and institutions from Switzerland, Denmark, Germany, the UK and the USA. There are no patents filed for the drug in Brazil, but four PCT applications have been filed. Progress of the patents numbers over the years may be known such as: year (patents number)–1976 (1); 1977 (1); 1980 (1); 1982 (2); 1991 (1); 1997 (2); 1998 (1); 2002 (1); 2005 (2); 2008 (2); 2009 (3).

Primaquine (CAS RN: 90-34-6)

According to SciFinder®, the first patent application for primaquine was filed in 1980 by the United States Department of the Army. Ten companies and institutions have filed the 11 process patents for the drug (six for its synthesis, three for its formulation, and two for its synthesis and formulation). Bayer Schering Pharma AG is the only assignee of two patents. Six countries are involved: the United States (three patents), Germany, France, and India (two apiece), and China and Spain (one each). The patents have been filed in 15 countries, but not in Brazil. Progress of the patents numbers over the years may be known such as: year (patents number)–1980 (1); 1983 (1); 1987 (1); 1988 (2); 2004 (1); 2005 (3); 2006 (1); 2007 (1).

Drugs for Chagas Disease

Benznidazol (CAS RN: 22994-85-0)

There is just one patent for the synthesis of benznidazole, the priority application having been filed by Hoffmann La-Roche in the United States in 1966. This patent has also been filed in the UK, Switzerland, Germany and France.

Nifurtimox (CAS RN: 23256-30-6)

There are only two companies with patents for this drug: Farbenfabriken Bayer AG (Germany), with a patent for the synthesis of the active ingredient filed in 1962, and Women and Infants Hospital of Rhode Island, with a patent for its formulation filed in 2006. These patents have been filed with the WIPO and with seven countries: Australia, Canada, China, Germany, France, the UK and the US); there are no patents for nifurtimox in Brazil.

Drugs for Schistosomiasis

Praziquantel (CAS RN: 55268-74-1)

16 process patents (14 for synthesis and two for formulation) were encountered for praziquantel, filed by 13 entities, all with one patent except Merck Patent (Germany), which holds four. This company was the first to patent its synthesis of praziquantel in 1973. There are no patents for this drug in Brazil, and there is one application filed with the PCT. The countries that hold the patents are China, India, Germany, France, Spain, South Korea and the United States. Progress of the patents numbers over the years may be known such as: year (patents number)–1973 (1); 1974 (1); 1980 (1); 1982 (2); 1983 (1); 1984 (1); 1986 (1); 2001 (1); 2005 (1); 2006 (2); 2007 (1); 2008 (2); 2010 (1).

Drugs for Leishmaniasis

Anfotericin B (CAS RN: 1397-89-3)

There are 42 process patents for amphotericin B–17 for its synthesis, 20 for its formulation, and five for its synthesis and formulation–filed by 32 companies and/or education and research institutions and two individuals. The first patent, held by Olin Mathieson Chemical Corp (USA) was granted in 1954. The country with most patents is the United States, with 19. In Brazil, three patents have been filed, by US companies Nektar Therapeutics Al (synthesis) and Insert Therapeutics (formulation), and by a Germany company, Biotechnologie - Gesellschaft Mittelhessen MbH (formulation). There are three patent applications filed under the PCT, which may or may not come to be filed in Brazil. Progress of the patents numbers over the years may be known such as: year (patents number)–1954 (1); 1968 (1); 1971 (3); 1977 (1); 1978 (1); 1984 (1); 1986 (1); 1987 (1); 1988 (1); 1989 (1); 1990 (1); 1991 (1); 1993 (3); 1994 (1); 1995 (1); 1997 (1); 1998 (1); 2000 (3); 2001 (2); 2002 (6); 2005 (3); 2006 (3); 2007 (1); 2008 (1); 2009 (2).

Meglumine Antimoniate (CAS RN: 133-51-7)

There are only three patents filed for meglumine antimoniate. The first, for its synthesis, was filed in 1992 by Iteve (Spain). The second, filed in 1999, is held by Universidade Federal de Minas Gerais (Brazil), and is also for a method for synthesizing the active ingredient. The third, for its formulation, was filed in 2009 by Suzhou Tianma Pharma Group Specialty Chemical Co. (China).

Amphotericin B Deoxycholate (CAS RN: 58501-21-6)

Although amphotericin B deoxycholate is on the SUS list of strategic products, we found no information on the first patent for this substance in any of the databases consulted. As explained earlier, there are 42 production patents for amphotericin B.

Drugs for Tuberculosis/Leprosy

Clofazimine (CAS RN: 2030-63-9)

Our search for chlofazimine patents in different databases only yielded information on the first patent. It was filed in 1956 by Geigy Chemical Corp in Switzerland and is also protected in the US, Germany and the UK.

Dapsone (CAS RN: 80-08-0)

32 process patents were identified for dapsone for medical use (24 for synthesis and eight for formulation). The first patent for the synthesis of the active ingredient was filed in 1938 in France by I. G. Farbenindustrie AG. No one company has an advantage in the number of patents, and as can be seen below for the trend over time, the number of patents filed over the years has remained constant at one a year. In Brazil, there is only one patent for the formulation of dapsone, held by Universidad Autonoma Metropolitana (Mexico). There are also three applications filed under the PCT, which could come to be filed in Brazil. Progress of the patents numbers over the years may be known such as: year (patents number)–1938 (1); 1939 (2); 1943 (1); 1946 (1); 1947 (1); 1950 (2); 1951 (1); 1953 (1); 1955 (1); 1956 (1); 1957 (2); 1958 (1); 1960 (1); 1962 (1) 1965 (1); 1969 (1); 1976 (1); 1980 (1); 1991 (1); 1992 (1); 1993 (1); 2003 (1); 2004 (1); 2006 (2); 2007 (1); 2008 (1); 2009 (2).

Ethambutol (CAS RN: 74-55-5)

Ethambutol has been the object of 16 process patents (ten for its synthesis, five for its formulation, and one for its synthesis and formulation). There are two companies that hold three patents each for its synthesis: PLIVA Tvornica Farmaceutskih i Kemijskih Proizvoda (Yugoslavia) and Societa Farmaceutici (Italy). The first patent was filed by a researcher from the former Czechoslovakia in 1962. The Table 1 shows the patent holders and respective priority years. There are no patents in Brazil and four PCT applications.

Table 1. Patent holders in Ethambutol

Assignee	Priority Year
Individual from Czechoslovakia	1962
Societa Farmaceutici Italia	1967
Societa Farmaceutici Italia	1969
Societa Farmaceutici Italia	1969
Individual from Italy	1971
PLIVA Tvornica Farmaceutskih i Kemijskih Proizvoda	1971
PLIVA Tvornica Farmaceutskih i Kemijskih Proizvoda	1972
PLIVA Tvornica Farmaceutskih i Kemijskih Proizvoda	1972
Beecham-Wuelfing G.m.b.H. und Co. K.-G.	1984
Norsk Hydro Asa	1997
Apsinterm	2002
The University of Akron	2005
Auspex Pharmaceuticals	2007
Ascendis Pharma AS	2008
The Brigham and Women's Hospital	2008
University of California	2009

Ethionamide (CAS RN: 536-33-4)

There are 31 process patents for ethionamide (28 for its synthesis, one for formulation, and two for synthesis and formulation). According to the SciFinder® database, the first patent was granted in 1954 in the United States to Farbenfabriken Bayer. There are no patents for this drug in Brazil. Progress of the patents numbers over the years may be known such as: year (patents number)–1954 (1); 1956 (2); 1957 (1); 1958 (2); 1959 (2); 1961 (1); 1962 (5); 1963 (6); 1964 (3); 1965 (1); 1966 (4); 1970 (1); 2006 (1); 2008 (1).

Isoniazid (CAS RN: 54-85-3)

There are 42 process patents for isoniazid for the pharmaceuticals area (27 for its synthesis, 12 for its formulation, and three for its synthesis and formulation). According to the Becker® database, the first patent was filed in 1952 by Hoffmann La-Roche. The chart below shows the number of patents filed each year. The leading countries are the United Kingdom, with 11 patents, and the United States, with seven. The main assignees are the Council of Scientific and Industrial Research (UK) and Distillers Co Ltd (UK), with three patents each. There are no patents in Brazil and there are no current PCT patent applications. Progress of the patents numbers over the years may be known such as: year (patents number)–1952 (3); 1953 (2); 1955 (6); 1956 (4); 1957 (3); 1958 (3); 1959 (1); 1960 (1); 1964 (1); 1967 (1); 1973 (1); 1980 (1); 1981 (1); 1983 (1); 1985 (1); 1993 (1); 1994 (1); 1995 (1); 1997 (1); 1999 (2); 2002 (2); 2003 (1); 2005 (3).

Pyrazinamide (CAS RN: 98-96-4)

Pyrazinamide is the object of 28 process patents (26 for synthesis and two for formulation). According to SciFinder®, the first patent was awarded to Merck & Co (USA) in 1935. The chart below shows the number of priority patent applications filed each year. The leading country is the United States, with eight patents, followed by Japan, with seven. Two patents (for synthesis) have been filed in Brazil, one by Swiss company Lonza and one by Nitto Chemical Industry (Japan). There is also one patent application filed under the PCT, which could be filed in Brazil. Progress of the patents numbers over the years may be known such as: year (patents number)–1935 (2); 1942 (1); 1943 (1); 1952 (1); 1953 (1); 1954 (1); 1970 (1); 1974 (1); 1976 (1); 1980 (1); 1983 (1); 1985 (1); 1987 (1); 1990 (1); 1993 (2); 1994 (1); 2001 (3); 2003 (1); 2004 (1); 2006 (1); 2007 (1); 2008 (2); 2009 (1).

Rifabutin (CAS RN: 72559-06-9)

There are 12 process patents for rifabutin, eight for its synthesis, two for its formulation, and two for its synthesis and formulation). The search of SciFinder® identified that the first patent was awarded in 1974 to US-based Pfizer. There are no patents in Brazil, and there are no current PCT applications. Progress of the patents numbers over the years may be known such as: year (patents number)–1974 (1); 1975 (1); 1978 (4); 1991 (1); 1994 (1); 1996 (1); 2001 (1); 2005 (1); 2007 (1).

Rifampicin (CAS RN: 13292-46-1)

There are 41 process patents for rifampicin (32 for synthesis, eight for formulation, and one for synthesis and formulation). Lepetit S.p.A. (Italy) was the pioneer in 1964. Today, Japan is the leader with 17 patents. There are no patents filed in Brazil and three applications currently under the PCT. Progress of the patents numbers over the years may be known such as: year (patents number)–1964 (2); 1967 (1); 1973 (2); 1976 (2); 1977 (3); 1978 (5); 1979 (4); 1980 (1); 1981 (3); 1987 (1); 1988 (1); 1989 (1); 1993 (1); 1996 (1); 1999 (1); 2002 (2); 2003 (2); 2004 (1); 2005 (1); 2008 (1); 2009 (4); 2010 (1).

Group 3: Chronic Non-Communicable Diseases

The third group from the SUS list of strategic products involves drugs designed for treating chronic non-communicable diseases. The diseases from this group and their respective drugs are:

- **Alzheimer's Disease:** Donepezil and rivastigmine;
- **Asthma:** Budesonide and formoterol;
- **Parkinson's Disease:** Cabergoline, entacapone, tolcapone, pramipexole and selegiline;
- Symptomatic treatment of psychoses, convulsive and epileptic crises, neuralgies and mood disorders: clozapine, olanzapine, primidon, quetiapine, topiramate and ziprasidone;
- **Rheumatism and Inflammations:** Leflunomide and mesalazin;
- **Immunosuppressants (Drugs Capable of Reducing or Suppressing Immune Reactions):** Everolimus, mycophenolate mofetil, mycophenolate sodium, tacrolimus and sirolimus;
- **Osteoporosis:** Calcitonin, calcitriol and raloxifene;
- **Pulmonary Hypertension:** Iloprost and sildenafil.

N.B. "Other uses" has been added to this group, which includes the following drugs:

- **Bromocriptine:** Used in the treatment of pituitary andenomas, Parkinson's disease, hyperprolactinemia, neuroleptic malignant syndrome and type 2 diabetes;
- **Sevelamer Hydrochloride:** Used in the control of hyperphosphatemia in chronic kidney disease;
- **Glatiramer Acetate:** Agent for the immunomodulatory treatment of multiple sclerosis;
- **Riluzole:** Used in the treatment of lateral amyotrophic sclerosis;
- **Somatostatin:** Used to control hemorrhaging in severe acute upper gastrointestinal bleeding and pancreatic surgery (to reduce complications); and
- Atorvastatin, simvastatin, pravastatin, fluvastatin and lovastatin: cholesterol-lowering drugs.

Figure 4 shows how much the term "non-communicable diseases" has been searched on Google since 2004. The darker the color of the country, the more searches have derived from there. Beside the map is a list of the main related terms searched in the same period.

In the following, we set forth information about the patent applications filed for the synthesis and formulation of each product in this group, the countries with the most patents, the main assignees, the year of the patent and its respective assignee. We also present the patents filed in Brazil and worldwide trends.

Drugs for Alzheimer's Disease

Donezepil (CAS RN: 120014-06-4)

Donepezil, used for treating Alzheimer's, has been the object of 57 process patents (42 for its synthesis and 15 for its formulation). The first patent, for its synthesis, was filed by Eisai Co (Japan) in 1987, and the same company is the leading assignee, with nine patents. The country with most patents is India,

Figure 4. Global interest in "non-communicable diseases" in the world

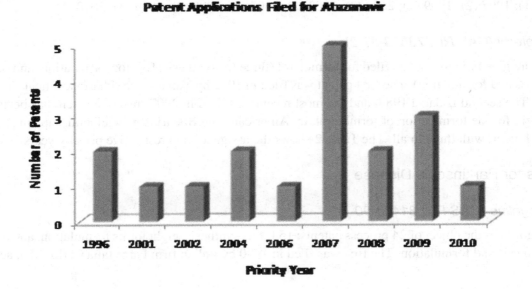

with 18, followed by the United States (12) and Japan (ten). Patenting patterns for donepezil can be seen in the graph below. There are two patents in Brazil, filed by US firm Pfizer (synthesis) and Japanese Takeda Chemical Industries (formulation). A further eight applications have been filed under the PCT. Progress of the patents numbers over the years may be known such as: year (patents number)–1987 (1); 1988 (1); 1990 (2); 1994 (1); 1995 (1); 1997 (1); 1998 (3); 2000 (1); 2002 (3); 2003 (3); 2004 (9); 2005 (5); 2006 (6); 2007 (5); 2008 (12); 2009 (3).

Rivastigmine (CAS RN: 123441-03-2)

There are 46 process patents for rivastigmine, a nootropic agent. 38 are for its synthesis, seven for it formulation, and one for a synthesis intermediate. The first patent, according to the Becker® database, was filed in 1985 by Yissum Research Development Co. The leading patent holder is the Shanghai Institute of Pharmaceutical Industry (China) with four patents.

China and India have the most patents for rivastigmine (16 and 12, respectively). There are two patents for its synthesis filed in Brazil: one by Emcure Pharmaceuticals Limited (India) and one by Ragactives (Spain). There are also seven PCT applications currently filed. Progress of the patents numbers over the years may be known such as: year (patents number)–1985 (1); 1987 (1); 2002 (2); 2003 (3); 2004 (4); 2005 (4); 2006 (6); 2007 (11); 2008 (5); 2009 (8); 2010 (1).

Drugs for Asthma

Budesonide (CAS RN: 51333-22-3)

There are 26 process patents for this antiasthmatic agent: 17 for synthesis, six for formulation, and three for synthesis and formulation). The first was filed in 1972 by Swedish firm Aktiebolag Bofors. The country with the most priority patent applications is the United States, with eight, followed by China and Italy (four each). There is only one patent filed in Brazil, by Nektar Therapeutics (USA), for its formulation, and there are five applications currently filed under the PCT. Progress of the patents numbers over the years may be known such as: year (patents number)–1972 (1); 1985 (1); 1988 (1); 1989 (1); 1991 (2); 1992 (1); 1997 (2); 1999 (1); 2002 (3); 2003 (3); 2007 (2); 2008 (4); 2009 (3); 2010 (1).

Formoterol (CAS RN: 73573-87-2)

There are nine process patents filed for formoterol (three for synthesis, five for formulation, and one for synthesis and formulation). The first patent was filed in 1972 by Yamanouchi Pharmaceutical Co, from Japan. The second is dated 1987, and the most recent was filed in 2007. Just one patent has been filed in Brazil, for the formulation of formoterol, by American firm Boehringer Ingelheim. Japan is the top patent holder, with three in all. The Table 2 shows the assignees and respective priority years.

Drugs for Parkinson's Disease

Cabergoline (CAS RN: 81409-90-7)

Cabergoline is the object of 24 process patents: 15 for its synthesis, eight for its formulation, and one for its synthesis and formulation. The first was filed in 1980 by Italian firm Farmitalia Carlo Erba, accord-

Table 2. Patent holders in Formoterol

Patent Holder	Priority
Yamanouchi Pharmaceutical Co.	1972
Sociedad Anon. Lasa Laboratorios	1987
Aktiebolaget Astra	1990
Saitama Daiichi Seiyaku K. K.	1997
Yamanouchi Pharmaceutical Co.	1997
New River Pharmaceuticals Inc.	2000
Boehringer Ingelheim Pharma G.m.b.H. & Co. K.-G.	2002
Natco Pharma Limited	2006
Argenta Discovery Ltd.	2007

ing to SciFinder®. Two patents for its synthesis have been filed in Brazil: one by Resolution Chemical Limited (UK) and one by Pharmacia & Upjohn (USA). There is also one PCT application. The pace of patenting for cabergoline from 1980 to 2008 may be known such as: year (patents number)–1980 (1); 1981 (2); 1992 (1); 1997 (1); 2000 (3); 2001 (2); 2003 (1); 2004 (3); 2005 (3); 2006 (3); 2007 (3); 2008 (1).

Entacapone (CAS RN: 130929-57-6)

Entacapone, used to treat Parkinson's disease, has 31 process patents: 26 for synthesis and five for formulation. A Finnish firm, Orion-Yhtyma Ou, was the first to file a patent for it, in 1986, but today the top assignee of patents for its synthesis is Wockhardt Limited, based in India. There is just one patent in Brazil for entacapone, filed by the leading assignee, and there are two PCT applications filed. Progress of the patents numbers over the years may be known such as: year (patents number)–1986 (1); 1989 (1); 2003 (4); 2004 (1); 2005 (2); 2006 (10); 2007 (7); 2009 (4); 2010 (1).

Tolcapone (CAS RN: 134308-13-7)

Only two patents for the spintese of tolcapone were identified, both filed by Swiss company Hoffmann La-Roche. The priority patent applications were filed in Switzerland (1986) and the European Union (1997), and the latter is also filed in Brazil.

Pramipexole (CAS RN: 104632-26-0)

There are 32 patents filed for this drug used to treat Parkinson's disease: 25 for its synthesis and seven for its formulation). The first one was filed in 1984 by a Germany company, Thomae. The country with the most patents is India, with 12, followed by the United States, with six. In Brazil there are two patents filed: one for its formulation, by Boehringer Ingelheim International (USA), and one for its synthesis, by Cipla Limited (India). There are three applications filed under the PCT. Progress of the patents numbers over the years may be known such as: year (patents number)–1984 (1); (000 (1); 2002 (1); 2003 (1); 2004 (8); 2005 (4); 2006 (6); 2007 (4); 2008 (2); 2009 (3); 2010 (1).

Selegiline (CAS RN: 14611-51-9)

Of the six process patents for the synthesis of selegiline, used to treat Parkinson's, three are held by the leader, Chinoin Gyogyszer es Vegyeszeti Termekek Gyara Rt (Hungary), which also filed the first patent in 1965, others in 1966 and 1982. Another companies like Belupo - Lijekovi i Kozmetika D.O.O. has one patent in 1999; Apsinterm Generics UK Limited in 2002 and Generics UK Limited in 2008.

There are no patents for selegiline in Brazil, and there is currently one PCT application.

Medications for the Symptomatic Treatment of Psychoses, Convulsive and Epileptic Crises, Neuralgies, and Mood Disorders

Clozapine (CAS RN: 5786-21-0)

There are a total of 18 process patents for this antipsychotic drug, 12 for its synthesis, four for its formulation, and two for its synthesis and formulation). The first patent was filed in 1960 by a Swiss company, Wander AG, but the leading assignee is now an American company, Allelix Biopharmaceuticals, with four patents. There are no patents in Brazil, while China is the country with the most patents filed. Progress of the patents numbers over the years may be known such as: year (patents number)–1960 (2); 1962 (1); 1971 (1); 1972 (1); 1977 (2); 1979 (1); 1992 (1); 1993 (1); 1994 (4); 2000 (1); 2002 (1); 2005 (1); 2008 (1).

Olanzapine (CAS RN: 132539-06-1)

Olanzapine is an antipsychotic that has been the target of 69 process patents, 34 for its synthesis and 35 for its formulation). The first was filed by Lilly Industries in 1990. Today, Eli Lilly (USA) is the leading assignee, with 33 patents. The top country is the United States, with 33, followed by India, with 11. 14 patents have been filed in Brazil, ten of which by Eli Lilly (two synthesis and eight formulation). The other four are for the synthesis of olanzapine, two filed by Adamed (Poland), one by Dr. Reddy's Laboratories (India) and one by Lek Pharmaceuticals (Slovenia). There are three patent applications filed under the PCT. Progress of the patents numbers over the years may be known such as: year (patents number)–1990 (1); 1991 (1); 1992 (1); 1995 (7); 1996 (8); 1997 (5); 1998 (2); 2000 (1); 2001 (4); 2002 (6); 2003 (5); 2004 (10); 2005 (3); 2006 (4); 2007 (3); 2008 (6); 2009 (1); 2011 (1).

Primidon (CAS RN: 125-33-7)

Primidon is an anticonvulsant that has been the object of 17 patents for its synthesis and one for its formulation. Imperial Chemical Industries was the first company to file a patent for it, in 1949 in Great Britain. There are no patents for this drug in Brazil and no applications were found in the PCT. Progress of the patents numbers over the years may be known such as: year (patents number)–1949 (1); 1951 (4); 1952 (2); 1954 (4); 1955 (1); 1959 (1); 1960 (1); 1961 (1); 1973 (1); 1978 (1); 2005 (1).

Quetiapine (CAS RN: 111974-69-7)

There are 55 process patents for this antipsychotic, 39 of which are for its synthesis, 11 for its formulation, and five for its synthesis and formulation. The first patent was filed in 1986 by ICI Americas in the UK. One patent has been filed in Brazil for its formulation, by Swedish firm Astrazeneca, and there are nine PCT applications filed. The top countries are the United States, with 19 patents, and India, with

15. Progress of the patents numbers over the years may be known such as: year (patents number)–1986 (1); 1987 (1); 1999 (1); 2000 (2); 2002 (2); 2003 (10); 2004 (7); 2005 (8); 2006 (2); 2007 (5); 2008 (9); 2009 (6); 2010 (1).

Topiramate (CAS RN: 97240-79-4)

This anticonvulsant has been the object of 27 process patents: 21 for its synthesis, four for its formulation, and two for its synthesis and formulation). The first patent was filed in 1983 by an American firm, McNeilab. The top country for topiramate patents is the United States (12), followed by India (eight). In Brazil, three patents have been filed, all by Ortho-MecNeil Pharmaceutical (USA) for the synthesis of the drug. There is also one PCT application. Progress of the patents numbers over the years may be known such as: year (patents number)–1983 (1); 1991 (2); 1995 (1); 2000 (1); 2001 (1); 2002 (2); 2003 (4); 2004 (4); 2005 (1); 2006 (5); 2007 (3); 2010 (2).

Ziprasidone (CAS RN: 146939-27-7)

There are 46 patents filed for the antipsychotic, ziprasidone, 26 for its synthesis, 15 for its formulation, and five for synthesis and formulation. Pfizer Inc. (USA) was the first to patent it (1987) and is also the leading assignee, with 13 patents. The top countries are the United States, with 18 patents, and India, with 16. In Brazil, there are seven patents for ziprasidone, all filed by Pfizer, four of which are for its synthesis and three for its formulation. There are four applications filed under the PCT. Progress of the patents numbers over the years may be known such as: year (patents number)–1987 (1); 1988 (1); 1992 (3); 1993 (1); 1996 (3); 1998 (1); 1999 (1); 2002 (5); 2003 (4); 2004 (9); 2005 (3); 2006 (5); 2007 (4); 2008 (3); 2009 (1); 2010 (1).

Drugs for Rheumatism and Inflammations

Leflunomide (CAS RN: 75706-12-6)

There are 22 process patents for leflunomide, nine of which are for its synthesis, 11 for its formulation, and two for its synthesis and formulation. Five patents are held by the leader and pioneer, Hoechst A-G (Germany), which filed the first patent in 1978. The country with the most patents is the USA, with nine. There are three patents filed in Brazil, one by Hoechst, for its formulation, one by Orchid Chemicals & Pharmaceiticals Limited (India), for its synthesis, and one by Aventis Pharma Deutschland (Germany), for its synthesis. There are no PCT applications. Progress of the patents numbers over the years may be known such as: year (patents number)–1978 (1); 1990 (1); 1991 (1); 1993 (1); 1994 (2); 1995 (1); 1999 (1); 2000 (2); 2001 (2); 2002 (4); 2006 (2); 2009 (3); 2010 (1).

Mesalazin (CAS RN: 89-57-6)

Mesalazin is an anti-inflammatory for which there are 46 process patents, of which 30 for synthesis, 15 for formulation, and one for synthesis and formulation). The first patent for its synthesis was filed by an individual from Czechoslovakia in 1957. The top assignees, with three patents each, are Institut Neftekhimii i Kataliza RAN Respublika Bashkortostan (Russia), the Jordanian Pharmaceutical Manufacturing Co, and Bayer. There are two patents filed in Brazil, one by B F Goodrich Diamalt (Germany) for synthesis and one by Giuliani International Limited (Italy) for formulation. Four applications are currently filed under the PCT. Progress of the patents numbers over the years may be known such as: year (patents number)–1957 (1); 1967 (1); 1975 (1); 1981 (1); 1983 (2); 1984 (1); 1985 (1); 1986 (5); 1988 (2); 1989 (1); 1990 (2); 1991 (1); 1992 (1); 1996 (1); 1997 (2); 1998 (3); 2000 (2); 2001 (1); 2002 (1); 2003 (1); 2004 (1); 2005 (4); 2007 (5); 2008 (3); 2009 (1); 2010 (1).

Immunosuppressants

Everolimus (CAS RN: 159351-69-6)

There are 15 process patents for this immunosuppressant (eight in synthesis and seven in formulation). Swiss firm Sandoz-Erfindungen Verwaltungsgesellschaft was the pioneer, in 1992, but the United States is now the leading country, with nine priority patent applications. No process patents for Brazil were identified, although one patent was found which appeared to be filed in the country, but detailed analysis showed that it was a medical device used in diagnosis, therapy or surgery. There are three PCT applications currently filed. Progress of the patents numbers over the years may be known such as: year (patents number)–1992 (1); 1995 (1); 1996 (1); 2000 (1); 2002 (1); 2003 (3); 2004 (2); 2007 (1); 2008 (1); 2009 (1); 2010 (1); 2011 (1).

Mycophenolate Mofetil (CAS RN: 128794-94-5)

There are 32 process patents for the immunosuppressant, mycophenolate mofetil: 23 for its synthesis, seven for its formulation, and two for its synthesis and formulation. The leading assignee is a US company, Syntex, with four patents, and is also the pioneer (first patent granted in 1987). The United States and India are the countries with the most patents: nine each. In Brazil there are three patents filed, one by Syntex (USA) and two by Ivax (Czech Republic), all for synthesis. There are six PCT applications currently filed. Progress of the patents numbers over the years may be known such as: year (patents number)–1987 (2); 1992 (1); 1994 (1); 1998 (1); 2001 (2); 2003 (3); 2004 (3); 2005 (5); 2006 (4); 2007 (7); 2008 (3).

Mycophenolate Sodium (CAS RN: 37415-62-6)

There are just seven process patents for the immunosuppressant mycophenolate sodium: five for synthesis, one for formulation, and one for synthesis and formulation. Novartis (Switzerland) filed the first patent in 1996. Indian company Biocon Limited is the only to have more than one patent, and Indian entities hold four of the seven patents. Two patents were found to be filed in Brazil: one by Biocon (synthesis) and the other by Novartis (formulation). There are also two patent applications filed under the PCT.

Tacrolimus (CAS RN: 104987-11-3)

Tacrolimus has been the target of 86 patents, of which 73 are for its synthesis, seven for its formulation, and six for its synthesis and formulation. A Japanese company, Fujisawa Pharmaceuticals, was awarded the first patent in 1984, and is the joint leader in this category, together with Merck & Co, with six patents each. The top country is the United States, with 33 priority patents, followed by South Korea (13) and India (12). There are six patents filed in Brazil: two by Fujisawa (synthesis), one by British firm Biotica Technology Ltd. (synthesis), one by Teva Magyarország Zrt (Hungary) (formulation), and one each by US-based Home Products (synthesis) and Ivax Corporation (synthesis). Ten patent applications are currently filed under the PCT. Progress of the patents numbers over the years may be known such as: year (patents number)–1984 (1); 1986 (1); 1987 (1); 1989 (3); 1990 (4); 1991 (1); 1992 (5); 1993 (5); 1994 (1); 1995 (2); 1996 (1); 1997 (3); 1999 (5); 2001 (2); 2002 (3); 2003 (8); 2004 (6); 2005 (5); 2006 (4); 2007 (4); 2008 (10); 2009 (10); 2010 (1).

Sirolimus (CAS RN: 53123-88-9)

Sirolimus has been the target of 72 process patents, the majority (49) for its synthesis, 18 for its formulation, and five for its synthesis and formulation. An American company, Wyeth, is the leading assignee with six patents, three of which (for synthesis) are protected in Brazil. Canadian Ayerst McKenna and Harrison Ltd. is the company that filed the first patent for sirolimus, in 1972. Alongside the three patents filed by the leader, five others are filed in Brazil, by American Home Products Corporation (USA), Biotica Technology Limited (UK), Isotechnika International (Canada), Novartis (Switzerland) and Sandoz-Erfindungen Verwaltungsgesellschaft (Switzerland), all for synthesis. There are currently five PCT applications. The top country is the United States, with 46 patents. Progress of the patents numbers over the years may be known such as: year (patents number)–1972 (1); 1989 (1); 1990 (1); 1991 (1); 1992 (3); 1993 (6); 1994 (2); 1995 (3); 1996 (3); 1997 (2); 1998 (1); 1999 (3); 2001 (3); 2002 (2); 2003 (12); 2004 (4); 2005 (5); 2006 (9); 2007 (1); 2008 (3); 2009 (4); 2010 (1); 2011 (1).

Drugs for Osteoporosis

Calcitonin (CAS RN: 9007-12-9)

Calcitonin, used for treating osteoporosis, has been the target of 204 process patents, of which 169 are for its synthesis, 28 for formulation, and seven for synthesis and formulation. The first patent was granted in 1968 to Ciba Ltd (Switzerland). The leading assignee is Armour Pharmaceutical (USA), with nine patents. The country with the most patents is the United States, with 96, followed by Japan, with 40. Ten patents have been filed in Brazil, two for synthesis by Institut Gustave Roussy (France), one for synthesis by The Scripps Research Institute (USA), one for synthesis by Transkaryotic Therapies (USA), one for synthesis by Tsumura and Co (Japan), one for synthesis by Akzo Nobel NV (Netherlands), one for formulation Amylin Pharmaceuticals (USA), one for synthesis by Daiichi Suntory Pharma (Japan), one for formulation by Societé de Conseils de Recherches et d'Applications Scientifiques (France) and one for synthesis by a British researcher. The patent applications filed under the PCT total 17. Progress of the patents numbers over the years may be known such as: year (patents number)–1968 (1); 1974 (1); 1976 (1); 1977 (2); 1978 (2); 1979 (1); 1980 (1); 1981 (1); 1982 (4); 1983 (5); 1984 (3); 1985 (7); 1986 (3); 1987 (9); 1988 (2); 1989 (9); 1990 (6); 1991 (8); 1992 (2); 1993 (8); 1994 (6); 1995 (5); 1996 (8); 1997 (6); 1998 (5); 1999 (7); 2000 (7); 2001 (12); 2002 (13); 2003 (13); 2004 (5); 2005 (6); 2006 (10); 2007 (9); 2008 (8); 2009 (8).

Calcitriol (CAS RN: 32222-06-3)

Osteoporosis drug calcitriol is the object of 85 process patents: 68 for synthesis, 14 for formulation, and three for synthesis and formulation. The top assignee is the Wisconsin Alumni Research Foundation (USA), with eight patents. The first patent was awarded in 1971 to Hoffmann La-Roche (Switzerland). Japan is the top country, with 37 patents, followed by the United States, with 31. There are three patents filed in Brazil, two by American company Pfizer (formulation) and one by The United States of America as Represented by the Administrator of the National Aeronautics and Space Administration (synthesis). There are four applications also available under the PCT. Progress of the patents numbers over the years may be known such as: year (patents number)–1971 (1); 1973 (1); 1975 (2); 1976 (2); 1978 (4); 1979 (1); 1981 (3); 1983 (1); 1984 (1); 1987 (1); 1988 (4); 1989 (1); 1990 (6); 1991 (3); 1992 (4); 1993 (4); 1994 (4); 1995 (4); 1996 (2); 1997 (3); 1998 (3); 1999 (6); 2000 (2); 2001 (2); 2002 (3); 2003 (6); 2004 (2); 2005 (1); 2006 (1); 2007 (1); 2008 (3); 2009 (3).

Raloxifene (CAS RN: 84449-90-1)

Raloxifene, used to treat osteoporosis, has been the object of 32 process patents, 23 for its synthesis and nine for its formulation. The earliest patent was filed in 1981 by Eli Lilly (USA), which is also the top assignee, with 19 patents. The United States is the leading country, with 23 patents in all. In Brazil, 11 patents have been filed (eight for synthesis and three for formulation), all by Eli Lilly. There are six patent applications filed under the PCT. Progress of the patents numbers over the years may be known such as: year (patents number)–1981 (2); 1992 (1); 1993 (1); 1994 (4); 1995 (5); 1996 (1); 1997 (3); 1999 (2); 2000 (2); 2002 (1); 2003 (1); 2005 (1); 2006 (1); 2007 (2); 2008 (1); 2009 (3); 2010 (1).

Drugs for Pulmonary Hypertension

Iloprost (CAS RN: 78919-13-8)

There are just three process patents for iloprost, two of which are held by a German company, Schering, which is also the company that filed the first patent in 1978, for synthesis and formulation. Its other patent, awarded in 1998, is for synthesis. In 1999 Teijin Limited (Japan) was granted a patent for its formulation, which was also filed in Brazil.

Sildenafil (CAS RN: 139755-83-2

There are 49 process patents for sildenafil (36 for its synthesis and 13 for its formulation). The top assignee is Pfizer (USA), with nine patents, the earliest of which dates back to 1990. China is the leading country, with 14 patents, followed by the UK, with eight. In Brazil, nine patents have been filed: six by Pfizer for synthesis, one by Mochida Pharmaceutical (Japan) for formulation, one by Torcan Chemical (Canada) for formulation and one by an individual Brazilian. There are three PCT applications currently filed. Progress of the patents numbers over the years may be known such as: year (patents number)–1990 (1); 1995 (1); 1996 (1); 1997 (1); 1998 (5); 1999 (12); 2000 (7); 2001 (5); 2002 (3); 2003 (1); 2004 (1); 2005 (1); 2006 (4); 2007 (2); 2008 (2); 2009 (2).

Drugs for Other Uses

Bromocriptine (CAS RN: 25614-03-3)

There are 17 process patents for bromocriptine: 12 for its synthesis, three for formulation, and two for synthesis and formulation). Sandoz (Switzerland) was the first company to be awarded a patent for this drug (1968) and is also the leading assignee, with three patents. Just one patent has been filed in Brazil for its synthesis by Sandoz. There is one PCT application. Progress of the patents numbers over the years may be known such as: year (patents number)–1968 (1); 1976 (1); 1978 (1); 1979 (1); 1981 (1); 1983 (2); 1985 (2); 1986 (1); 1988 (1); 1990 (1); 1991 (1); 1995 (1); 2000 (1); 2004 (2).

Sevelamer Hydrochloride (CAS RN: 152751-57-0)

Sevelamer hydrochloride has been the target of 19 process patents, four for its synthesis, 12 for formulation, and three for synthesis and formulation). According to SciFinder®, the earliest patent was filed in 1991 by a Japanese company, Nitto Boseki Co, but for food applications. As such, we here consider the first patents to be from 1993, filed by Geltex (USA) for the formulation of a medication containing sevelamer hydrochloride for oral administration. Geltex Pharmaceuticals (USA) is the top assignee, with nine patents in the pharmaceuticals area. There are two patents in Brazil, both for the formulation of sevelamer hydrochloride: one filed by the leading assignee and one by Genzyme Corporation (USA). Five applications are currently filed under the PCT. Progress of the patents numbers over the years may be known such as: year (patents number)–1993 (2); 1994 (2); 1997 (3); 1998 (3); 2005 (1); 2006 (2); 2007 (1); 2008 (4); 2009 (1).

Glatiramer (CAS RN: 28704-27-0)

There are 19 patents filed for glatiramer for pharmaceutical processes, of which 11 are for synthesis, six for formulation, and two for synthesis and formulation. The first patent was filed by Yeda Research and Development, Israel, in 1971. There are two companies with three patents each: Momenta Pharmaceuticals (USA) and Teva Pharmaceutical Industries (Israel). The top country is the United States. There are currently six patent applications filed under the PCT. In Brazil, two patents have been filed, both by Teva Pharmaceuticals Industries, one for the synthesis of glatiramer, and one for its synthesis and formulation. The number of new patents filed since 1971 may be known such as: year (patents number)–1971 (1); 1998 (1); 2000 (1); 2001 (1); 2002 (1); 2004 (3); 2005 (1); 2006 (2); 2007 (3); 2008 (3); 2009 (2).

Riluzole (CAS RN: 1744-22-5)

There are ten process patents for riluzole: four for its synthesis, four for its formulation, and two for synthesis and formulation). The only company with two patents is France-based Rhone-Poulenc Santé (one each for formulation and synthesis), and this company was also the first one to file a patent for riluzole, in 1980. There is one patent filed in Brazil, for its synthesis (by American company Tularik), and there are two PCT applications. The Table 3 shows the companies that hold patents for riluzole and the years in which they were filed.

Somatostatin (CAS RN: 51110-01-1)

Somatostatin has been the target of 172 process patents: 106 for its synthesis, 41 for its formulation, and 25 for its synthesis and formulation. The country with the most patents is the USA, with 107, and it is a US company, American Home Products, that is the top assignee, with 27 patents, and the pioneer (first patent granted in 1974), according to SciFinder®. There are ten patents filed in Brazil. Five of these are for synthesis, filed by Actogenix N.V (Belgium), Amgen Inc (USA), Biomeasure (USA), Sandoz Ltd (Switzerland), and an individual American researcher; and five for formulation, filed by DuPont Merck Pharmaceutical Co (USA), Nobex Corporation (USA), Novartis A.-G (Switzerland), Societé de Conseils de Recherches et d'Applications Scientifiques S.A.S (France) and an individual American researcher.

Table 3. Patent holders in Riluzole

Assignee	Priority Year
Pharmindustrie	1980
Rhone-Poulenc Sante	1987
Warner-Lambert Co.	1987
Rhone-Poulenc Sante	1988
Tularik Inc.	2000
Dr. Reddy's Laboratories Limited	2006
Rottapharm S.p.A.	2007
Ascendis Pharma AS	2009
Edmond Pharma S.r.l.	2009
Farmak	2009

11 applications are currently filed under the PCT. Progress of the patents numbers over the years may be known such as: year (patents number)–1974 (1); 1975 (10); 1976 (12); 1977 (17); 1978 (8); 1979 (16); 1980 (1); 1981 (3); 1982 (6); 1983 (2); 1984 (2); 1985 (4); 1986 (2); 1987 (2); 1988 (4); 1989 (5); 1990 (1); 1991 (3); 1992 (4); 1993 (5); 1994 (3); 1995 (7); 1996 (4); 1997 (2); 1998 (3); 1999 (3); 2000 (6); 2001 (4); 2002 (3); 2003 (6); 2004 (3); 2005 (4); 2006 (1); 2007 (2); 2008 (9); 2009 (2); 2010 (2).

Cholesterol-Lowering Drugs

Atorvastatin (CAS RN: 134523-00-5)

There are 114 process patents for atorvastatin, of which 84 are for its synthesis, 26 for its formulation, and four for its synthesis and formulation. The first patent was awarded to an American company, and the companies with the most patents (eight each) are Israeli Teva Pharmaceuticals Industries and US-based Warner-Lambert Company. The latter was awarded the first patent in 1986. There are 17 patents filed in Brazil, six by Warner Lambert Company (five for synthesis and one for formulation), two by Teva Pharmaceuticals Industries (one for formulation and one for synthesis), two by Pfizer (USA), for synthesis, and one each by Lek Pharmaceuticals (Slovenia–synthesis), Avecia Limited (UK–synthesis), Ciba Specialty Chemicals Holding (Switzerland–synthesis), DSM IP Assets (Netherlands–synthesis), Bristol-Myers Squibb (USA–synthesis), Nicox (France–formulation) and Vital Health Sciences Pty (Australia –synthesis). Seven PCT applications are currently filed. Progress of the patents numbers over the years may be known such as: year (patents number)–1986 (1); 1989 (1); 1997 (1); 1998 (4); 1999 (4); 2000 (7); 2001 (8); 2002 (11); 2003 (16); 2004 (13); 2005 (17); 2006 (9); 2007 (12); 2008 (9); 2009 (1).

Simvastatin (CAS RN: 79902-63-9)

126 process patents have been filed for simvastatin, 104 of which are for its synthesis, 17 for its formulation, and five for its synthesis and formulation. The first patent was awarded in 1980 to Merck & Co (USA), which is the leader with nine patents. The United States holds the most patents (37), followed by India, with 33. There are seven patents filed in Brazil, all for the synthesis of simvastatin: two by Lupin Limited (India), and one apiece by DSM IP Assets (Netherlands), Cheil Jedang Corporation (South

Korea), CJ Corporation (South Korea), Teva Pharmaceuticals (Israel) and Bristol-Myers Squibb (USA). There are currently 15 PCT applications. The development of patenting for simvastatin over the years may be known such as: year (patents number)–1980 (2); 1983 (1); 1987 (1); 1990 (1); 1991 (2); 1993 (1); 1994 (1); 1995 (1); 1996 (2); 1997 (7); 1998 (9); 1999 (8); 2000 (7); 2001 (13); 2002 (7); 2003 (10); 2004 (12); 2005 (10); 2006 (10); 2007 (10); 2008 (6); 2009 (6); 2011 (1).

Pravastatin (CAS RN: 81093-37-0)

There are 86 process patents for pravastatin (72 for synthesis, 12 for formulation, and 12 for synthesis and formulation). Sankyo (Japan) is the company that filed the first patent, in 1980. The leading patent holders are the United States (26), the European Patent Office (17) and Japan (18). No priority patent applications have been filed in Brazil, but there are eight patents filed there: six for its synthesis, by Sankyo (Japan), Bristol-Myers Squibb (USA), Biocon India, Gyogyszerkutato Intezet Kft (Hungary), Institute for Drug Research (Hungary), Vital Health Sciences Pty (Australia); one for its formulation by Nicox AS (France); and one for its synthesis and formulation by Teva Gyogyszergyar Zartkoeruen Mukoedo Reszvenytarsasag (Hungary). Nine patent applications are current filed under the PCT. Patenting of pravastatin over the years may be known such as: year (patents number)–1980 (1); 1989 (1); 1992 (2); 1993 (1); 1995(3); 1996 (1); 1997 (2); 1998 (6); 1999 (7); 2000 (6); 2001 (12); 2002 (5); 2003 (9); 2004 (5); 2005 (4); 2006 (5); 2007 (6); 2008 (5); 2009 (3); 2010 (1); 2011 (1).

Fluvastatin (CAS RN: 93957-54-1)

Fluvastatin has been the target of 45 process patents, of which 33 are for synthesis, 11 for formulation, and one for synthesis and formulation). Sandoz, from Switzerland, filed the first patent in the United States in 1982. Lek Pharmaceuticals, from Slovenia, is the company with the most patents (four). In Brazil, four patents have been filed: one by Lek Pharmaceuticals (synthesis), one by Israeli company Teva Pharmaceutical Industries (synthesis), one by US-based Bristol-Myers Squibb (synthesis) and one by a French company, Nicox AS (formulation). There are three PCT applications currently filed. The new patents filed for fluvastatin over the years may be known such as: year (patents number)–1982 (1); 1986 (1); 1995 (1); 1998 (2); 1999 (1); 2000 (1); 2001 (1); 2002 (2); 2003 (4); 2004 (3); 2005 (11); 2006 (5); 2007 (9); 2008 (1); 2009 (2).

Lovastatin (CAS RN: 75330-75-5)

There are 121 process patents for lovastatin (95 for synthesis, 22 for formulation, and four for synthesis and formulation). The first company to file a patent for this drug, in 1979, was Merck & Co (USA), and this company is also the leading assignee, with 37 patents. No priority patent applications have been filed in Brazil, but there are nine patents filed in the country, all for the synthesis of lovastatin: two by Battelle Memorial Institute (USA) and one each by Gist-Brocades BV (Netherlands), Ranbaxy Laboratories (India), Lupin Limited (India), Teva Pharmaceutical Industries (Israel), Bristol-Myers Squibb (USA), CJ Corporation (South Korea) and Novopharm (Canada). There are presently nine PCT applications filed. Progress of the patents numbers over the years may be known such as: year (patents number)–1979 (2); 1980 (1); 1981 (1); 1983 (3); 1984 (1); 1985 (1); 1986 (1); 1987 (1); 1988 (1); 1989 (2); 1992 (2); 1993 (7); 1994 (2); 1995 (6); 1996 (5); 1997 (8); 1998 (3); 1999 (9); 2000 (7); 2001 (7); 2002 (5); 2003 (5); 2004 (7); 2005 (7); 2006 (7); 2007 (6); 2008 (5); 2009 (8); 2010 (1).

Group 4: Biological Pathways

This group covers medications whose drugs are manufactured via biological pathways. These include:

- **Monoclonal Antibodies:** Adalimumab, dasatinib, imatinib, infliximab, nilotinib, rituximab and trastuzumab;
- **Enzymes:** Dornase alpha and glucocerebrosidase;
- **Hormones:** Insulin-like growth factor, filgrastim, chorionic and serum gonadotropin, goserelin, glucagon, follicle-stimulating hormone, human insulin, leuprorelin and somatotropin; and
- **Proteins:** Etanercept, procoagulant factors, interferons, octreotide and botulinum toxin.

It's not possible shows the graph and map for this group in "searched on Google." Occurs due, the technology in this field, interestingly, only started to emerge this decade (2011), for which reason there are insufficient data to conduct a global technology foresight study.

In the following, we set forth information about the patent applications filed for the synthesis and formulation of each product in this group, the countries with the most patents, the main assignees, the year of the patent and its respective assignee. We also present the patents filed in Brazil and worldwide trends.

Monoclonal Antibodies

Adalimumab (CAS RN: 331731-18-1)

Adalimumab has been the target of 27 process patents: 18 for its synthesis, two for formulation, and seven for synthesis and formulation. The first patent was awarded in 1996 to BASF (Germany). The country with the most patents is the United States, with 26, and Abbott Laboratories is the leading company, with eight patents. There are two patents filed in Brazil, one by BASF, related to the synthesis of adalimumab, and one by Abbott (USA) for its formulation. There are currently 12 PCT applications filed. There are presently nine PCT applications filed. Progress of the patents numbers over the years may be known such as: year (patents number)–1996 (1); 1997 (1); 2004 (2); 2005 (3); 2006 (7); 2007 (4); 2008 (3); 2009 (5); 2010 (1).

Dasatinib (CAS RN: 302962-49-8)

There are 14 process patents for dasatinib, of which eight are for synthesis, two for formulation, and four for synthesis and formulation. US company Bristol-Myers Squibb was the first to file a patent for dasatinib, in 1999, in the United States, and also owns the most patents (five). There are two patents filed in Brazil, both by Bristol-Myers Squibb, one for its synthesis and other for its synthesis and formulation. There are also five patent applications filed under the PCT. Progress of the patents numbers over the years may be known such as: year (patents number)–1999 (1); 2004 (3); 2005 (1); 2006 (1); 2008 (2); 2009 (4); 2010 (2).

Imatinib (CAS RN: 152459-95-5)

Imatinib has been the target of 61 process patents: 36 for its synthesis, one for a synthesis intermediate, 13 for its formulation, and 11 for its synthesis and formulation). US-based Ciba-Geigy was the first company to file a patent for imatinib, in Switzerland in 1992. The top assignee is Natco Pharma (India), with seven patents, and India is also the country with the most priority patents (18). Four patents have been filed in Brazil: two for synthesis, filed by Novartis (Switzerland), another for synthesis filed by Cipla Limited (India), and one for formulation, by Gilead Sciences (USA). Ten patent applications are currently filed under the PCT. Progress of the patents numbers over the years may be known such as: year (patents number)–1992 (1); 2002 (1); 2003 (7); 2004 (4); 2005 (1); 2006 (6); 2007 (14); 2008 (9); 2009 (13); 2010 (5).

Infliximab (CAS RN: 170277-31-3)

There are 24 process patents for infliximab: 12 for synthesis, five for formulation, and seven for synthesis and formulation). Centocor (USA) was the first company to file a patent for it, in the United States in 1991. The US is also the country with the most priority applications (19). There are two patents filed in Brazil, one by Abbott Biotechnology (Bermuda) for synthesis and formulation, and one by Neose Technologies (USA) for synthesis. There are also seven PCT applications filed. Progress of the patents numbers over the years may be known such as: year (patents number)–1991 (1); 1999 (3); 2001 (3); 2003 (1); 2005 (3); 2006 (4); 2007 (2); 2008 (1); 2009 (6).

Nilotinib (CAS RN: 641571-10-0)

Eight process patents have been filed for nilotinib: five for its synthesis and three for its synthesis and formulation. Novartis (Switzerland) was awarded the first patent in 2002 and is also the company with the most patents (four). In Brazil, two patents have been filed for its synthesis and two for its synthesis and formulation, all by Novartis. There are three patent applications filed under the PCT. The Table 4 shows the assignees and respective priority dates.

Rituximab (CAS RN: 174722-31-7)

Rituximab is the object of 60 process patents, 33 for its synthesis, 17 for its formulation, and ten for its synthesis and formulation. Idec Pharmaceuticals Corporation (USA) filed the first patent application for rituximab in 1992 in the United States. It and Genetech are the top assignees, with six patents each. The

Table 4. Patent holders in Nilotinib

Assignee	Priority Year
Novartis A.-G.	2002
Novartis A.-G.	2005
Novartis A.-G.	2005
Novartis A.-G.	2005
Teva Pharmaceutical Industries Ltd.	2008
Teva Pharmaceutical Industries Ltd.	2008
Avila Therapeutics	2008
Targegen	2005

leading country is the United States, where 48 of the patents were first filed. In Brazil, eight patents have been filed, all by American firms, four of which by Xencor (three for synthesis and one for synthesis and formulation), two by Neose Technologies (both for synthesis), one by Immunogen (formulation) and one by Genentech (formulation). There are 16 PCT applications currently filed. Progress of the patents numbers over the years may be known such as: year (patents number)–1992 (1); 1999 (1); 2000 (3); 2001 (6); 2002 (3); 2003 (6); 2004 (4); 2005 (8); 2006 (6); 2007 (8); 2008 (5); 2009 (8); 2010 (1).

Trastuzumab (CAS RN: 180288-69-1)

Trastuzumab is the target of 97 process patents (48 for its synthesis, 27 for its formulation, and 22 for its synthesis and formulation). An American company, Chiron Corporation, was the first to file a patent application for trastuzumab, in 1984, according to the Becker® database. The top country is the United States, with 76 patents. In Brazil, 11 patents have been filed: three for synthesis by Genentech (USA), two for synthesis and one for synthesis and formulation by Xencor (USA), one for synthesis and one for formulation by Immunogen (USA), two for synthesis by Neose Technologies (USA), and one for synthesis and formulation by Syntarga BV (Netherlands). There are currently 38 PCT applications filed. Progress of the patents numbers over the years may be known such as: year (patents number)–1984 (1); 1988 (1); 1999 (1); 2000 (2); 2001 (4); 2002 (3); 2003 (9); 2004 (10); 2005 (8); 2006 (12); 2007 (11); 2008 (11); 2009 (22); 2010 (2).

Enzymes

Dornase Alpha (CAS RN: 143831-71-4)

Our search of the databases revealed five patents filed for dornase alpha. The first patent was granted in 1995 to Genentech (USA). The priority application was filed in the United States, and the same patent was filed in 18 countries: Austria, Australia, Bulgaria, Brazil, Canada, Czech Republic, Spain, Hungary, Israel, Japan, Norway, New Zealand, Poland, Portugal, Romania, Russia, Slovakia, South Africa, the European Patent Office and the World Intellectual Property Organization.

Alongside Genentech, the other assignees are Altus Biologics (USA), Momenta Pharmaceuticals (USA) (with two patents) and Roche Diagnostics (USA).

Glucocerebrosidase (CAS RN: 37228-64-1)

There are 86 process patents for glucocerebrosidase, 64 of which are for its synthesis, 19 for its formulation, and three for its synthesis and formulation. The first patent was filed in 1974 by an individual researcher from the United States. Genzyme Corporation is the top assignee, with eight patents, followed by Neose Technologies with five, both from the United States. Brazil has been the target of six patents for its synthesis (three by Neose Technologies, one by German firm Merck Patent GmbH, one by US-based The Scripps Research Institute, and one by Transkaryotic Therapies, also American) and one for its formulation, by Athersys (USA). There are currently 12 PCT applications filed. Progress of the patents numbers over the years may be known such as: year (patents number)–1974 (1); 1981 (1); 1991 (2); 1992 (2); 1994 (3); 1995 (2); 1997 (2); 1998 (5); 1999 (4); 2000 (9); 2001 (7); 2002 (7); 2003 (6); 2004 (5); 2005 (4); 2006 (9); 2007 (6); 2008 (6); 2009 (2); 2010 (3).

Hormones

Insulin-Like Growth Factor (IGH1) (CAS RN: 67763-96)

IDH1 has been the target of 195 process patents: 135 for its synthesis, 42 for its formulation, and 18 for its synthesis and formulation. The first patent application for this substance was filed in 1979 by the Nichols Institute (USA), but when we examined the document we found that it was for insulin production, and therefore falls outside the scope of this study. There were two patents filed in 1983, both for the synthesis of this product, by American companies, Genentech and Amgen.

Genentech is the leading assignee, with 15 patents. Six patents have been filed in Brazil for the synthesis of IDH1: two by Genentech, one by the Scripps Research Institute (USA), one by Human Genome Sciences (USA), one by Pharmacia & Upjohn Company (USA), and one by Crucell Holland (Netherlands). There are also three for its formulation: one each by Dow Agrosciences (USA), Octapharma (Switzerland), and Cambridge University Technical Services (UK), and one for its synthesis and formulation, filed by Acetogenix (Belgium). There are 19 applications filed under the PCT. Progress of the patents numbers over the years may be known such as: year (patents number)–1983 (2); 1984 (1); 1985 (1); 1986 (1); 1987 (11); 1988 (1); 1989 (3); 1990 (6); 1991 (8); 1992 (5); 1993 (14); 1994 (7); 1995 (13); 1996 (5); 1997 (5); 1998 (7); 1999 (1); 2000 (6); 2001 (4); 2002 (9); 2003 (9); 2004 (9); 2005 (12); 2006 (20); 2007 (9); 2008 (11); 2009 (9); 2010 (6).

Filgrastim (CAS RN: 121181-53-1)

Filgrastim has been the object of 13 process patents (four for its synthesis and nine for its formulation). The first patent was granted in 1985 to Kirin-Amgen (USA). The majority (nine) of the priority applications have been filed in the USA. Just one patent is filed in Brazil, for the formulation of filgrastim, by Fresenius Kabi Deutschland GmbH (Germany). There are three PCT applications currently filed. Progress of the patents numbers over the years may be known such as: year (patents number)–1985 (1); 1994 (1); 1999 (1); 2002 (1); 2003 (1); 2004 (2); 2006 (1); 2007 (1); 2008 (2); 2009 (2).

Chorionic Gonadotropin (HCG) (CAS RN: 9002-61-3)

There are 128 process patents for chorionic gonadotropin: 78 for its synthesis, 41 for its formulation, and nine for its synthesis and formulation. The first company to file a patent for it was Hoffmann La-Roche (Switzerland), in 1972. The top country for priority patent applications is the United States, with 53. 13 patents have been filed in Brazil, as well as one priority application for its synthesis by Comissão Nacional de Energia Nuclear. Of the 13 patents filed by foreign firms, 11 are for synthesis: three by Applied Research Systems ARS Holding (Netherlands), two by Washington University (USA), and one apiece by Neose Technologies (USA), Akzo Nobel (Netherlands), Athersys (USA), Crucell Holland (Netherlands), Leland Stanford Junior University (USA), and Yeda Research and Development (Israel). The remaining patents, for its formulation, are held by two American companies: Mountain View Pharmaceuticals and Summa Medical. There are currently 11 patent applications filed under the PCT. Progress of the patents numbers over the years may be known such as: year (patents number)–1973 (1); 1974 (1); 1978 (1); 1979 (3); 1980 (4); 1981 (3); 982 (2); 1983 (2); 1984 (1); 1985 (3); 1987 (1); 1988 (3); 1989 (4); 1990 (1); 1991 (3); 1993 (3); 1994 (3); 1995 (3); 1996 (9); 1997 (3); 1998 (4); 1999 (4); 2000 (9); 2001 (4); 2002 (8); 2003 (8); 2004 (5); 2005 (10); 2006 (3); 2007 (7); 2008 (5); 2009 (4); 2010 (3).

Serum Gonadotropin (PMSG) (CAS RN: 9002-70-4)

There are seven process patents for serum gonadotropin (PMSG): four for synthesis and three for formulation. Observe that the first patent for PMSG was filed by a Polish company, Drwalewskie Zaklady Przemyslu Bioweterynaryjnego and there are no patents filed in Brazil and no PCT applications at present. Follow assignees and respective priority dates: Drwalewskie Zaklady Przemyslu Bioweterynaryjnego in 1977; Commonwealth Serum Laboratories Commission in 1980; individual assignees, Germany in 1981; Akademie der Landwirtschaftswissenschaften der DDR in 1984; Biotechnology Australia Pty. Ltd. in 1985; Teikoku Hormone Mfg Co Ltd. in 1994 and Ningbo Sansheng Pharmacy Co. in 2006.

Goserelin (CAS RN: 65807-02-5)

15 process patents have been filed for goserelin: 12 for its synthesis, two for its formulation, and one for its synthesis and formulation. The first, granted in 1976, was filed by Imperial Chemical Industries (UK), which is also the leading assignee, with three patents. No patents for goserelin have been filed in Brazil, but there are three applications filed under the PCT. Progress of the patents numbers over the years may be known such as: year (patents number)–1976 (1); 1991 (2); 1995 (1); 1996 (1); 1999 (1); 2000 (1); 2004 (1); 2005 (1); 2006 (1); 2008 (2); 2009 (2); 2010 (1).

Glucagon (CAS RN: 9007-92-5)

There are 142 process patents for the hormone, glucagon, of which 106 are for its synthesis, 27 for its formulation, and nine for its synthesis and formulation. The first patent dates back to 1953, filed by Eli Lilly and Co. There were few patent applications filed for glucagon synthesis until 2000, when the average rose to eight a year. The top country for priority patent applications is the United States, with 79, followed by Denmark (23) and Japan (11). A great number of the assignees are biotechnology companies. Ten patents have been filed in Brazil, seven of which are for the synthesis of glucagon. These were filed by the top assignee, Novo Nordisk A/S (Denmark), with three, and US firms Athersys, Novocell, Transkaryotic Therapies and Wyeth, all with one each. The remaining three patents are for its formulation: one each by Biotechnologie - Gesellschaft Mittelhessen MbH (Germany), Nobex Corporation (USA) and Societe de Conseils de Recherches et d'Applications Scientifique (France). There are 19 PCT applications currently filed. Progress of the patents numbers over the years may be known such as: year (patents number)–1953 (1); 1968 (1); 1970 (1); 1971 (1); 1973 (1); 1975 (2); 1976 (3); 1977 (4); 1978 (1); 1980 (3); 1982 (1); 1985 (3); 1986 (3); 1990 (3); 1991 (1); 1993 (5); 1994 (6); 1995 (10); 1996 (6); 1997 (5); 1998 (3); 1999 (6); 2000 (4); 2001 (6); 2002 (18); 2003 (10); 2004 (2); 2005 (6); 2006 (4); 2007 (6); 2008 (7); 2009 (10); 2010 (1).

Follicle-Stimulating Hormone (FSH) (CAS RN: 9002-68-0)

Follicle-stimulating hormone has been the target of 167 process patents: 117 for its synthesis, 43 for its formulation, and seven for its synthesis and formulation. According to SciFinder®, the first patent for its synthesis was filed in 1968 by Monsanto. Meanwhile, the Merck Index has Genentech as the owner of the first patent, granted in 1992. The top country is the United States (95 patents), and the pattern of patenting over the years can be seen in the chart below. Four priority patent applications have been filed in Brazil: by Applied Research Systems ARS Holding N.V (Netherlands), in formulation, and by Comissão Nacional de Energia Nuclear, Fundação de Amparo a Pesquisa do Estado de Minas Gerais e

Fundação Universidade de Brasília, all in synthesis. A further 23 patents have been filed in the country (19 for synthesis and four for formulation). There are 24 PCT applications filed at the time of writing. Progress of the patents numbers over the years may be known such as: year (patents number)–1968 (1); 1971 (1); 1978 (1); 1980 (1); 1982 (1); 1984 (1); 1985 (2); 1986 (4); 1987 (2); 1988 (3); 1989 (2); 1991 (2); 1992 (1); 1994 (7); 1995 (2); 1996 (3); 1997 (8); 1998 (4); 1999 (13); 2000 (7); 2001 (5); 2002 (15); 2003 (13); 2004 (13); 2005 (14); 2006 (9); 2007 (11); 2008 (9); 2009 (9); 2010 (3).

Human Insulin (CAS RN: 11061-68-0)

128 process patents have been filed for insulin (85 for synthesis, 35 for formulation, and eight for synthesis and formulation). The leading assignee is Novo Nordisk (Denmark), with 18 patents. The first company to file a patent application for insulin was Merck & Co (USA) in 1965. The graphic below showing patenting of human insulin demonstrates an upturn in activity in recent years. 17 patents were filed in Brazil (ten for synthesis and seven for formulation), although these technologies have all be sold to Novo Nordisk (Denmark). There are 20 patent applications currently filed under the PCT. Progress of the patents numbers over the years may be known such as: year (patents number)–1965 (1); 1972 (3); 1974 (2); 1978 (2); 1979 (2); 1980 (7); 1981 (4); 1982 (5); 1983 (2); 1984 (1); 1985 (2); 1986 (6); 1988 (2); 1990 (1); 1991 (1); 1992 (6); 1993 (3); 1994 (4); 1995 (4); 1996 (3); 1997 (4); 1998 (5); 1999 (5); 2000 (1); 2001 (5); 2002 (1); 2003 (2); 2004 (2); 2005 (5); 2006 (14); 2007 (8); 2008 (6); 2009 (8).

Leuprorelin (CAS RN: 53714-56-0)

Leuprorelin has been the object of 33 process patents (25 for synthesis, five for formulation, and three for synthesis and formulation). A Japanese firm, Takeda Chemical Industries, was the first company to file a patent application for leuprorelin, in 1973. Today, the top country is the United States, with nine patents, followed by China, with seven. The chart below shows leuprorelin patenting over time. Just one patent–for its synthesis–has been filed in Brazil, by Syntonix Pharmaceuticals Inc (USA), in 2004. There are six PCT applications filed. Progress of the patents numbers over the years may be known such as: year (patents number)–1973 (2); 1975 (1); 1980 (1); 1994 (2); 1995 (1); 1996 (1); 1997 (1); 1999 (2); 2002 (1); 2003 (2); 2005 (5); 2006 (2); 2007 (3); 2008 (5); 2009 (3).

Somatotropin (CAS RN: 9002-72-6)

Somatotropin has been the target of the highest number of process patents: 394 in all, of which 290 are for its synthesis, 78 for its formulation, and 26 for its synthesis and formulation. The first patent was filed in 1968 by Upjohn Co. There is also one priority patent application held by a Brazilian entity (Comissão de Energia Nuclear), for its synthesis. The leading assignee is Novo Nordisk, with 24 patents, followed by Genentech and Ambrix, with ten apiece. 44 patents have been filed in Brazil, the top assignee being Ambrix (USA), with four (three in synthesis, and one in synthesis and formulation). There are 30 PCT applications currently filed. The leading country is the United States, with 208 patents, followed by Japan (32), China (25) and South Korea (24). Progress of the patents numbers over the years may be known such as: year (patents number)–1968 (1); 1970 (1); 1973 (1); 1975 (1); 1980 (2); 1981 (1); 1982 (6); 1983 (1); 1984 (2); 1985 (6); 1986 (6); 1987 (10); 1988 (9); 1989 (7); 1990 (8); 1991 (4); 1992 (7); 1993 (11); 1994 (8); 1995 (16); 1996 (11); 1997 (12); 1998 (10); 1999 (14); 2000 (21); 2001 (21); 2002 (33); 2003 (35); 2004 (24); 2005 (17); 2006 (23); 2007 (16); 2008 (16); 2009 (28); 2010 (5).

Proteins

Etanercept (CAS RN: 185243-69-0)

There are 25 process patents for etanercept: 16 for its synthesis, five for its formulation, and four for its synthesis and formulation. The first patent was granted in 1989 to Immunex Corporation (USA). Only three countries/regions hold priority patents: the United States, with 21, the European Patent Office with three, and India with one. Two patents have been filed in Brazil by Neose Technologies (USA), both for the synthesis of etanercept. There are six PCT applications currently filed. Progress of the patents numbers over the years may be known such as: year (patents number)–1989 (1); 1997 (1); 1999 (1); 2000 (1); 2001 (2); 2002 (3); 2003 (3); 2004 (1); 2005 (2); 2006 (1); 2007 (3); 2008 (1); 2009 (5).

Procoagulant Factors (CAS RN Not Available)

No patents for the synthesis of procoagulants were found in the Scifinder® and Becker® databases.

Interferons (CAS RN: 9008-11-1)

No patents for the synthesis of interferons were found in the Scifinder® and Becker® databases.

Octreotide (CAS RN: 83150-76-9)

There are 60 process patents for octreotide: 30 for its synthesis, 25 for its formulation, and five for its synthesis and formulation. Sandoz (Switzerland) was the first company to file an application for a patent for octreotide, in 1979. The top country is the United States, with 26 patents, followed by China, with nine. It's possible note a rise in the number of patent applications for processes as of 2000. Two patents have been filed in Brazil for its formulation: one by Quest Pharmaceutical Services (USA) and the other by Akzo Nobel (Netherlands). There are nine patent applications filed under the PCT. Progress of the patents numbers over the years may be known such as: year (patents number)–1979 (1); 1986 (1); 1988 (1); 1989 (1); 1992 (1); 1996 (1); 1997 (1); 1998 (1); 1999 (2); 2000 (9); 2001 (6); 2002 (3); 2003 (2); 2004 (5); 2005 (5); 2006 (6); 2007 (1); 2008 (8); 2009 (3); 2010 (1); 2011 (1).

Botulinum Toxin (CAS RN: 93384-43-1)

Botulinum toxin is the target of 62 process patents: 40 for its synthesis, 14 for its formulation, and eight for its synthesis and formulation. The leading countries are the United States, with 34 patents, and the UK, with nine. The SciFinder® database identifies the first patent has having been granted to Ophidian Pharmaceuticals (USA) in 1989. Nine patents have been filed in Brazil, eight of which are for its synthesis: two by Biotecon Therapeutics GmbH (Germany) and one apiece by the leading assignee, Allergan (USA), Alphavax (USA), Merz Pharma GmbH & Co (Germany), Toxogen GmbH (Germany), Ophidian Pharmaceuticals (USA), and The Speywood Laboratory Limited and Microbiological Research Authority (UK partnership). The other patent is for its formulation, filed by Merz Pharma GmbH & Co. There are 13 patent applications filed under the PCT. Progress of the patents numbers over the years may be known such as: year (patents number)–1989 (1); 1991 (1); 1993 (1); 1995 (3); 1996 (2); 1997 (1); 1998 (2); 1999 (3); 2000 (2); 2002 (4); 2003 (2); 2004 (9); 2005 (4); 2006 (7); 2007 (5); 2008 (1); 2009 (13); 2010 (1).

CONCLUSION

Big data is difficult to work using most relational database management system, howsoever becomes great ally to determine public policies that promote intensity in science research and contribute significantly to innovation and technological development of the countries. Cluster engineering proves effective assistance in this area of knowledge. Nonetheless, the urgent need for treatment of information to aid in the science management and decision makers to improve the health care of their populations.

The intensity with which companies and scientists devote their energy to developing and filing patents to protect their innovations demonstrates how strategically important certain technologies are. In this sense, by observing the progress of certain products over the years, it is possible to deduce the technological importance of the products/processes in question, which indicates where most effort is concentrated. However, technologies that are not protected in a given country or which expire may then be produced generically and incremental innovations may be made, etc.

Looking at group 1 (antiretrovirals), it can be seen that the first patents were granted very recently (starting in the 1990's), which means that only as of the 2010's will the production of generics start to be possible. A clear indication of the trends in technological innovations can also be seen from the patenting patterns.

Group 2 contains the drugs for treating neglected diseases. This group is the target of the fewest patents of all the four groups studied. Only two antibiotics, amphotericin and rifampicin, have been the target of over 40 patents. On average, the others have no more than 11 process patents. This shows the scant interest in investments in technological breakthroughs for this area of public health.

Group 3 contains a significant range of drugs for what are jointly known as chronic non-communicable diseases. It can be seen that over time, the drugs from this group have been the target of a number of process patents for their synthesis or formulation. This intensity demonstrates the degree of technological progress being made by several companies. This could be explained by the prolonged length of time it takes to treat such diseases and the aging of the world population, with a corresponding rise in diseases such as Alzheimer's, Parkinson's, osteoporosis and high cholesterol.

Group 4 contains drugs manufactured by biological pathways. The first patents for monoclonal antibodies were awarded in the 1990s, except nilotinib, for which the first patent was granted in 2002. Amongst the enzymes, there is just one patent for dornase alpha, filed in 1995 by Genetech, while glucocerebrosidase has been the target of multiple patents since 1974. As for hormones and proteins, the first patents date back to the 1990's.

This technology foresight study investigating the number of patents for processes / formulations of products on the SUS list of strategic drugs showed that there are many options open for the production of drugs and/or medications in Brazil, using processes / formulations that are not protected in Brazil. With the listing of these products in directive no. 1284 (published by the Ministry of Health), the Brazilian government has defined them as strategic and priority, indicating that it will maintain its policy to foster the domestic production of these products in the long term.

REFERENCES

Alvares, L., Quoniam, L., & Boutet, C.-V. (2011). Representação cartográfica dinâmica online: análise da atividade editorial em inteligência econômica na França. *Encontros Bibli: Revista Eletrônica de Biblioteconomia e Ciência da Informação, 16*(32), 94–106. doi:10.5007/1518-2924.2011v16n32p94

Antunes, A. M. S., & Magalhães, J. L. (2008). *Patenteamento & prospecção tecnológica no setor farmacêutico.* Rio de Janeiro, Brazil: Editora Interciência.

Bastos, Q. C., Moreira, A. C., & Antunes, A. M. S. (2008). Patentes de compostos químico-farmacêuticos - A proteção de compostos químicos - Farmacêuticos com fórmulas Markush. *Biotecnologia Ciencia & Desenvolvimento, 37*, 60–63.

Beau, F. (2009). *Renseignement, systèmes d'information et organisation des connaissances.* Revue Internationale d'Intelligence Economique, Série Publications Numériques. Retrieved from http://r2ie.fr.nf, juillet

Brasil. (2010). *Dispõe sobre a lista de produtos estratégicos, no âmbito do sistema único de saúde, com a finalidade de colaborar com o desenvolvimento do complexo industrial da saúde.*–Portaria n° 1.284, de 26 de maio de 2010. Altera o Anexo da Portaria n° 978/GM/MS, de 19 de maio de 2008, publicada no Diário Oficial da União n° 99, de 28 de maio de 2008, Seção 1, página 46.

Brasil. (2012). *Portal do governo Brasileiro.* Retrieved from www.brasil.gov.br

Carpineto, C., Osiński, S., Romano, G., & Weiss, D. (2009). A survey of web clustering engines. *ACM Comput. Surv., 41*(3), 17:1–17:38. doi:10.1145/1541880.1541884

Cartaxo, R. J. A. (2011). *Metodologia de priorização para produção nacional dos medicamentos pertencentes à lista do sistema único de saúde.* (Master's dissertation). Instituto Nacional da Propriedade Industrial. Rio de Janeiro, Brazil.

Castro, A. L. S. (2002). O valor da informação: Um desafio permanente. *Revista de Ciência da Informa\ccão, 3*(3).

DND. *i*–Drugs for Neglected Disease initiative. (2012). *Portal website.* Retrieved from www.dndi.org

Gadelha, C. A. G., Costa, L., Borges, T., & Maldonado, J. (2012). O complexo econômico-industrial da saúde: Elementos para uma articulação virtuosa entre saúde e desenvolvimento. *Saúde em Debate, 36*, 21–30.

Huberman, B. A. (2012). Sociology of science: Big data deserve a bigger audience. *Nature, 482*(7385), 308–308. doi:10.1038/482308d PMID:22337040

Huyghe, F.-B. (2008). *Web 2.0: Influence, outils et réseaux.* Revue Internationale d'Intelligence Economique, Série Publications Numériques. Retrieved from http://r2ie.fr.nf

Lynch, C. (2008). Big data: How do your data grow? *Nature, 455*(7209), 28–29. doi:10.1038/455028a PMID:18769419

Magalhães, J. L., Antunes, A. M. S., & Boechat, N. (2012). *Technological trends in the pharmaceutical industry: The matter of neglected tropical diseases–An overview of the research, development & innovation in the Brazil*. Synergia Editora.

Magalhães, J.L., Boechat, N., & Antunes, A.M.S. (2008). An overview of the Brazilian pharmaceutical production status. *Chemistry Today, 26*(4).

Mendes, F. M. L., Cartaxo, R. J. A., & Antunes, A. M. S. (2012). Estruturas-chave na synthesis de antir-retrovirais. *Revista Virtual de Química, 4*, 329–342.

Miller, J. P. (2012). *Millenium intelligence: Understanding and conducting competitive intelligence in the digital age*. CyberAge Books.

Milne, G. W. A. (Ed.). (2002). Drugs: Synonymes & properties (2nd ed.). Inglaterra: Ashgate Publishing Limited.

Palmeira Filho, P. L., Antunes, A. M. S., & Bomtempo, J. V. (2012). The pharmaceutical industry in Brazil: Is innovation the next step for the domestic Industry? *Chimica Oggi, 30*, 87–89.

Pierret, J.D., Dolfi, F., Quoniam, L., Boutin, E., & Riccio, E.L. (2005). Découverte de connaissances dans les bases de données bibliographiques: Modèles expérimentaux autour de la première hypothèse de Swanson. *The International Journal of Information Science for Decision Making, 20*.

Quoniam, L. (2011). Competitive intelligence 2.0. In *Organization, Innovation and Territory*. New York: John Wiley & Sons Inc.

Quoniam, L. (2012). Utiliser les medias sociaux comme un levier d'efficacité de sa veille compétitive. Conférence sur Invitation présenté à 2eme éd.: Marcus Evans: Intelligence Compétitive et Management des Connaissances, mars 27. Paris.

Scifinder Scholar. (n.d.). *A division of the American chemical society*. Retrieved from https://scifinder.cas.org/

Takeuchi, H., & Nonaka, I. (2004). *Gestão do conhecimento*. Porto Alegre, Brazil: Bookman.

The Merck Index. (2006). An encyclopedia of chemicals, drugs, and biologicals (14a ed.). New York: Merck Research Laboratories Division of Merck & Co., Inc.

ENDNOTES

[1]   In Brazil, there are national and transnational private and public drugs laboratories. The public ones are called Official Pharmaceuticals Laboratories and are maintained by the federal or state governments. There are 21 such official laboratories in the country (Magalhães, 2011).

[2]   According to the World Health Organization (WHO) there are 17 such disease, which affect one billion people around the world, and are more prevalent in tropical countries but are a great threat to developed nations, such as tuberculosis, leishmaniasis, malaria, Chagas disease, etc. (WHO, 2010).

3   Process patents can be searched in this database. However, there are many patent documents that do not contain the structures of the chemical structures in the product pathways, and these were not considered in this chapter.

4 The CAS Registry Number is a unique number in the Chemical Abstracts Service database, run by the American Chemical Society.

5   Commercial software owned by Search Technology, Inc.

Chapter 9
Harvesting Deep Web Data Through Produser Involvement

Tomasz Kaczmarek
Poznań University of Economics, Poland

Dawid Grzegorz Węckowski
Poznań University of Economics, Poland

ABSTRACT

Acquiring the data from the deep Web is a complex process, which requires understanding of Website navigation issues, data extraction, and integration techniques. Currently existing solutions to automate it are not ready to cover the whole deep Web and require skills and knowledge to be applied in practice. However, several systems were created, which approach the problem by involving end users who are able to bring the data from the deep Web to the surface while creating solutions for their own information needs. The authors study these systems in the chapter from the end user perspective, investigating their interfaces, languages that they expose to end users, and the platforms that accompany the systems to involve end users and allow them to share the results of their work.

INTRODUCTION

Produsers category is a group of highly involved, creative users of the Web applications, which are also content and functionality creators. The concept was derived from the 'prosumers' term, which describes exceptionally well-informed and critical consumers, that contribute to product development. The notion of 'produsage' was created to distinguish a group of Web users, that engage in "...collaborative and continuous building and extending of existing content in pursuit for further improvement" (Bruns, 2006). There is a number of characteristic features of these users and their activity, discussed in further publications on produsers (Bruns, 2007; Ritzer & Jurgenson, 2010), such as evolution of content that they create, collaborative effort, or their approach to intellectual property. One area where creativity of produsers is employed is deep Web harvesting. Deep Web consists of the databases, that are accessible via Web interface to humans, but poorly indexed by regular search engines and, in consequence, not available through regular Web search. It contains valuable information that is not available on its reverse

DOI: 10.4018/978-1-5225-3163-0.ch009

– surface Web. In order to acquire this information (prices and stock amounts for products, statistical data, bibliographical information and many other types of information) significant knowledge and effort is necessary, that exceeds beyond querying established Web search engines. First, the sources need to be identified or found, then the user has to understand and be able to use the query interface for a given source, and only afterwards, he is able to obtain the Web pages containing actual data, which often require further processing to be useful. Therefore getting the data from the deep Web is a complex process, which requires understanding of Website navigation issues, data extraction, and integration techniques. Due to lack of fully automated tools in the style of search engines, it has to be carried out manually to a large extent. Researchers in the area are constantly looking for solutions to decrease the complexity and provide convenient interfaces to solve the problem. Produsers, with their drive to make their creations accessible and reusable, and higher awareness of the technical issues that need to be solved, engage in surfacing the data and make it more available for a wider audience. Several systems were created, that approach the problem by involving produsers and their higher-than-standard abilities, together with their need for the data which are otherwise inaccessible. We study these systems together with their interfaces and underlying formalisms (to assess the level of knowledge and expertise required to use them) as well as motivation model for the users to take part in such endeavours.

DEEP WEB STRUCTURE

The Deep Web notion (a.k.a. the Hidden Web) refers to Web pages that are not directly accessible by the usage of URLs, but are rather dynamically generated upon HTML form submitting (Madhavan et al., 2008). Web page retrieval from the Deep Web involves filling the form with desired values, which will influence the content of delivered Web page. Apart from the result processing, the challenging part is the automatic determination of HTML form values, that can generate useful outcome.

As it was shown in the studies (He et al., 2007), the Deep Web is very extensive and versatile. In 2007 it was estimated to embrace over 300,000 sites, 450,000 databases and 1,250,000 interfaces, and still expanding at high rate, e.g. increasing 3 – 7 times between 2000 and 2004. The Deep Web pages are distributed across wide range of subject areas, with significant share of e-commerce sites. Although the non-commerce sites are gradually being hidden behind HTML forms. The Deep Web pages are mostly structured, providing the data objects in attribute-value pairs. This feature comes from the back-end structure of Deep Web sites, that use databases running in relational or objective paradigm. As the generated Web pages are the result of database queries, which provides data in highly structured manner, the Web pages design is noticeably influenced by the data structures. This is reflected in table-like layouts or database-style tuples on the Web pages. Also the structure of Deep Web sites tend to be quite shallow (He et al., 2007), about 94% of the Deep Web databases is located not deeper than on the 3rd level of a Website.

The ability of Web crawlers to index Deep Web pages is limited, although some efforts are made in this area. The problem is that new approaches had to be developed, and the large base of research work on surface Web is inapplicable to the deep Web due to differences in using basic building blocks of the Web - pages and links. The classical approaches to Web search were treating the Web as a repository of documents, and hyperlinks in the documents were used to traverse the Web to get access to more documents. Later on, the nature of the Web, being a graph of interlinked documents, was used to improve the search results. Analysing graph structure allowed to improve the accuracy of search. The Web graph structure can be easily analysed for the surface Web, however introduction of Web forms distorts the graph and, if they lead to the deep Web, changes the purpose of links and pages. In the deep Web source the main role of links is not to point at Web resources, but to mimic the structure of the underlying data that is presented in Web pages. Moreover, the sets of interlinked Web pages may change dynamically, in response to changes to the underlying database. Therefore Web objects in the invisible Web are more volatile and not addressable as resources in comparison to objects in the visible Web (an important deviation from this difference is the emergence of so called REST-ful applications, where one of the main underlying assumptions is to expose the data in such a way that each piece has an unique identifier in the form of regular Web URL address). Trying to address a deep Web resource by a link is more prone to ending up with a dead link, because these resources most often are not designed to be addressable by regular URLs.

The above difference together with the fact that deep Web pages rarely are about textual content but rather present data items, invalidates most of the techniques devised to improve Web search results. Additionally major Web search engines may cover about one-third of the Deep Web data (He et al., 2007). Still there is a considerable overlap of the indexes between various search engine, causing that prevalent part of the Deep Web totally hidden. As the possibility of being found with search engine can be perceived as a competitive advantage for Deep Web site owner (e.g. online store), several mechanisms are being used for delivering not indexable data to Web crawlers (Madhavan et al., 2008, 2009). The directory services, that try to index the Deep Web resources, perform even worse, with coverage ranging from 0.2% to 15.6% (He et al., 2007).

Information on the surface Web is mostly textual, while the deep Web includes, to large extent, numerical and properly structured data. Furthermore, information sources on the deep Web are allegedly of higher quality, which stems from the structuring of the information (following the line of thinking: valuable information is likely to be provided in a structured way and the structure itself includes some value). Additionally deep Web enables data owners to limit access to the information by using access rights even on the level of single information item, reflecting the security systems employed in database management systems. Deep Web often serves as a way to expose or give access to proprietary, legacy, or non-Web enabled systems. Various repositories that were accessible until now only via specialized protocols are currently being brought to the Web as deep Web data sources.

It is worth noting that from the end user's point of view, the differences between surface and deep Web are blurry. Most end users do not even realize when they enter the deep Web. Typical activities like searching for products in Web stores, logging in or filling online surveys allow end users to reach for deep Web resources and are as natural as navigating a link, especially with modern approach to build Web sites to resemble desktop applications which buries the differences even deeper.

DEEP WEB HARVESTING

An important problem in addressing the deep Web challenge is its size. There are literally millions of HTML forms on the Web. They are embedded in the Websites in hundreds of languages and are gateways to databases in hundreds of domains. The mechanism capable of harvesting this data would have to be scalable, efficient and extremely flexible. It would have to figure out what to ask for from every of the forms (Khare et al., 2010). This is another challenge, since the product of all possible values that can be entered into the form are countless and only small fraction of them is relevant for a given database (Noor et al., 2011). There is also a problem of form fields that have open domain or continuous domain (like floating point numbers) – some heuristics would have to be applied to be able to query automatically such sources (Madhavan et al., 2008; Mundluru and Xia, 2008).

As prominent researchers in the field state: "There are two common approaches to offering access to Deep-Web content. The first approach (essentially a data integration solution) is to create vertical search engines for specific domains (e.g. cars, books, or real estate). In this approach we could create a mediator form for each domain and semantic mappings between individual data sources and the mediator form. The second approach is surfacing, which pre-computes the most relevant form submissions for all interesting HTML forms. The URLs resulting from these submissions are generated off-line and indexed like any other HTML page. This approach enables leveraging the existing search engine infrastructure and hence the seamless inclusion of Deep Web pages" (Madhavan et al., 2008). The problems with the first approach are that integrating data from various sources requires mapping, which are hard to maintain manually and hard to obtain automatically. Additionally domain boundaries are not fixed or even discrete, which further aggravates the problem. Second, it requires identifying the source domain to ask relevant queries (in a relevant language) which is hard without was background knowledge provided to such mechanism. The second approach, although more suitable for current search engine infrastructure, leads to limited coverage of the deep Web, because it does not work for the sources which require user login or complex user session management. For such sources the URL does not correspond to a resource – they are not addressable in a traditional way.

The problem of harvesting deep Web data shares many characteristics also with general data integration problem. For example, subsequent queries to the source could return partially overlapping result sets, which would require removal of duplicates. Numberous articles are devoted to techniques that optimize the source access patterns in terms of number of queries to ask and their coverage, so that most data is obtained with smallest possible number of queries (Calì & Martinenghi, 2010; Sheng et al., 2012).

END USER DEVELOPMENT

End user development in general ranges from customization of software, through configuration, to end user programming. The goal is to enable end users to develop systems for their needs, however complexity and the amount of knowledge required to do it often overwhelms the users. They need to express their custom build solutions in some language and one of the key problems in the domain is a compromise that has to be made when designing such language – the compromise between complexity and power (Fischer et al., 2004). The problem is learning new language, or the time necessary to spend on studying the language in comparison to the time needed to carry out the task that is to be automated. There languages can be also classified according to their scope and the cost of learning. The goal of end user development is to devise languages with high scope and low learning costs. It seems that there is a limit in reducing the cost if one wants to stick to a certain scope of the language. Machine learning and rule induction techniques were also applied to allow the end users to give examples to the system, that should learn how to carry out the task at hand. However, there is another problem with such approach – the systems built in this way are prone to making errors. It is embedded in their design and unavoidable in general. Only the number of errors can be reduced.

But learning a language is only part of the problem. There are other skills required from the end user to successfully develop a program. One of them is data modelling or tightly involved ability to create abstractions (Fischer et al., 2004). End users are by definition very knowledgeable in their domain and are abstracting within the scope of their domain comes easier. However it is more problematic to carry these abstractions into the domain of language and abstract data structures which are often required by the programming environment where end user development is carried out.

PRODUSERS IN THE DEEP WEB

One of the aspects of end user development is social creativity, where the resources of a single person are not enough to solve the problem and only consolidated input from a number of community members leads to the solution. Two flavours of such activity can be distinguished - when cooperation between the community members is required, or when they can contribute separately. The case of the latter is involved with addressing the problems of deep Web harvesting mentioned above. Due to high number of deep Web sources and problems with full automation of deep Web harvesting a number of systems and languages were proposed to allow end users to automate access to the data sources that are most relevant for them. These approaches allow end users to create wrappers for Web sources. The purpose of a wrapper is to extract from a Web page (or broader – deep Web source) only relevant data, discarding all the content and markup that is not interesting for the end user (advertisements, menus, HTML tags). Over the course of last 15 years, a number of approaches to wrapper creation were proposed. Natural language processing, formal grammars, machine learning, information retrieval or knowledge engineering methods were applied to create wrappers (Teixeira et al., 2002). Only few of them were targeted at end users, while most remained on a level of scientific prototype for which a significant knowledge was required to use.

An important feature of the wrapper is to be resistant to small changes of the Web page structure and content, which occur with different frequency in the Web environment. A wrapper should be capable of extracting information from similar pages, or in the extreme case, from different pages but containing information of the same structure and meaning. A simplest possible wrapper which cuts substrings from the document content based on the number of symbols from the document beginning is not resistant at all and fails almost immediately for common Web sources, whoever from the end user perspective it is easy to create.

Manual development of wrappers has several drawbacks. Most importantly, the wrappers created manually, relying on textual content of the document, are often complex and hard to maintain. Once the document content changes, it is quite probable that the wrapper would have to be updated, resulting in further complications being introduced. It accumulates the burden of subsequent changes finally becoming a undecipherable mixture of cryptic instructions operating on strings. It is also hard to build such wrappers in a component and modular way, or reuse parts of wrappers due to tight connection between the wrapper code and technical solutions for generating documents used in a particular source.

Another important aspect of extracting information from a deep Web source is navigation between the source pages. As mentioned earlier, it is often necessary to pass through a Web form before getting to the pages containing interesting data. Various approaches were also proposed to deal with this issue: hierarchical extraction (Knoblock et al., 2003), use of navigation algebras (Mecca et al., 1998), finite state machines (Kaczmarek, 2006), or Web site graph (Ramanath and Haritsa, 2000; Flejter, 2012).

Scientists were aware of these problems and tried to address them by developing methods for automated wrapper generation, which would decrease the effort required for wrapper creation and maintenance and at the same time increase wrapper effectiveness (Teixeira et al., 2002). We may observe in this domain a similar trade-off to the one in general end user development, between low cost of creating and maintaining a wrapper in a given language and broad scope and effectiveness of the wrapper.

This would not solve however the problem of large number of relevant sources that are available on the deep Web. A full-scale automation is still being pursued in the domain of wrapper creation, yet some solution for the current state of affairs was needed. Therefore, the idea of involving produsers was introduced. A large number of end users could be involved into creating wrappers for equally numerous sources, provided that the wrapper definition language is friendly enough and there are incentives for participating in such coordinated endeavours. The prime incentive could be that of mutual benefit: I am able to use the structured data exposed ('surfaced') by somebody else's wrapper, provided that I share my wrapper online and allow others to use it too.

DEEP WEB HARVESTING SOLUTIONS FOR PRODUSERS

We selected the systems for the survey based on their popularity and availability. The list below reflects, to the best of our knowledge, all of the significant systems currently available on the Web. There might be new systems arising, as the domain is expanding, however their position is probably less established at the moment, than the ones listed here.

Chickenfoot

Chickenfoot is an add-on for the Mozilla Firefox browser (available for download at http://groups.csail. mit.edu/uid/chickenfoot/install.html), which consists of a library, that extends the browser's built-in JavaScript engine, and an runtime environment that allows produsers to run Chickenfoot programs in the browser.

Chickenfoot Language

Chickenfoot users are offered with full-featured scripting language, with prototype-based object-oriented system and extensive set of libraries. Thus, users only need to know the JavaScript, which is quite popular, to create Chickenfoot programs. All JavaScript predefined variables (as window or document) are available within the Chickenfoot, so even JavaScript code, that was meant to be use within Web sites can be reused in Chickenfoot. Additionally, JavaScript mechanisms of Web navigation, submitting forms or changing DOM elements, can extend the Chickenfoot interactions with Web pages.

Chickenfoot scripts are executed with additional privileges to be able to surpass the standard JavaScript limitations, that origin from Web browsers security policy. To be able to extract and integrate data from different Web pages, the scripts have access to the whole browser API, all visited Web sites, as well as to the user's file system.

Pattern Matching

Pattern matching is the basic, yet powerful, feature of the Chickenfoot (Little and Miller, 2006). To operate on an element of a Web page, a kind of unambiguous description of the element is required, for its identification. To that end, Chickenfoot supports two kinds of patterns – keyword patterns and text constraint patterns (Bolin et al., 2005). The keyword patterns are simple expressions, that consist of the name of the Web page element that is being search, and a text label that is associated with that element. For example "search button" matches a button with "search" in its label, and the "query form" looks for a form with a "query" keyword. Sometimes the keyword matching can be even more simplified, when the usage of a Chickenfoot command implies the type of the element that is to be found. For example click("Find") performs the left-click action on a link or button that is labelled with "Find" keyword. The text constraint patterns are built from a set of primitive patterns, matching different types of page content (e.g. paragraph, link, table), a keywords that are bind to the elements, and operators describing placement relations between the elements, like contains, just before, starts. The expressions are derived from an experimental Web browser called LAPIS (Miller and Myers, 2000), and tend to describe the elements with a form close to natural language, e.g. "second row in first table."

For locating individual elements on a Web page the find command can be used, which can get as an argument an arbitrary pattern, which can be both keyword pattern and text constraint pattern. It results with a Match object, which represents first pattern match and allows for iterating over next matching elements. The Listing shows a simple example of the find command usage.

```
// pattern matching test
if (find(pattern).hasMatch) {... }

// pattern match count
find(pattern).count

// iterate over matched elements
for (m=find(pattern);
     m.hasMatch;
     m = m.next) {... }
```

The Match object represents a continuous part of a Web page, allowing for further processing with the use of DOM manipulating methods. For example, an URL address can be retrieved from a found link as follows: find("link").element.href. Also the find command can be nested to be used on a part of a Web page and not to the whole of the document.

Navigation and Web Page Interface

Chickenfoot is also featured with various commands for interacting with Web page interfaces, like buttons or checkboxes, and for navigation management (Rasmussen, 2008). With the use of click command the mouse left-click event can be send to any clickable element, causing the same effect as the usage of regular computer mouse by a Web browser user. For example, on the page http://us.yahoo.com one can perform actions such as:

- Click("Search") – which performs a button click.
- Click("SIGN IN") – which performs a link click.

The keyword patterns do not have to be the exact value of a button or hyperlink label, but it needs to be unique for the page. That is why a command click("SIGN") would be ambiguous, as there is another link called "Sign Up." Additionally, command click can identify clickable image objects with their alt attribute, as well as it can take an attribute in a form of Match object, that results from the find command, like click(find(link just before textarea)).

For simulating user input, the enter command is provided, which can fill a text field on a Web page. Just as the click command, it can identity Web page elements with the use of pattern matching, but the pattern is checked against the caption attribute of all text fields or against nearby labels. This can be used e.g. for the purpose of logging into a Web site – for the it can be done as follows:

```
enter("My e-mail address is:", "user@example.com")
enter("Yes, I have a password:", "mySecret")
```

In the case when a page consist only one text field, which is common for search engines pages, the pattern can be omitted and the field will be chosen automatically, as in this search example for http://search.carrot2.org/stable/search:

```
enter("igi global")
click("Search")
```

Checkboxes and radio buttons can be manipulated with the use of check and unckeck commands, which get a single argument of keyword pattern that describes the fields:

```
check("Yes, I have read the license")
uncheck("Remember me")
```

Also the list boxes or drop-down lists can be accessed in similar manner with the pick command, which searches the HTML code for <select> elements. If the value of an element is unambiguous within the page, only one argument is required for the command: pick("Poland"). Otherwise, an additional parameter is needed to identify appropriate list, e.g. pick("Country", "Poland")

All the elements for clicking and form manipulating can be executed as methods of Match or Document objects, so the interaction can be easily limited to selected area on the page (Bolin, 2005).

```
f = find("Search form")
f.enter("Search field", "Poznan")
f.click("Search")
```

Except from navigating through Web pages with the use of link clicks and form submissions, Chickenfoot scripts can perform direct navigation using go command, for example go(http://www.fsf.org/). The prefix "http://" can be automatically added if the input is not a properly formated URL address. Additionally, Chickenfoot allows for navigation tasks that are common form many Web browsers, like back, forward, or reload.

Web pages can also be processed without displaying their content, one can create additional objects of type Document by executing fetch command: doc = fetch("kie.ue.poznan.pl"). Using the resulting object, it is possible to run any regular Chickenfoot command, e.g. for data extraction and integration, in the context of fetched but not displayed Web page, as shown in the Listing.

```
with (fetch("www.google.com"))
{
    enter(''snowboard'')
    click(''Search with Google'')
    n = find("number just after about").text
}
```

Web pages resulting from executing commands fetch, go or click are being downloaded asynchronously, while Chickenfoot scripts are working. This means that there can be several independent fetches at one time, when one is executed after another, but no one is waiting for the previous ones to finish downloads. Although, if subsequent task needs a reference to already downloaded document, e.g. pick, the execution is suspended until whole document is available. For more flexibility, there are also wait and ready functions for use with Document objects.

Web Page Modification

Chickenfoot offers a set of three simple commands for modification of Web page content and structure: insert, remove, and replace. The insert command takes two arguments – the place in the Web page structure, where the insertion is to be performed, and the content that is to be inserted. In the simplest form, the place can be described by text constraint pattern and the content is an HTML code fragment, e.g. insert("just before button", "Click me!"). The location can also be derived from a Match object but it needs to point to a specific place in the document, rather than a range, or a page element, using before and after commands:

```
b = find("button")
insert(before(b), "<b>Click me!</b>")}
```

The value being inserted can originate from another page, which can be a way of cross-page data integration:

```
table = page1.find("scores")
insert("just after results", table)}
```

The other Web page modification commands can be used similarly. The remove command deletes a region of the page that is defined by a text constraint pattern or a Match object, like remove("advertisement"). While the replace command turns a specified part of the page into another one. It can be used for nesting HTML entities, as in the keyword highlighting example:

```
word = find("UEP")
replace(word, "<b>"+word+"</b>")
```

Individual elements of a Web page interface, like buttons or links, can be generated by Chickenfoot constructors and appended to the Web page. Link is the constructor for creating hyperlinks, it takes two arguments: HTML code snippet that will be displayed inside the link and the event handler, which will be executed on link click event, e.g.: new Link("<i>Show more</i>", showMore). The event handler can be a JavaScript function, as usually in HTML onclick attribute, or a Chickenfoot command. Buttons can be generated accordingly, but with the use of the Button constructor. Other elements of the Web page interface can be added with the use of insert command and appropriate fragment of HTML code, although any JavaScript function located in this code will be executed in the standard JavaScript environment, not as the privileged Chickenfoot code. A Chickenfoot procedure can be added afterwards for any extracted HTML element with the onClick command, for example: onClick(button, showMore).

Programming Environment

The programming environment of Chickenfoot, placed in the side-panel of the Mozilla Firefox browser, is shown in Figure 1.

In the upper part the Chickenfoot editor can be found, which serves for creating and modifying scripts, that can be both simple Chickenfoot expressions and extensive programs with methods and class definitions. The editor simplifies the use of Chickenfoot scripts, since the code is directly accessible and it can be modified at any time, without any complicated procedures to attach the script to a Web page.

In the lower part of the panel one can find a tabbed area with additional settings concerning script execution. The first one, Output is the standard output console for Chickenfoot scripts, it stores the results

Figure 1. Chickenfoot programming environment

of method execution as well as generated error messages. The Patterns tab is designed to help end user (produser) to construct and validate keyword and text constraint patterns, by highlighting the elements that match a pattern on a current page. It also contains a set of primitive patterns, available in the patterns library, that match some HTML elements. The third tab—Triggers—allows for installing Chickenfoot scripts in the browser for regular use. For manual execution, the Chickenfoot scripts can be installed as bookmarks and run with a single click, as any other bookmark. In case of automatic execution, a script has to be associated with an URL pattern, e.g. http://ue.poznan.pl/*. If the URL of a Web page that is being visited matches the pattern, the associated script is executed. The Triggers tab offers an interface for adding and removing scripts that are to be run on defined page, for temporary disabling the scripts and viewing errors (Bolin et al., 2005).

Chickenfoot provides a producer with a platform for extracting data from Web page, for integration data from a different source, for accessing and processing Deep Web pages, that can be result of defined sequence of interaction with standard user interface. It strive for giving a regular user the possibilities and potential of scripting languages for processing Web page content and structure with minimal needs for technical skills in particular language. The solutions, such as JavaScript, Java, or Curl (Müffke, 2001), despite of having long history in Web browsers, they are designed for programmers only. Chickenfoot gives a regular users the possibility of harvesting Web resources, that can be customised for individual needs. It is being realised in three main areas:

- Automation user operations on a Web page interface.
- Integration of data from multiple Web pages.
- Adjusting Web page content and structure.

Additionally, the whole processing is placed in a well-known environment of the Web browser, where one can view and inspect the results of scripts that are being executed, without knowing and analysing the HTML code. It is in contrast to other solutions for Web documents processing, that come out of the Web browser environment, like the ones that are using Perl, Python or WebL languages (Kistler, 1998), as well as screen-scrapping techniques (Maron, 2003), in which it is required to have a good knowledge of a Web page source code and a fluency in HTML analysing. Apart from that, all operations are being done outside the natural context of Web page rendering (i.e. Web browser), which makes it hard to work with HTTP supporting technologies, like cookie files or proxy servers, which are vital for Deep Web applications. The main idea behind the Chickenfoot solution is that the user (or produser) should not be forced to see into the source code of a Web page to be able to process it, customise and automate the interaction (Bolin and Miller, 2005).

Greasemonkey

Similar to the previous solution, Greasemonkey is an add-on module for the Mozilla Firefox Web browser. It allows users to add their own scripts (called user scripts) in the JavaScript language to any Web page, allowing this way for dynamic changes of the HTML code (DHTML). This scripts can influence any element on a Web page, including the content and structure of the Web page, its functioning and the ways of interaction it provides. The Greasemonkey scripts are executed every time a user is visiting the Web page, and the changes made to the Web page are in the immediately included, without showing any difference with comparison to the native scripts coming from a Web server. Greasemonkey programs can be used for adding new functionalities to the Web pages, for adjusting the look and feel of presented content, for integration of heterogeneous data sources and for many other tasks (McFarlane, 2005).

Functionality

Greasemonkey allows for integration of many distributed resources from different Web pages. Thanks to this mechanism, it is possible to retrieve data from Web pages that are backed by different technologies, including Deep Web pages, to extend the content of other Web pages with retrieved data, and to integrate scripts with HTML code, without significant differences between Greasemonkey and the scripts from Web pages authors. Greasemonkey provides the users with means for reusing the whole source code of a page and additional available data, including HTML as well as JavaScript and CSS, data that are being passed to the Web page. Greasemonkey scripts can also make requests to a Web server for receiving new data. Some examples of the Greasemonkey usage can be (Krishnakumar and Chatzopoulou, 2007):

- Filling forms and managing user inputs.
- Parsing Web page content and saving it in a machine readable format.
- Adding the possibility to download files from popular services publishing such files, like http://www.youtube.com.
- Blocking annoying advertisements in social services sites.
- Changing the way an e-mail box looks.

Technical Remarks

The majority of the Greasemonkey scripts is written with the use of JavaScript code that is specific for the Web page, for which the modifications are designed, and are managing the Web page content by the Document Object Model (DOM) interface. A user script is just a regular JavaScript code with some additional information concerning the conditions which trigger the execution of the code. Every user script can have one or many target Web pages, which are described by a list of URL, that contains wildcards in the form of asterisk (*). When a user visits a Web page that correspond with an element on the list, Greasemonkey runs the relevant scripts, which influence the appearance and behaviour of the Web page.

Greasemonkey API

User scripts in Greasemonkey can perform any operation that is available within the JavaScript code. Additionally they can include some specific functionalities that are only available for Greasemonkey scripts, thanks to the Greasemonkey Application Programming Interface (API). For example, the scripts can retrieve external Web resources, with the use of XmlHttpRequest object of the Ajax technology. The resources can then be integrated to any other Web page structure, without the restrictions of the Web browser's security policy concerning same-origin of scripting source code and the HTML document (Pilgrim, 2005b). The Greasemonkey API methods are the following:

- GM_log – writes the script logs to the console.
- GM_getValue – retrieves a configuration value, specific for the script.
- GM_setValue – sets a configuration value, specific for the script.

- GM_registerMenuCommand – adds a value to the User Script Commands menu.
- GM_xmlhttpRequest – constructs HTTP request.

Limitations

User scripts, in any way, can neither harm the computer that are being run at, nor can corrupt the data on the hard drive, but improperly written source code can slow down the browser, and even—if it is written for that purpose—it can spy on the users, logging their activities in the browser. That is why users are warned to be careful while installing and using scripts that comes from unknown or untrusted sources. With the use of such scripts it is possible to steal user passwords from the logging forms and sending it to a remote server, as well as other undesirable actions, that can be harmful for the user (Pilgrim, 2005a).

Smart Bookmarks

The system of Smart Bookmarks was implemented as a side bar for Web browsers. With the use of this mechanism, Web users can save links to visited Web pages in a form of bookmarks, return to previously saved pages and to view and edit the graphical representation of saved bookmarks. Smart Bookmarks continuously monitors and records the interactions between a user and subsequent visited Web pages, and running in background it stores the data about the interactions. When a Web page is saved in form of a bookmark, the system automatically defines the sequence of actions that are need to be generated to come back to the Web page, and saves the sequence in the bookmark.

After creating a bookmark, subsequent events, that are stored within it, can be replayed with a simple click, which effects in executing an appropriate navigational path for generation the original Web page that was bookmarked. Additionally, the user can indicate which values that are being used during the navigation path traversal, suppose to be set manually before the automation mechanism starts.

To be more expressive in terms of indicating which action are to be executed after running selected bookmark, the user is provided with a graphical representation of the bookmark. It consists of images of every operation, highlighting the part of the page to which the operation refers. The Smart Bookmarks system allows users for easy editing of the bookmarks, after being created – it is possible for a user to fully control the code that is to be executed or to dynamically edit a bookmark by recording the user actions that are being performed.

There is an issue in terms of automatic recording of user actions and replaying them afterwards, concerning the side effects, which the user would not want to repeat. For example, when the user buys a book in an online store or subscribes to a news group, he/she is not willing to repeat this action when a bookmark is replayed. That is why the graphical representation allows for significant restriction of the number of unwanted operations and the mistakes made during the automation.

Action History Recording

While a user visits Web pages, the Smart Bookmarks system continuously records the user's actions. However, unlike the standard browsing history that can be found in a Web browser, Smart Bookmarks records not only the URLs but also the events, that refer to clicks or form filling. The events registering is being done with the use of event listeners, that are installed internally into browser, and can record:

- **Click:** Mouse click on a button or a hyperlink.
- **Change:** Change of a value inside a HTML form, e.g. a change of a text value in a text box.
- **Load:** New Web page fetch.

When any of such events occurs, it is recorded in the action history, together with a description of the Web page element that the event referred to (e.g. a button or drop-down list). This description consists of several elements, that are further used for bookmark generation:

- A label, describing a Web page component.
- An XPath expression, that identifies the placement of the element inside the DOM tree model of the page.
- A picture of the element, together with some context.

The label of the element is usually extracted from the Web page content, and if the element contains its own label, as in case of buttons or hyperlinks, the label is constructed based on the value of the text and value attributes, or the alt and title attributes, in case of images. For check boxes and radio buttons, the label is looked for, similarly to the algorithm, that can be found in the Koala system (Little et al., 2007):

1. At first, the system checks whether one of the previous sibling of the element has a not hidden and not empty text.
2. If the label is not found after the first step, in the same way the ancestors' previous siblings are being checked.

This algorithm is effective for cases in which the label is located left of, or above the element.

As an alternative form of object representation, the system generates an XPath scheme, which is represented as a sequence of elements' names with the positions of descendants. In this way, a path is created, that leads from the root of the DOM tree to the given element. An example of such path is the following:

```
/html/body/table[2]/tr[3]/form/div[0]/input
```

While creating a bookmark, such XPath scheme is used in case when the label cannot be determined.

Finally, the Smart Bookmarks system generates also a screen picture, that represents the action performed – it retrieves the appropriate element graphic and stores it as a PNG bitmap. For events such as load the picture contains the whole Web page, while for other actions it is only the main element, which is influenced by the event together with 50-pixel surrounding. Figure 2 shows an exemplary bookmark representation, with action graphics.

Separate history is saved for every opened tab in a browser and when a tab is closed, the history is removed. The history is not permanently saved until the user creates a bookmark in the system.

Creating a Bookmark From Action History

When a user creates a Smart Bookmark to the given page, the system has to extract, from the whole history, the sequence of actions that will lead back to the page. It is true that the whole history could serve

Figure 2. Smart bookmarks example

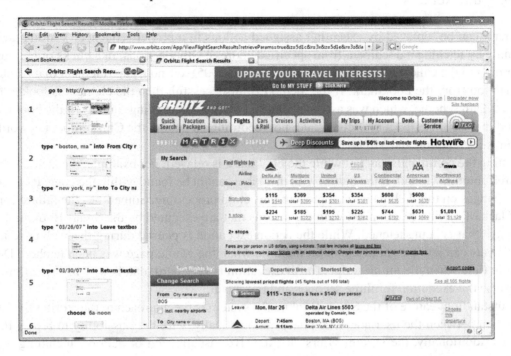

as the needed action sequence, since it begins from a fixed position (an URL address, from which the tab started) and it ends on a desired Web page. However, the whole history can be very long, that is why the system tries to find the shortest set of actions from the end of the history, that will successfully result in the desired Web page. It is done by finding the closest fixed and reachable URL from the history, form the latest. While visiting those pages, the cookie files are temporarily blocked, to simulate the situation in the future, when they will be not available.

The URL address is reachable if the fetch generates the same or very similar Web page, that the user got, when the action history was made. Even reachable pages can be slightly different when re-fetched in short period, e.g. some different advertisement can be rendered. The Smart Bookmark system analyses the changes, and assumes that they should be relatively small, comparing to the whole page. To compare two versions of a Web page, the distance between DOM trees is calculated (Marian, 2002), which indicates how many operations of insertion, deletion or replacing the DOM elements is required to transform the original version to the one that was re-fetched. The cost of insertion or deletion subtree D is measured as a sum of weights of nodes in the subtree, denoted by wD, while the element node has a weight 1, and the text node containing n characters is given as $log\ n$. The holistic change between the original page S and the re-fetched page P is the sum of weights of elements that differs between two documents, divided by the sum of weights of the both documents' trees ($wS+wP$). If S and P are identical, the measure takes the value 0, which means lack of changes. However, if S and P are totally different, that the smallest set of changes to transform S into P includes deleting all elements of S and replacing them with whole P, the measure has the value 1. The Smart Bookmarks system uses the value of 0.1 as a boundary to assess, whether the pages are similar enough. If the value of the measure is less than 0.1, than the URL address is assumed to be reachable.

Replaying the Actions

A bookmark can be replayed by executing assigned actions in a proper sequence. Visiting an URL is done simply by fetching a document from specified address. Other actions, like clicks or text input, are run according to the Chickenfoot algorithm (Bolin et al., 2005) to find a page element that is relevant to the description from the bookmark. If the method is unsuccessful, then the element is looked for with the use of XPath scheme, which was assigned during bookmark recording. Finally, if the bookmark was edited and the user inserted a new command, not recording an action, the Chickenfoot keyword search algorithm is used (Little and Miller, 2006).

Executing the commands can fail while the bookmark is relayed. For example, the action of clicking the "Search" button will fail, if the button with that label cannot be found within the page. It can be result of some changes on the Web pages that prevent the action processing. Sometimes the failure can be the result of lack of synchronisation between the actions that are executed by the Smart Bookmark system and the page that is being fetched. While the action execution is paused during the Web page fetching, some elements can still be not available in the time when the whole page was been fetched. Detecting the point in time when the initial scripts finish execution is very hard, that is why in case of failure, the system pause the execution for three seconds and ties again.

The outstanding feature of the Smart Bookmarks system is the approach to the storing the sequence of interaction between the user and Web pages, automatically, with the possibility to replay them and customise. Additionally, the system offers an extensive visualisation of actions, including text help, screenshots, and animations. The rich graphics is designed for greater user involvement, ease of understanding the mechanisms and sharing the bookmarks. Also the text representation of the bookmark action, allows user to edit the bookmark behaviour, without the knowledge of script languages (Hupp and Miller, 2007).

Co-Scripter

CoScripter is a system for recording, automating, and sharing processes performed in a Web browser. An example of such process could be logging in to a photo sharing portal, searching for photos on some topic (specified in the script) and print the first one that appears in the results. It is available as a plugin for Firefox browser, which displays a sidebar with subsequent steps of the process to be performed. The tool can record the steps by capturing user's behaviour, but it is also possible to enter or edit the steps manually. Similar to previous solutions, it supports Web actions such as:

- Navigating to a Web address.
- Clicking on buttons.
- Entering values into Web forms.
- Navigating thorough available links.

The commands refer to the elements that they should be performed on by the names of the elements which are visible to the browser user, rather than by some abstract addressing scheme. The advantage, from the users' point of view, is that the language for the commands is based on a simplified restricted English, with easily understandable meaning and syntax of commands. Co-Scripter is also flexible in interpreting several synonyms for Web page elements (see Figure 3).

Figure 3. Co-scripter during execution of a script

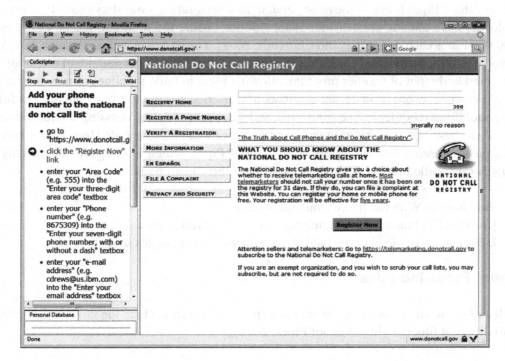

An important feature of the whole system is the Web portal for sharing the recorded scripts - it is open and by default all scripts created by Co-Scripter are shared if the user chooses to save them to the portal. Currently there are more than 6000 scripts recorded, which were created in the last 5 years. A big advantage of Co-Scripter is its ability to mimic user's steps on a live Web pages, which solves numerous technical problems, which occur, if a deep Web harvesting system is not simulating the browser behaviour correctly. However, Co-Scripter lacks any support for data extraction or integration, and therefore needs to supplemented in these respects by the tools for digging out the data from the Web pages. It is also of limited applicability for large-scale data harvesting, since it lacks extensive support for Web site navigation templates.

Yahoo! Pipes

Yahoo! Pipes is a tool that has a very different nature from all previously mentioned solutions. As one can read on the Yahoo! Pipes Website "Pipes is a free online service that lets you remix popular feed types and create data mashups using a visual editor. You can use Pipes to run your own Web projects, or publish and share your own Web services without ever having to write a line of code." (Yahoo! Pipes, 2012). As a mashup-related solution, Yahoo! Pipes allows for manipulating and composing various data sources, especially from the Web, or functionality to the end of creating new services or sources of processed data that can be published in return. A common task for mashups is extracting data from several feeds, combining them and filtering according to some criteria, and publish them on a Web page (Stolee and Elbaum, 2011).

The Yahoo! Pipes is one of the most popular mashup solution – statistics shows that more than 90,000 developers have already created individual solutions using the tool, and the pipes are executed over 5,000,000 times each day (Jones and Churchill, 2009). The name, as well as the idea of Yahoo! Pipes, is derived from Unix command-line tool called pipe, which can connect a standard output of one program with a standard input of another program, allowing users to build pipelines of transformation, in which data going out from one module, are automatically inserted as a input data for another module. Similarly, the Yahoo! Pipes modules can be connected, and the results of data processing at one module can be send to another phase of transformation that can take place in another module (Jones and Churchill, 2009).

Figure 4 presents the user interface of Yahoo! Pipes, which is designed for creating and editing mashups (also called pipes). The editor consists of three main parts:

- **Side Menu:** With the list of available modules.
- **Canvas:** For placing, connecting and setting up selected modules.
- **Debugger:** For viewing the output information from modules in real time.

Yahoo! Pipes Modules

The list of all available modules can be found in the side menu, where the modules are grouped according to different functionality (Yahoo! Pipes, 2012):

Figure 4. Yahoo! pipes user interface

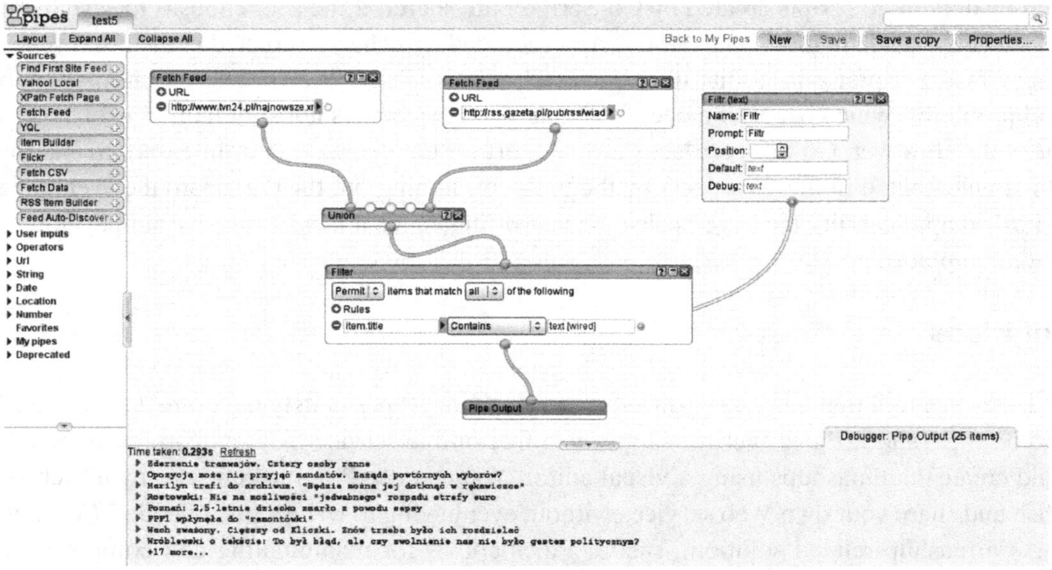

Sources

Are data sources (such as Yahoo Search, Atoms, XML or CSV documents) that return an RSS feed.

User Inputs

Are input fields that your Pipe's users can fill in at runtime.

Operators

Are basic features like foreach, sort, count, and filter.

URL

Contains modules for building and manipulating URLs

String

Contains modules for handling strings

Date

Contains modules for manipulating dates

In this menu, one can find also a list of favourites pipes, including pipes from other users, that can be placed in the pipeline just as every other building block element, that would be chosen from module list. With this feature, processing of a pipe can get more complicated without disturbances of low-level views – a pipe can integrate, multilevel pipes, which hide complex processing details in one object.

Building a Mashup

Using Yahoo! Pipes, building a mashup application is rather straightforward. The main work area is the canvas, which serves for assembling individual modules in a coherent processing pipeline. Modules from the side menu can be drag-and-dropped on the canvas area, where they can be manually or automatically arranged. Using a mouse, one can establish a connections between input and output ports of each module, in this way allowing the data to flow between the connected modules. Modules can also have some configuration parameters, which can be set by hand or the value can be derived from previous processing results of another modules. The canvas allows users to work with subpipes – the previously created pipes that can be used as regular module component. With the use of the provided interface, one can arrange the subpipes as a whole, or can go deeper in the subpipe structure to edit its internal processing behaviour. All modules should eventually be connected with the output module, which aggregates all processing results, and represents the outcome of the whole pipe (Yahoo! Pipes, 2012).

While creating a pipe, the debugger console extremely helpful, as it can show data that is to be processed on every stage of the pipeline. Clicking on a module element, that is already placed on the canvas, one can see the debugger console refreshing and showing the results, that the module will deliver, with the use of data that it finds on the Web or receive from the other modules. Using the debugger console, a produser can inspect in real time the performance of the solution that is being built (Yahoo! Pipes, 2012).

Sharing Pipes

Each pipe (mashup application) is defined by a unique identifier, and is available under specified URL. Any user can publish own pipes in the public directory, where other users can find it, view and reuse it. Yahoo! Pipes follow an open security model, where any user can access any pipe if he/she knows the pipe's URL. This policy is intended to foster the learning-by-example process among produsers, and to increase the level of reusing the best pipes. Users can use the "View Source" option to any pipe application, to be able to inspect internal structure of the pipe. This way users can share their in-development pipes, view and modify each other pipes, and collaboratively debug problems. If a pipe is modified by a non-owner, a local copy of the pipe is created, allowing a parallel work on any type of application (Jones and Churchill, 2009).

Yahoo! Pipes is providing produsers with powerful tool for harvesting Web resources. One can create a processing pipelines, edit it and debug in real time. A wide range of supported input data formats makes the tool extremely flexible, and the open security model fosters reliable and full-featured application development.

DISCUSSION AND CONCLUSION

All the systems gathered in this survey share one feature: they enable sharing of the deep Web data acquisition procedures created by produsers. Other than that, they are intended for slightly different use cases and differ in approach and features. Chickenfoot is primarily a Web automation tool, which can be used for mining the deep Web. Therefore it is targeted at ease of navigation on the Web pages but extraction of the data, it's integration and further processing requires programming effort and is less supported.

The primary use case for Greasemonkey is Web page customization using JavaScript, which directly impacts the accessibility of the solution. Its capabilities allow to prepare scripts to mine the deep Web; however, there are little specific tools, that would support integration of the data and processing. Its strength is the portal to share scripts and ease of adoption for new users - they are managed by the browser plugin.

Smart Bookmarks were targeted at first for solving the bookmarking problem on the dynamic Websites, that inhibit traditional linking by URL. Similar problem is present in the deep Web mining activity – data is often not accessible to the outside world under a given URL. Therefore Smart Bookmarks can be used to ease access to the deep Web, yet due to its primary goal is less suited to process the obtained information.

Co-Scripter is similar to Chickenfoot in that it is primarily Web automation tool, which is especially targeted at ease of use. It fits perfectly to automate the access to the data and sharing of the created automation scripts (again through a portal open for the users). To close the processing loop it would be necessary however to supplement it with data extraction tools, that would actually make the data available for other applications.

Yahoo! Pipes on the other hand is an information stream processing tool, which is particularly good at processing, integrating, and filtering the streams of data or textual information from various sources. Slightly less suited for connecting and navigating to arbitrary Websites; it excels at exposing the processed data.

The solutions for harvesting deep Web data presented in the article fall into one category of tools – that allow for end user development of scripts to navigate and extract information from Web pages or feeds. Although the internal mechanisms of the tools differ, they share common characteristics. They provide commands to execute common operations for navigation and extraction, allow for simple data integration or transformation, and provide little means for cooperation among the users, except from possibility to share the scripts publicly. They are thus targeted for specific audience – the users that can satisfy their information needs from deep Web sources. The approaches could be extended at least in two directions. One is adding semantics to the extracted data; the other is surfacing deep Web resources. It would be beneficial for search engines to be able to index the data surfaced with the scripts created using the described tools, however without the added meaning, the data is even less useful, than the partially surfaced deep Web sources. It would be also useful to mine the library of scripts created by community of users for common access patterns, source domains, or meaningful queries. For that to happen, open sharing platform would be necessary and the incentives and motivation for produsers to contribute their work for the benefit of accessing deep Web.

REFERENCES

Bolin, M. (2005). *End-user programming for the web*. (Master's thesis). Massachusetts Institute of Technology, Cambridge, MA.

Bolin, M., & Miller, R. C. (2005). Naming page elements in end-user web automation. In *Proceedings of the First Workshop on End-User Software Engineering*, (pp. 1–5). New York, NY: ACM.

Bolin, M., Webber, M., Rha, P., Wilson, T., & Miller, R. C. (2005). Automation and customization of rendered web pages. In *Proceedings of the 18th Annual ACM Symposium on User Interface Software and Technology*, (pp. 163–172). New York, NY: ACM.

Bruns, A. (2006). Cultural attitudes towards communication and technology. In *Towards Produsage: Futures for User-Led Content Production*. Tartu, Estonia: Academic Press.

Bruns, A. (2007). Produsage. In *Proceedings of the 6th ACM SIGCHI Conference on Creativity & Cognition, C&C '07*, (pp. 99–106). New York, NY: ACM.

Calì, A., & Martinenghi, D. (2010). Querying the deep web. In *Proceedings of the 13th International Conference on Extending Database Technology, EDBT '10*, (pp. 724–727). New York, NY: ACM.

Fischer, G., Giaccardi, E., Ye, Y., Sutcliffe, A. G., & Mehandjiev, N. (2004). Meta-design: A manifesto for end-user development. *Communications of the ACM, 47*(9), 33–37. doi:10.1145/1015864.1015884

Flejter, D. (2012). *Semi-automatic web information extraction*. (PhD thesis). Poznań University of Economics, Poznan, Poland.

He, B., Patel, M., Zhang, Z., & Chang, K. C.-C. (2007). Accessing the deep web. *Communications of the ACM*, *50*(5), 94–101. doi:10.1145/1230819.1241670

Hupp, D., & Miller, R. C. (2007). Smart bookmarks: Automatic retroactive macro recording on the web. In *Proceedings of the 20th Annual ACM Symposium on User Interface Software and Technology*, (pp. 81–90). New York, NY: ACM.

Jones, M. C., & Churchill, E. F. (2009). Conversations in developer communities: A preliminary analysis of the Yahoo! pipes community. In *Proceedings of the Fourth International Conference on Communities and Technologies*, (pp. 195–204). New York: ACM.

Kaczmarek, T. (2006). *Integracja danych z głebokiego internetu dla potrzeb analizy otoczenia przedsiebiorstwa*. (PhD thesis). Poznan University of Economics, Poznan, Poland.

Khare, R., An, Y., & Song, I.-Y. (2010). Understanding deep web search interfaces: A survey. *SIGMOD Record*, *39*(1), 33–40. doi:10.1145/1860702.1860708

Kistler, T. (1998). Webl - A programming language for the web. In *Computer Networks and ISDN Systems* (pp. 259–270). London: Elsevier. doi:10.1016/S0169-7552(98)00018-X

Knoblock, C. A., Muslea, I., Lerman, K., & Minton, S. (2003). *Accurately and reliably extracting data from the web: A machine learning approach* (pp. 275–287). Academic Press. doi:10.1007/978-3-7908-1772-0_17

Krishnakumar, A., & Chatzopoulou, D. (2007). *Greasemonkey script extensions to web pages*.

Little, G., Lau, T. A., Cypher, A., Lin, J., Haber, E. M., & Kandogan, E. (2007). Koala: Capture, share, automate, personalize business processes on the Web. In *Proceedings of the SIGCHI Conference on Human Factors in Computing Systems*, (pp. 943–946). New York: ACM.

Little, G., & Miller, R. C. (2006). Translating keyword commands into executable code. In *Proceedings of the 19th Annual ACM Symposium on User Interface Software and Technology*, (pp. 135–144). New York, NY: ACM.

Madhavan, J., Afanasiev, L., Antova, L., & Halevy, A. Y. (2009). *Harnessing the deep web: Present and future*. CoRR, abs/0909.1785.

Madhavan, J., Ko, D., Kot, Ł., Ganapathy, V., Rasmussen, A., & Halevy, A. (2008). Google's deep web crawl. *Proceedings of VLDB Endowment*, *1*(2), 1241–1252.

Marian, A. (2002). Detecting changes in xml documents. In *Proceedings of the 18th International Conference on Data Engineering*, (p. 41). Washington, DC: IEEE Computer Society.

Maron, M. (2003). *Screen scraping with finite state machines. project for programming techniques*.

McFarlane, N. (2005). Fixing web sites with greasemonkey. *Linux Journal*, (138), 1.

Mecca, G., Mendelzon, A. O., & Merialdo, P. (1998). Efficient queries over web views. *Lecture Notes in Computer Science*, 1377.

Miller, R. C., & Myers, B. A. (2000). Integrating a command shell into a web browser. In *Proceedings of the Annual Conference on USENIX Annual Technical Conference, ATEC '00*, (p. 15). Berkeley, CA: USENIX Association.

Müffke, F. (2001). The curl programming environment. [–ff.]. *Dr. Dobb's Journal, 26*(9), 66.

Mundluru, D., & Xia, X. (2008). Experiences in crawling deep web in the context of local search. In *Proceedings of the 2nd International Workshop on Geographic Information Retrieval, GIR '08*, (pp. 35–42). New York, NY: ACM.

Noor, U., Rashid, Z., & Rauf, A. (2011). A survey of automatic deep web classification techniques. *International Journal of Computers and Applications, 19*(6), 43–50. doi:10.5120/2362-3099

Pilgrim, M. (2005a). *Dive into greasemonkey.*

Pilgrim, M. (2005b). *Greasemonkey hacks: Tips and tools for remixing the web with firefox.*

Ramanath, M., & Haritsa, J. R. (2000). Diaspora: A highly distributed web-query processing system. *World Wide Web (Bussum), 3*(2), 111–124. doi:10.1023/A:1019233713818

Rasmussen, B. (2008). *Rewrite the web with chickenfoot.*

Ritzer, G., & Jurgenson, N. (2010). Production, consumption, prosumption: The nature of capitalism in the age of the digital 'prosumer'. *Journal of Consumer Culture, 10*(1), 13–36. doi:10.1177/1469540509354673

Sheng, C., Zhang, N., Tao, Y., & Jin, X. (2012). Optimal algorithms for crawling a hidden database in the web. In M. Ozsoyoglu (Ed.), *Proceedings of the VLDB Endowment (PVLDB)*. VLDB.

Stolee, K. T., & Elbaum, S. (2011). Refactoring pipe-like mashups for end-user programmers. In *Proceedings of the 33rd International Conference on Software Engineering, ICSE '11*, (pp. 81–90). New York: ACM.

Teixeira, J. S., Ribeiro-Neto, B. A., Laender, A. H. F., & da Silva, A. S. (2002). A brief survey of web data extraction tools. *SIGMOD Record, 31*(2), 84–93. doi:10.1145/565117.565137

Yahoo! Pipes. (2012). Retrieved from http://pipes.yahoo.com

KEY TERMS AND DEFINITIONS

Deep Web: Consists of the databases, that are accessible via Web interface to humans, but poorly indexed by regular search engines and, in consequence, not available through regular Web search. The Web pages generated from these databases are not present in search engines because the engines do not know how to query such data sources.

End-User Development: Involving end-users in extending or changing the application in some way when it is already deployed and used. It ranges from customization of software (change of layout, look or small changes of functionality), through configuration (selection of functionality), to end-user programming (writing macros, plugins, extensions).

Mashup: An application combining either data or services available on the Web. The data are usually provided by services too. A mashup is usually created using some high-level language or a specialized platform. Many mashups operate by putting some data with geographical context on a map or combining data from a number of sources and put them on a chart.

Produsers: A group of highly involved, creative users of the Web applications, which are also content and functionality creators and contribute to the Web by posting, commenting, publishing video, extending applications, contributing data or even creating and making applications available on the Web.

Surface Web: Consists of Web pages that can be obtained from regular search engines. Some pages may belong both to surface Web (because they were exposed or surfaced by publishing links on some other page) and deep Web (because they are generated from a database based on a query).

Web Mining (Web Harvesting): An activity of acquiring content or data from the Web. It usually involves identifying the source of data, understanding its scope and query capabilities, using source query interface, navigating through the returned pages and extracting data into some structured form.

Web Source: A page or a whole Website exposing textual content or data in some semistructured form. A free text article does not constitute a Web source usually. Examples: blog with a number of posts, forum, RSS stream, news portal, e-shop, statistical data Website, Web service or REST-full service.

Wrapper: A program written to mine data or content from a particular Website. It is tightly bound to this Website and hardly applicable to any other source. At the same time, it should be resistant to small changes of the Web page structure and content, which occur within a Website from time to time.

This research was previously published in Frameworks of IT Prosumption for Business Development edited by Małgorzata Pańkowska, pages 200-221, copyright year 2014 by Business Science Reference (an imprint of IGI Global).

Chapter 10
Web Harvesting:
Web Data Extraction Techniques for Deep Web Pages

B. Umamageswari
New Prince Shri Bhavani College of Engineering and Technology, India

R. Kalpana
Pondicherry Engineering College, India

ABSTRACT

Web mining is done on huge amounts of data extracted from WWW. Many researchers have developed several state-of-the-art approaches for web data extraction. So far in the literature, the focus is mainly on the techniques used for data region extraction. Applications which are fed with the extracted data, require fetching data spread across multiple web pages which should be crawled automatically. For this to happen, we need to extract not only data regions, but also the navigation links. Data extraction techniques are designed for specific HTML tags; which questions their universal applicability for carrying out information extraction from differently formatted web pages. This chapter focuses on various web data extraction techniques available for different kinds of data rich pages, classification of web data extraction techniques and comparison of those techniques across many useful dimensions.

INTRODUCTION

The information available on the World Wide Web has grown to several zettabytes according to Richard Currier (2013). Estimated size of pages indexed in Google in the last three months is shown in Figure 1. The structured information such as lists and tables containing the target data of interest is embedded in semi-structured web pages which complicates automated extraction.

Many mining applications depend on the data available in this huge repository. The process of automatically retrieving data from websites is known as web data extraction aka Web scraping or Web harvesting. Applications include business intelligence, product intelligence, market intelligence, data analytics, data mashup, meta-search, meta-query etc. Information on WWW is available in different forms. The classification is shown in Figure 2.

DOI: 10.4018/978-1-5225-3163-0.ch010

Figure 1. Size of pages indexed in Google (http://www.worldwidewebsize.com/)

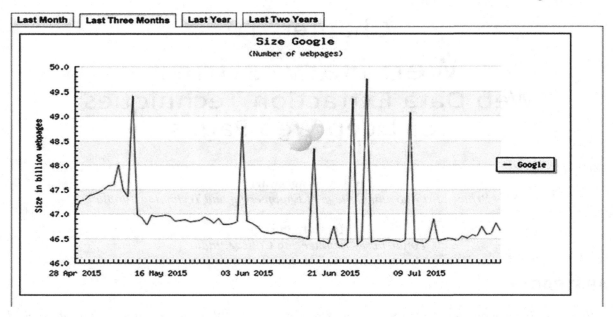

Figure 2. Classification of different forms of information available on WWW

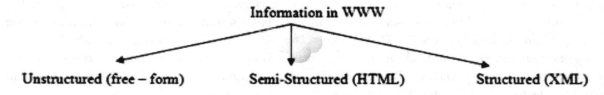

Techniques used for information extraction depends upon the representation of information in WWW. Text mining is a domain which focuses on processing unstructured information. On the other end, extraction of data from structured representation such as XML document can be handled easily using several APIs for ex., JAXP. Our focus is on semi-structured information presented in the form of HTML pages. HTML (Hyper Text Markup Language) is used initially for formatting data and therefore the information is not structured which makes the extraction task cumbersome. Many techniques have been proposed to perform information extraction from HTML pages. Detailed discussion of such techniques is available in the next section.

HTML documents can be represented in various forms. 1. String/Text – Source code of HTML document where a web page is represented using its source code. Certain data extraction tools like OLERA and Trinity etc. use the source code and apply string comparison techniques for information extraction. 2. DOM tree – Many techniques in the literature such as Thresher, DELA, MDR, TPC etc. use DOM tree representation for extraction of information from HTML pages where an HTML page is represented as a tree of HTML elements. 3. Visual (CSS Box) – When the HTML documents are rendered by the browser, each tag is represented as a CSS box. The position and size of box are used by some techniques such as ViDE, ViPER etc for information extraction. 4. Rendered form – it represents the form after being rendered by browsers and tools like Chickenfoot makes use of it for web data extraction which enables user without knowledge in HTML code of the website, to extract data. Figure 3 represents the various representations of HTML documents.

Presentation of Data in HTML Pages

Information is presented in various forms such as tabular form, lists (ordered list, unordered list, definition list, etc.), paragraph, etc. Most of the techniques in the literature are designed for information extraction from a specific presentation format, for ex., Google Set by Tong et al. (2008) is used for extraction from a list, whereas techniques like WWT found by Gupta et al. (2009) are used for information extraction from tabular format and many techniques in the literature such as IEPAD, MDR, OLERA, DELA, DEPTA, ROAD RUNNER etc. are designed for extracting data records. All these formats are in general referred to as web list according to Gatterbauer et al. (2007).

Web List Definition

As defined by Gatterbauer et al. (2007): A list is a series of similar data items or data records. A list is a series of similar data items or data records. A list can be either one-dimensional or two-dimensional; in both variants, no hierarchical or other semantic relationships in between individual list items are implied except for a possible ordering of the items.

Many techniques are designed for information extraction from data rich pages. Therefore, we are going to survey the techniques available for information extraction for different types of data rich pages. There are two types of data rich pages:

Figure 3. Various representations HTML documents

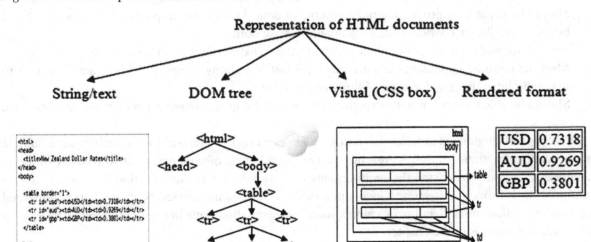

- List pages:
  - ○ Contains a list of one or more data records.
  - ○ Data records may be flat or nested.
  - ○ Similar data records compose a data region.
- Detail pages:
  - ○ Contains details about a single object.
  - ○ Can have relevant as well as other irrelevant information.

Deep vs. Surface Web

Search engines can be used to retrieve pages that are indexed. Crawlers are used to crawl through the links and get the appropriate pages that match the search keywords. All these pages are part of surface web. We get more appropriate information when we do a keyword search in the target web sites directly through form submission. In the back end, the database is queried which results in retrieval of appropriate records which are embedded in HTML template pages and returned to the end user as search results. For ex, book search in Amazon.com using keywords java programming. These template generated web pages are termed as deep web pages and search engines are not capable of retrieving them. Web data extractors play a key role in extracting structured data embedded in template generated web pages which can be fed to many data analytics and data mining applications.

Challenges of Web Data Extraction

Web data extraction systems makes use of techniques derived from Natural Language Processing, Information Retrieval and Machine Learning. Web data extraction system should be applicable to multiple application domains. i.e. it should be domain independent.

Challenges of web data extractors are:

- Requires high degree of human intervention to improve accuracy.
- There exists trade off between level of automation and level of accuracy.
- Should be capable of processing huge volume of data. This is very important for competitive and business intelligence where time critical analysis are done.
- Should not violate the access policies when trying to extract data from social web.
- Machine learning approaches require huge amount of training samples and is a laborious task to manually label them and it is also highly error-prone.
- Should be able to cope up with structural changes that happen frequently with www applications.

This chapter is organized as follows. Section 2 elaborates various state-of-the-art techniques available for web data extraction. Section 3 presents the two broad areas of application of web data extraction techniques. Section 4 discusses the requirements of a web data extractor. Section 5 presents various traditional IR (Information Retrieval) evaluation metrics and custom metrics. Section 6 lists commercial web data extraction tools. Section 7 explores future research directions in the field of web data extraction. Section 8 concludes the chapter.

WEB DATA EXTRACTION TECHNIQUES

General Picture of Web Data Extraction Task

Data in web pages are presented in user-friendly formats and therefore, it is difficult for automated processed to retrieve them, since the structuring of data is done in various ways. The process of extracting data from unstructured or semi-structured web pages and then storing in structured format in RDBMS or other structured file formats such.csv,.xls etc. is known as web data extraction. The general picture of web data extraction is shown in Figure 4.

Data available on world wide web, embedded in HTML pages are referred to as Web data. Web data extraction techniques are broadly classified into two types:

- Data Extraction from free-form text.
- Data Extraction from semi-structured documents.

Data Extraction from Free-Form Text

Tools under this category learn extraction rules and it is used for data extraction from free-form text. All these tools use filtering, POS tagging, semantic tagging in order to determine extraction rules. Most widely used tools in the literature, under this category are:

Figure 4. General picture of web data extraction

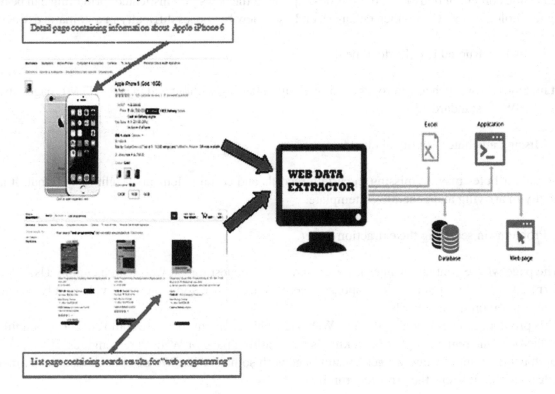

- **WHISK by Soderland (1999):** It is a tool which uses training examples for learning a set of extraction rules. It iteratively learns rule starting from the empty set. It requires manual tagging of attributes. Extraction rules are expressed in the form of regular expression and the technique is capable of extracting multiple records from a document.
- **SRV by Freitag et al. (2000):** This tool can extract only one record from a document. It uses simple or relational token oriented features. Simple feature maps a token to any individual value where as relational feature maps a token to another token. Used for field-level extraction.
- **RAPIER (Robust Automated Production of Information Extraction Rules) by Califf et al. (2003):** It automatically determines extraction rule when provided the input document and a template indicating the data to be extracted. It extracts only one record of a document. It can be used to perform field-level extraction.

Data Extraction From Semi-Structured Document

Web Pages are written using HTML (HyperText Markup Language). HTML is semi-structured which might introduce error during extraction process.

Possible Errors include:

- Presentation of unstructured data.

Structure or format helps user to easily understand and extract information and it helps data extraction tools greatly to find out target of extraction task. For ex, digital newspaper. Each row has a headline followed by the content or body that contains description of the news. Sophisticated formatting can be done using technologies like CSS which enhances end user view but poses difficulty in automatic extraction.

- Badly constructed HTML documents.

It includes errors such as improper nesting of tags, start tag without end tag etc. HTML pages should follow the W3C standard.

- Missing attributes / optional elements

Some attributes may be missing in certain records and certain elements might be optional. It adds difficulty in arriving at a generalized template.

- Problems in selecting the extraction target.

The page whose content changes for each and every request for ex, web search engine. Ususaly we perform a keyword search and the response web page may have some pictures, videos, advertisement etc., depending on the keywords.

This problem can be shown choosing a Web page which content structure could change depending on some factors. One real example of this kind is the resulting page of Web search engines. If we perform a search using an input value we get a result page with some entries. We need to choose the extraction sample such that it keeps the error to a minimum.*f*.

- Problems using scripts or dynamic content.

Dynamic contents can be created using web 2.0 specifications like AJAX, javascript etc. It cannot be treated just like static HTML content because changes happen at any time when the page is loaded. The change can be structural or visual and it may introduce errors during data extraction process which should be taken care of.

Therefore, an ideal web page for data extraction should have the following characteristics:

- It should have structured data representation f.
- HTML code should obey the W3C standard.
- It should not contain nested data elements.
- Used Flash or scripts should not contain data to be extracted f.
- CSS Styles should be used to format elements.

Data Extraction from semi-structured documents can be classified further across four different dimensions:

- Based on the number of input pages it requires.
- Based on the level of human intervention, it requires. (Manual, Wrapper Induction/ semi-supervised, automatic/Unsupervised).
  - **Manually Constructed:** It requires a very high level of human intervention.
  - **Supervised:** Labeled sample is provided based on which wrappers are induced automatically. Therefore, the level of human intervention is high.
  - **Semi Supervised:** Templates are deduced automatically. But human intervention is required for labeling the attributes. Therefore, the level of human intervention is medium.
  - **Unsupervised:** Very little or no human intervention is needed.
- Based on the features or techniques used for data extraction.
- Based on level of extraction.

Level of extraction can be any of these four categories: field-level, record-level, page-level and site-level. The four categories along with the classification of techniques based on level of extraction are shown in Figure 5.

Semi – structured data embedded in web pages are formatted using different HTML tags. We are interested specifically in data regions. Usually, a collection of similar items is formatted as a list using tags such as <OL> (Ordered List), <UL> (Unordered List) and <DL> (Definition List) or as tables (<TABLE>) or as data records using (<DIV>,<SPAN> etc.). In general, they can be referred to as web list according to Gatterbauer et al. (2007).

Representation of Web List and Web List Extraction Techniques

A Web list can be in the form of lists, tables or data records. A web page with different types of web lists is as shown in Figure 6. Navigation list takes us to a similar set of web pages containing data regions of interest. Data region contains one or more data records. Data record contains one or more data items.

Figure 5. Categories of levels of extraction

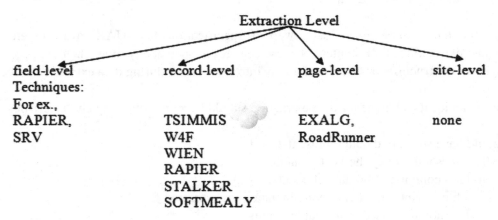

Figure 6. A web page containing different types of web list

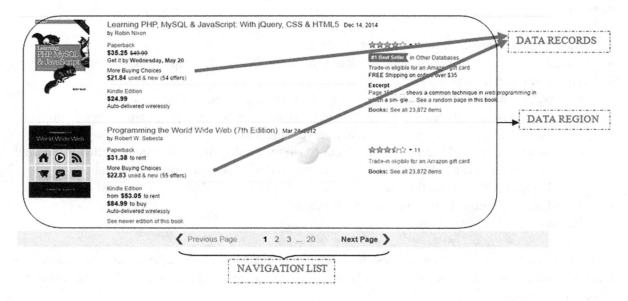

List and Web Tables Extraction Technique

Google Sets by Tong et al. (2002): This tool is used to generate lists, given a small number of examples of list items. It uses HTML tags to identify lists in a page. It can be used to extract records enclosed within UL, OL, and DL and H1-H6 tags.

Lerman et al. (2001) proposed a technique for automatic data extraction from lists and tables found in web pages. It is based on unsupervised learning algorithm that exploits the regularities found in structure of lists and organization of data for carrying out the extraction task. The limitation of their approach is that the technique requires several pages for identifying list.

Table detection: Wang and Hu (2002) had concluded from their studies genuine tables in most web pages are those enclosed between <table> and </table> tags. They have used a machine learning approach based on layout features, content type feature and word group feature for table detection and extraction.

WWT: This is an unsupervised technique developed by Gupta et al. (2009) for extracting rows from unstructured web lists and to combine multiple lists into a single unified merged table.

Data Region Extractors

Sleiman et al. (2013), have given a detailed survey of several region extractors. The survey is about study of region extractors, along different dimensions such as domain for which it is designed, input to the tool, algorithm used, effectiveness etc. We are going to use that as a foundation for exploring widely used characteristics, when selecting a data extractor for performing IE tasks. Data region consists of a collection of data records. Usually data records are the subject of interest during data extraction. Figure 7 represents an overall classification of data region extractors.

Manually Constructed Extractors/ Web Wrappers

In this category of tools, the user should have profound programming knowledge in order to create wrappers manually using languages such as PERL or specially designed languages.

TSIMMIS by Hammer et al. (1997): In this system, a specification file written using some declarative language which tells where the data of interest is located and how it should be represented as objects, is given as input and it outputs the extracted data in the form of OEM (Object Exchange Model).

W4F by Sahuguet et al. (2001) (World Wide Web Wrapper Factory): It is a JTK used in wrapper generation for which an HTML document from which data need to be extracted is given as input and it outputs NSL (Nested String List) structures. First, the input HTML document is converted into a DOM tree and then extraction rules are applied to the parse tree to obtain NSL structure which is exported to the higher-level application according to the mapping rules.

Supervised Extraction Techniques

It requires comparatively less human intervention compared to previous technique. Here, the user need not manually create a wrapper. Instead, a set of labelled, web pages, is given as input and the system produces wrapper automatically. Some of widely used tools based on this technique are:

WIEN by Kushmerick et al. (1997) (Wrapper Induction for information ExtractioN): In this paper, the authors introduced wrapper induction, which can construct wrappers automatically by generalizing from example query responses. They have used the PAC model which is used in determining bounds on

Figure 7. Classification of data region extractors

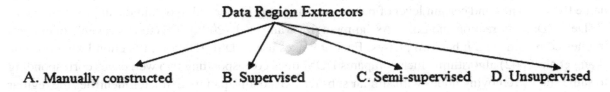

the number of examples needed. They have used oracles for labeling examples. They also used HLRT, a wrapper class designed for retrieving information expressed in tabular form.

SoftMealy by Hsu et al. (1998): Hsu et al. introduced FST (Finite State Transducer) in order to handle variant extraction structures. FST is made of body transducer which is used to extract the data region and tuple transducer for extracting data records within a data region.

STALKER by Muslea et al. (1999) (Learning Extraction Rules for Semistructured, Web-based Information Sources): This technique is also applicable to differently structured documents and the authors have introduced a concept called Embedded Catalog (EC) formalism. EC of a web page is represented in the form of a tree structure where the leaves represent the attributes to be extracted and the internal nodes represent the list of tuples. It uses a list iteration rule in order to divide the list into individual tuples.

Semi-Supervised Extraction Techniques

Unlike the supervised technique in which labeled examples are needed, these tools require post-effort (i.e. manual labeling after extraction). These techniques are suitable for record-level extraction. User's effort is needed to specify extraction targets using GUI. Therefore, these techniques are classified under semi-supervised extraction techniques.

IEPAD by Chang et al. (2001) (Information Extraction based on PAttern Discovery): This tool is built upon the hypothesis that web pages generated from single server-side template will be having data records structured in a similar way. Thus, this technique uses repetitive patterns to learn template from a set of unlabeled pages. It uses PAT (Pattern Tree) data structure to discover repetitive pattern corresponding to the web page.

OLERA by Chang et al. (2004): It generates extraction rules from roughly labeled examples. It is capable of learning extraction rule, even from a page containing a single data record. This technique uses multiple string alignment technique to find the extraction pattern.

Thresher by Hogue et al. (2005): Users should highlight the data region of interest and label them. It uses tree edit distance, whereas OLERA by Chang et al. (2004) uses string edit distance to find the extraction pattern. Tree edit distance between two trees A and B is the cost associated with the minimum set of operations needed to transform A to B. Here, the set of operations can be node insertion, removal and replacement.

Unsupervised Extraction Techniques

These techniques neither require labeled examples nor user interaction for wrapper induction. Certain un-supervised techniques are used for page-level extraction, such as RoadRunner by Crescenzi et al. (2002), EXALG by Arasu et al. (2003), FivaTech by Kayed et al. (2001) whereas certain others like DeLa Wang et al. (2003) and DEPTA by Zhai et al. (2005) are used for record-level extraction. Since, these techniques do not require user to select data regions of interest, they are extracted automatically by identifying and removing templates. Determining schema is cumbersome and it is up to the user to name the attributes and certain level of post-processing may be needed to obtain the appropriate data.

DeLa (Data Extraction and Label Assignment) by Wang et al. (2003): This tool is capable of extracting nested records and it has two phases: First, it makes use of DSE (Data-rich Section Extraction) by Wang et al. (2002) algorithm which compares DOM trees corresponding two web pages corresponding to same site by removing nodes with similar sub-trees. Secondly, pattern extractor identifies the regular expression. The regular expression is used to discover data objects and then some heuristics such as form element labels and table column names are used to label the columns of the data table.

RoadRunner by Crescenzi et al. (2002): This tool uses ACME (Align, Collapse, Match and Extract) technique in order to induce wrapper from a set of web pages by identifying similarities and differences between them. The outcome of the step is a wrapper which is a pattern used during data extraction.

EXALG (EXtraction ALGorithm): Arasu et al. (2003) presented an approach EXALG for data extraction from template generated web pages which consists of two major steps: i. Differentiating roles and ii. Equivalence classes (EC). According to the authors, if a same token occurs along different paths, then their roles will be different and tokens having the same frequencies of occurrence belong to the same equivalence class. Finally, ECs are used to build the template which is used for data extraction.

DEPTA by Zhai et al. (2005) (Data Extraction Based on Partial Tree Alignment): The authors used visual information for segmenting data records in a web page and used a novel technique called partial tree alignment for extracting data items from identified records. They have used a measure called string edit distance as in OLERA by Chang et al. (2004) for string comparison. The edit distance of two strings, s1 and s2, is defined as the minimum number of mutations required to change one to another where the mutation can be i. change a letter, ii. insert a letter, iii. delete a letter.

MDR by Liu et al. (2004) (Mining Data Records): This technique is used for retrieving data records. It is based on the hypothesis that data records pertaining to similar data objects are formatted using similar HTML tags. It has 3 steps:

- Constructing DOM tree of the page.
- Using a heuristic that each data region should have at least two or more data records with similar structures for data region identification.
- Extracting data records within data regions.

MDR by Liu et al. (2004) is found to be a useful technique in data region extraction and many researchers NET by Liu et al. (2005), ViPER by Simon et al. (2005), PAT by Zhai et al. (2005) used MDR as part of their work.

TPC Miao et al. (2009) (Tag Path Clustering): This technique can be applied only to web pages that satisfy the assumption that a data region should contain data records that are rendered similarly, visually aligned and contain atleast 3 HTML tags. It has the following steps:

- Construct DOM tree and determine DOM paths for every node.
- Determine the triple (p,s,O), where p is a DOM path, s is a visual signal vector which is a binary vector; it contains 1 in position i if the DOM path to the tag at position i is same as p and 0, otherwise and O is a group of individual occurrences of nodes whose DOM path is p.
- Construct a similarity matrix representing visual signals and apply spectral clustering by Ng at al. (2001) to group identical visual signals. Then, find a maximal ancestor for each cluster.
- Identify nested data records using the heuristic that if a visual signal occurs at each point where data records are separated, then the text enclosed by this visual signal represents the relationship between these data records.

STAVIES by Papadakis et al. (2005) (A System for Information Extraction from Unknown Web Data Sources through Automatic Web Wrapper Generation using Clustering Techniques): This technique is used in the automatic data region discovery and data record extraction. It is based on the assumption that the most relevant information is available in leaf nodes and data records have identical structure. HTML code is converted to its strict XHTML version and DOM tree is built. Then, the leaf nodes are extracted and the data region is located by performing hierarchical clustering of leaf nodes and the clusters identified within the data region are returned as data records.

DSE by Wang et al. (2002) (Data-Rich Section Extraction): This technique is based on the assumption that all web pages in a website have similar headers, footers, menus etc. whereas they differ in data regions unless they belong to the same section. After the user provides an input document, then the technique finds a document that can be reached from this document based on a similarity measure computed using URLs. Then, both web pages are transformed into DOM trees. It then, searches for matching node in DOM trees. Removal of those nodes results in two pruned trees constituting data regions. This technique is used in DeLa by Wang et al. (2003).

MSE by Zhao et al. (2006) (Multiple Section Extraction): This technique is based on the assumption that data records in a data region appear consecutively and their content lines are not similar. It is given a set of documents as input. It makes use of two algorithms, namely: Multirecord Extractor (MRE) and Data Section Extractor (DSE) by Wang et al. (2002). MRE is used to discover data regions and DSE by Wang et al. (2002) is used to identify data records composing data regions.

RST by Bing et al. (2011) (Record Segmentation Tree): This technique assumes that similar data records present contiguously form a data region and data records within a data region are formatted using similar tags and they all share a same parent node in the tag tree. The advantage of this technique is that it can handle embedded region and nested region. And also, the authors have introduced a new measure called token-based edit distance. The technique has two major steps, namely record region detection and record segmentation and it determines the similarity between subtrees dynamically and the similarity measure takes into account, the features of the current record region.

FiVaTech by Kayed et al. (2010) (Page-level web data extraction from template pages): It is an unsupervised approach for carrying out page-level extraction task. First, it converts the input web pages to DOM trees. Then, it performs tree merging, which constitutes four steps, namely peer node recognition (i.e. nodes with same names are compared to identify whether they are peer subtrees), multiple string alignment, tandem repeat mining and optional merging. The final step is a schema and template deduction and data extraction.

Trinity by Sleiman et al. (2014) (On Using Trinary Trees for Unsupervised Web Data Extraction): The authors have devised a technique for data extraction based on the hypothesis that templates are shared across web pages and when templates are removed, we get the needed data. The algorithm for construction of trinary tree requires atleast two web pages. It compares the string representation of web pages to find the longest matching substring. The portion of the string before the matching pattern is considered as prefix. The portion of the string in between the matching pattern and its next occurrence is considered as separator and the portion of the string after the matching pattern is considered as suffix. At each step, a node is expanded to the above three nodes. Once the trinary tree is constructed, regular expression is deduced and then, it is used for extracting data.

Table 1 represents the comparison of different data region extraction techniques along different dimensions such as number of input pages required, the level of human intervention needed, features used for data extraction, level of extraction and limitations.

Visual Information Based Extraction Techniques

These techniques utilize several visual clues for data region identification and extraction.

NET by Liu et al. (2005) (Flat and Nested Data Records Extraction): Liu et al. proposed a technique for extraction of both flat and nested records. According to their technique, first a tag tree is built using visual clues and then a post-order traversal of tree is performed in order to match sub trees using tree edit distance method and visual clues. Finally, data records are found and data items are aligned.

VIPS by Cai et al. (2003) (VIPS: a Vision-based Page Segmentation Algorithm): This technique uses visual clues such as position, background color, foreground color etc. It involves traversing DOM tree enriched with visual clues and the authors have used 12 heuristics, few to say, if the background color of a node differs from its child nodes then that child is a sub-region; if a table is not having any sub-region, then the adjacent cell also won't be having sub-region and so on. Once sub-regions are identified, they are organized to form tree structure representing the containment relationships and then the tree is returned as output.

VIDE by Liu et al. (2010) (A Vision-Based Approach for Deep Web Data Extraction): It uses Vision based Data Records Extraction technique aka ViDRE by Liu et al. (2006). First, it creates a tree of data regions using VIPS by Cai et al. (2003). Secondly, it finds the largest region present lowest in the tree. Then, the technique groups similar sub-regions using similarity function which is calculated based on features of images, links and text. Then it finds the bounding rectangle for each group. It then creates extraction rule which is given by (x,y,w,h) where x, y represents location of the region and w, h denotes width and height of the bounding box.

ViNTs by Zhao et al. (2005) (Visual Information aNd Tag structure): Learns rules and extract data records from web documents returned by search engine. ViNTs is used for wrapper generation in many search engines for ex., it is used in AllInOneNews by Liu et al. (2007) metasearch engine. Input to the system is set of web pages with atleast four data records and a web page without any data record. First, the input documents are rendered using a browser and css box model of each node is used to extract content lines. A suffix tree is used to find a repetitive pattern that occurs atleast 3 times. Each pattern is used as a separator for dividing the input web page into several regions. It, then learns the extraction rule and finally it selects and merges rules.

Hybrid Information Extraction Techniques

HyLiEn by Fumarola et al. (2011) (Hybrid approach for automatic List discovery and Extraction on the Web): The authors have made a survey of existing list extraction techniques and have shown that existing techniques is not suitable for carrying out general list extraction task by Weninger et al. (2010). They have concluded that DOM based processing alone is insufficient and therefore, they proposed a hybrid approach using visual alignment of list items and non-visual information such as DOM structure of visually aligned items. First, generate the rendered box tree structure for the input web page. Then, generate candidates using visual features and pruning is done using DOM tree structure to eliminate false candidates and finally, list is extracted and returned.

APPLICATIONS

Based on real time applications, Web data extraction techniques can be broadly classified into two types:Organization or Enterprise level techniques and Social web level techniques.

At the organization level, it is useful in performing business engineering, competitive data analysis and helps in making critical business decisions.

At the social web level, it can be used to determine market analysis of human buying behaviors at a large scale. Social media and online social network data can also be analyzed which has significant use in business intelligence, product intelligence and competitive intelligence.

Organization or Enterprise Level Application

Personalized Advertising

End-user will be presented with thematic advertisements along with the content of the web page, ensuring increase in interest towards the advertisement. Ex. Google Adsense.

Customer Help Desk

Usually customer care receives lot of unstructured information in the form of queries, emails, customer phone conversation transcripts, customer review sites etc. Extracting information, classifying and storing them in structured form helps organizations in making important business decisions.

Building Relational Database

It involves collecting information from multiple online sources and integrating them. For ex, Commercial product or services companies want to compare pricing other aspects with their competitors.

Business Intelligence and Competitive Intelligence

Baumgartner et al. (2009) analyzed how to apply Web data extraction techniques and tools to improve market analysis. They discussed about how to acquire the unstructured and semi-structured information using the Lixto Suite and then to perform ETL (Extract, Transform and Load).

Social Applications

Due to the advancements of web 2.0 specifications, many websites evolved which led people to share thoughts, opinions, photos, recipes etc.

Social Networks

Social network consists of millions of people representing relationships between nodes where nodes may represent an entity, groups or organization and edges reprensents relationships between nodes. Ex., Facebook, Twitter, Flikr etc. Social networks are useful to both academic and industrial community.

Therefore, Social Networks stay as a field where we can apply web data extraction systems. Applications include obtaining information from relationships between nodes, learning distribution of ties and checking the theory of six degrees of separation, mining patterns from statistical data, finding heuristics. Another interesting application is social bookmarking, a new kind of knowledge sharing, allows user to define hierarchy known as folksonomy and the bookmarks are referred to as tags. Extracting information from social bookmarks is much faster compared to HTML-aware extraction systems

Comparative Shopping

One of the interesting application of Social Web which is used by many commercial organizations is the comparative shopping. It provides a platform to compare prices, features, user experience etc. These services rely on Web data extraction using websites as input.

Mashup Scenarios

A mashup is defined as a website or web application that integrates content of a number of websites of interest. The content is obtained via APIs, embedding RSS or Atom Feeds. To access deep web, complex form queries and web services containing several operations encapsulating application logic can be used.

Opinion Mining

User opinions are expressed in natural language in blogs in the form of reviews, comments, tags, charts etc. Since it is expressed in natural language, they are unstructured and therefore extraction of such information poses serious problem.

Mining of Citation Databases

Web data extraction can be applied to citation databases like Google Scholar, CiteSeer etc. in order to collect scientific digital publications, extract references and citations and build a structured database where users can compare, count number of citations, search etc.

REQUIREMENTS OF A WEB DATA EXTRACTOR

Robust

Web pages structure and content changes frequently and the wrapper should be able to extract data despite those changes. When the wrappers are hand-crafted, we can use the human intelligence to create robust wrappers. In order to create robust wrappers in case of wrapper induction, it should be based on rendered model rathen than source code for ex., class selector, id selector etc.

For ex, consider the following source code,

```
<div id="item" class="content">
 <h3 id="name"> Item Name </h3>
```

```
<div> Dealer <strong id="dealer"> Dealer </strong> </div>
<div> Cost: &rp; <strong id="price"> 100 </strong> </div>
</div>
```

A human developer may decide to use #item (id selector) for selecting the region representing an item rather than class selector.content because ID selector is unique. An induced wrapper won't be able to recognize this and also, different shopping websites may use different names. Thus, induced wrappers should be based on rendered model so that even if the structure and layout changes, the labeling remains the same i.e. price will always be labeled with Price. Technologies like HTML5 contains semantic tags like <time>, <header>, <footer> etc which adds meaning to the document and paves way to design robust wrappers.

Session Management

Web data extractors if integrated onto browser then it handles session management automatically. Session management is needed in websites where multiple requests are made by the client within a session and server wants to keep track of user requests. In case of any disruption, user will be able to proceed from where he has left rather than starting from the scratch. Cookies are small files stored in client machine used for session management. For ex, a client after logging in to a site successfully, the server sends a response which contains cookies that will be stored in the client side. Subsequent requests from the client to the same server includes the stored cookies which are used by the server for identifying the client. In case of disconnection, the server won't ask the client to log on again. When a web data extractor is part of a browser, it need not handle sessions since they will be handled by browser itself whereas if it is itself a HTTP client then it is important that it should support cookies and session management.

Websites With Dynamic Content

Certain websites use scripting languages to present the content dynamically i.e page responds to user initiated events like onmouseover, onmousemove etc. It is easy for designing a wrapper for static web page compared to dynamic web page. In case of dynamic pages, extractor needs to execute scripting code and capture events.

Data Modeling

Extracted data can be structured into different formats such as CSV, XML, RDBMS etc.

Performance

Extractor should not consume too much of resources. Also, it should not be too fast. Otherwise, it results in sending too many requests to the same server resulting in overload which might result in legal action.

User Friendliness

Wrappers should be user friendly. If the end user is not a technical expert, then wrappers should have a rich GUI that helps user in choosing the extraction targets. Certain wrappers require profound programming skills.

$$\text{Prescision (P)} = \frac{tp}{tp + fp} \quad \text{Recall} \left(R \right) \frac{tp}{tp + fn} \text{ F1 (or) F- measure} = \frac{2PR}{P + R}$$

Table 1. Comparison of data region extraction techniques across different dimensions

Data Region Extraction Systems	No. of Input Pages Needed	Level of Human Intervention	Features Used for Data Extraction	Limitations	Level of Extraction
TSIMMIS	Single page	Very High, requires sound programming knowledge to write wrappers.	Extraction rules	Requires reconstruction of extraction rule depending upon the structure of the web page	Record-level
W4F	Single Page	Very High, Extraction rules expressed using HEL (HTML Extraction Language) to be written manually.	DOM tree, Extraction rules.	Requires higher level of human intervention.	Record-level
WIEN	Single page	High, Requires manual labeling.	Uses a family of six wrapper classes	Attribute Ordering is required. Therefore, cannot handle missing attributes and permutation of attributes.	Record-level
SOFTMEALY	Single page	High, Requires manual labeling.	Finite State Transducer (FST) for handling missing attributes and attributes permutations.	Cannot handle pages having different structure.	Record-level
STALKER	Single page	High, Requires hand crafting extraction rules.	Uses Node Extraction Rule and List Extraction Rule.	Uses multiple pass scans to handle missing attributes and attributes permutations	Record-level
IEPAD	Single page with multiple records	Medium, Requires manual tagging of extracted template pattern.	PAT trees (binary suffix tree used for identifying repetitive pattern) are used. Center Star Algorithm is used to align strings.	Can be used only for record level extractions. Cannot be used for pages containing single record.	Record-level
OLERA	Single page	Medium, requires labeled examples.	Uses multiple string alignment technique in order to generalize the extraction pattern.	User need to mark the information block of interest.	Record-level
THRESHER	Single page	Medium, requires user highlight the information of interest and label them.	Uses tree edit distance between DOM subtrees for wrapper generation.	Requires substantial manual effort.	Record-level
DELA	Multiple pages with multiple records	Low	DOM trees for Data-rich Section Extraction. Pattern Extractor.	Applicable only for web pages containing more than one data record.	Record-level
ROADRUNNER	Multiple Pages	Low	ACME matching technique is used.	Requires multiple pages for template deduction.	Page-level
EXALG	Multiple Pages	Low	Differentiating roles and equivalence classes (EC) are used.	Requires multiple pages for template deduction.	Page-level

continued on following page

Table 1. Continued

Data Region Extraction Systems	No. of Input Pages Needed	Level of Human Intervention	Features Used for Data Extraction	Limitations	Level of Extraction
DEPT	Single page with multiple records	Low	HTML TAG tree is used. String Edit Distance is used for substring comparison.	Applicable only for web pages containing more than one data record. Cannot handle nested data records.	Record-level
MDR	Single page with multiple records	Low	DOM tree and combinatorial algorithm is used.	Applicable only for web pages containing atleast two or more data records. HTML tag dependent. Does not align data items.	Record-level
TPC	Single page with multiple records	Low	DOM tree and spectral clustering technique are used	Works only for web pages that satisfy the assumption that data records in a data region are rendered similarly and visually aligned and contains atleast 3 HTML tags.	Record-level
STAVIES	Single page with multiple records	Low	DOM tree based. Hierarchical clustering of leaf nodes is done.	Assumes that most information is available in leaf nodes. Suitable only for pages containing identical data record structure.	Record-level
DSE	Single page with multiple records.	Low	DOM tree based.	Requires atleast two web pages with similarly structured data regions.	Page-level
MSE	Multiple pages.	Low	Uses two algorithms: MRE – Multi-Record Extractor and DSE – Dynamic Section Extractor.	Requires atleast two documents.	Record-level
RST	Singe page with two or more records.	Low	DOM tree based. Token-based tree edit distance is used to calculate similarity.	Web page should have more than one data record.	Record-level
FivaTech	Multiple pages containing single or multiple data records.	Low	Tree matching, Tree alignment and mining techniques.	Does not work for malformed HTML pages. Effectiveness highly depends on peer nodes identification.	Page-level
TRINITY	Multiple pages containing single or multiple records.	Low	Trinary tree is obtained by comparing web pages which are used for deducing regular expression.	User has to perform semantic labeling. It does not works well with templates having alternating formatting for the same data.	Record-level

Evaluating Accuracy of Web Data Extraction

The data set used for determining efficiency of various web data extraction techniques are not domain specific. Data rich pages from various domains such as real estate, job search, shopping, sports, movies, restaurants etc. are used. Two commonly used metrics in order to evaluate effectiveness of any information retrieval approach are precision and recall. F-Measure is calculated using the precision and recall values. The traditional metrics used for measuring effectiveness of information extractors are shown in Table 4.

Data Sets commonly used include RISE pubic repository, repositories used in EXALG by Arasu et al. (2003) and RoadRunner byCrescenzi et al. (2002) techniques.

Table 2. Comparison of visual clue based and hybrid data region extraction techniques across different dimensions

Web Data Extraction Systems	No. of Input Pages Needed	Level of human Intervention	Features Used for Data Extraction	Limitations	Level of Extraction
NET	Single	Low	Post order traversal of visual based tree is used for Flat and Nested record extraction.	Works only for data records.	Record-level
VIPS	Single page with more than one record.	Low	Visual Layout information.	Browser dependent and presence of many small images results in extraction of too many regions.	Record-level
VIDE	Single page with 2 or more records.	Low	Visual rendering of DOM tree boxes, namely AF (Appearance Feature and Layout Feature) are used. Some non-visual information such as same text, frequent symbols and data type are also used.	Cannot handle multi data region deep web pages.	Record-level
ViNTs	Multiple pages with 4 or more records.	Low	Visual rendering of DOM tree boxes.	Cannot be applied to web pages having fewer than 4 data records.	Record-level
HyLiEn	Single page with multiple records.	Low	Visual alignment of items and non-visual information such as DOM structure.	Cannot handle noisy data.	Record-level

For Data Region Extractors

Precision (P) is defined as the ratio of number of regions extracted correctly to the total number of extracted data regions. Recall (R) is defined as the ratio of number of data regions retrieved correctly to the total number of data regions available. F-Measure is defined as weighted harmonic mean of precision and recall. F-Measure aka F1= 2 (P*R)/(P+R).

For List Extractors

Precision (P) is defined as the ratio of number of lists extracted correctly to the total number of lists extracted. Recall (R) is defined as the ratio of number of lists extracted correctly to the total number of lists present in the web page.

Custom Metric

Liu et al. (2010) have proposed a metric called revision in order to measure the performance of an automated extraction algorithm. It represents the percentage of web databases for which the automated extraction solution fails to achieve perfect extraction.

Commercial Web Data Extractors

Table 3 lists the features of various commercial web data extractors:

Table 3. Data extraction tool features

	Input Variables	Script Usage	Output Formats	Complexity	Dynamic Pages	Single / Multiple Pages	Error Treatment	Execution Time	HTML / Other Formats
Dapper	Yes	No	XML, RSS, HTML, Google Gadget, Netvibes Module, PageFlake, Google Maps, Image Loop, Icalendar, Atom Feed, CSV, JSON, XSL, YAML, email	Low	Yes	No	No	Very Good	HTML
XWRAP	No	No	Java	Medium	Yes	No	No	Good	HTML
Lixto	Yes	Yes	XML	Medium	Yes	Yes	No	Very good	HTML
Web Harvest	No	No	XML	Medium	Yes	No	No	Good	HTML
Win Task	By script	Yes	File, Excel, DB	Medium	No	Yes	No	Good	HTML and other formats
Automation Anywhere	No	No	File, Excel, DB, EXE	Low	No	Yes	No	Good	HTML and other formats
Web content extractor	No	No	File, Excel, DB, SQL script File, MySQL script File, HTML, XML, HTTP submit	Low	No	No	No	Poor	HTML

Table 4. Tradional metrics to characterize the effectiveness of information retrieval

Expected		
Extracted	tp – true positive	fp – false positive
	tn – true negative	fn – false negative

Dapper

This tools helps in generating fully server based wrappers and also allows building reusable wrapper repository. It uses ML techniques(Machine Learning) for generation of wrappers and mainly focuses on web pages that can be reached without deep navigation. The tool learns the structure of web page from both positive and negative examples given in the form of labelled web pages and testing is done on similarly structured web pages. Wrappers can be hosted as RESTful web services and can be accessed using web service clients. It also offers commercial APIs.

Denodo6

Denado offers sophisticated GUI for configuring wrappers and allows processing of DOM events while navigating web pages. It supports extraction from deep web pages. It provides a tool called Aracne for document crawling and indexing. It also offers wrapper maintenance functionalities.

Lixto

This tool offers a fully interactive wrapper generation framework. It provides a scalable data transformation environment. It suits well for data extraction from dynamic web applications developed using web 2.0 specifications. It is capable of simulating clicks on DOM elements. Expression Language ELOG is used for data extraction. It can be embedded in Mozilla browser.

Kapowtech

This tool offers a Java-based visual development environment for developing web wrappers. It has a proprietary browser and it has a GUI built on top of a procedural scripting language and stores data in RDBMS.

WebQL

It is a query language used for writing wrappers. WebQL uses HTML DOM tree rather than traditional browser. It also offers IP address anonymization environment.

WinTask

WinTask is a windows tool used for data extraction from websites. It can be used like browser to launch a URL, send userid and password if it is a secure site, perform searches and navigate to web pages which acts as extraction targets. User interaction requires knowing scripts and we need to buy it for unlimited access.

Automation Anywhere

This tool has a sophisticated UI which can record user clicks and movement of mouse. It creates navigation sequence and extract target data. Templates can also be used to realize concrete taks or use the task editor that helps user to create pre-determined action sequences. We need to buy the software to get unlimited access to it.

Web Content Extractor

Allows user to create a project for each extraction site, extracts data and store it in project database. The extracted data can be exported into various formats like txt, HTML, XML, Access and Microsoft Excel (CSV). Only trial version is available as free download. We need to buy the software to get unlimited access just like the previous two softwares.

XWRAP

This tool has a toolkit which has three components: Object and Element Extraction, filter interface extraction and code generation. To use this tool, user need to enter the URL of target website and it also supports customization of extraction process. We need a Java web server like Apache Tomcat to launch XWRAP.

Webharvest

Webharvest is a java based open source web data extraction tool. This tool can be used to collect web pages and extract data from them. It makes use of well established web technologies shuch as XSLT, XQuery and Regular expressions. It is helpful for extraction of data from HTML or XML based websites which constitue the major part of World Wide Web.

FUTURE RESEARCH DIRECTIONS

Generic Web Data Extraction

Manual labeling is tedious and cumbersome task and therefore fully automated web data extraction is of interest to many users. Research challenges in this direction are:

1. How to make accurate extraction of need data (i.e. to how to deal with false positives).
2. How to deal with exponentially increase in size of extraction targets.
3. How to bring in semantic knowledge to the extraction process in order to improve accuracy.

Auto-Adapting Wrappers

Wrappers should get automatically adapted to change in layout and code change of web pages. Auto-adapting wrappers should be capable of healing from such changes by using the knowledge of previous versions of web pages. It should be capable of repairing extraction rules accordingly.

Wrapping From Visual Layouts

Many wrappers were based on HTML code or DOM tree structure and there are few recent approaches which makes use of CSS box model i.e. visual rendering of web pages in browser and it is useful when the extraction targets are layout oriented such as web tables and it also allows creation of domain independent wrappers.

Data Extraction From Non-HTML File Formats

Deducing wrappers for documents in formats like PDF and PostScript is of interest in the recent years. It is guided by visual reasoning process over white space and Gestalt theory which is completely different from designing wrappers for web pages and it can also use algorithms from document understanding community.

Learning to Deal With Web Interactions

The tool can be enhanced with automatic recording of user interactions, making use of efficient wrapping languages which helps in recording, executing and generalizing macros of web interactions so that it models the workflow integration process. Ex. Booking a ticket transaction.

Web Form Understanding and Mapping

To deal with deep web pages, wrappers must be capable of filling out complex web search forms and usage of query interfaces. Such systems should be capable of understanding different form element types, contents and labels and map them to corresponding meta form and vice versa. It should be capable of learning abstract representation of search forms.

CONCLUSION

Customized web documents makes data extraction task cumbersome. This motivated several researchers in designing state-of-the-art techniques for extraction of information from data rich pages. Many data mining and data analytics applications are fed using data, extracted from WWW. Data rich pages are organized in two different ways: i. Detail pages containing information about a single object of interest ii. List pages formatted as tables, data regions containing data records or unordered/ordered lists. Chang et al. (2006) and Laender et. al (2002) have surveyed several state-of-the-art approaches available for information extraction whereas Sleiman et. al (2013) have paid attention to techniques used for data region extraction. This chapter is about techniques available for web data extraction from any sort of data rich pages, need not be specifically data regions. And therefore, it also elaborates on techniques available for list extraction. Finally, comparison of all the above techniques based on dimensions such as the number of input pages needed, level of human intervention, features used for data extraction, level of extraction and limitations had been done. The following are the concluding remarks of this chapter:

- Most of the data rich region extractors rely on DOM tree / Visually rendered tag tree. Therefore, these techniques are applicable only for web pages formatted using HTML.
- There are four classes of information extractors: hand-crafted, supervised, semi-supervised and unsupervised. Much of the research focus is on unsupervised technique because human intervention makes the extraction process time-consuming, specific and error-prone.
- It is very difficult to compare the techniques because evaluation is done on different data sets. Developing data set repository in order to make a fair evaluation of various techniques is required.
- Customizing and personalizing web pages using fast developing web technologies imposes difficulty in carrying out extraction task and therefore, developing an extraction technique that goes well with all, differently formatted web pages is still an active research topic.

REFERENCES

Arasu, A., & Garcia-Molina, H. (2003). Extracting structured data from Web pages. *Proceedings of the ACM SIGMOD International Conference on Management of Data.*

Baumgartner, R., Gatterbauer, W., & Gottlob, G. (2009). Web data extraction system. Encyclopedia of Database Systems, 3465-3471.

Bing, L., Lam, W., & Gu, Y. (2011). Towards a Unified Solution: Data Record Region Detection and Segmentation. *Proc. 20th ACM Int'l Conf. Information and Knowledge Management (CIKM)*. doi:10.1145/2063576.2063761

Bolin, M. (2005). *End-user programming for the web*. (Master's thesis). Massachusetts Institute of Technology.

Cai, D., Yu, S., & Wen, J.-R. Ma & W.-Y. (2003). Extracting Content Structure for Web Pages based on Visual Representation. In *Proc. Fifth Asia Pacific Web Conf.(APWeb)*.

Califf, M., & Mooney, R. (2003). Bottom-up Relational Learning of Pattern Matching Rules for Information Extraction. *Journal of Machine Learning Research*, 177–210.

Chang, C.-H., Kayed, M., Girgis, M. R., & Shaalan, K. F. (2006). A Survey of Web Information Extraction Systems. *IEEE Transactions on Knowledge and Data Engineering, 18*(10), 1411–1428. doi:10.1109/TKDE.2006.152

Chang, C.-H., & Kuo, S.-C. (2004). OLERA: A Semi-Supervised Approach for Web Data Extraction with Visual Support. *IEEE Intelligent Systems, 19*(6), 56–64. doi:10.1109/MIS.2004.71

Chang, C.-H., & Lui, S.-C. (2001). IEPAD: Information Extraction based on Pattern Discovery. *Proceedings of the Tenth International Conference on World Wide Web (WWW), Hong-Kong*. doi:10.1145/371920.372182

Crescenzi, V., Mecca, G., & Merialdo, P. (2002). *Roadrunner: Automatic Data Extraction from Data-Intensive Websites*. SIGMOD. doi:10.1145/564691.564778

Currier. (2013). *The amount of data generated worldwide will reach four zettabytes*. Retrieved May 19,2015 from https://vsatglobalseriesblog.wordpress.com/2013/06/21/in-2013-the-amount-of-data-generated-worldwide-will-reach-four-zettabytes/

Estimated size of Google's index. (n.d.). Retrieved August 1, 2015, from http://www.worldwidewebsize.com/

Freitag, D. (2000). Machine Learning for Information Extraction from Informal Domains. *Machine Learning*, *39*(2/3), 169–202. doi:10.1023/A:1007601113994

Fumarola, F., Weninger, T., Barber, R., Malerba, D., & Han, J. (2011). Extracting general lists from web documents: A hybrid approach. *IEA/AIE,* (1), 285–294.

Gatterbauer, W., Bohunsky, P., Herzog, M., Krupl, B., & Pollak, B. (2007). *Towards Domain-Independent Information Extraction from Web Tables*. New York: ACM.

Gupta, R., & Sarawagi, S. (2009). *Answering table augmentation queries from unstructured lists on the web*. PVLDB.

Hammer, J., McHugh, J., & Gracia-Molina, H. (1997). Semistructured data: The TSIMISS experience. *Proceedings of the First East-Europen Symposium on Advances in Databases and Information Systems*.

Hogue, A., & Karger, D. (2005). Thresher: Automating the Unwrapping of Semantic Content from the World Wide. *Proceedings of the 14th International Conference on World Wide Web (WWW)*. doi:10.1145/1060745.1060762

Hsu, C.-N., & Dung, M. (1998). Generating Finite-State Transducers for Semi-Structured Data Extraction from the Web. *Journal of Information Systems*, *23*(8), 521–538. doi:10.1016/S0306-4379(98)00027-1

Kayed, M., & Chang, C.-H. (2010). FiVaTech: Page-level web data extraction from template pages. *IEEE Transactions on Knowledge and Data Engineering*, *22*(2), 249–263. doi:10.1109/TKDE.2009.82

Kushmerick, N., Weld, D., & Doorenbos, R. (1997). Wrapper Induction for Information Extraction. *Proceedings of the Fifteenth International Conference on Artificial Intelligence*.

Laender, F.-H.-A., Ribeiro-Neto, B.-A., da Silva, A.-S., & Teixeira, J.-S. (2002). A Brief Survey of Web Data Extraction Tools. *ACM SIGMOD*, *31*(2), 84–93. doi:10.1145/565117.565137

Lerman, K., Knoblock, C., & Minton, S. (2001). Automatic Data Extraction from Lists and Tables in Web Sources. *Proceedings of the workshop on Advances in Text Extraction and Mining (IJCAI-2001)*.

Liu, B., Grossman, R.-L., & Zhai, Y. (2004). Mining Web Pages for Data Records. *IEEE Intelligent Systems*, *19*(6), 49–55. doi:10.1109/MIS.2004.68

Liu, B., & Zhai, Y. (2005). NET − A System for Extracting Web Data from Flat and Nested Data Records. *WISE*, *2005*, 487–495.

Liu, K.-L., Meng, W., Qiu, J., Yu, C.-T., Raghavan, V., Wu, Z., & Zhao, H. et al. (2007). AllInOneNews: Development and Evaluation of a Large-Scale News Metasearch Engine. *Proceedings ACM SIGMOD International Conference Management of Data*. doi:10.1145/1247480.1247601

Liu, W., Meng, X., & Meng, W. (2006). Vision-Based Web Data Records Extraction. *Proceedings International Workshop Web and Databases (WebDB)*.

Liu, W., Meng, X., & Meng, W. (2010). ViDE: A Vision based approach for Deep Web Data Extraction. *IEEE Transactions on Knowledge and Data Engineering, 22*(3), 447–460. doi:10.1109/TKDE.2009.109

Miao, G., Tatemura, J., Hsiung, W.-P., Sawires, A., & Moser, L. E. (2009). Extracting Data Records from the Web using Tag Path Clustering. *Proceedings International Conference World Wide Web (WWW)*. doi:10.1145/1526709.1526841

Muslea, I., Minton, S., & Knoblock, C. (1999). A Hierarchical Approach to Wrapper Induction. *Proceedings of the Third International Conference on Autonomous Agents* (AA-99). doi:10.1145/301136.301191

Ng, A.-Y., Jordan, M.-I., & Weiss, Y. (2001). *On Spectral Clustering:Analysis and an Algorithm. In Proceedings Neural Information Processing Systems* (pp. 849–856). NIPS.

Papadakis, N., Skoutas, D., Topoulos, K.-R., & Varvarigou, T.-A. (2005). STAVIES: A System for Information Extraction from Unknown Web Data Sources through Automatic Web Wrapper Generation using Clustering Techniques. *IEEE Transactions on Knowledge and Data Engineering, 17*(12), 1638–1652. doi:10.1109/TKDE.2005.203

RISE: Repository of Online Information Sources Used in Information Extraction Tasks. (n.d.). Retrieved May 19,2015 from http://www.isi.edu/integration/RISE/

Sahuguet, A., & Azavant, F. (2001). Building Intelligent Web Applications using Lightweight Wrappers. *IEEE Transactions on Data and Knowledge Engineering, 36*(3), 283–316. doi:10.1016/S0169-023X(00)00051-3

Simon, K., & Lausen, G. (2005). ViPER: Augmenting Automatic Information Extraction with Visual perceptions. *Proceedings 14th ACM International Conference on Information and Knowledge Management (CIKM)*. doi:10.1145/1099554.1099672

Sleiman, H.-A., & Corchuelo, R. (2013). A survey of region extractors from web documents. *IEEE Transactions on Knowledge and Data Engineering, 25*(9), 1960–1981. doi:10.1109/TKDE.2012.135

Sleiman, H.-A., & Corchuelo, R. (2014). Trinity: On Using Trinary Trees for Unsupervised Web Data Extraction. *IEEE Transactions on Knowledge and Data Engineering, 26*(6), 1544–1556. doi:10.1109/TKDE.2013.161

Soderland, S. (1999). Learning information extraction rules for semi-structured and free text. *Machine Learning, 34*(1-3), 233–272. doi:10.1023/A:1007562322031

Tong, S., & Dean, J. (2008). *System and methods for automatically creating lists*. US Patent: 7350187.

Wang, J., & Lochovsky, F.-H. (2002). Data-Rich Section Extraction from HTML Pages. *Proceedings of the Third International Conference on Web Information Systems Engineering (WISE)*.

Wang, J., & Lochovsky, F.-H. (2003). Data extraction and Label Assignment for Web databases. *Proceedings of the Twelfth International Conference on World Wide Web (WWW)*. doi:10.1145/775152.775179

Wang, Y., & Hu, J. (2002), A.machine learning based approach for table detection on the web. *Eleventh International World Wide Web Conference*. doi:10.1145/511446.511478

Weninger, T., Fumarola, F., Barber, R., Han, J., & Malerba, D. (2010). Unexpected Results in Automatic List Extraction on the web. *SIGKDD Explorations*, *12*(2).

Zhai, Y., & Liu, B. (2005). Web Data Extraction Based on Partial Tree Alignment. *Proceedings of the 14th International Conference on World Wide Web (WWW)*. doi:10.1145/1060745.1060761

Zhao, H., Meng, W., Wu, Z., Raghavan, V., & Yu, C.-T. (2005). Fully Automatic Wrapper Generation for Search Engines. *Proceedings of the International Conference on World Wide Web (WWW)*. doi:10.1145/1060745.1060760

Zhao, H., Meng, W., & Yu, C.-T. (2006). Automatic Extraction of Dynamic Record Sections from Search Engine Result Pages. *Proceedings of the 32nd International Conference on Very Large Data Bases (VLDB)*.

ADDITIONAL READING

Cohen, W. W. (2003). Learning and discovering structure in web pages. *IEEE Data Eng. Bul.*, (26), pp. 3–10.

Embley, D.-W., Campbell, D.-M., Jiang, Y.-S., Liddle, S.-W., Ng, Y.-K., Quass, D., & Smith, R.-D. (1999). Conceptual model-based data extraction. *Journal Data & Knowledge Engineering*, *31*(3), 227–251. doi:10.1016/S0169-023X(99)00027-0

Gupta, S., Kaiser, G., Neistadt, D., & Grimm, P. (2003). DOM based Content Extraction of HTML Documents. *WWW '03 Proceedings of the 12th international conference on World Wide Web*, pp. 207 – 214.

Hu, Y., Xin, G., Song, R., Hu, G., Shi, S., Cao, Y., & Li, H. (2005). Title Extraction from bodies of HTML documents and its application to web page retrieval. *SIGIR '05 Proceedings of the 28th annual international ACM SIGIR conference on Research and development in information retrieval*, pp. 250 – 257.

Mantratzis, C., Orgun, M., & Classidy, S. (2005). Separating XHTML content from navigation clutter using DOM-structure block analysis. *HYPERTEXT '05 Proceedings of the sixteenth ACM conference on Hypertext and hypermedia*, pp. 145 – 147.

Weninger, T., Hsu, H.-W., & Han, J. (2010). CETR: Content Extraction via Tag Ratios. *Proceedings of the 19th International Conference on World Wide Web*, pp. 971-980. doi:10.1145/1772690.1772789

Zhang, Y., Mukherjee, R., & Soetarman, B. (2012). Concept Extraction for Online Shopping. *ICEC'12 Proceedings of the 14th Annual International Conference on Electronic Commerce*, pp. 48 – 53.

Ziegler, C.-N., Vogele, C., & Viermetz, M. (2009). Distilling Informative Content from HTML News Pages. *WI-IAT '09 Proceedings of the 2009 IEEE/WIC/ACM International Joint Conference on Web Intelligence and Intelligent Agent Technology*, (01), pp. 707 – 712.

KEY TERMS AND DEFINITIONS

DOM Tree: Nodes of documents like HTML, XML etc. are organized in the form of tree structure called DOM tree and the tree structure can be accessed by using Document Object Model API.

Hyper Text Markup Language: A semistructured format for defining content of webpages in WWW.

Information Retrieval: A process of obtaining information resources relevant to an information need from the collection of resources.

Precision: Precision indicates what proportion of the retrieved documents is relevant.

Recall: Recall indicates what proportion of all the relevant documents have been retrieved from the collection.

Resilience: It is defined as the ability to withstand change.

Server-Side Template: HTML template used in server-side for generating web pages, by embedding data records retrieved from database.

Supervised: It is a method which requires manually labeled training samples for web data extraction.

Unsupervised: This method automatically deduces the template for data extraction and makes use of it for data extraction.

Web Harvesting: The process of automatically retrieving data from websites is known as web harvesting or web scraping.

Web Wrapper: A procedure, that might implement one or many different classes of algorithms, which seeks and finds data required by a human user, extracting them from unstructured (or semistructured) Web sources, and transforming them into structured data, merging and unifying this information for further processing, in a semi-automatic or fully automatic way.

This research was previously published in Web Usage Mining Techniques and Applications Across Industries edited by A.V. Senthil Kumar, pages 351-378, copyright year 2017 by Information Science Reference (an imprint of IGI Global).

Chapter 11

Effectiveness of Web Usage Mining Techniques in Business Application

Ahmed El Azab
Institute of Statistical Studies and Research, Egypt

Mahmood A. Mahmood
Institute of Statistical Studies and Research, Egypt

Abd El-Aziz
Institute of Statistical Studies and Research, Egypt

ABSTRACT

Web usage mining techniques and applications across industries is still exploratory and, despite an increase in academic research, there are challenge of analyze web which quantitatively capture web users' common interests and characterize their underlying tasks. This chapter addresses the problem of how to support web usage mining techniques and applications across industries by combining language of web pages and algorithms that used in web data mining. Existing research in web usage mining techniques tend to focus on finding out how each techniques can apply in different industries fields. However, there is little evidence that researchers have approached the issue of web usage mining across industries. Consequently, the aim of this chapter is to provide an overview of how the web usage mining techniques and applications across industries can be supported.

INTRODUCTION

Nowadays, with the evolution of technology, supported by global and speedy communication network online Web services, has been growth rapidly in the form of created content presents new opportunities and challenges to both producers and consumers of information, the volumes of click stream and client information gathered by Web-based associations in their everyday operations has come to galactic extents.

DOI: 10.4018/978-1-5225-3163-0.ch011

Web Usage Mining deals with understanding user behavior in interacting with the web site. The aim is to obtain information that may assist web site recognition to better suit the user. The logs include information about the referring pages, user identification, time a user spends at a site and the sequence of pages visited (Rani, 2013).

Data extraction is a field that is concerned with obtaining information from different online databases and services web resources including websites. According of the dynamic nature of the World Wide Web so it become important to find tools for data extraction. end users and application programs have some difficulties when it comes to finding useful data (MOHAPATRA, 2004)

Since 1980 the attempt researches to extract data from the Web are. Two of strategies emerged learning techniques and knowledge engineering techniques also called learning-based and rule-based approaches, respectively. These approaches depends on domain expertise it need programming experience and a good knowledge of the domain in which the data extraction system (Ferrara, E., De Meo, P., Fiumara, G., & Baumgartner, R., 2014)

On the same way, (Tomasz Kaczmarek,et al) in ((Kaczmarek, 2010)) present method part of the extra Spec system called EXT was based on hierarchical execution of XPath commands and regular expressions depending on the structure of processed documents. EXT is capable of processing webpages written in the Polish language in order to extract the information relevant for the needs of expert programmer and team building. But this method not includes development of text processing techniques to cope with fields that are manually filled by humans (Kaczmarek, 2010)

Also web usage mining benefits the capitalist people in some area such as business, industrials and insurance to take a good decision by apply web usage mining recommender system.

Recommender systems have become an important research area since the appearance of the first papers on collaborative filtering in the mid-1990s, The interest in this area still remains high because it constitutes a problem-rich research area and because of the abundance of practical applications that help users to deal with information overload and provide personalized recommendations, content, and services to them. although the roots of recommender systems can be traced back to the extensive work in cognitive science, approximation theory, information retrieval, forecasting theories, and also have links to management science and to consumer choice modeling in marketing, recommender systems emerged as an independent research area in the mid-1990s when researchers started focusing on recommendation problems that explicitly rely on the ratings structure (Mahmood A. Mahmood N. E.-B., 2014).According that recommender system tends to make use of different sources of information (collaborative, social, demographic, content, knowledge-based, geographic, sensors, tags, implicit and explicit data acquisition, etc.), An important research subject in the recommender system field focuses on providing explanations that justify the recommendations the user has received. This is an important aspect of a recommender system because it aids in maintaining a higher degree of user confidence in the results generated by the systems (Mahmood A. Mahmood N. E.-B., 2014) Mahmood and et al in (Mahmood A. Mahmood E. A.-S.-B., 2013)).presented Recommender System for Ground-Level Ozone Predictions. The obtained results demonstrate the effectiveness and the reliability of the proposed recommender system. Resulted experimental values of ground-level Ozone predicted by the proposed recommender system showed similar behavior as the actual tested values of the ground-level Ozone dataset.

Samar and et al in (Samar Mahmoud, 2013) presented An Intelligent Recommender System for Drinking Water Quality to evaluate the performance of the presented recommender system, 5 parameters developed and validated between the year 2000 to 2013, were used. The initial seven years of data was used to develop the forecasting models and the remaining data was used for testing and verifying these models. The obtained results demonstrate the effectiveness and the reliability of the proposed recommender system. Based on the data resulted, the average PH level prediction in a certain time is characterized by a mean absolute error of 0.34. In addition, both experimentally resulted and actual dataset values existed in the healthy region of the PH level for drinking water, which is within the range 6.5 to 8.0 according to the World Health Organization (WHO) drinking water guidelines.

This chapter organized as follows: First sections gives an overview on web mining and web mining taxonomy and its applications. Also Section describes the issues of web usage mining. Also Section 4 introduces Web Usage Mining Languages and Algorithms. On the same way Section explains Effective Web usage mining in Business. Finally, Section presents and discusses the conclusion.

WEB MINING: AN OVERVIEW

There are many definition for web mining the Most popular definition of Web mining is "the application of data mining techniques to extract knowledge from web data, i.e. web content, web structure, and web usage data." As shown in Figure 1. (Rani, 2013) (T. Srivastava, P. Desikan, V. Kumar, 2005) see Figure 1.

Figure 1. Diagram of web mining taxonomy

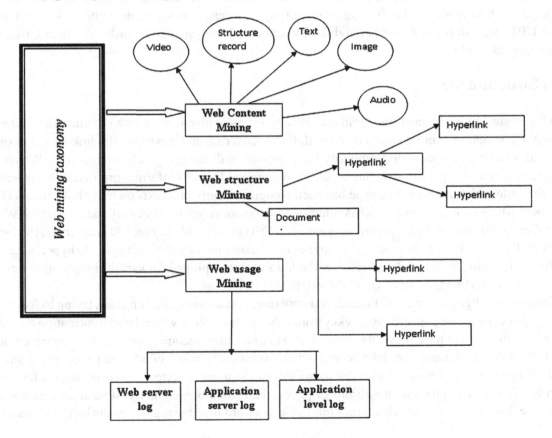

Web Content Mining

Most Web content mining and information retrieval applications involve measuring similarity among two or more documents.

Web Content Mining is the process of retrieving the information from web document into more structure forms. It is related to Data Mining because many Data Mining techniques can be applied in Web Content Mining (Gupta, V., & Lehal, G. S. 2009).

Also Vector representation facilitates similarity computations using vector-space operations (such as Cosine of the angle between two vectors).

For Examples Search engines: measure the similarity between a query (represented as a vector) and the indexed document vectors to return a ranked list of relevant documents.

Document clustering: group documents based on similarity or dissimilarity (distance) among them.

Document categorization: measure the similarity of a new document to be classified with representations of existing categories (such as the mean vector representing a group of document vectors) (Janssens, 2007)

Personalization: recommend documents or items based their similarity to a representation of the user's profile (may be a term vector representing concepts or terms of interest to the user)

Web mining is one of the applications and it's used to discover patterns from the web. The research of the web mining is based on interdisciplinary field and it used techniques from data mining, text mining, databases, statistics, machine learning, multimedia, etc. Web mining has interest based on three categories such as clustering i.e. finding natural groups of users, pages, etc., next one is associations i.e. which URLs tend to request together and finally sequential analysis i.e. the order in which URLs tend to be accessed (Mehtaa, 2012).

Web Structure Mining

Web Structure Mining discovering similarity between sites or discovering web communities Is the target of Web Structure Mining which deals with the discovering and modeling the link structure of the web. This can help in discovering similarity between sites or discovering web communities. Which web structure use of the hyperlink structure of the Web as an (additional) information source the hyperlinks play vital role which pointing to a page has been recognized early on. Texts on hyperlinks in an HTML document which called Anchor which Anchor of predecessor pages were already indexed by the World-Wide Web Worm, one of the first search engines and Web crawlers (McBryan, 1994). Spertus (1997)cited in (Patel, P., Jena, B., & Sahoo, B, 2014) suggested a taxonomy of different types of (hyper-)links that can be found on the Web and discusses how the links can be exploited for various information retrieval tasks on the Web (Patel, P., Jena, B., & Sahoo, B, 2014).

There are challgenes appear with confused structure, people use search engines, trying to focus their search by querying using specific terms/keywords. At the beginning, where large information contained in the Web did not yet have these big parts, search engines used manually-built lists covering common topics. First they maintained an index, containing a list for every word, of all Web pages containing this word. This index was then used in order to answer to the users' queries. However, after a few years, when the Web evolved including millions of pages, the manual maintenance of such indices was very expensive. The automated search engines relying in keyword matching, give results including hundreds (or more) Web pages, most of them of low quality. The need for ranking somehow the importance and relevance of the results was more than evident.

Search engines such as AltaVista, Lycos, Infoseek, HotBot and Excite use some simple heuristics in order to accomplish a page ranking. Such heuristics take into consideration the number of times the term appears in the document, if it appears at the beginning of the text, or at areas considered more important (such as headings, italics, etc) (Fürnkranz, Johannes, 2002).

Web Usage Mining

Web Usage Mining deals with understanding user behavior in interacting with the web site. The aim is to obtain information that may assist web site recognition to better suit the user. The logs include information about the referring pages, user identification, time a user spends at a site and the sequence of pages visited.

There are three main tasks for performing Web Usage Mining or Web Usage Analysis. the tasks for each step and discusses the challenges involved (Rani, 2013).

Preprocessing

The web usage dataset collection, perform preprocessing on the dataset. Because, the data collected from the web is normally diverse, heterogeneous and unstructured. Therefore, it is necessary to do the pre-processing like filtering unnecessary and irrelevant data, predicting and filling the missing values, removing noise, resolving inconsistence before applying the algorithm. Data pre-processing consists of the following processes such as, Data cleaning, User identification, Session identification and Path completion (Choudhary, Durga, and Shreya Sharma., 2015)

Pre-processing consists of converting the usage, content, and structure information contained in the various available data sources into the data abstractions necessary for pattern discovery.

Usage Preprocessing

Difficult task in the Web Usage Mining process is Usage preprocessing, such as the incompleteness of the available data. Unless a client side tracking mechanism is used, only the IP address, agent, and server side click stream are available to identify users server sessions (Srivastava J. C., 2000).

There are some of the typically encountered problems such as:

- **Single IP address/Multiple Server Sessions:** Internet service providers (ISPs) typically have a pool of proxy servers that users access the Web through. A single proxy server may have several users accessing a Web site, potentially over the same time period.
- **Multiple IP Address/Single Server Session:** Some ISPs or privacy tools randomly assign each request from a user to one of several IP addresses. In this case, a single server session can have multiple IP addresses.
- **Multiple IP Address/Single User:** A user that accesses the Web from different machines will have a different IP address from session to session. This makes tracking repeat visits from the same user difficult.

- **Multiple Agent/Singe User:** Again, a user that uses more than one browser, even on the same machine, will appear as multiple users. Assuming each user has now been identified (through cookies, logins, or IP/agent/path analysis), the click-stream for each user must be divided into sessions (Srivastava J. C., 2000). When page request from other servers are not available, it is difficult to know when a user has left a Web site. A thirty minute timeout is often used as the default method of breaking a user's click-stream into sessions. When a session ID is embedded in each URI, the definition of a session is set by the content server. While the exact content served as a result of each user action is often available from the request field in the server logs, it is sometimes necessary to have access to the content server information as well. Since content servers can maintain state variables for each active session, the information necessary to determine exactly what content is served by a user request is not always available in the URI. The final problem encountered when preprocessing usage data is that of inferring cached page references (Mohamed, 2011).

The only verifiable method of tracking cached page views is to monitor usage from the client side. The referrer field for each request can be used to detect some of the instances when cached pages have been viewed.

Content Preprocessing

Content preprocessing consists of converting the text, image, scripts, and other files such as multimedia into forms that are useful for the Web Usage Mining process. Often, this consists of performing content mining such as classification or clustering. While applying data mining to the content of Web sites is an interesting area of research in its own right, in the context of Web Usage Mining the content of a site can be used to filter the input to, or output from the pattern discovery algorithms. For example, results of a classification algorithm could be used to limit the discovered patterns to those containing page views about a certain subject or class of products. (Witten, I. H., Frank, E., 2005). Page views can be intended to convey information (through text, graphics, or other multimedia), gather information from the user, allow navigation (through a list of hypertext links), or some combination uses. The intended use of a page view can also filter the sessions before or after pattern discovery. In order to run content mining algorithms on page views~ the information must first be converted into a quantifiable format. Some version of the vector space model is typically used to accomplish this. Text files can be broken up into vectors of words. Keywords or text descriptions can be substituted for graphics or multimedia. The content of static page views can be easily preprocessed by parsing the HTML and reformatting the information or running additional algorithms as desired. Dynamic page views present more of a challenge. Content servers that employ personalization techniques and/or draw upon databases to construct the page views may be capable of forming more page views than can be practically preprocessed. A given set of server sessions may only access a fraction of the page views possible for a large dynamic site. Also the content may be revised on a regular basis. The content of each page view to be preprocessed must be "assembled", either by an HTTP request from a crawler, or a combination of template, script, and database accesses. If only the portion of page views that are accessed are preprocessed, the output of any classification or clustering algorithms may be skewed (Witten, I. H., Frank, E., 2005).

Structure Preprocessing

The structure of a site is created by the hypertext links between page views. The structure can be obtained and preprocessed in the same manner as the content of a site. Again, dynamic content (and therefore links) pose more problems than static page views. Pattern Discovery Pattern discovery draws upon methods and algorithms developed from several fields such as statistics, data mining, machine learning and pattern recognition. However, it is not the intent of this paper to describe all the available algorithms and techniques derived from these fields.

The kinds of mining activities that have been applied to the Web domain. Methods developed from other fields must take into consideration the different kinds of data abstractions and prior knowledge available for Web Mining. For example, in association rule discovery, the notion of a transaction for market-basket analysis does not take into consideration the order in which items are selected. However, in Web Usage Mining, a server session is an ordered sequence of pages requested by a user. Furthermore, due to the difficulty in identifying unique sessions, additional prior knowledge is required (Okoli et al., 2012).

Statistical Analysis

Statistical techniques are the most common method to extract knowledge about visitors to a Web site. By analyzing the session file, one can perform different kinds of descriptive statistical analyses (frequency, mean, median, etc.) on variables such as page views, viewing time and length of a navigational path. Many Web traffic analysis tools produce a periodic report containing statistical information such as the most frequently accessed pages, average view time of a page or average length of a path through a site (Jaideep Srivastava, 2000).

Application of Web Data Mining

Web data mining can successfully fix information extraction and the following features incorporated with the web mining program must be fixed if we need to use data mining successfully in creating Web intelligence (Mohamed., 2011).

Web Search-Engine Data Mining

For website optimization web crawls on indexes Websites, and builds and stores large keyword-based indices that help identify sets of Websites that contain specific keywords and phrases. By using a set of tightly restricted keywords and phrases, an experienced user can quickly identify appropriate documents. However, current keyword-based search engines suffer from several deficiencies. First, a subject of any breadth can easily contain tens of thousands of records. This can lead to a look for website returning many document entries (Witten, I. H., Frank, E., 2005), many of which are only partially appropriate to the subject or contain only poor-quality materials. Second, many highly appropriate records may not contain keywords and phrases that explicitly define the subject, a trend known as the polysemy problem. For example, the keyword and key phrase information exploration may turn up many Websites related to other exploration industries, yet fail to identify appropriate papers on knowledge discovery, mathematical analysis, or machine learning because they did not contain the information exploration keyword and key phrase. Depending on these observations, data mining should be integrated with the web search engine service to enhance the excellence of Web searches To do so, For example, a look for the keyword and key phrase information exploration can consist of a few alternatives so that an index-based web search engine can perform a parallel search that will obtain a larger set of records than the search phrases alone would return. The search engine then can look for the set of appropriate Web records obtained so far to select a smaller set of highly appropriate and authoritative records to present to the user. Web-linkage and Web dynamics analysis thus provide the basis for discovering high-quality records.

Web Link Structure Analyzing

Keyword and key phrase or subject, such as investment, an individual would like to find web pages that are not only extremely appropriate, but trustworthy and of high quality. Instantly determining trustworthy Websites for a certain subject will improve a Web search's excellence. The secret of power conceals in Website linkages. These hyperlinks contain quantity of hidden human annotation that can help instantly infer the idea of power. When a Web page's writer makes a web page link directing to another Website, this action can be considered as an approval of that web page. The combined approval of a given web page by different writers on the Web can indicate the value of the site and lead normally to the development of trustworthy Web pages. First, not every web page link symbolizes the approval for a search. Web-page writers make some links for other requirements, such as routing or to provide as compensated ads. Overall, though, if most hyperlinks operate as recommendations, the combined viewpoint will still control. Second, a power that belongs to a professional or aggressive interest will hardly ever have its Web page point to competing authorities' pages. (T. Sunil Kumar; Dr. K. Suvarchala, 2012)

For example, manufacture will likely avoid supporting a product by guaranteeing that no links to that product in their Websites appears. These qualities of web link components have led researchers to consider another essential Website category: locations. A hub is just one Website or web page set that provides selections of links to authorities. Although it may not be popular, or may have only a few links directing to it, a hub provides hyperlinks to a selection of popular websites on a typical subject. These web pages can be list of suggested links on individual home pages, such as suggested referrals websites from a course home-page or a expertly constructed source list on a commercial site A hub unquestioningly confers authority status on websites that focus on a specific subject. Generally, a good hub points to many excellent authorities, and, on the other hand, a page that many good locations point to can be considered a good authority. Such a common encouragement relationship between locations and authorities helps users my own trustworthy. Websites performs development of high quality Web components and sources. Techniques for determining trustworthy Web pages and locations have led to the development of the PageRank1 and HITS3 methods.Some over the counter available Web search engines, such as Google, are built around such methods. By assessing Web links and textual perspective information, these systems can generate better-quality look for results than term-index look for engines.

Automatically Classifying

Web documents Although Yahoo and similar Web listing service systems use human visitors to categorize Web records, inexpensive and improved speed make automated category highly suitable. Common category methods use good and bad illustrations as training sets, then determine each papers a category brand from a set of defined subject groups depending on pre classified papers illustrations. For example, designers can use Yahoo's taxonomy and its associated records as exercising and test places to obtain a

Web papers category program. This program groups new Web records by giving groups from the same taxonomy. Developers can obtain great results using typical keyword-based papers category methods, such as Bayesian category, support vector machine, decision-tree introduction, and keyword and key phrase centered organization analysis to categorize Web records. Since hyperlinks contain high quality semantic signs to a page's subject, such semantic information can help achieve even better precision than that possible with genuine keyword-based category. However, since the back-linked web pages around a documents may be loud and thus contain unrelated subjects, innocent use of terms in a document's web page link community can lower precision. For example, many personal home pages may have climate. com connected simply as a save, even though these web pages have no importance to the subject of climate. Tests have shown that combining solid mathematical designs such as Markov unique areas with pleasure brands can considerably improve Web papers category precision. As opposed to many other category techniques, automated category usually does not clearly specify adverse examples: category a pre classified papers connected to, but not which records a certain category definitely limits. Thus, preferably, a Web documents category program should not require clearly marked adverse illustrations. Using positive illustrations alone can be especially useful in Web papers category, forcing some scientists to recommend a category method based on a enhanced support-vector machine program (T. Sunil kumar; Dr. K. Suvarchala, 2012)

Web Page Content and Semantic Structure Mining

Completely automated removal of Website components and semantic material can be difficult given the present restrictions on computerized natural-language parsing. However, semiautomatic techniques can identify a large part of such components. Professionals may still need to specify what types of components and semantic material a particular web page type can have. Then a page-structure-extraction system can evaluate the Website to see whether and how a segment's content suits into one of the components. Designers also can evaluate individual reviews to enhance the training and evaluate procedures and enhance the quality of produced Website components and contents. Specific research of Website exploration systems shows that different types of web pages have different semantic components. For example, a department's home-page, a professor's homepage, and a job marketing web page can all have different components First, to identify the relevant and interesting framework to draw out, either an expert personally identifies this framework for a given Website category, techniques develop to instantly generate such a framework from a set of relabeled Website examples. Second, designers can use Website framework and content removal methods for automatic removal based on Website classes, possible semantic components, and other semantic information. Web page category identification allows to draft out semantic components and material, while getting such components allows validating which category the produced pages are part of. Such a connection mutually increases both procedures. Third, semantic page structure and content recognition will greatly enhance the in depth analysis of Web page contents and the building of a multilayered Web information base. (T. Sunil kumar; Dr. K. Suvarchala, 2012)

Dynamic Web Mining

Web mining can also recognize as dynamics web. How the Web changes in the perspective of its material, components, and accessibility styles. Saving certain pieces of traditional details related to these Web exploration factors helps in discovering changes in material and linkages. In this case, we can evaluate pictures from different time postage stamps to recognize the up-dates. However, as opposed to relational data source systems, the Internet's wide depth and large shop of details create it nearly difficult to consistently shop past pictures or upgrade records (Yu-Hui Tao, 2007).

These restrictions create discovering such changes generally infeasible. Mining Web accessibility activities, on the other hand, is both possible and, in many programs, quite useful. With this strategy, customers can mine Web log information to discover Web page access styles. Assessing and discovering regularities in Web log information can enhance the quality and distribution of Internet information services to the end individual, enhance Web hosting server system performance, and recognize customers for electronic industry. A Web hosting server usually signs up a Web log entry for every Web page accessed. This accessibility includes the asked for URL, the IP address from which the request is started, and a time seal. Web-based e-commerce hosts gather many Web accessibility log details. Popular Web sites can register Web log details that variety hundreds of megabytes each day. Web log directories provide rich details about Web characteristics. Opening these details requires innovative Web log exploration techniques. The success of such programs relies on what and how much legitimate and efficient knowledge we can find out from the raw details. Often, researchers must clean, reduce, and convert these details to recover and evaluate significant and useful details. Second, scientists can use the available URL, time, IP deal with, and Web page content details to create a multidimensional view on the Web log data source and execute a multidimensional OLAP research to find the top customers, top utilized websites, most frequently utilized times, and so on. These results will help find out customers, marketplaces, and other organizations. Third, exploring Web log records can expose organization styles, successive styles, and Web accessibility styles.

Issues of Web Usage Mining

According to Data Mining News, as of 1999, the data mining industry was valued at $1 billion also according to Herb Edelstein, by 1998, the data mining tool market was at $45 million, a 100% increase from 1997. It has been estimated by Internet News that the number of adults using credit cards to purchase goods and services online more than doubled between 1998 and 1999. Furthermore, the report included that by the third quarter of 1999, 19.2 million adults used their credit cards to make online transactions, compared to 9.3 million in 1998 and only 4.9 million in 1997. As such, online transactions are increasing in record numbers.

In the Healthcare E-commerce industry, a recent study showed that by 2004, this industry would surpass the $370 Billion mark in online transactions. Compared with travel, finance, and even the steel industry, healthcare e-commerce is a late bloomer, says the report from Forrester Research (Aldana, 2000), Web mining will be a growing technology as more companies are investing their futures in the Internet. Just in advertising alone, companies are spending most of their revenues trying to publicize their sites and try to attract as many potential customers as they can. With increasing online transactions and the potential of attaining a large set of customers through the Internet, it is no surprise that most Internet companies are devoting most of their sources of revenue to advertising costs.

In the recent years, Internet companies have accumulated over $1 billion in advertising. Advertising by dot.com companies saw growth nearly triple in the third quarter of 1999 compared to the same time period from last year according to a study by Competitive Media Reporting. Including the holiday season, CMR predicted that dotcom's have more than doubled their spending on advertising than the $649.2

million spent offline for all of 1998. According to the CKS Group, they estimated online advertising spending to be $301 million in 1996.

Information Extraction Approaches

Researchers began to use statistical techniques and machine learning algorithms to automatically create information extraction systems for new domains. In the following subsections, overviews of information extraction approaches are presented. In general, approaches of information extraction can be under the category of either supervised, weakly supervised, or unsupervised learning approaches. Supervised learning can be applied for extracting different information including patterns, rules, and sequential information. Moreover, weakly supervised and unsupervised learning methods for information extraction are applied for more global or discourse-oriented approaches to information extraction. The following subsections will demonstrate the work performed by researchers in this field. (Ravi, 2015)

Limitation and Challenges in Web Data Mining

Web information presentation is a noteworthy test in current patterns of data extraction. The conventional plans for getting to the gigantic measures of information that live on the Web on a very basic level expect the content situated, watchword based perspective of Web pages. To accomplish the obliged data we require a high potential web mining procedures to beat the crucial issues. an information situated deliberation will empower another scope of functionalities. Second, at the administration level. Flow web hunt mining backings decisive word, connection address and substance based web look, where information mining will assume an imperative part. Be that as it may, these web crawlers still can't give astounding, astute administrations as a result of a few impediments in web mining which adds to the issue (Marc Bousquet, Katherine Wills, 2003)

Quality of Keyword-Based Searches

The quality of keyword-based searches suffers from several inadequacies such as a search often returns many answers, especially if the keywords posed include words from popular categories such as sports, politics, or entertainment. It overloaded keyword semantics and it can return low-quality results. For instance, contingent upon the connection, a Mac could be a natural product, squeeze, organization or PC and a pursuit can miss numerous exceedingly related pages that don't unequivocally contain the postured essential words and, a quest for the term information mining can miss numerous much respected machine learning or measurable information examination pages (NOOR, 2008)

Effective of Deep-Web Extraction

A research analysts estimated that searchable databases on the Web numbered more than 100,000. These databases provide high-quality, well-maintained information, but are not effectively accessible. Because current Web crawlers cannot query these databases, the data they contain remains invisible to traditional search engines. Conceptually, the deep Web provides an extremely large collection of autonomous and heterogeneous databases, each supporting specific query interfaces with different schema and query constraints. To effectively extract the deep Web, we must integrate these databases and implement efficient web mining approaches (Jiawei Han Kevin, 2002)

- **Self-Organized and Constructed Directories:** A content or type-oriented Web information directory presents an organized picture of a Web sector and supports a semantics-based information search [9], which makes such a directory highly desirable. For example, following organization links like Country > Sports > Football > Players makes searches more efficient. Unfortunately, developers construct such directories manually which limit coverage of these costly directories provide and developers cannot easily scale or adapt them.
- **Semantics-Based Query:** Most keyword- based search engines provide a small set of options for possible keyword combinations, such as Google and Yahoo, provide more advanced search primitives, including ——with exact phrases, without certain words, with restrictions on date and domain site type (Liu, 2003)
- **Human Activities Feedback:** Web page authors provide links to authoritative Web pages and also traverse those Web pages they find most interesting or of highest quality [10][2]. Unfortunately, while human activities and interests change over time, Web links may not be updated to reflect these trends. For example, significant events—such as the 2012 Olympic or the tsunami attack on Japan can change Web site access patterns dramatically, a change that Web linkages often fail to reflect. We have yet to use such human-traversal information for the dynamic, automatic adjustment of Web information services. (Jiawei Han, 2002).
- **Multidimensional Data Analysis and Mining:** Because current Web searches rely on keyword based indices, not the actual data the Web pages contain, search engines provide only limited support for multidimensional Web information analysis and data mining. These challenges and limitation have promoted research into efficiently and effectively discovering and using Internet resources, a quest in which web data mining play an important role (Lancaster, 2003)

Web Mining Tasks

Web mining is the Data Mining technique that automatically discovers or extracts the information from web documents, it consists of following tasks:-

1. **Resource Finding:** It involves the task of retrieving intended web documents. It is the process by which it had been extract the data either online or offline resources available on web.
2. **Information Selection and Pre-Processing:** It involves the automatic selection and pre processing of specific information from retrieved web resources. This process transforms the original retrieved data into information. The data is transformed into useful information by using suitable transformation. The transformation could be renewal of stop words, or it may be aimed for obtaining the desired representation such as finding particular format of data.
3. **Generalization:** It automatically discovers general patterns at individual web sites as well as across multiple sites. Data Mining techniques and machine learning are used in generalization.
4. **Analysis:** It involves the validation and interpretation of the mined patterns. It plays an important role in pattern mining. A human plays an important role in information on knowledge discovery process on web (Thirumala Sree Govada, 2014).

The process of web mining shown in Figure 2.

According to Table 1 there are difference between comparison of WCM, WSM and WUM

Web Usage Mining: Languages and Algorithms

XML languages and a web data mining application which utilizes them to extract complex structural information.

Extensible Graph Markup and Modeling Language (XGMML) is an XML 1.0 application based on Graph Modeling Language (GML) which is used for graph description. XG-MML uses tags to describe nodes and edges of a graph. The purpose of XGMML is to make possible the exchange of graphs between different authoring and browsing tools for graphs. Theconversion of graphs written in GML to XGMML is straight forward. Using Extensible Stylesheet Language (XSL) with XGMML allows the translation of graphs to different formats.

Which Web data mining is one of the current hot topics in computer science. Mining data that has been collected from web server logfiles, is not only useful for studying customer choices, but also helps

Figure 2. Diagram of the Process of web mining

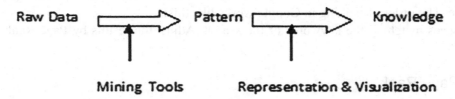

Table 1. Comparison WCM,WSM,WUM

Specifications	Web Content Mining (WCM)	Web Structure Mining	Web Usage Mining
View of data	Structured, Semi Structured and Unstructured	Linking of structure	Interactive data
Type of data used in mining	Primary	Primary	Secondary
Main data	Text document, Hypertext Document	Link Structure	Server Logs, Browser Logs
Representation	Bag of Words, n-grams, Terms, phrases, Concepts or Ontology, Relational, Edge Labeled Graph	Graph	Relational Table, Graph
Method	Machine learning, Statistical Method, Proprietary Algorithm, Association Rules	Proprietary Algorithm,	Machine Learning Statistical Method
Tasks	It describes the discovery of useful information from the web content/ documents.	It tries to discover the model underlying the link structure of the web.	It tries to make sense of data generated by web surfer"s session or behaviour.
Scope	In IR view of data the scope is global while in DB view it is local	Global	Global

to better organize web pages. This is accomplished by knowing which web pages are most frequently accessed by the web surfers (Punin, et al.,2002).

Link Analysis Algorithms

There are many algorithms (Aggarwal, 2013) used in web mining.Three Popular algorithms Page Rank, Weighted Page Rank and Weighted Page Content Rank are discussed below.

Page Rank

Page Rank is a numeric value that represents how important a page is on the web. Page Rank is the Google's method of measuring a page's "importance." When all other factors such as Title tag and keywords are taken into account, Google uses Page Rank to adjust

Results so that more "important" pages move up in the results page of a user's search result display. Google Fig.s that when a page links to another page, it is effectively casting a vote for the other page. Google calculates a page's importance from the votes cast for it. How important each vote is taken into account when a page's Page Rank is calculated. It matters because it is one of the factors that determine a page's ranking in the search results. It isn't the only factor that Google uses to rank pages, but it is an important one. The order of ranking in Google works like this:

Find all pages matching the keywords of the search. Adjust the results by Page Rank scores (Aggarwal, 2013)

Weighted Page Rank

Extended Page Rank algorithm- Weighted Page Rank assigns large rank value to more important pages instead of dividing the rankvalue of a page evenly among its outlink pages. The importanceis assigned in terms of weight values to incoming and outgoing links denoted as and respectively. is calculated on the basis of number of incoming links to page n and the number of incoming links to all reference pages of page m.

In is number of incoming links of page n, Ip is number of incoming (Tamanna. 2007).

Weighted Page Content Rank

Weighted Page Content Rank Algorithm (WPCR) is a proposed page ranking algorithm which is used to give a sorted order to the web pages returned by a search engine in response to a user query. WPCR is a numerical value based on which the web pages are given an order. This algorithm employs web structure mining as well as web content mining techniques. Web structure mining is used to calculate the importance of the page and web content mining is used to find how much relevant a page is? Importance here means the popularity of the page i.e. how many pages are pointing to or are referred by this particular page. It can be calculated based on the number of inlinks and outlinks of the page. Relevancy means matching of the page with the fired query. If a page is maximally matched to the query, that becomes more relevant (Aggarwal, 2013)

Comparison of Algorithms

According the rapidly development algorithms were used at web mining we present the difference between coomon three algorithms which Table 2 shows the difference between above three algorithms

The GSP Algorithm

The GSP algorithm, is intended for mining Generalized Sequential Patterns. It extends previous proposal by handling time constraints and taxonomies.

For solving The problem of mining association rules has been refined considering a database storing behavioral facts which occur over time to individuals of the studied population. Thus facts are provided with a time stamp. The concept of sequential pattern is introduced to capture typical behaviors over time, i.e. behaviours sufficiently repeated by individuals to be relevant for the decision maker (Masseglia, 2000).

The PSP Approach

There are problem of a web server log file florent Masseglia, et al., split the problem of mining sequential patterns from a web server log file into the following phases (Masseglia, 2000):-

1. Sort Phase

converts the original access log file into a database d of datasequences is aim of this phase which the access log file is sorted with ip address as a major key and transaction time as the minor key. Further-

Table 2. Comparison of page rank and weighted page rank

Contents	Page Rank	Weighted Page	Weighted Page Content Rank
Mining Technique Used	WSM	WSM	WSM and WCM
Complexity	O(logn)	<O(logn)	<O(logn)
Working Procedure	Computes Scores at index time. Results are sorted on the importance of pages	Assigns large value to more important pages instead of diving the rank value of a page evenly among its outlink pages.	Gives sorted order to the web pages returned by a search engine as a numerical value in response to a user query.
Input/Output parameters	Backlinks	Backlinks and forward links	Backlinks Forward links and content
Advantages	It provides important information about given query by diving rank value equally among its outlink pages	It provides important information about given query and assigning importance in terms of weight values to incoming an outgoing links	It provides important information and relevancy about a given query by using web structure and web content mining
Search Engine	Google	Google	Research Model
Limitations	(1) Page Rank is equally distributed to outgoing links (2) It is purely based on the number of inlinks and outlinks.	(1) While some pages may be irrelevant to a given query, it still receives the highest rank (2) There is a less determination of the relevancy of the pages to a given query	No limitation best as comparison to Page Rank and Weighted Page Rank

more, by group together entries that are sufficiently close according to the user-specified Δt in order to provide temporal transactions. such a transaction is therefore the set of all url names and their access times for the same client where successive log entries are within Δt. a unique time stamp is associated with each such transaction and each url is mapped into integer in order to efficiently manipulate the structure (Ezeife, 2005)

2. Sequence Phase

The general algorithm is utilized to locate the successive arrangements in the database. Methodology continues the key standards of GSP. its inventiveness is to utilize an alternate various leveled structure than in gsp for sorting out hopeful groupings, to enhance productivity of recoveries. the general calculation is like the one in gsp. at every stride, the db is perused for tallying the backing of current competitors (method applicant confirmation). at that point the regular arrangement set can be manufactured. from this set, new competitors are displayed for being managed at the following step (method applicant era). the calculation stops when the longest successive arrangements, installed in the db are found along these lines the hopeful era method yields a vacant arrangement of new applicants. Backing is a capacity giving for every applicant its including quality put away the tree structure (Masseglia, 2000)

Effective Web Mining in Business

Web mining techniques were the major functional areas of businesses. Some examples of deployed systems as well as frameworks for emerging applications yet-to-be-built are discussed. However, the examples are no means to be regarded as solutions to all problems within the framework of business function they are cited in. Their purpose is to illustrate that Web mining techniques have been applied successfully to handle certain kind of problems, providing the evidence of its utility also Neeraj Raheja and V.K.Katiyar cited in (Desikan, P, 2009). proposes an approach for web usage mining based upon web log partition. Neeraj Raheja and V.K.Katiyar have result show how It takes less time and provides popular results in accordance with the existing approach. Some more results may be obtained if the number of cluster formed are changed approach can be changed to 6, 8 or more. However recall and precision may be affected by changing the number of clusters i.e. either may be improved or decayed (Karypis, et al 2000)

Marketing

Marketing is typically defined as: "Marketing is the ongoing process of moving people closer to making a decision to purchase, use, follow or conform to someone else's products, services or values. Simply, if it doesn't facilitate a 'sale', then it's not marketing" Marketing is responsible for keeping the enterprise attentive to market trends, as well as keeping the sales unit aware of where the target segment is. In the following examples, Web mining techniques have been utilized for showcasing items to a client furthermore to recognize conceivable new territories of potential business sector for a venture. Item proposal recommending items to buy is a key issue for all organizations. As the client driven methodology drives the present plans of action, customary block and-mortar stores need to depend on information gathered unequivocally from clients through reviews to offer client driven recommendations.

Product Area and Trend Analysis John Ralston Saul, the Canadian author, essayist and philosopher noted: Businesses would definitely like to see such projections onto the future. Specially, identifying new product areas based on trends is a key for any business to capture markets Adapted from (Al-Azmi, 2013)

Human Resources

In any enterprise, the expansive obligation of Human Resource office is to accurately coordinate the privilege talented work force with the right capacity. HR is additionally dependable to set up approaches, rules and to give devices to representatives and administration to empower a charming work air, solid culture, sound and spare environment, and to guarantee that the association's representatives are reliably getting roused. The accompanying application analyzes how to viably oversee human asset office by keeping up the perfect measure of workforce as far as expense viability. It delineates the utilization of Web mining strategies to decrease pointless human workload.HR Call Centres Human resource departments of large companies often face the task of answering the numerous questions of various employees. As the extent of the organization develops and because of globalization, the assignment turns out to be more troublesome as they not just need to handle the quantity of workers, additionally consider different issues, for example, topographically neighborhood strategies and issues. The majority of these errands are noteworthy to the human asset division as it is their obligation to keep their representatives fulfilled and very much –inform. A possible and popular approach to handle this problem is to have "call-centres" that provide the informative service to the employees. With the advent of Web, most companies have tried to put all their policy information on Web sites for easy perusal by the employees. However, it has been observed that over time, more and more employees seek the advice of the representatives (Regis, 2008).

Sales Management

In an enterprise, sales dealing with the trusts for its diverse divisions and undertakings with the point of amplifying benefit and minimizing the danger. Money related administration itself includes two sorts of issues. The principal kind manages the stores gave to the organization from different sources. These stores could be long haul, (for example, proprietorship value) or short-term, (for example, financing from banks). The second kind manages 'reserve administration'. Here, the objectives include distinguishing issues, for example, methodologies, timetables, and hazard avoidance; for the endeavor to settle on a choice on the amount to contribute and when. In the accompanying case, advancements, for example, web and novel strategies, for example, Web mining can assist focus misrepresentation in exchanges to help an undertaking diminish.

Business opportunity risk evaluation With growing competitive markets, better understanding of customer's requirements and matching those to the enterprise's offerings have gained prominence in an enterprise's decision making processes. Important financial and business forecasts are affected by decisions in such processes and hence these decisions highly influence how an enterprise plans to support its market. For example, a lot of historical data about business sales opportunities are gathered by enterprises for one such analysis. Traditionally, this information of an enterprise's offerings, competitor's offerings and the market's demands are analyzed manually by human experts, using statistical methods, usually using a multi-step process. Correct analysis in such a multi-step process is of prime importance. For example, classifying good (profitable) opportunities as bad (non-profitable) makes the predictions pessimistic and results in lost revenue, whereas classifying bad opportunities (non-profitable) as good opportunities ties up an enterprise's resources, in addition to asking for unrealistic goals (Soley, 2003).

Business Financial Management

Financial Management in a venture manages dealing with the trusts for its diverse divisions and undertakings with the point of amplifying benefit and minimizing the danger. Money related administration itself includes two sorts of issues. The principal kind manages the stores gave to the organization from different sources. These stores could be long haul, (for example, proprietorship value) or short-term, (for example, financing from banks). The second kind manages 'reserve administration'. Here, the objectives include distinguishing issues, for example, methodologies, timetables, and hazard avoidance; for the endeavor to settle on a choice on the amount to contribute and when. In the accompanying case, advancements, for example, web and novel strategies, for example, Web mining can assist focus misrepresentation in exchanges to help an undertaking diminish its risks (Gupta, V., & Lehal, G. S. , 2009).

Role of web mining in e-commerce Financial had AnalysesIt includes reviewing of costs and revenues, calculation and comparative analysis of corporate income statements, analysis of corporate balance sheet and profitability, cash flow statement, analysis of financial markets and sophisticated controlling. Web mining can be an effective tool (Arti, 2015).

Fraud Analysis

Fraud analysis is a large problem faced by many businesses ranging from the telecommunications industry to Web-based stores. Fraud is defined as the use of false representations to gain an unjust advantage or abuse of an organization's resources, such as illegal access to an organization's finances. For example, credit card fraud causes the loss of millions of dollars to credit card management companies like Visa and MasterCard. This motivates organizations to analyze data in order to identify fraud. However, since large amounts of data are necessary for fraud analysis, it becomes difficult for an organization to manually identify fraud from legitimate transactions. This motivates current research in automated analysis of such data, in order to reduce manual screening of individual transactions for fraudulent activity. There are two approaches to reducing fraud - fraud prevention, taking appropriate steps to prevent a fraud from occurring, and fraud detection, identifying fraud as soon as it occurs, thus enabling a quick corrective response. Since it is difficult to predict when a fraud has occurred, fraud detection techniques are usually applied in parallel with fraud prevention techniques (De Decker, 2007).

Fraud Analysis (Case Study)

Ahmed ELAzab (ElAzab. et al, 2015) introduce an approach for detecting fake accounts on Twitter social network, the proposed approach was based on determining the effective features for the detection process. The attributes have been collected from different research, they have been filtered by extensive analysis as a first stage, and then the features have been weighted. Different experiments have been conducted to reach the minimum set of attributes with perceiving the best accuracy results. From more than 22 attributes, the proposed approach has reached only seven effective attributes for fake accounts detection. Although we claim that these attributes can succeed in discovering the fake accounts in other social networks such as Facebook with minor changes according to the unique nature of each social network, however, we need to prepare a dataset to prove our claim. Moreover, providing an analysis to the tweets content of the user can provide more accurate results in the detection process.

Social Media Mining

In general, information extraction is a field that is concerned with obtaining information from different sources. Focusing on online sources such as online databases and web resources services including websites, according of the dynamic nature of the World Wide Web, it became important to find tools for information extraction from the web as end users and application programs have some difficulties when it comes to finding useful information (Alim, Sophia, et al, 2011).

Extracting information from social media had applied different learning approaches as HTML is the common language for implementing Web pages and it is widely supported by The World Wide Web Consortium (W3C). HTML pages can be as a form of semi-structured data in which information follows a nested structure (Ferrara, 2014). This section present different research that have been presented to apply different information extraction approaches on social media.

Culotta, Bekkerman, and McCallumin (Culotta, 2004)had created a system which used the collection of statistical and learning components using real email of two users. In the work of Aron Culotta, et. Al., he depended on the expert-findings, and social network analysis. However,the analysis which is performed by the proposed system lacked a suitable level of reliability and some important information were not considered such as fake email or fake content.

Generally the evolution of technology, supported by global and speedy communication network online Web services, has been growing rapidly which presents new opportunities and challenges to both producers and consumers of information. The volumes of click stream and client information, gathered by web-based associations in their everyday operations, have come to galactic extents. Analysis of such information helps these organizations to focus on the life-time estimation of customers (Mobasher, 2006)

Data mining technique that automatically discovers or extracts the information from web documents in general usually consists of following tasks (Srivastava, Desikan, & Kumar, 2005); (Bhisikar & Sahu, 2013).

- **Resource Finding:** It involves the task of retrieving intended web documents. It is the process by which we extract the data either online or offline resources available on web.
- **Information Selection and Pre-Processing:** It involves the automatic selection and preprocessing of specific information from retrieved web resources. This process transforms the original retrieved data into information. The data is transformed into useful information by using suitable transformation. The transformation could be renewal of stop words, or it may be aimed for obtaining the desired representation such as finding particular format of data.
- **Generalization:** It automatically discovers general patterns at individual web sites as well as across multiple sites. Data Mining techniques and machine learning are used in generalization
- **Analysis:** It involves the validation and interpretation of the mined patterns. It plays an important role in pattern mining. A human plays an important role in information on knowledge discovery process on web

However, in the extraction process, many issues arise for the target of discovering useful information from online pages. One of these issues considering data representation, as website pages can be found in different formats. HTML is designed for present unstructured information, while XML and XHTML are intended for more organized information which elements help the parsers of web crawlers to communicate with the site pages' substance all the more proficiently (Alim, Sophia, et al, 2011)

Production: Shipping and Inventory

Inventory is characterized as the estimation of products available at a certain time case, in an endeavor. Stock can be in distinctive structures like crude material before the company's quality expansion, in procedure amid generation stage, as completed item in its stockroom or in a retail location's conveyance focus holding up to be sold. Stock typically brings about non-esteem added taking care of expenses identified with tied-up capital, protection costs, administration related expense furthermore other outdated stock expenses. Stock administration is characterized as an arrangement of exercises used to do the right stock in ideal spot at perfect time with right amount and right cost. In the accompanying sample application ion, we discuss how Web mining has aided in inventory management (Fernie, 2009)

Predictive Inventory Management in order to help business perform just-in-time inventory, an inventory management system is required to analyze transaction data and accordingly find clusters, each of which is composed of similar items. Since one of significant costs for a business is to maintain an inventory to support sales as well as customers, a successful inventory management helps business decrease cost and increase profit without losing customer satisfaction. An inventory management system should be able to foresee the customers' demand and trends about sale as well; that is, what most customers will buy. (Desikan, P, 2009)

Web Mining in E-Commerce

Ahmad et al, in (Siddiqui, 2013) Tasnim Siddiqui model web mining integrated with the electronic commerce application to improve the performance of e-commerce applications. First Ahmad et al have discussed some important mining techniques which are used in data mining. Then Ahmad et al explained the proposed architecture which contains mainly four components business data, data obtained from consumer's interaction, data warehouse and data analysis. After finishing the task by data analysis

Module it'll produce report which can be utilized by the consumers as well as the e-commerce application owners.

Utilizing Mining to Gain Business Advantages

KFC/Pizza (Al-Azmi, 2013) Hut in Singapore have more than 120 outlets, with a workforce of 5000 Representatives. As a universal fast food establishment, they convey sustenance and refreshments to clients through outlets, drive-through, and by home conveyance. To manage such workload, KFC/Pizza Cabin have utilized a BI instrument; the device was becoming progressively wasteful with every month. Device didn't meet with time necessities to convey business reports. It was additionally had issues with execution benchmarking, in addition to day by day reports over numerous frameworks was dreary. KFC/Pizza Cabin most essential day by day operation was to figure installments required for every day paid laborers, for example, convey staff. The utilized BI instrument, chiefs would take hours and needed to work for additional hours to total up pay accurately. At long last, the old framework reporting was backing off KFC/Pizza Cabin capacity to match and adjust to present and quick changes. Arrangement was to discover another BI apparatus that was present day. KFC/Pizza Hut contracted with Zap, a BI seller, utilizing their item Zap Business Intelligence (Qaqaya, 2008). New arrangement was electronic; it was moreover connected to other outside sources. Corporate information distribution center was rebuilt as to incorporate the point of offers POS, advertising, HR, and the corporate own one of a kind production network. In September 2009, following two month of testing, KFC/Pizza Hut ran live with the new BI apparatus. The workers and administrators were for the most part content with the new instrument. As it was online, and it offered cutting edge BI abilities like dashboards, moment report era, KPI benchmarking, scoreboards, and an extremely easy to understand interface. The advantages of the new device were huge. The change included improved business sector spending, through live upgrades; KFC/Pizza Hut promptly reacted and balanced its promoting effort and offers. Eatery arranging and outlet area administrations were taking into account reports given for the instrument, to adapt to KFC/Pizza Hut procedure of being near its Clients. Client administration was exceptionally enhanced, particularly the home conveyance administration, as the instrument precisely catch the parameters of such conveyances to streamline the conveyance process. In expansion, the POS incorporation into the information distribution center permitted KFC/Pizza Hut to deal with its arrangements what's more, offers per outlet; diverse clients at distinctive areas had exceptionally changed requests.

In brief Web mining extends analysis much further by combining other corporate information with Web traffic data. Practical applications of Web mining technology are abundant, and are by no means the limit to this technology (Arti, 2015). Web mining tools can be extended and programmed to answer almost any question. It can be applied in following areas:

1. Web mining can provide companies managerial insight into visitor profiles, which help top management take strategic actions accordingly.
2. The company can obtain some subjective measurements through Web Mining on the effectiveness of their marketing campaign or marketing research, which will help the business to improve and align their marketing strategies timely.
3. In the business world, structure mining can be quite useful in determining the connection between two or more business Web sites.
4. This allows accounting, customer profile, inventory, and demographic information to be correlated with Web browsing. (Mitta, 2013)
5. Knowledge discovery is obtained from artificial intelligence and machine learning, which uses a datasearch process, to extract information from the data, as well as the relationship between data elements and models from which to discover business rules and business facts. In Knowledge discovery we can use data visualization tools and navigation tools to help developers analyse the data before mining, to further enhance data mining capabilities, visualization systems can be presented with a graphical analysis of multivariate data to help business analysts, knowledge discovery (Arti, 2015).

ADDITIONAL READING

The Deep Web is a part of the internet not accessible to link-crawling search engines like Google. The only way a user can access this portion of the internet is by typing a directed query into a web search form, thereby retrieving content within a database that is not linked. In layman's terms, the only way to access the Deep Web is by conducting a search that is within a particular website.

The Deep Web allows access to my tool box. As Fake ID, Malware, Drugs, Arms, Assassination Services, People trafficking (Kapoor, A., 2011).

The dark Web is the portion of the deep Web that has been intentionally hidden and is inaccessible through standard Web browsers. Dark Web sites serve as a platform for Internet users for whom anonymity is essential, since they not only provide protection from unauthorized users, but also usually include encryption to prevent monitoring. A relatively known source for content that resides on the dark Web is found in the Tor network. The Tor network is an anonymous network that can only be accessed with a special Web browser, called the Tor browser (Tor 2014a). First debuted as The Onion Routing (Tor) project in 2002 by the US Naval Research Laboratory, it was a method for communicating online anonymously. Another network, I2P, provides many of the same features that Tor does. However, I2P was designed to be a network within the Internet, with traffic staying contained in its borders. Tor provides better anonymous access to the open Internet and I2P provides a more robust and reliable "network within the network" (van Eeten, 2012)The dark web is using for The ability to traverse the Internet with complete anonymity nurtures a platform ripe for what are considered illegal activities in some countries, including controlled substance marketplaces, credit card fraud and identity theft and leaks of sensitive information.

The Dark Web refers to any web page that has been concealed to hide in plain sight or reside within a separate, but public layer of the standard internet. The internet is built around web pages that reference other web pages; if you have a destination web page which has no inbound links you have concealed that page and it cannot be found by users or search engines. One example of this would be a blog posting that has not been published yet. The blog post may exist on the public internet, but unless you know the exact URL, it will never be found. Other examples of Dark Web content and techniques include: Search boxes that will reveal a web page or answer if a special keyword is searched. Try this by searching "distance from Sioux Falls to New York" on Google. Sub-domain names that are never linked to; for example, "internal.brightplanet.com" Relying on special HTTP headers to show a different version of a web page Images that are published but never actually referenced, for example "/image/logo_back.gif" Virtual private networks are another aspect of the Dark Web that exists within the public internet, which often requires additional software to access. TOR (The Onion Router) is a great example. Hidden within the public web is an entire network of different content which can only be accessed by using the TOR network. While personal freedom and privacy are admirable goals of the TOR network, the ability to traverse the internet with complete anonymity nurtures a platform ripe for what is considered illegal activity in some countries, including: Controlled substance marketplaces Armories selling all kinds of weapons Child pornography Unauthorized leaks of sensitive information Money laundering Copyright infringement Credit Card fraud and identity theft Users must use an anonymizer to access TOR Network/ Dark Web websites. The Silk Road, an online marketplace/infamous drug bazaar on the Dark Web, is inaccessible using a normal search engine or web browser (van Eeten, 2012).

FUTURE RESEARCH DIRECTIONS

Web mining techniques were the major functional areas of businesses so Web mining and extract information role important need to be analyze by measure the credibility of information propagated through web.

On the other web mining need to be integrated with the electronic commerce application to improve the performance of e-commerce applications

CONCLUSION

In this chapter, we introduced an overview for web mining, web mining taxonomies, web mining applications, and web mining challenges and limitations. Web usage mining presented in particular, issues of web usage mining, and web usage mining language and algorithms, and finally presented the effectiveness of web usage mining in some area of business such as (Production, Fraud analysis, Business Financial Management, Sales Management, Marketing, Human resource, etc...).

REFERENCES

Aggarwal, Shruti, & Gurpreet. (2013). Improving the Efficiency of Weighted Page Content Rank Algorithm using Clustering Method. *International Journal of Computer Science & Communication Networks, 3*, 231–239.

Aggarwal, S. G. (2013). *Improving the Efficiency of Weighted Page Content Rank Algorithm using Clustering Method*. Academic Press.

Al-Azmi, A. A. (2013). *Data, text and web mining for business intelligence: A survey*. arXiv preprint arXiv:1304.3563

Aldana, W. A. (2000). *Data mining industry: emerging trends and new opportunities*. (Doctoral dissertation). Massachusetts Institute of Technology, Dept. of Electrical Engineering and Computer Science.

Alim, S. (2011). Online social network profile data extraction for vulnerability analysis. *International Journal of Internet Technology and Secured Transactions, 3*(2).

Arti, S. C. (2015). Role of Web Mining in E-Commerce. *International Journal of Advanced Research in Computer and Communication Engineering*.

Bhisikar, P., & Sahu, P. (2013). Overview on Web Mining and Different Technique for Web Personalisation. *International Journal of Engineering Research and Applications, 3*(2).

Bousquet & Wills. (2003). *The Politics of Information The Electronic Mediation of Social Change*. Alt-X Press.

Chaabane, A., Manils, P., & Kaafar, M. A. (2010, September). Digging into anonymous traffic: A deep analysis of the tor anonymizing network. In *Network and System Security (NSS), 2010 4th International Conference on* (pp. 167-174). IEEE. doi:10.1109/NSS.2010.47

Choudhary & Sharma. (2015). Review Paper on Web Content Mining. *International Journal of Research in Engineering and Applied Sciences, 5*(6), 172-176.

Culotta, A. B. (2004). *Extracting social networks and contact information from email and the web.* Academic Press.

De Decker, B. D. (2007). *Advanced Applications for e-ID Cards in Flanders.* Academic Press.

Desikan, P. (2009). *Web Mining for Business Computing.* Academic Press.

El Azab, A., Idrees, A. M., Mahmoud, M. A., & Hefny, H. (2015). Fake Account Detection in Twitter Based on Minimum Weighted Feature set. *World Academy of Science, Engineering and Technology, International Journal of Computer, Electrical, Automation Control and Information Engineering, 10*(1), 13–18.

Ezeife, C. I., & Lu, Y. (2005). Mining web log sequential patterns with position coded pre-order linked wap-tree. *Data Mining and Knowledge Discovery, 10*(1), 5–38. doi:10.1007/s10618-005-0248-3

Fernie, J. (2009). *Logistics and retail management:. emerging issues and new challenges in the retail supply chain.* Kogan Page Publishers.

Ferrara, E. D., De Meo, P., Fiumara, G., & Baumgartner, R. (2014). Web data extraction, applications and techniques. A survey. *Knowledge-Based Systems, 70*, 301–323. doi:10.1016/j.knosys.2014.07.007

Fürnkranz, J. (2002). Web Structure Mining. Exploiting the Graph Structure of the World Wide Web. *Österreichische Gesellschaft für Artificial Intelligence*, 17-26.

Gupta, V., & Lehal, G. S. (2009). A survey of text mining techniques and applications. *Journal of Emerging Technologies in Web Intelligence, 1*(1), 60-76.

Han, J., Cheng, H., Xin, D., & Yan, X. (2007). Frequent pattern mining: Current status and future directions. *Data Mining and Knowledge Discovery, 15*(1), 55–86. doi:10.1007/s10618-006-0059-1

Hassan, H. A. (2014). Query Answering Approach Based on Document Summarization. Query Answering Approach Based on Document Summarization. *International Open Access Journal of Modern Engineering Research, 4*(12).

Hassan, H. D. (2015). Arabic Documents classification method a Step towards Efficient Documents Summarization. *International Journal on Recent and Innovation Trends in Computing and Communication*, 351-359.

Hussein, M. K., & Mousa, M. H. (2010). An Effective Web Mining Algorithm using Link Analysis. *International Journal of Computer Science and Information Technologies, 1*(3), 190-197.

Jaideep Srivastava, R. C.-N. (2000). Web Usage Mining: Discovery and Applications of Usage. *SIGKDD Explorations, 1*(2), 12.

Janssens, F. (2007). *Clustering of scientific fields by integrating text mining and bibliometrics.* Academic Press.

Jiawei Han, K.-C. C. (2002). Data Mining for Web Intelligence. *IEEE International Conference on Data Mining.*

Jiawei Han Kevin, C.-C. C. (2002). *Data Mining for Web Intelligence*. University of Illinois at Urbana-Champaign.

Kaczmarek, T. Z. (2010). Information extraction from web pages for the needs of expert finding. Studies in Logic, Grammar and Rethoric, Logic Philosophy and Computer Science, 141-157.

Kapoor, A., & Solanki, R. (2011). The Susceptible Network. *IITM Journal of Information Technology, 54*.

Kumar & Suvarchala. (2012). A Study: Web Data Mining Challenges and Application for. *IOSR Journal of Computer Engineering, 7*(3), 24-29.

Lancaster, F. W. (2003). *Indexing and abstracting in theory and practice*. London: Facet.

Liu, B. G. (2003). Mining data records in Web pages. In *Proceedings of the ninth ACM SIGKDD international conference on Knowledge discovery and data mining* (pp. 601-606). ACM.. doi:10.1145/956750.956826

Mahmood, A., & Mahmood, E. A.-S.-B. (2013). Recommender system for ground-level Ozone predictions in Kuwait. *IEEE Federated Conference on Computer Science and Information Systems*.

Mahmood, A., & Mahmood, N. E.-B. (2014). An Intel Innovations in Bio-inspired Computing and Applications. Springer.

Masseglia, F. P. (2000). *An efficient algorithm for web usage mining. Networking and Information Systems Journal*.

Mehtaa, P. P. (2012). Web Personalization Concept and Research Issue. *International Journal of Information and Education Technology*.

Mobasher, B. (2006). Web Usage Mining. In *Web Data Mining: Exploring Hyperlinks, Contents and Usage Data*. Academic Press.

Mohamed, F. (2011). Business Intelligence for Emerging e-Business Applications. *Journal of Emerging Technologies in Web Intelligence*.

Mohapatra, R. (2004). *Information extraction from dynamic web sources*. Doctoral dissertation.

Noor, A. B. (2008). Semantic Web: Data Representation. In Partial Fulfillment of the Requirement for the Degree of Master in Information Technology.

Okoli, C., Mehdi, M., & Mesgari, M. (2012). *The people's encyclopedia under the gaze of the sages. A systematic review of scholarly research on Wikipedia*. Academic Press.

Patel, P., Jena, B., & Sahoo, B. (2014). Knowledge Discovery on Web Information Repository. *IJACTA, 1*(2),049-56.

Qaqaya, H. (2008). *The effects of anti-competitive business practices on developing countries and their development prospects*. Academic Press.

Rani, P. (2013). A Review of Web Page Ranking Algorithm. *Revi International Journal of Advanced Research in Computer Engineering & Technology*.

Ravi, K., & Ravi, V. (2015). A survey on opinion mining and sentiment analysis: Tasks, approaches and applications. *Knowledge-Based Systems*, *89*, 14–46. doi:10.1016/j.knosys.2015.06.015

Regis, R. (2008). *Strategic human resource management and development*. Excel Books India. Excel Books India.

Samar Mahmoud, N. E.-B. (2013). An Intelligent Recommender System for Drinking Water Quality. *International Conference on Hybrid Intelligent Systems (HIS)*.

Shoemaker, P., & Reese, S. D. (2011). *Mediating the message*. Routledge.

Siddiqui, A. T. (2013). *Web Mining Techniques in E-Commerce Applications*. arXiv preprint arXiv:1311.7388

Soley, M. (2003). Culture as an issue in knowledge sharing: A means of competitive advantage. *Electronic Journal of Knowledge Management*, *1*(2), 205-212.

Srivastava, J. C., Cooley, R., Deshpande, M., & Tan, P.-N. (2000). Web usage mining: Discovery and applications of usage patterns from web data. *ACM SIGKDD Explorations Newsletter*, *1*(2), 12–23. doi:10.1145/846183.846188

Srivastava, T., Desikan, P., & Kumar, V. (2005). Web Mining – Concepts, Applications and Research Directions. Foundations and Advances in Data Mining. *Studies in Fuzziness and Soft Computing*, *180*, 275–307. doi:10.1007/11362197_10

Srivastava, T., Desikan, P., & Kumar, V. (2005). Web Mining – Concepts, Applications and Foundations and Advances in Data Mining. *Studies in Fuzziness and Soft Computing*, *180*, 275–307. doi:10.1007/11362197_10

Stevenson, M., & Greenwood, M. A. (May 2006). Learning Information Extraction Patterns Using WordNet. *Proceeding of The Third International WordNet Conference*.

Thirumala Sree Govada, N. L. (2014). Comparative study of various Page Ranking Algorithms in Web Content Mining (WCM). *International Journal of Advanced Research*, *2*(7), 457–464.

van Eeten, M. J., & Mueller, M. (2012). Where is the governance in Internet governance? *New Media & Society*.

Witten, I. H., & Frank, E. (2005). *Data Mining: Practical machine learning tools and techniques*. Morgan Kaufmann.

Yi, L., Liu, B., & Li, X. (2003, August). Eliminating noisy information in web pages for data mining. In *Proceedings of the ninth ACM SIGKDD international conference on Knowledge discovery and data mining* (pp. 296-305). ACM. doi:10.1145/956750.956785

Yu-Hui Tao, T.-P. H.-M. (2007). Web usage mining with intentional browsing data. *International Journal of Expert*.

KEY TERMS AND DEFINITIONS

Data Extraction: Data extraction is a field that is concerned with obtaining information from different online databases and services web resources including websites. According of the dynamic nature of the World Wide Web so it become important to find tools for data extraction. end users and application programs have some difficulties when it comes to finding useful data.

Fraud Analysis: Fraud analysis is a large problem faced by many businesses ranging from the telecommunications industry to Web-based stores. Fraud is defined as the use of false representations to gain an unjust advantage or abuse of an organization's resources, such as illegal access to an organization's finances.

I2P: Was designed to be a network within the Internet, with traffic staying contained in its borders. Tor provides better anonymous access to the open Internet and I2P provides a more robust and reliable "network within the network."

Page Rank: Page Rank is a numeric value that represents how important a page is on the web. Page Rank is the Google's method of measuring a page's "importance." When all other factors such as Title tag and keywords are taken into account, Google uses Page Rank to adjust.

The Deep Web: A part of the internet not accessible to link-crawling search engines like Google. The only way a user can access this portion of the internet is by typing a directed query into a web search form, thereby retrieving content within a database that is not linked. In layman's terms, the only way to access the Deep Web is by conducting a search that is within a particular website.

The GSP Algorithm: GSP algorithm is intended for mining Generalized Sequential Patterns. It extends previous proposal by handling time constraints and taxonomies.

Web Content Mining: Web Content Mining is the process of retrieving the information from web document into more structure forms. It is related to Data Mining because many Data Mining techniques can be applied in Web Content Mining.

Weighted Page Content Rank Algorithm (WPCR): A proposed page ranking algorithm which is used to give a sorted order to the web pages returned by a search engine in response to a user query. WPCR is a numerical value based on which the web pages are given an order.

XGMML: Extensible Graph Markup and Modeling Language) is an XML 1.0 application based on Graph Modeling Language (GML) which is used for graph description. XG-MML uses tags to describe nodes and edges of a graph. The purpose of XGMML is to make possible the exchange of graphs between different authoring and browsing tools for graphs. The conversion of graphs written in GML to XGMML is straight forward. Using Extensible Stylesheet Language (XSL) with XGMML allows the translation of graphs to different formats.

This research was previously published in Web Usage Mining Techniques and Applications Across Industries edited by A.V. Senthil Kumar, pages 324-350, copyright year 2017 by Information Science Reference (an imprint of IGI Global).

Section 3
Online Identity

Chapter 12
In Plaintext:
Electronic Profiling in Public Online Spaces

Shalin Hai-Jew
Kansas State University, USA

ABSTRACT

People have long gone online to groom their online identities, to communicate some aspects of themselves in the real. The information shared is purposive and strategic. Inevitably, the information is selective and incomplete. The cyber may evoke something about the physical only to a degree, in the cyber-physical confluence. In an asymmetrical information environment, those who have the most accurate and requisite information often have the advantage. It is said that much of intelligence is conducted using Open-Source Intelligence (OSINT), which suggests a need for reading between the lines of publicly released information; indeed, much of life is conducted in online public spaces. A number of tools enable the extraction and analysis of information from public sites. When used in combination, these tools may create a fairly clear sense of the online presences of various individuals or organizations or networks online for increased transparency. This chapter describes some of the tools (Maltego Radium™ and Network Overview, Discovery, and Exploration for Excel/NodeXL™) that may be used to increase the knowability of others in the creation of various profiles. This includes some light applications of "inference attacks" based on publicly available information. Further information may be captured from the Hidden Web through tools designed to crawl that understructure, and this potential is addressed a little as well.

INTRODUCTION

A related trend of our times is that troves of dossiers on the private lives and inner beings of ordinary people, collected over digital networks, are packaged into a new private form of elite money. The actual data in these troves need not be valid. In fact, it might be better that it is not valid, for actual knowledge brings liabilities. -- Jaron Lanier in Who Owns the Future? (2013, p. 108)

Correlation of seemingly innocuous information can create inference chains that tell much more about individuals than they are aware of revealing. -- Gerald Friedland, Gregor Maier, Robin Sommer, and

DOI: 10.4018/978-1-5225-3163-0.ch012

Nicholas Weaver's "Sherlock Holmes' Evil Twin: On the Impact of Global Inference for Online Privacy" (2011)

In professional lives, opportunities to collaborate with others arise with fair regularity, including with organizations and individuals about whom one has no direct prior experiences. While most have an interest in maintaining some basic public-facing profiles and do share information strategically through the WWW and Internet. These public electronic realms are high-noise environments, with the concomitant challenges of clear sense-making and accurate signals detection. The problem is how to more accurately read online signaling to create effective electronic profiles.

The value of consuming others' self-authored contents is limited because most people offer information that shows themselves in optimal light. Even when individuals are fully candid, self-reportage is limited because of human limitations in perception and cognition; for example, people have been found to employ "an unconscious defense mechanism used to reduce anxiety by denying thoughts, feelings, or facts that are consciously intolerable" (Varki & Brower, 2013, p. 17), which suggests that any information that threatens the ego will often be disavowed or ignored. Donath (2007) differentiates between inherently reliable signals [such as index signals (directly related to traits), and "strategic" or "handicap" signals (costly to produce to show the capability of the signaler to afford such "wastage"; theoretically sufficiently costly to outweigh potential signals of deceptively producing such a signal)] and less reliable ones [such as "conventional" signals in human communications, which have an arbitrary relationship between the signal and the actual underlying quality] (Donath, 2007, p. 234). This author makes the point that "very few signals are impossible to fake" given human ingenuity (Donath, 2007, p. 234). Conventional signals are then less reliable because they are open to deceptive manipulations (Shami, Ehrlich, Gay, & Hancock, 2009). These signals are a common feature of social grooming or "fronting." Online depictions are a form of cheap vs. costly signaling. Greenberg (2012) writes:

Forget these conflicting parallel realities. The Internet is neither fundamentally private nor fundamentally public, anonymous or onymous. Those who behave a certain way online and use certain services will have no privacy, while those who behave another way and use other services can be very, very hard to identify—harder to identify now, in many ways, than ever in communication's history (pp. 6 - 7).

If online spaces are "digital enclosures" that are panopticons open to surveillance and monitoring (Andrejevic, 2007), these offer space for going beyond surface understandings of others. Online, there are explicit and implicit systems that are used for understanding reputations. The challenge then is to exploit high-dimensionality data in a way that is accurate and that scales. Balanced against outsider knowing is the core concept of privacy, the suggestion that individuals and groups may choose to self-reveal what they choose to about themselves to others according to their own free will; privacy is conceptualized as the right to be left alone and to limit others' access to oneself and one's personal information. There are varying types of privacy: spatial, bodily, informational, and communicative, among others; these suggest the need for physical anonymity and safety, informational confidentiality, unobservability in various contexts, and protection of information and reputations. "Privacy" is both a social and a legal concept. In other words, the work of electronic profiling must be balanced against others' privacy rights, but solving this balance may well be an intractable challenge.

People and organizations may have various reasons to "go to ground." Generally speaking, "anonymity" refers to the ability to function in a certain realm or mixed realms without disclosing actual personally identifiable information (PII) or unique identifiers, and ultimately user identity. This concept is often used with the assumption that people should be able to choose what they want to disclose and to keep secret the rest from those around them. Pseudonymity refers to the ability to maintain long-term anonymity without disclosure of actual real-world identity. Onymity refers to the phenomenon of bearing a name, possibly in a non-detachable or non-separable way from the self. Theoretically, there may be traceable and untraceable anonymity and pseudonymity. Traceable anonymity means that someone somewhere knows and can connect an individual to an alias. Here, the anonymity is revocable: an example could be a government law enforcement agency asking a commercial service provider to identify a user who is anonymous to the broader public. Untraceable anonymity means that no one anywhere knows about the connection between an individual to an alias (except the individual). Traceable pseudonymity means that someone somewhere knows who the real individual is behind a pseudonym; by contrast, untraceable pseudonymity means that no one anywhere knows who the real individual is behind a pseudonym (except for the individual). Researchers have noted that pseudonyms may be used over time to build up a reputation like any other online personality. Unlinkability refers to the ability to use multiple resources and / or identities without having these connected to the same user. Unobservability refers to the ability to use a resource or service without allowing others to see that use. In the adversarial approach in information technologies (IT) research and development work, coders and engineers have designed various schemes for both offense and defense in terms of data access (encryption and data masking vs. decryption and data un-masking; data certitude and security vs. uncertainty and error); identity management (obfuscation or masking vs. traceability); safe communications (encryption vs. interception and decryption); information security (protection vs. man-in-the-middle and other attacks); mobility tracking (trace and analysis vs. spatial obfuscation), and others. Is untraceable anonymity or pseudonymity possible? Is this possible in time (with the assumption of improving analytical techniques and technologies in the future)? With retroactive analysis, will everything be knowable in terms of "wayback" search and analysis and linkage? Certainly, various law enforcement, military, intelligence, and other organizations are hard at work to make sure that this is not possible—in order to fulfill their respective tasks. After all, if people may untraceably function online, in underground economies, in criminal enterprises, in terrorist plots, they could unleash chaos through non-accountability (Greenberg, 2012). As such, it is difficult to conceptualize the possibility of absolute untraceability of electronic identity, whether for individuals or for groups. In a pervasive computing environment, with so many devices and signals moving through wires and the air, this work of knowability and unknowability is in constant tension.

Figure 1, "Public Electronic Information from Various Sectors," shows that public electronic information is created in a number of sectors. This diagram is drawn to show overlaps from all four quadrants. It is assumed that each of the entities in all four quadrants hold private data in reserve, with a continuum of protected in-access to public access. The willingness to invest moneys to probe for particular information may affect the range of data available up to a point; the further willingness to go beyond legal means may increase access to data. Those who would like to remain unobserved do not use one methodology or tool in isolation. Active efforts to evade detection, such as using encryption, proxy servers, virtual private networks, pseudonymous identities or anonymous credentials, anonymous remailers, unusually long passwords, and other strategies, would be sufficient to put off most (except the hardiest and technology-endowed) researchers in the public space. This chapter assumes only public and legal access through publicly available technology tools and methods.

Figure 1. Public electronic information from various sectors

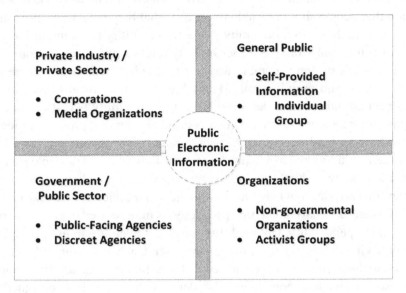

Table 1 proposes a utilitarian conceptualization for going public or private. The default state is understood as privacy or non-revelation of information, with going public related to the effort in making data public. This conceptualization may be helpful in interpreting the information that is public.

REVIEW OF THE LITERATURE

The online environment is a constantly changing one, with an evolving set of information exploitation capabilities available to the broader public. In academia, white-hat documentation of others using publicly available information is done to learn about others without causing harm. The same tools—social network analysis, inference attacks, big data analysis, and other methods—may be used for a variety of ends.

Table 1. Motivations for going public vs. going private

Public	Private
• Reputation building and maintenance • Outreach to constituents and stakeholders • Sparking behaviors through ideas and messages (activism, buying, selling, marketing, or acquiring resources, etc.) • Professional responsibility • Socializing • Making purchases • Collecting information	• Following laws • Protecting people's privacy • Protecting non-public information • Maintaining degrees of freedom (self-determination) in current and future decision-making • Protection of innovations • Maintaining a personal life • Increasing safety and protection of the self and others • Hiding information irrelevant to the public • Avoiding the risks to information revelation

Social Network Analysis (SNA) and Electronic SNA

There are ways to extract information from social media platforms to understand apparent relationships and social ties (edge relations) through social network analysis (SNA) and electronic social network analysis (ESNA). Research in social networks assumes some core concepts. One assumption is that people are social beings, and they have social needs which must be met through interacting with others. People preferentially attach to others: they are most comfortable with those like themselves (homophily), but they will engage with others heterophilously when necessary to work across domains (such as on cross-functional teams). People are seen to be hierarchical, with defined leadership and followership tendencies. Much of people's real-world interactions are moved from the physical world into cyberspace where people congregate, communicate, collaborate, and socialize. Various tools and methods are applied to the capture, analysis, and visualization of these social networks, in order to understand others' systems, the members within the network, the activities in the network, and other details. There are thoughts that latent information may be extracted, such as sleeper entities or nodes who are highly influential in actuality (even if they may not seem so from an external view). By implication, individuals may be understood by the company they keep. Organizations may be understood by the membership they attract and the behaviors and communications they display. Social networks are portrayed as node-link (vertices-edges) diagrams in two dimensions (2D) or three dimensions (3D). The focal or core node is the main focus, and his or her ego neighborhood is comprised of the direct ties that link to him or her through online behaviors (such as direct communications, such as followership). Social networks may be visualized beyond the one-step ego neighborhood to examine transitivity (the likelihood of the directly connected nodes or "alters" to connect to each other; those networks with higher transitivity have higher connectivity among these social agents). These connections may be carried out to multiple degrees. An undirected network involves one in which the links are non-directional; a directed network is one in which the links have arrows on the ends showing which way relationships are going (or if the relationships are reciprocal, with arrows on both ends of a link). Dense-tie and sparse-tie networks have different advantages and short-comings for different purposes. Not all ties are created equal either. Some are thicker to indicate a greater amount of connectivity in terms of trust, formality, longevity, or amount of movement of transmissible goods. Tie strength may be indicated by line thickness or an annotation like a number.

Extracting social network information enables structure mining, which involves an analysis of the hierarchies and interrelationships in such networks. A "social graph census" of the social network identifies various types of structural relationships within the social network. Influential nodes, for example, are conceptualized as having high in-degree (nodes that feed information and resources into that influential node) but low out-degree (few other entities to whom the powerful entity is beholden). Whiskers are subgraphs (or islands or cliques) that are more densely interconnected among themselves but less connected to the overall larger network (usually by only a connector link or two). Pendant nodes are those that are connected to a social network by one tie only, and these tend to be on the periphery. Isolate or singleton nodes are zero-degree nodes; they are part of the network's periphery but do not directly interact with the other members.

Electronic social network analysis is based on both data and metadata (information about information), both the contents of the exchanges and the structures of the interrelationships between entities based on their actual interactions. One underlying concept to SNA is that there is a cost to creating and maintaining relationships, and in that sense, there must be a rationale for that connection; there are natural limits to the sizes of people's social groups per the Dunbar number, so people tend to be selective and preferential. Another concept is that there are hidden relationships that are non-apparent without the uses of particular analytical tools, a few of which will be explored here. Social network analysis includes an analysis of the structure of social networks (social graphs or topologies) in terms of those who are most central in a network as compared to others who are peripheral; the types of communities or clusters within it, and other structural features. Only some phenomena have a strong correlation with the network structure while others do not. There is also content mining in terms of analyzing the messages and resources that move through particular social networks.

With sufficient access to relevant information and big data analysis, public information may be interpreted for latent (or hidden or as-yet-undiscovered) information, identities, relationships, inferences, and predictivity. There are various strategies to analyze public data to "predict undisclosed private information" (Lindamood, Heatherly, Kantacioglu, & Thuraisingham, 2009, p. 1145). Popular latent identities are for "sleeper" experts or influencers in a social network.

Social Network Evolutions Over Time

While social networks are captured as a static slice-in-time with many of these tools, the networks themselves are actually dynamic. They change at various speeds, with members cycling in and out, and leadership changing. One intriguing study found that in large social networks that there were three main components: a giant component in the middle (with a tightly connected core of active individuals who make up the network's core), a middle region comprised of small clusters (usually formed around star individuals), and then an outer periphery with isolate nodes or singletons (those loners with zero degree or no connectivity). Over time, the middle region subgraphs which presented as stars (one charismatic individual as a hub surrounded by acolytes) tended to either merge with the main mass or disappear once the charismatic individual at the hub stopped cultivating the particular small subgraphs (Kumar, Novak, & Tomkins, 2006). These researchers found a low likelihood of extant subgraphs or islands forming more connections through bridging nodes or linking outreaches.

The likelihood that two isolated communities will merge together is unexpectedly low. Evolution in the middle region is characterized by two processes: isolated communities grow by a single user at a time, and then may eventually be merged into the giant component; these processes capture the majority of activity within the middle region. Furthermore, we present a structural finding showing that almost all the isolated communities are in fact stars: a single charismatic individual (in the online sense) linked to a varying number of other users who have very few other connections (Kumar, Novak, & Tomkins, 2006, p. 612).

Kumar, Novak, and Tomkins (2006) suggest different ways that those at the core join the network (based on their interest in the core purpose of the community) and those on the periphery (who they speculate may have been invited by friends, colleagues, or acquaintances) tend to be moving their extant networks online but without an interest in necessarily connecting with those outside that group based on preferential attachment.

One analytical approach involves a datamining technique known as an "inference attack" or "inference chaining," which is often augmented with customized computer programs, in which data is analyzed for sensitive information value with high confidence (of veracity). Indeed, the IT security literature is replete with measures and countermeasures over information knowability via inference attacks and countermeasures to obfuscate information. Inference attacks may be done by cross-referencing large data sets against each other to re-identify individuals; various research studies have found that people may be re-identified often with only a few data points. People's search terms on search engines have been used to create whole-person profiles. This "aggregation problem" is made worse with the sharing of personal attributes of individuals in their social network profiles, which create a "significant privacy concern" (Chivers, 2005). He explains:

Authentication by attribute, rather than identity, requires an authority such as the user's organization to vouch for the attribute, and a temporary binding between the user and the target service that avoids providing further information (Chivers, 2005, p. 19).

Collected electronic data may offer "high resolution data portraits" (Andrejevic, Sept. 20, 2007). Friedland, Maier, Sommer, and Weaver (2011) describe the uses of a variety of sources for "global inference attacks." Individual social actors who may be private may be interpreted by those who are around them, who may leak data purposefully or accidentally. In the same way, "dark" networks that strive to be hidden may be inferred in part by the parts around them that are public. These electronic data doubles or data *doppelgangers* may be revealing of their human counterparts. After all, the wide availability of personally identifiable information enables full-on "doxing" (documentation) attacks by those who may want to find compromising information of others in order to publicly shame them or to commit fraud or to harass or directly harm others.

Inferring Authorship and Identity Through Stylometry

There is analysis of writing styles (stylometry based on various variables such as underlying semi-invariant linguistic patterns) that may lead to the identification of various anonymous authors, with a high degree of certitude (McDonald, Afroz, Caliskan, Stolerman, & Greenstadt, 2012); computing tools have been able to identify writings which have been purposefully obfuscated and those which are imitative, with varying degrees of confidence. Such stylometry analyses have been applied to microblogging as well. Web-based inference is an attack on redaction systems whereby the redacted document is linked with other publicly available documents to infer the removed parts. (Thi & Safavi-Naini, 2012), to see the hidden.

Inferring Relationships From Conversations

Researchers have been developing ways to infer types and depths of relationships based on the language used in online intercommunications. People with lower power than another with greater power tends to align (or mirror) his or her language to the individual with greater power; further, when that power status changes, there are corollary changes in language. Such relationships may be observed cross-domains as well. In online spaces, in terms of emails, wikis, blogs, short message services, and microblogs, and via text, video, and audio file types, people exchange information in a natural language or abbreviated SMS way—and in the exchange may be revealing leadership and followership roles based on status differences. Transactional closeness may be interpreted for relationship, from acquaintanceship to "friend of a friend" (FOAF) and to other levels of intimacy.

Inferring Life Patterns From Location Information

Another form of inference analysis involves accessing movement profiles from online sites and creating time- and location-based trails from apps on mobile devices and cell phones. These mobile phones work like "wearable sensors that in the aggregate show patterns which may be interpreted for the 'social patterns in daily user activity' and which show relationships, socially significant locations, and organizational rhythms (Eagle & Pentland, 2006, p. 255). This data exhaust may provide individual insights about a person's habits. Heatmaps in work places may show where an individual spends the most time. Digital badging in high security buildings is used to identify individuals going into anomalous locations in order to notify security (and counterintelligence) of possible security breaches and individuals who may raise concerns. There is structure in routines, and anomalies are potential red flags of potential malevolent interests and actions. Researchers have shown how "proximity frequencies" may reveal relationships, with couples demonstrating nearness. This may also be collected globally to understand the behaviors of people en masse and their convergences at certain physical or spatial locales at certain times of day and night. With hundreds of millions of handsets sold annually, these devices provide another stream of electronic analysis information.

A groundbreaking study found that tracking mobile phones continuously over 9 months—as a way to simulate wearable sensors—enabled researchers to "accurately analyze, predict, and cluster multimodal data from individuals and communities within the social network of a population" and from an individual's primary eigenbehaviors was able to, at mid-day extrapolate and predict the individual's behaviors for the rest of the day with 79% accuracy (Eagle & Pentland, 2009). The researchers were also able to predict close relationships based on observed similarities between the individuals and groups (Eagle & Pentland, 2009, p. 1057). Given human habituating and patterning, sufficient observations could be analyzed to accurately predict human behaviors. Behavioral data over time not only may be analyzed to describe roles but also to infer affiliations.

A recent study found that people's mobility traces tend to be highly unique. These researchers studied 15 months of human mobility data for 1.5 million individuals. With sufficient time-data collections, the authors could uniquely identify 95% of the individuals, even absent any other defining information.

In fact, in a dataset where the location of an individual is specified hourly, and with a spatial resolution equal to that given by the carrier's antennas, four spatio-temporal points are enough to uniquely identity 95% of the individuals (de Montjoye, Hidalgo, Verleysen, & Blondel, 2013, p. 1).

Further, even coarse data sets provide little anonymity, they assert (de Montjoye, Hidalgo, Verleysen, & Blondel, 2013, p. 2).

Facial recognition software is being applied to public information on the Internet. The identification of people's faces (as a hard-to-disguise biometric feature) in social networking platforms has added another layer of knowability to help researchers capture identities and reveal inter-relationships (Friedland, Maier, Sommer, & Weaver, 2011). Combined with exif (exchangeable image file format) data, such images may place people in certain locations at certain times.

It is important to note that such digital traces may be captured and mixed. These do not have to be conceptualized as separate data sets. Information may be historical, current and real-time, as well as projecting—into the future. Data may be short-term or longitudinal. Social network captures of ego neighborhoods (even those multiple degrees out) may include n = "all," a core definition of "big data". Electronic data capture may create a sense of a whole person or a whole community. Theoretically, these ideas and practices may apply to whole locales, states, regions, countries, or supra-nation systems. These approaches scale, with sufficient human and computing power.

EXPANDING KNOWABILITY

The work of reality mining involves capturing empirical data observed in the wild in order to see what may be accurately learned from that. With the increasing amounts of personal and institutional information placed online, there is a growing sense of what is "knowable" as compared to what is truly private. What follows then are various data crawls of the Web to show some of what is knowable—beyond keyword searches on search engines and other basic research. This also serves as a review of some aspects of Maltego Radium's capabilities in mapping various public networks online. There is also a little information about Network Overview, Discovery, and Exploration for Excel (NodeXL™), an open-source and free tool created under the auspices of the Social Media Research Foundation and made available from Microsoft's CodePlex.

To create a sample graph, entrepreneur and investor Jeff Bezos, CEO of Amazon.com, was chosen for this data crawl. As a well-known individual, he likely has many who are interested in contacting him. His is a fairly disambiguated or original name. The Maltego Radium "machine" was run without filtering out other emails (so as not to head off other potential leads), but at a later point, it would be important to prune out such accounts. The crawl identifies j@amazon.com as his email. In Figure 2, "Linking a Person to an Email Address," there are phone numbers, individuals, a uniform resource locator (URL), and other information from this search.

A "company stalker" machine captures the main email addresses linked to a particular company. Beginning with just a name, the Maltego Radium software identifies linked email accounts, telephones, and websites. This puts companies, even those which are fairly private and protective, within reach of alumni organizations, for example. Figure 3, "A 'Company Stalker' View of www.wikipedia.org," provides many points of connection or contact that do not show up on the public-facing site directly.

In another scenario, a university may want to identify individuals who represent a non-profit organization and its staff. A "company stalker" machine may reveal some of the main individuals who may be broadly reached, even if their names do not appear directly on a website. Figure 4, "A 'Company Stalker' View of www.educause.edu" provides a number of access points.

The actual "footprinting" of a URL surfaces a range of technical information of the host machines, IP addresses, and technologies used to create and deliver the online contents linked to the URL. Figure 5 offers a view of some of the collected information during a machine run.

A Level 3 footprint crawl is the most intensive one possible within Maltego Radium. Figure 6, "Bubble View of a Level 3 Footprint Crawl of Educause.edu" shows a screen capture of one such crawl with the bubble visualization, which is a dynamic and evocative one as the information is in-coming. To provide a sense of the possibilities of viewing this harvested data, a triptych follows that shows a global view of this data visualization and then the zoomed-in views, in Figure 7, "A Triptych Showing a Constellation of Complexity in a Level 3 Footprint Crawl of Educause.edu".

Figure 2. Linking a person to an email address

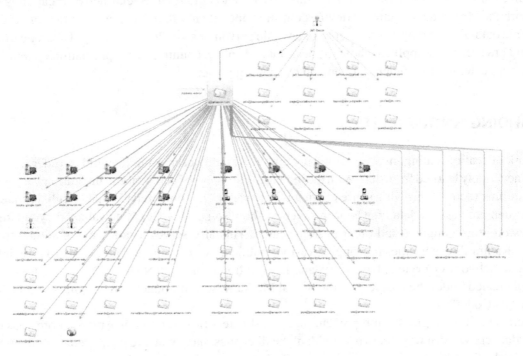

Figure 3. A "company stalker" view of www.wikipedia.org

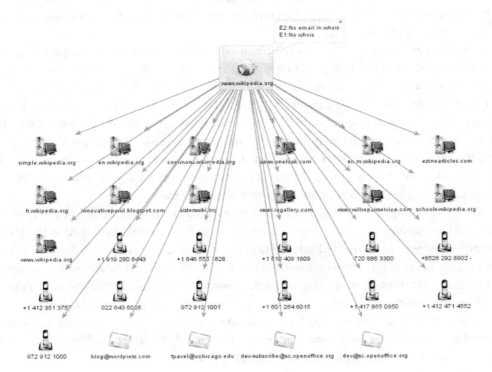

Figure 4. A "company stalker" view of www.educause.edu

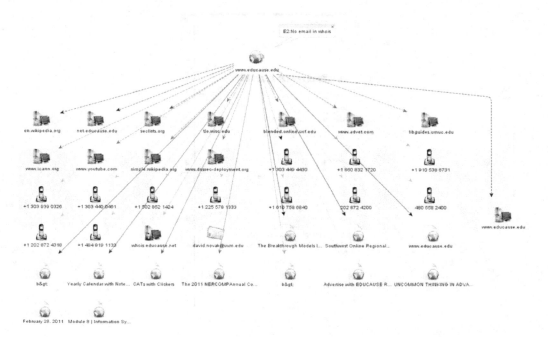

While the top levels of a network may be informative, researchers may probe deeper into various segments of the network (subgraphs or islands)…and may explore specific nodes or entities.

Online Explorations

Another approach involves identifying emergent events or understanding microblogged conversations around trending topics through a hashtag analysis. A "hashtag" involves the usage of the <#> sign and alpha-numeric text to help organize conversations, so that discussants may follow the gist of fast-moving and distributed conversations. The application programming interface (API) of various social media platforms enable such sites to harvest public data. Figure 8, "The Exploration of #MOOCs as a Hashtag Phrase on Twitter™" shows a hashtag search around massive open online courses through #MOOCs. The connections here show some of the discussants in this ad hoc network that has formed around this conversation topic. In which Twitter Digger searches (using Maltego Radium), whole phrases and user names and other elements may be used as the base search term, to pull out self-organizing structures based on emergent issues. Such analyses may show surprising interest groups coalescing (or dividing) around particular issues.

The world's most popular microblogging site, Twitter also offers a geolocation feature. This means that locations may be captured in the various types of Twitter crawls that may be done. In Figure 9, "A Twitter Geo Location Crawl of the edXOnline Twitter Account," this structured graph shows a search of the edXOnline user account on Twitter (located online at https://twitter.com/edXOnline). The various physical locations tied to this account include Seattle, Tuscon, Jacksonville, Albuquerque, Colorado

Figure 5. A "footprinting" view of www.educause.edu

Figure 6. Bubble view of a Level 3 footprint crawl of Educause.edu

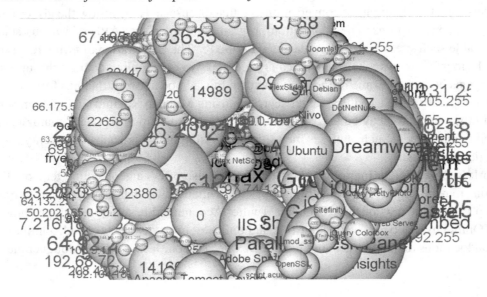

Figure 7. A triptych showing a constellation of complexity in a Level 3 footprint crawl of Educause.edu

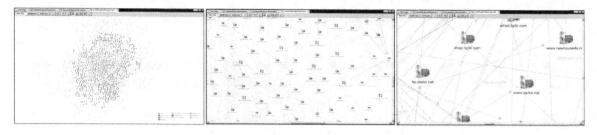

Figure 8. The exploration of #MOOCs as a hashtag phrase on Twitter™

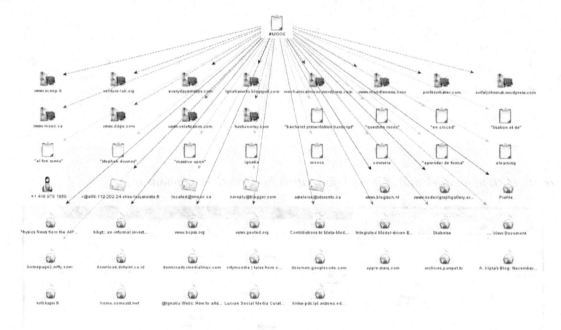

Springs, Omaha, Minneapolis, Chicago, Cambridge, Reading, Serbia, and Ukraine. Various related phone numbers, human identities, documents, URLs, and other elements were surfaced as well.

For the technologists that want to understand the underlying technologies used to build a particular site, it is possible to specify a URL in order to discover the network and domain information as well as the technologies used to build the site. Figure 10, "URL to Network and Domain Information for CreativeCommons.org," shows the various tools and languages used on a site.

Maltego Radium™ enables a domain crawl of locations in the world that then lead to electronic presences, email accounts, URLs, email accounts, telephone numbers, and other elements. Figure 11, "A Domain Crawl of Pretoria, South Africa (Organic Layout Mode)" uses proximity to the center focal node as an indicator of connectivity and linkage.

The domain crawl of a physical location in the world (anywhere on Earth that has networks on the Web) can offer a broad view of the various related electronic entities. Figure 12 shows a larger organic layout mode of the domain crawl of Pretoria, South Africa.

Figure 9. A Twitter geo location crawl of the edXOnline Twitter account

Figure 10. URL to network and domain information for CreativeCommons.org

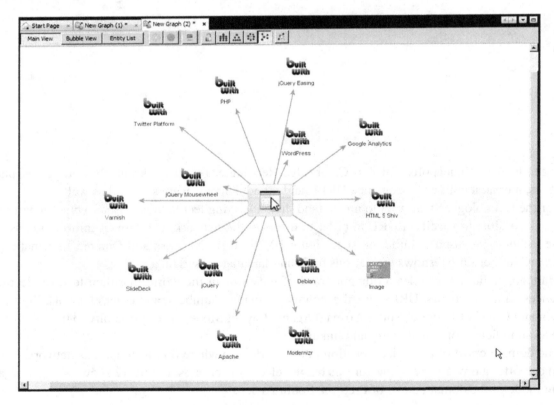

Figure 11. A domain crawl of Pretoria, South Africa (organic layout mode)

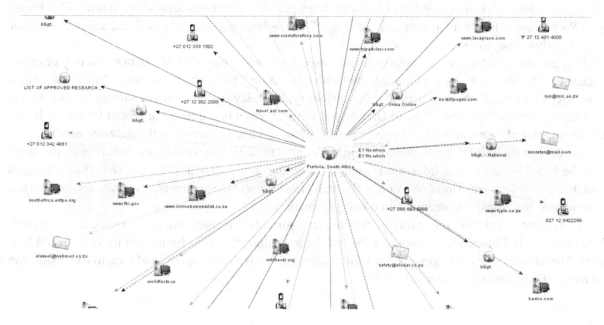

Figure 12. A domain crawl of Pretoria, South Africa (a holistic view of the organic layout mode)

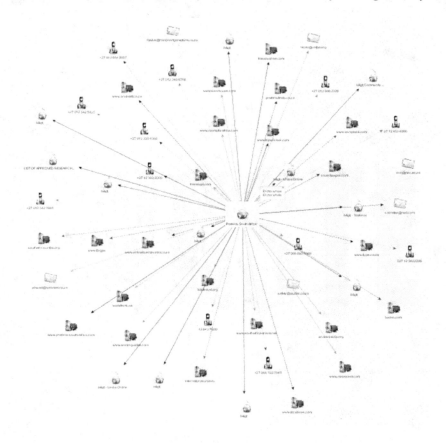

For this crawl, in order to better understand a professional organization, its temporary website (http://blogs.jccc.edu/c2c/) was crawled in order to see what presences the organization has online. This Figure 13, "Web Connectivity for Colleague 2 Colleague" shows both the original crawl and a side connection to its Facebook presence.

It is possible to identify the various devices used on a network as part of a data extraction or crawl. Figure 14, "A Topeka, Kansas, Domain Crawl with a Focus on URLs, Phone Numbers, Email Addresses, and Discovered Files" shows a listing of the various types of devices used on the domain for this region.

Figure 15, "A CNN.com Crawl to Understand Gist" shows a broad range of global locations. It also shows popular phrases on the site to give readers a gist of what the nature of the network may be.

In Maltego Radium™, a search may begin with a so-called Twit or Twit entity. In this case, the target was the U.S. Department of Education (usedgov) user account on Twitter (Figure 16). The initial goal was just to see what was findable. A once-through crawl shows other connected websites, search terms, individuals, locations, documents, and other information.

A "transform" refers to the ability to change one information element online to a wide range of other types of data. In Figure 17, "Evaluating the "Maltego Radium™" Twit Entity and its Web-Based Network," the data extraction begins with a Twitter account, leads to a company, and then to a website with its many affiliations with other sites.

Figure 13. Web connectivity for Colleague 2 Colleague

Figure 14. A Topeka, Kansas, domain crawl with a focus on URLs, phone numbers, email addresses, and discovered files

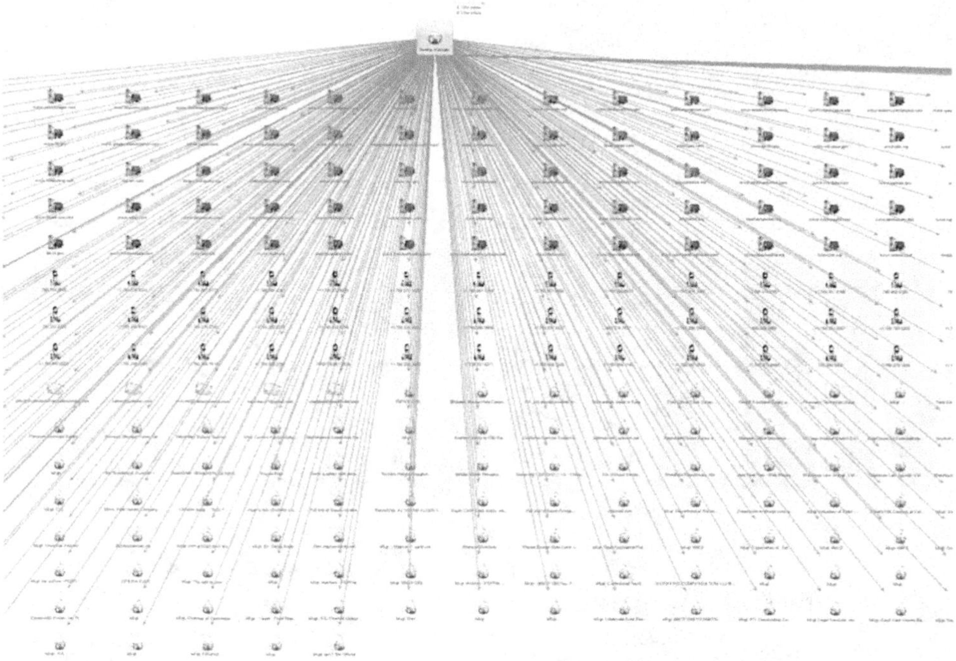

A crawl of the GitHub user network on Twitter (including its presence on Facebook as a side connection) shows the software's use of exif (exchangeable image file) formatted data, with geolocation tags and other information often including many of the recording device's settings during the moments of capture. Such crawls may extract images from a site (Figure 18).

The regional non-profit organization Colleague 2 Colleague hosts the annual Summer Institute on Distance Learning and Instructional Technology (SIDLIT) for the sharing of technological knowledge. The organization created an account to share microblogs (Tweets, in this case) of the event. To understand who might be running this account and their various locales, it may help to run a Twitter Digger exploration. Figure19, "A SIDLIT EventGraph using Twitter Digger in Maltego Radium™" captures related email accounts, locations, individuals, documents, as well as Internet infrastructure.

A similar type of event-related account was created for the BlackHat conference by the organizers there (Figure 20). The freeware tool, Network Overview, Discovery, and Exploration for Excel (NodeXL™), was used to map their network. The social network data was displayed using the Fruchterman-Reingold force-based layout algorithm, and then the nodes (vertices) were placed on a grid to aid in the visualization of the various social networks and communities that are in this ego neighborhood. The initial parameters of the data extraction of BlackHatEvents's user network was 2 degrees (the ego neighborhood and the alters' ego neighborhoods), with a 9,999-persons limit. At the time of the crawl, the official BlackHat-Events account (https://twitter.com/BlackHatEvents) had 2,684 Tweets (microblogs), 1,661 following

Figure 15. A CNN.com crawl to understand gist

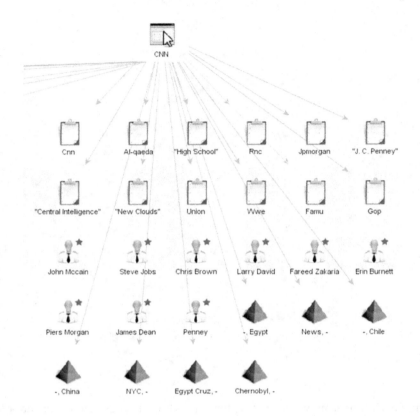

Figure 16. U.S. Department of Education presence on Twitter (usedgov)

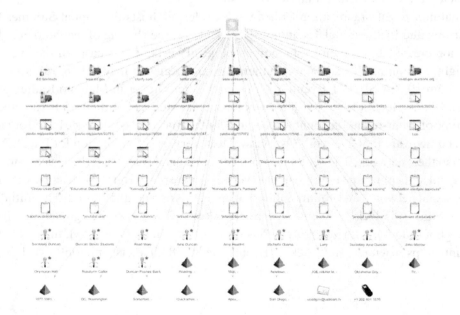

Figure 17. Evaluating the "Maltego Radium™" Twit entity and its Web-based network

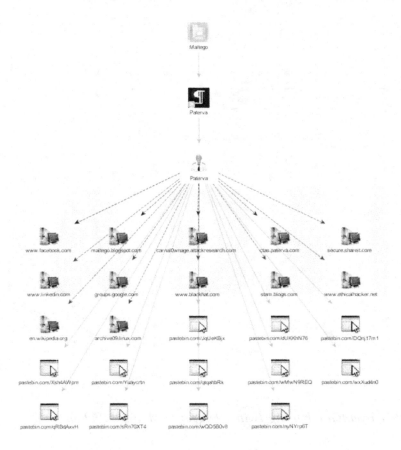

(accounts that the BlackHatEvents were following on Twitter), and 38.798 followers (accounts following BlackHatEvents). From this directed network, seven (7) clusters were identified.

At Figure 21, "An Interactive Graph of the BlackHatEvents User Network on Twitter on the NodeXL Graph Gallery Site (a GraphML version)," the interactive graph of the BlackHatEvents user network may be seen on the NodeXL Graph Gallery site. A mouseover effect reveals the specific node at each location. The inset shows that scrolling in further reveals all the vertices or nodes identified by formal name in that particular region. This social graph visualization stems from raw data. The underlying graph metrics table with more information about the actual social network is shown at Table 2: Black-HatEvents User Network on Twitter (Graph Metrics). This extraction found 14.963 vertices, with 16,310 unique edges, to show a sparsely connected network. In terms of the breadth of this social network, the maximum geodesic distance from furthest node to furthest node was 4. This suggests that the farthest path would be three hops away. The average geodesic distance was 2.4, so most nodes were within pretty easy reach of each other.

Figure 18. GitHub affiliation in Twitter with a side connection to Facebook

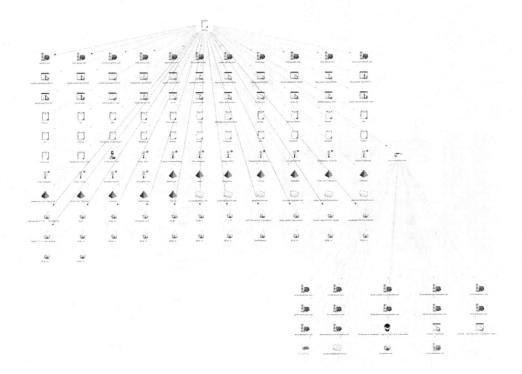

Figure 19. A SIDLIT EventGraph using Twitter Digger in Maltego Radium™

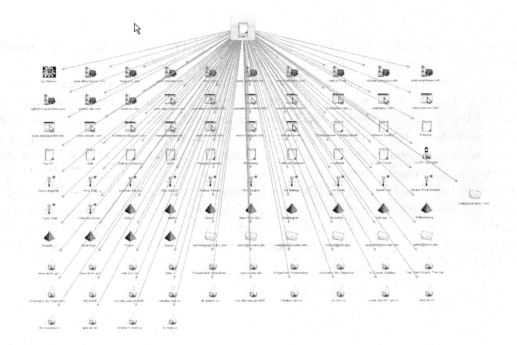

Figure 20. BlackHatEvents user network on Twitter (graphed with the Fruchterman-Reingold force-based layout algorithm and then placed on a grid)

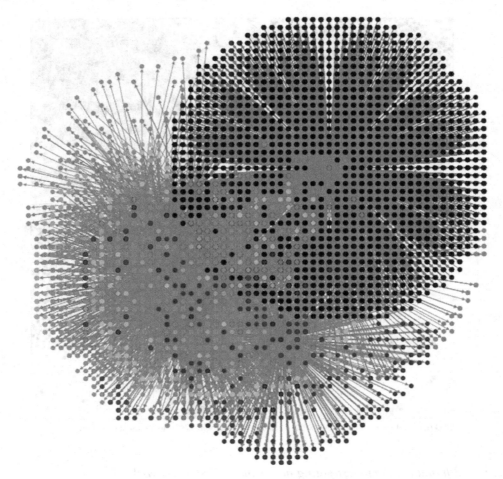

Layering Searches Within the Program

Searches are not limited to the initial "machine" or "transform" that is conducted. A recent domain crawl of the United States Department of Agriculture (USDA) site is shown in Figure 22, "Breadth and Depth: Investigating Nodes in the USDA Network."

In Figure 22, there are multiple pull-out nodes from the main original machine crawl. These branching nodes show more details. A legend of this graph is shown at the bottom right. This legend shows high-dimensionality data or data of various types extracted through various transforms. This view is a higher level view to provide a "forest" version of the structured tree. Scrolling into the image reveals more details. Another way to examine the specific data is in the form of the "entity list," which may be extracted in table or workbook or text formats, among others. This enables a micro data view. This corresponding table may be visualized in the redacted Figure 23: A Corresponding "Entity List" for the USDA Network.

Figure 21. An interactive graph of the BlackHatEvents user network on Twitter on the NodeXL graph gallery site (a GraphML version)

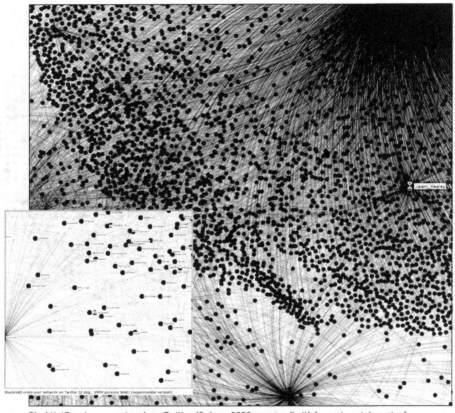

BlackHatEvents user network on Twitter (2 deg., 9999-persons limit) (experimental version)

Figure 22. Breadth and depth: Investigating nodes in the USDA network

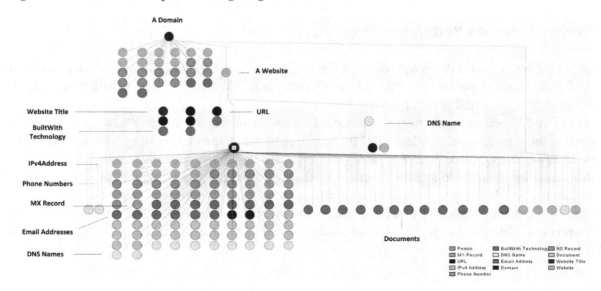

Table 2. BlackHatEvents user network on Twitter (graph metrics)

Graph Type	Directed
Vertices	14963
Unique Edges	16310
Edges With Duplicates	0
Total Edges	16310
Self-Loops	0
Reciprocated Vertex Pair Ratio	0.002458513
Reciprocated Edge Ratio	0.004904966
Connected Components	1
Single-Vertex Connected Components	0
Maximum Vertices in a Connected Component	14963
Maximum Edges in a Connected Component	16310
Maximum Geodesic Distance (Diameter)	4
Average Geodesic Distance	2.422124
Graph Density	7.28527E-05
Modularity	Not Applicable
NodeXL Version	1.0.1.245

By account, that could mean human, cyborg (human and 'bot), and 'bot.

Figure 23. A corresponding "entity list" for the USDA network

To further show how multiple data extractions may be done, Figure 24, "A Graph of a Person-to-Email "Machine" with Links to Related Websites" shows how an initial machine linking a person to an email may be further extended to linking to various connected websites to the email.

As a backstory, only four (4) hits were found on Google for this individual, which is quite sparse. Further transforms were done to try to link to a person. This led to a number of other leads. This visualization was rendered in a zoomed-out format in order to protect the privacy details of the individuals. The converse may also be done: linking an email account to an actual person. Figure 25, "A Graph of an Email Account to a Person," shows how an email account links to various domains and websites, which link to various persons. Some transforms will link directly to individuals.

Another approach combining "machines" and "transforms" may involve placing dual or multiple nodes on the work space to see what overlapping entities may be found. In this case. An alias and a person were placed on the workspace, and crawls were performed. This initial probe found three overlapping websites shared between the two initial entities, in Figure 26, "Dual Node Crawl for Shared Connections." The visualization shows both intra-network (within) and inter-network (between) information.

Additional crawls may be done at each entity level (node) to disambiguate each entity and further sub-relationships. (This tool enables studies of individual nodes to deep levels of fine-grained granularity. Each node is understood to have assumed "biases" that affect how the node behaves. Nodes may be thought of as having a threshold at which point it may be triggered to accept a particular influence, in terms of percolation theory. Percolation is the concept of how anything transmissible may move through social networks. There are various theories of information propagation through social networks.) If graphs become too unwieldy, they may be broken off into their own Maltego Radium™ files. This work requires a level of thoroughness but also select precision. Over-collection will mean that analysts will be sorting through that collected data for usable information. There are risks of collecting too much or too little.

Figure 24. A graph of a person-to-email "machine" with links to related Websites

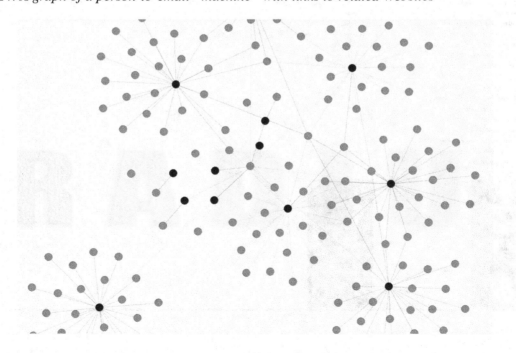

Figure 25. A graph of an email account to a person

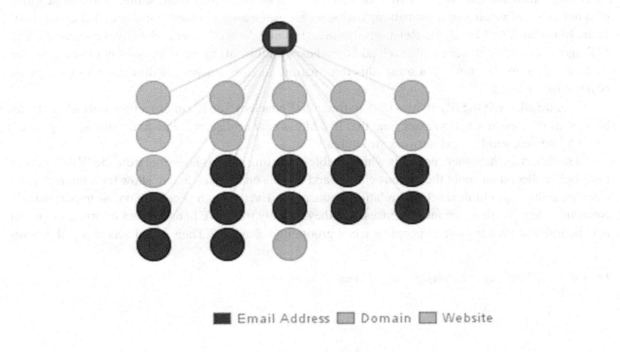

Figure 26. Dual node crawl for shared connections

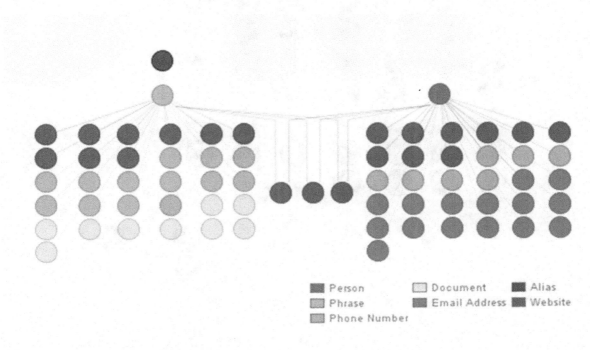

A data extraction may begin with a mere email address which may then be linked to a wide range of other types of electronic information: URLs, websites, email addresses, phone numbers, and a domain. In Figure 27, "Identifying Relationships to an Email Address," other nodes may be explored. The Maltego Radium™ software pulls such additional explorations off to the side, so as not to confuse the contents of the initial crawl. In a sense, this information suggests where an individual may go with his or her email account.

In Figure 28, "A Static IP Address Data Extraction (Redacted)," an IP (Internet Protocol) address may be used as the base node in a search, and that IP address may be disambiguate to locations, telephones, email addresses, and Internet network structures.

To summarize, then, there are tools which enable extracting various networks from the WWW. These tools help collect data about the various entities and objects on the Web and to show their interrelationships for online (and limited offline) relational coherence. Even though people go online to purposively communicate with their various audiences, and they actively work to edit and redact information, much may be inferred even in spite of people's social grooming behaviors. (Their actual acts at social groom-

Figure 27. Identifying relationships to an email address

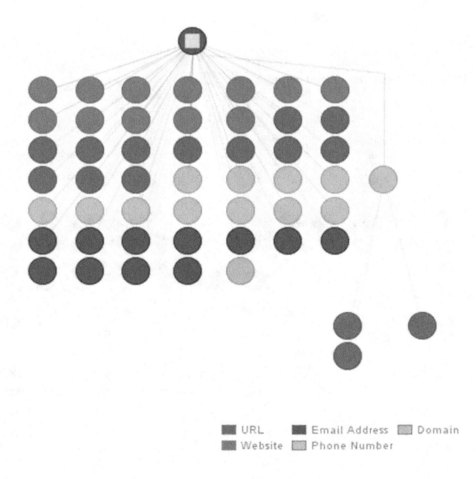

Figure 28. A static IP address data extraction (redacted)

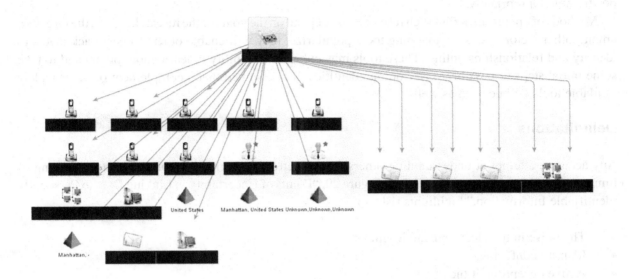

ing and other contrivances are very psychologically revealing in and of themselves.) With site scraping and other methods for data extraction, there are capabilities to map IP addresses to various locations, documents, telephone numbers, and network structures and machines. There are ways to link aliases to personally identifiable information and then contact information from that alias. There are ways to correlate across sites and identities. There are ways to create content networks from microblogging sites and identify emergent communities around particular discussions. Real-world physical locations may have their main domains mapped to understand the electronic Web presence of various locales. There is much interplay between public and private channels in electronic spaces.

These capabilities may be applied to learning contexts in rich ways and through various "use cases". For example, in massive open online courses (MOOCs), various communities of practice may be extracted and studied, with influential student leaders contacted for more support (for them and the other learners who rely on them) or information about how to improve the learning. Latent experts may be identified from various networks. Aliases may be de-anonymized into recognizable individuals who may be reached through their contact information. People who post to a wiki or a blog may be re-identified by their IP addresses and contacted for further interchanges. (That said, there are limits to using such tools to verify whether electronic or virtual identities actually match with real-world people. An actual example relates to faux student accounts that were created apparently to pursue opportunities for fraud. One university could look for evidence to see if the accounts tied to actual individuals. They could identify suspicious accounts. However, they had to take extra steps to identify whether electronic accounts linked to actual people—which actually required multiple other steps—such as direct phone calls and ties to physical addresses.)

Such tools may be turned around on the self and on one's own organizations (as a form of sousveillance, viewing or surveiling an organization from inside; participant surveillance). This tactic may increase self-awareness and learning about what others from the outside can see. In terms of enlightened self-interest, individuals and organizations benefit from knowing what others can know about them and positioning appropriately.

Methods of operationalizing such research will depend on the goals of the researchers and the target(s), among other factors. As such mapping tools popularize, they will enable others to peel back layers to identity and relationships online. These tools may enhance the ability to learn about others and to take some initial steps to possibly verify online identities. It is assumed that a complement of other widely available tools will be used as well.

Delimitations

Any accurate attempt at understanding others from electronic data must involve the understanding of limitations to the publicly collected data. Figure 29, "Points of Uncertainty in Linking Data to Personally Identifiable Information," highlights risks to

- The noise in the electronic environment,
- Identity confusions,
- Active deception of the target,
- Limitations of the tools, and
- Researcher / user error.

These elements may all play a role in confusing online information.

For those who are collecting data exhaust, digital traces, and noisy information (much of it "conventional signals"), it can be hard to know the actual informational value of the data. In order to ensure accuracy, researchers have to use due care to know what is knowable and what is not knowable from what they have. They strive to attain and analyze harder-to-fake signals. If they are going to extrapolate from the

Figure 29. Points of uncertainty in linking data to personally identifiable information

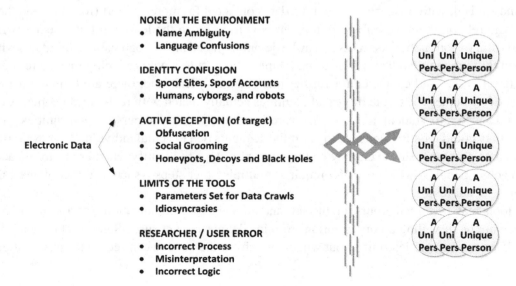

data, they have to understand the limits of those extrapolations. The cyber-physical confluence implies that electronic signaling and presence may indicate something about the real-world. Indeed, the electronic proxy or stand-in for the individual may indicate something about offline lives, but the confluence is clearly not one-for-one. Further, information is constantly changing; likewise, people and organizations themselves are dynamic. What is accurate for a particular moment will not likely be so after a certain period of time. Figure 30, "A Continuum for Assessing Validity of Backstopped Electronic Identities" depicts a conceptualization of a continuum in terms of the level of confidence that may be attained with the collected information. At one end, an electronic identity may be poorly backstopped to a real-world individual. At the other end may be a somewhat higher level of certitude of identity.

One way to standardize an approach about where to understand the confidence level for linking electronic information to an individual or group is to list the evidentiary chains. While there may be many indicators linking online information to an electronic identity, these tools cannot actually prove that that individual is actually real. Optimally, it would help to have actual verification of identity with legal law enforcement standards. Otherwise, there will just be whispers and impressions (Table 3).

It may help to systematize the steps to a data extraction. Figure 31, "A Preliminary Decision Tree of Electronic Profiling," provides an overview of the general steps to these data extractions.

This work would not be sufficiently complete without addressing recent revelations of the work of world-class cryptanalysts and spies, whose quotidian work is to break into protected systems and learn what others hope to keep secret. In the aftermath of the "NSA-leaker" Edward Snowden revelations in mid-2013 about how compromised various encryption systems are (compromisable by a range of intelligence agencies), the truth is that there are still many blocks to accessing people's information for people

Figure 30. A continuum for assessing validity of backstopped electronic identities

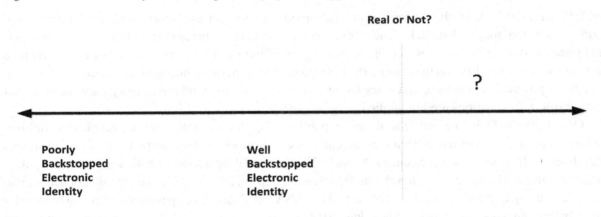

Table 3. Reasons for and against linking electronic information to an individual or group

Reasons For Linking Electronic Information to an Individual or Group	Neutral (as-yet undetermined)	Reasons Against Linking Electronic Information to an Individual or Group

Figure 31. A preliminary decision tree of electronic profiling

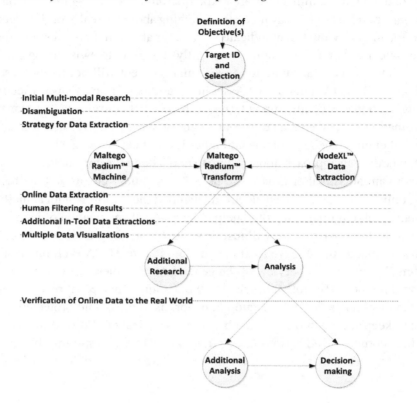

with lesser powers. A number of hurdles prevent broad access to private information: legal liabilities of corporations that may leak data; high-level encryptions (that are not breakable without massive computing power and other capabilities); complex training, and funding. There has to be savvy to differentiate appearances from reality and to consider the limitations that stem from the gappiness in tool capabilities, the cyber-physical confluence, and other factors. Analysts have to avoid the illusory naïve realism that may result if due cautions are not applied.

One truism in IT is that public tools and capabilities lag those of intelligence agencies by multiple decades because competitive advantages are embargoed for years (or even perpetuity). Those in signals intelligence, like the National Security Agency (NSA), benefit by access to both what is in the public academic literature and in protected channels (Schneier, Sept. 4, 2013). Those who would hope to remain nameless are up against a powerful adversary in the NSA with brute-force password guessing reportedly at "a trillion guesses per second" (Snowden, 2013, as cited in Maass, 2013). Even a single slip-up can be devastatingly unforgiving in terms of revealing identity. To successfully extract useful information from the WWW and Internet and then to effective exploit that information requires a lot of work. The public does not know what they do not know except through the rare glimpses and slippages in information from the hidden sides of society. Defining the boundaries of what is or is not feasible in the "black" realm is often a simple guessing game. Much information about individuals is held in private—by those in mega-corporations and in government, particularly law enforcement.

FUTURE RESEARCH DIRECTIONS

The data extraction and analysis presented here shows the capabilities of a few tools as applied to the Surface Web, which is built on the capabilities of browsers that connect http links. This field would benefit from other research showing ways to apply technologies such as those used here to positive use. There will likely be continuing works on measures and countermeasures in terms of knowability and unknowability.

Underlying the Surface Web is the Hidden or Dark Web, which is comprised of databases not searchable with the main browsers today. This Hidden Web is thought to be orders of magnitude bigger than the WWW and is said to contain thousands of terabytes of data. There are limited portals to enable some basic crawls of this Hidden Web—some created by organizations that wish to make their data more accessible and others which enable more federated searches (such as Pipl).

There is plenty of other work advancing capabilities to increase accurate knowability (even in the face of sophisticated deceptions), to push forward what David Rice (2008) terms "an asymmetry of intimacy" between technologies and people (with the first capturing and "knowing" much more than people realize). In a sense, there should never be full trust because of the potential for data leakage and compromise. This is so, too, with "knowability," because there is always noise and a lack of certitude, a degree of doubt. In mainline journalism, there have been various stories about people used as "sensor networks" to detect large-scale phenomena such as epidemic outbreaks or political unrest. There is use of microblogging sites as digital nervous systems with content messaging contents and sentiment analyzed by machines. As part of U.S. government high-innovation "skunkworks" projects, there is a move to see every moving object in entire cities (Greenberg, 2012, p. 174).

CONCLUSION

Much information by and about people is exchanged in plaintext or unencrypted format, in the clear, where any who are paying attention may capture the information for any number of ends. Electronic social network analysis and inference chaining are common ways to infer non-definitive information from online social media platforms and sites. Inferences have been made from individual and group social presences online. Further analyses of the communications and location data have been shown to potentially contribute even more information. The collection and fusion of information enables knowledge that may well be beyond what most common users imagine. Once information is in the wild, it is irrecoverably gone. For all the privacy metrics and testing regimes of various sites, all systems are vulnerable to as-yet unknown exploits and future capabilities.

Any high-value endeavor will require a higher level of research depth and formal learning than what is shown here. There is a value in going with professional investigators to track other information that may better inform the decision-making of an individual or organization. While the costs for their services may be non-trivial, their work itself is important to properly inform choices.

Extractions of social networks from social media platforms are used in various ways by various industries already to profile individuals. Recent news coverage suggests that some lending entities consider social network connections as part of a mass of data points to consider a person's suitability (fitness) for a loan, in the context of big data crunching (Lobosco, 2013). Social acquaintances online who have poor credit scores may negatively affect those on their direct social networks (or ego neighborhoods).

The nature of inferences is elusive, with connections that may be associative, inexact, and non-causal. Any predictive models extrapolated from real-world networks will have to be balanced against the extremes of over-fitting and underfitting. Overfitting refers to describing a model too closely to the facts of what was observed, causing too tight of demands (and then resulting in a lack of transferability or generalizability of the model) or underfitting, having too loose of demands for the model (or allowing for a range of features without actual support from the real-world research).

ACKNOWLEDGMENT

Some of the images in this chapter were re-created using Maltego Tungsten, the follow-on technology after Maltego Radium.

REFERENCES

Andrejevic, M. (2007, September 20). *Book discussion on iSpy: Surveillance and power in the interactive era.* C-Span Video Library. Retrieved Aug. 18, 2013, from http://www.c-spanvideo.org/program/201320-1

Chivers, H. (2005). *Personal attributes and privacy: How to ensure that private attribute management is not subverted by datamining.* Berlin: Springer-Verlag. Retrieved September 8, 2013, from http://link.springer.com/chapter/10.1007%2F0-387-24486-7_2#page-1

De Montjoye, Y.-A., Hidalgo, C. A., Verleysen, M., & Blondel, V. D. (2013). Unique in the crowd: The privacy bounds of human mobility. *Scientific Reports, 3*(1376), 1–5. PMID:23524645

Donath, J. (2007). Signals in social supernets. *Journal of Computer-Mediated Communication, 13,* 235–251. doi:10.1111/j.1083-6101.2007.00394.x

Eagle, N., & Pentland, A. S. (2006). Reality mining: Sensing complex social systems. *Personal and Ubiquitous Computing, 10,* 255–268. doi:10.1007/s00779-005-0046-3

Eagle, N., & Pentland, A. S. (2009). Eigenbehaviors: Identifying structure in routine. *Behavioral Ecology and Sociobiology, 63,* 1057–1066. doi:10.1007/s00265-009-0739-0

Friedland, G., Maier, G., Sommer, R., & Weaver, N. (2011). Sherlock Holmes' evil twin: On the impact of global inference for online privacy. [Marin County, CA: NSPW.]. *Proceedings of NSPW, 11,* 105–114.

Greenberg, A. (2012). *This machine kills secrets: How wikileakers, cypherpunks, and hacktivists aim to free the world's information.* New York: Dutton.

Kumar, R., Novak, J., & Tomkins, A. (2006). Structure and evolution of online social networks. In *Proceedings of KDD '06* (pp. 611-617). Philadelphia, PA: ACM.

Lanier, J. (2013). *Who owns the future?* New York: Simon & Schuster.

Lindamood, J., Heatherly, R., Kantarcioglu, M., & Thuraisingham, B. (2011). Inferring private information using social network data. In *Proceedings of WWW 2009.* Madrid: ACM Digital Library. Retrieved September 14, 2013, from http://dl.acm.org/citation.cfm?id=1526899

Lobosco, K. (2013, August 26). *Facebook friends could change your credit score*. CNN Money. Retrieved Aug. 26, 2013, from http://money.cnn.com/2013/08/26/technology/social/facebook-credit-score/index. html?hpt=hp_t2

Maass, P. (2013, August 13). How Laura Poitras helped Snowden spill his secrets. *The New York Times*. Retrieved Sept. 14, 2013, from http://www.nytimes.com/2013/08/18/magazine/laura-poitras-snowden. html?pagewanted=all&_r=0

McDonald, A. W. E., Afroz, S., Caliskan, A., Stolerman, A., & Greenstadt, R. (2012). Use fewer instances of the letter 'I': Toward writing style anonymization. In S. Fischer-Hübner & M. Wright (Eds.), *PETS 2012 (LNCS)* (Vol. 7384, pp. 299–318). Berlin: Springer-Verlag.

Rice, D. (2008). *Geekonomics: The real cost of insecure software*. Boston: Pearson Education.

Schneier, B. (2013). What exactly are the NSA's 'groundbreaking cryptanalytic capabilities'? *Wired Magazine*. Retrieved September 7, 2013, from http://www.wired.com/opinion/2013/09/black-budget-what-exactly-are-the-nsas-cryptanalytic-capabilities/

Shami, N. S., Ehrlich, K., Gary, G., & Hancock, J. T. (2009). Making sense of strangers' expertise from signals in digital artifacts. In *Proceedings of CHI 2009—Expertise/People Finding* (pp. 69-78). Boston, MA: ACM.

Thi, H. L., & Safavi-Naini, R. (2012). An information theoretic framework for web inference detection. [Raleigh, NC: AISec.]. *Proceedings of AISec, 12*, 25–35. doi:10.1145/2381896.2381902

Varki, A., & Brower, D. (2013). *Denial: Self-deception, false beliefs, and the origins of the human mind*. New York: Hachette Book Group.

ADDITIONAL READING

Andrejevic, M. (2009). iSpy: Surveillance and Power in the Interactive Era. Lawrence: University Press of Kansas.

Bamford, J. (1983). *(1982, 1983). The Puzzle Palace: Inside the National Security Agency, America's Most Secret Intelligence Organization. New York: Houghton Mifflin Company (1982)*. New York: Penguin Books.

Bamford, J. (2008). *The Shadow Factory: The Ultra-Secret NSA from 9/11 to the Eavesdropping on America*. New York: Random House.

KEY TERMS AND DEFINITIONS

Anonymity: A state of not being knowable or identifiable, through information hiding or obfuscation.
Backstop: A support, an evidentiary support for a faked identity.
Content Mining: The analysis of content for meaning.

Cybernetics: The interdisciplinary study of system dynamics.

Cyber-Physical Confluence: The overlap between virtual and physical (offline) spaces.

Data Crawl: The extraction of data from an online system.

Deep Web (Hidden Web, Invisible Web, Deep Net, Undernet): WWW content that is not typically indexed by standard search engines; thought to be many times the size of the Surface Web, with research suggesting that there may be 300,000 deep Web sites in 2004 and potentially 7,500 terabytes of data.

Denial: An unconscious defense mechanism which prevents people from acknowledging pain-causing realities, feelings, or thoughts.

Doxing Attack: Gathering private and personal information about others in order to exploit vulnerabilities or flaws.

Emergent: The state of coming into existence or arising or forming.

Encryption: Encoding messages so that they are not readable by those for whom the message was written.

Geolocation: The locating of an individual or thing to a real-world geographic location.

Hashtag: A brief word or phrase prefaced with "#" used as a metadata tag (to coalesce microblogging entries).

Hidden Web (Deep Web, Invisible Web, Deep Net, Undernet): The often-private information that is hosted on the Internet (or intranet) or on the Web that is not seeable or findable using popular browsers, with contents thought to be 7,500 terabytes in size (in 2001).

Inference: A form of logic which draws generalizations and transferable conclusions from a set of information.

Inference Exposure: The degree to which a website or dataset is vulnerable to an "inference attack"; the degree of unintended information revelation possible through inference analysis.

Machine: A sequence of computer codes (macros) used to extract information from the WWW and Internet (a term used in Maltego Radium™).

Macro: A computer instruction that contains a number of computer scripts as part of it.

Massive Open Online Course (MOOC): A large-scale online course which is both human-and machine-mediated.

Narrowcasting: Projecting information to a small and targeted group (vs. broadcasting).

Network: A connected system of nodes and links comprising a structure of intercommunications.

Network Footprint: The electronic manifestation of a network.

Open-Source Intelligence (OSINT): Relevant information collected from publicly available sources; public intelligence.

Overfitting a Model: Applying too tight demands for an empirical model by only asserting what is observed.

Personally Identifiable Information (PII): Information that leads to the irrefutable identification of an actual person; also "individually identifiable data."

Profiling: Description of an entity or individual.

Pseudonymity: Long-term use of a false name and maintenance of actual anonymity.

Reserve: Privacy from strangers.

Social Media Platform: An online space where people interact over time including microblogging sites, social networking sites, shared work sites, and other spaces (accessed by mobile and Web-based technologies).

Social Network: A social structure containing people as social actors.

Sociotechnical System (STS): Online spaces on which people interact and socialize.

Sousveillance: Participant surveillance; surveiling a system from within.

Structure Mining: The analysis of structures of interrelationships for meaning.

Surface Web: The World Wide Web reachable with current-stage browsers.

Traceability: The capability of discerning the history of, and identifying and finding a particular thing (including digital presence).

Transform: The act of converting one type of information to another type such as an online graphic to a URL or to a matching telephone number (a term used in Maltego Radium™).

Triangulation: Using in-depth comparisons of various data sources to verify information.

Underfitting a Model: Applying too loose demands for an empirical model by asserting behaviors without actual data support.

Unique Identifier: Information that serves to differentiate one object from every other of its kind.

Unlinkability: The state of not being able to relate a particular digital artifact or data exhaust trail to an individual.

Use Case: A projected scenario in which a particular information technology (IT) tool may be used (usually defined in a series of specific steps and interactions).

This research was previously published in Remote Workforce Training edited by Shalin Hai-Jew, pages 231-264, copyright year 2014 by Business Science Reference (an imprint of IGI Global).

Chapter 13
Becoming Anonymous:
A Politics of Masking

Maria-Carolina Cambre
King's University College at Western University Ontario, Canada

ABSTRACT

In a new global topography of cultural movements, repressed layers of populations come to historical consciousness and demand autonomy and sovereignty: many are finding ways to engage through online communities. In the wake of rapid global and social change, groups increasingly organized and operated independently of the control and planning of states are taking shape. Elaborating these so-called "processes" as manifested by those behind Guy Fawkes's mask is a key concern in this study. The author builds theoretical insights on the shifting semiotic vocabulary of the Guy Fawkes Mask used by the niche online community of Anonymous as a disruptive insertion of online visual communication.

INTRODUCTION

Today I took off my face and became #anonymous 1 am 1 of all.

A faceless soldier for those with no army #OPEgypt #egypt #jan25 anon #legion (Twitter Handle: Anonymous_2D (Feb 4, 2011 at 23:30.22))

We have the ability to operate with efficiency in the digital realm.

And our protection comes from the fact that we have grown out of the fabric of humanity itself.

We cannot be stopped because we are not restricted by your rules.

We cannot be beaten because we are not playing your game.

DOI: 10.4018/978-1-5225-3163-0.ch013

Each of us has our Own Path, but each of us shares the Same Goal.(Anonymous YouTube Video, www. youtube.com 2013-05-12 original link deleted)

The screenshot in Figure 1 is one of a multitude of illustrations posted by various online group administrators claiming to be associated or linked with the now infamous online set of actors identifying themselves with the name "Anonymous" or Anons. The image symbolizes some of the key ideas behind this loose collective: identity in/as non-identity, and action as transformative. It also gestures toward the history of the coalescing of this collection of actors in that they had to take up a face upon "emerging" from the Internet. Like other photographic statements posted by Anonymous-related social media users, it makes a reference to "truth."

This image depicts a young white male with a laptop who, in the process of typing, literally has his face drawn in and through the screen. The visage emerging on the other side of the screen is a representation of the now well-known Guy Fawkes Mask (herein referred to as the V-mask). However, we can see that the hair of the subject is continuous, figuratively indicating that it is still *him* essentially. In the image, it is unclear whether the subject's face is only attracted to the screen and pulled into it, or if he is also venturing into that other space, perhaps as a function of the ability or desire to "see the truth." As a parallel, one might ask the same of Lewis Carroll's character, Alice from his children's book, *Through the Looking-Glass, and What Alice Found There*. Why does Alice step through the looking glass and *how* does she do it? In the 1871 classic, Alice sighs, "How nice it would be if we could only get through into Looking-glass House! I'm sure it's got, oh! Such beautiful things in it! Let's pretend there's a way of getting through into it…" (1990, p. 4).

Figure 1. Originally posted by the Facebook page, "World wide freedom" and then shared by "Anonymous PICTURES." (No comments below, shared 19 times and "liked" 55 times) (Screenshot by C. CAMBRE May 30, 2013. Retrieved from https://www.facebook.com/AnonPictures.)

Carroll's Alice is clearly very imaginative, her favourite words as noted on the same page are "let's pretend," but she is also very curious. On the oddly ironic day of the fourth of November (i.e. the day before Guy Fawkes Night), Alice is pulled into the mirror by curiosity, but her own imagination is the vehicle that makes it possible. Imagination/creativity and curiosity also play key roles in the emergence of Anonymous as what might be seen as an enigmatic online community. Following a similar impulse, this next image (Figure 2) brings into play not only the notion of the screen/mirror but also the theme of identity more directly. The back and part profile of a white male in his late 20's or early 30's is shown bending forward and looking into a mirror. Lying on a small shelf are some kind of toiletries and in the reflection, a shower frame recedes into the background. It is a banal and mundane setting recalling daily routines in all their ordinariness. However, the image looking back at the protagonist is extremely unusual. The hooded figure wearing the V-mask represents an as-if of the looker's face. It is also an encounter with alterity in a play with identity/non-identity. Somehow there is recognition and misrecognition simultaneously through the creation of this alternative space. But there is also a gesture toward what will emerge as a repeated notion for members, and that is, that they "live there" in the virtual realm, in/beyond the screen: that is home. Again, the play of presence and absence is felt, since home is a non-concrete place.

The magic screen is an ancient trope: myths and stories from the world over are littered with enchanted portals into heterotopic spaces, from mirrors to pools. Through their adventures in these alternate worlds, characters are transformed and become able to *see otherwise*. Metaphorically, the image in figure one implies that the interface of the screen provides a transgressive technological vehicle for the subject to experience and witness another world, which follows different rules according to the second epigraph:

Figure 2. Posted by the Facebook page: "Anonymous PICTURES." (1 comments below, shared 37 times and "liked" 75 times) (Screenshot by C. CAMBRE, May 30, 2013. Retrieved from https://www.facebook. com/AnonPictures.)

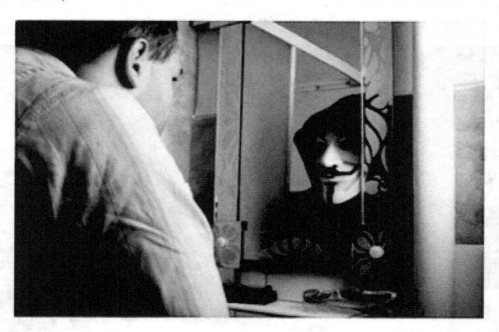

"we are not restricted by your rules." These online experiences then prompt actors to emerge transformed as agents in the material world. One might ask, what then, are *your* rules? Clearly there are insiders and outsiders and a way of belonging. Or is it so clear?

APPROACH AND RATIONALE

The "network society" (Castells, 1996; Negroponte, 1996; Turkle, 1995) informs, reflects, and shapes other kinds of educational and social practices in everyday life. As a result, the cultural politics of digital media has global implications. As Coleman (2010) wrote, "it would be a mistake to overlook how digital media have cultivated new modes of communication and selfhood; reorganized social perceptions…and established collective interests …and projects" (p. 490). But understanding groups dependent on digital technologies for their existence is a not only a minefield for research in terms of a litany of limitations, such as varying degrees of anonymity, ephemerality, and changeability, but also tends to overwhelm the capacity of a researcher's tools: "Despite the massive amount of data and new forms of visibility shored up by computational media, many of these worlds remain veiled, cloaked and difficult to decipher" (p. 498). Scholars need to respond to these challenges creatively with flexible/emergent research designs.

In a new global topography of cultural movements, repressed layers of populations come to historical consciousness, and demand autonomy and sovereignty: many are finding ways to engage through online communities. In the wake of rapid global and social change, groups are taking shape that are increasingly organized and operated independently of the control and planning of states. Elaborating these so-called "processes" as manifested by those behind Guy Fawkes' mask is a key concern in this study. Often existing in a moral and legal gray area, "Today Anonymous is associated with an irreverent, insurgent brand of activist politics" (Coleman, 2012, p. 1), Anonymous' activities, however disparate and paradoxical on their surface, have tapped into a "deep disenchantment with the political status quo" (p. 3). And yet, "Anonymous manages to achieve spectacular visibility and individual invisibility at once" (p. 9).

As Coleman (2010) notes in her review of the literature, increasingly scholars are approaching digital practices, subjects, and communication modalities through ethnographic lenses "(Baron, 2008; Biao, 2007; Boellstorff, 2008; English-Leuck, 2002; Juris, 2008; Malaby, 2009; Senft, 2008; Taylor, 2006). Yet, much of this work continues to confound sharp boundaries between off-line and online contexts (Kelty, 2008; Sreberny & Khiabany, 2010)" (p. 492). In her survey of the growing body of ethnographic work on digital media, Coleman provisionally identifies three overlapping categories based primarily on their varying frames of analysis. The first focuses on cultural politics of media vis-à-vis digital media, which includes a sociological perspective on identity categories and an examination of how those are both formed and informed through digital technologies. The second, is termed "vernacular cultures of digital media" (p. 488) to express a focus on examining how communication forms are organized around qualities proper to digital media and the political economy of digital media. Research itself is transformed by virtue of finding ways to address such digital forms as flowing/intermittent comment lists, and Internet memes. The third, which Coleman (2010) calls prosaics of digital media, refers to work that interrogates the effects of digital media integration on social and material practices, habits, and discourses.

Because my subject is an assemblage that came into being online, it necessarily includes and is materially dominated by both the second and third categories. The vernacular of digital media is crucial as I interact with the data through social media and must essentially immigrate to the Internet in order to do so and learn the symbology of Anonymous to some extent in order to comprehend at some level the interactions between members. Prosaics, the third of these categories, is used in the sense ascribed to Bakhtin by Morson and Emerson when they identify in Bakhtin's thought that which can be seen as the non-everydayness of the everyday. This formulation encourages a revival of the potential fruitfulness of a micro-sociology focusing on the unexpectedly creative, participatory, and non-totalizing and radical imagination at the core of everyday life and by extension communication. As I am examining daily postings, prosaics play a significant role. However, the first of Coleman's categories is most closely tied to the thrust of this phase of the study. By examining this kind of amorphous group gestating primarily in the digital realm, its practices and communicative modalities, I hope to contribute to developing work in "digital ontologies" and teasing out a "community's overall structure of priorities and issues" (Srinivasan, 2006, p. 510) through the ways these are visually transferred to public spheres (Coleman, 2010).

METHODOLOGY AND METHODS

As research on online communities grows, more and more people are paying attention to niche assemblages such as *Anonymous*, who have garnered a globally distributed and ever-fluctuating membership, not to mention international press coverage. While tracing the interlocking thematic tensions in the self-representation of Anonymous online through diverse texts and images, I will draw on the thinking of Michel Foucault, Alphonso Lingis, and others to help describe this 'history of the present' where *something* comes (is always becoming) into being by virtue of sharing their technology. More specifically, this paper does not pretend to be traditional ethnography nor an atomistic discourse analysis; it does, however, aim at valuing informal texts and images as part of a wider discourse and at a critical recovery of narratives that can shed light on the nature of the ongoing evolution of this particular assemblage.

Through sustained social media presence, I attend to the patterns in image publication especially by those positioning themselves as members of Anonymous. I proceed in the spirit of attending to the "odd," "queer," or "fishy" postings, that in themselves are "quite insignificant… but which nonetheless… denatures the scene of the crime and… renders the whole picture strange" (Zizek, p. 53, in Kaomea, 2000). Identifying these clues is a process that by its very nature is messy and incomplete; still it provides points of traction from which a researcher can get a different view of the kaleidoscopic terrain. As ruptures, these "odd" moments participate in the larger framework of a Foucauldian genealogy. The "live" online genealogy that I undertake here is underwritten and contextualized by a broader study I have initiated that combines this approach with digital ethnography (see Coleman, 2010) and critical visual sociology. Taken together, these processes of data collection and analysis honour a post-structural orientation to inquiry.

While one might find an opposition between a genealogical approach and what is clearly a more horizontal rhizomatic process of connection and multiplication, I want to stress that the way I understand the word genealogy here is more akin to that which produces and is related to, rather than conjuring a family tree-like image. I found this approach useful as a starting point because it does not ignore the fluid movements and shifting meanings and values contained in discourses that are often temporary and ephemeral and, at times, contradictory. It might be described with Foucault's (1977) genealogical language as "a field of entangled and confused parchments" (p. 139). In addition, a genealogy does not identify a fixed starting point or any rigid meaning. Rather, the genealogist who listens to history will find otherwise: "behind things: not a timeless and essential secret, but the secret that they have no essence or that their essence was fabricated in a piecemeal fashion from alien forms" (p. 142).

Michael Mahon (1992) writes, the Foucauldian genealogist's task "is to afflict the comfortable by dredging up what has been forgotten, whether actively or passively. He or she counteracts the prevailing social amnesia by emancipating subjected historical knowledges" (p. 120). An understanding of "what it means to say what we say" entails three procedures, an examination of the continuities or "systems which are still ours today," the "ruptural effects" or breaks and discontinuities, and the contingencies, accidents and impacts of the immediate and local (p. 121). Foucault sees discursive formations as "historical events" rather than universal structures. In other words, they correspond to a specific intersection of time and space and are produced by circumstance. As a result, discourses provide a view of the *interplay* of variables.

Representations, insists Edward Said (1994), necessarily include an element of interpretation, "in any instance of at least written language, there is no such thing as a delivered presence, but a re-presence, or a representation" (p. 21). Utterances, as well as texts, are constructions containing ideological structures consciously or unconsciously serving a purpose in a specific context and must be interrogated "not only in terms of who represents but also in terms of who is being represented for what purpose, at which historical moment, for which location, using which strategies, and in what tone of address" (Shohat, 1995, p. 173).

On one level, I ask what the nature of social engagement is, and on another, what is at stake when groups such as Anonymous are created and sustained anonymously? Somehow managing different languages, identities, social codes, and ability in online environments and cultures can occur while controlling self-revelation. More specifically, I ask what are the politics of anonymity and masking of identity, vis-à-vis the Internet, and what are its pedagogical models? By tracing some of the continuities, discontinuities, and contingencies in the contexts and characteristics of the discursive texts/images about faces and masking Anonymous as used by a wide range of people, some characteristics of this entity emerge. However, given the condition of anonymity and temporariness of many participants, this study has important limitations, for example, it cannot be exhaustive in the sense that a true historical study might be. Because of the quantity and richness of data in this kind of study, time will also be a limiting factor. And, of course, the researcher, as an instrument, is always limited by inevitable biases in the interpretation process for both data and theory.

DATA COLLECTION AND STRATEGIES OF ANALYSIS

With Anonymous uprisings as a heuristic, I undertake a specific socio-cultural reading of masking as developed within online cultures in response to difficult social, economic, and political conditions. This will go beyond the counter-cultural nature of these trends to address specific visual vocabularies and cultural architectures signifying social struggle as well as innovative educational practices. It is my contention that the ability of Anonymous to transgress linguistic and geographic borders prompts the questioning of existing representational categories and identities.

Although I began collecting images about two years ago, in the last 18 months, using sustained participation-observation and tracking of events and discourses of online cultures focused on anti-establishment newsfeeds operated by self-identified Anonymous administrators, I amassed a collection of 1013 (and growing) images (screen captures and downloads) that were posted, or shared by Facebook page administrators claiming some link to Anonymous and featuring the V-mask. My criteria were simple, to collect all the V-mask images that were publicly shared in those feeds and to add new related feeds as they appeared and when links were posted to check on Twitter, Sound Clouds, YouTube, and online news pages or blogs to crosscheck information and build mini-background stories related to different images.

In terms of media forms, the images posted could be photographs, screen captures, digital art, and occasionally written references to the mask. The content of these images ranges from collages, sketches, and graffiti to altered photographs or digital art. All of these images are public statements or messages, that is, they are meant to be seen and that they have been either partially or fully crafted (whether through photo editing software such as Photoshop, or simple cropping).

While I began with approximately 10 feeds, they eventually snowballed to over 32, but in reality represent many more because each one follows an ever-changing number of other sites and cross-posts from there. The pages I follow include: Anonymous PICTURES, World wide freedom, Anonymous News Network, Anon Arts International, Anonymous ART of Revolution, Divided ByNothing, Occupy London, Occupy Chicago, Anonymous, Wake Up, it's a MaTriX, Anarchist Memes, Anonymous Freedom Art, Cryp0nymous News Network, Antisec., Occupy Bahrain, Anonymous Portugal Internacional, Anonymous INDIA, Sono Antifascista E Odio Gli Infami E I Traditori, فن المقاومة Art of resistance, Anonymous Việt Nam and others.

Each page has an undisclosed number of administrators who do not always identify themselves, cryptically or otherwise, and who are also subject to change and inconsistency in posting. Still, there are strong trends in terms of themes and repetition in the images, which enable a stage of categorical analysis. In *Qualitative Evaluation and Research Methods*, Quinn Patton (1990) explained two ways of representing patterns that emerge from the data in inductive analysis:

First, the analyst can use the categories developed and articulated by the people studied to organize presentation of particular themes. Second, the analyst may also become aware of categories or patterns for which the people studies did not have labels or terms, and the analyst develops terms to describe these inductively generated categories. (p. 390)

If a term or expression is repeatedly used, it becomes necessary to evaluate what is meant by the term and attempt to deduce how users understand it. In this strategy of analysis, patterns of repetition in the data not only allow indigenous and sensitizing concepts to emerge and to be identified, but also to reveal organizing themes in the participants' construction of their worlds of experience or as typologies.

The online research experience I am sharing is more or less like standing in a room in the massive labyrinth of the Internet, opening a number of related portals and watching what comes through. While the collection is not very significant in terms of breadth or depth then, it is important in terms of statements that are repeatedly stressed and in terms of the gradual establishment of some kind of picture of "who we say we are." There is an observable effort to find a point of reference or traction for all the people who continually join Anonymous, or begin posting as if they are part of Anonymous.

I have tentatively sorted the 1013 images into seven broad and overlapping sets indigenous to the image thematics emerging by virtue of repetition. Within each set I examine subsets both within and across groupings in terms of the quadrant in Table 1.

Table 1.

Sensitizing typologies	Indigenous typologies
Sensitizing themes	Indigenous themes

For the purposes of this chapter I will touch on three indigenous themes within the forms of self-representation and visual identity taken on by this faceless group, and expand on them with sensitizing concepts. Thus, the three themes mask/face, community/anonymity, and surveillance/freedom, which overlap and inform each other and, while taken up in particularistic ways depending on context, hold universalistic features in terms of their significance for Anonymous.

WHAT IS ANONYMOUS?

As I explore here the possibility of considering Anonymous a community, I will refer to Anons as a mobile-tiered assemblage to reflect what I will describe as fluid, formless, and circumstantially connected sets of actors. At times referred to as a group, or collective, Anonymous lacks the cohesion to be well understood with the ideas these terms evoke. Indeed they are most often identified by what they are not as in this Soundcloud recording (2013) posted online by *Anonymous ART of revolution* titled "Welcome to Anonymous":

You cannot join Anonymous. Nobody can join Anonymous.

Anonymous is not an organization. It is not a club, a party or even a movement. There is no charter, no manifest, no membership fees. Anonymous has no leaders, no gurus, no ideologists. In fact, it does not even have a fixed ideology. (online audio)

It is needless to note the non-having of an ideology it itself an ideology. Claiming such may also be a mask. However these negations are followed by specific affirmations in this case:

All we are is people who travel a short distance together – much like commuters who meet in a bus or tram: For a brief period of time we have the same route, share a common goal, purpose or dislike. And on this journey together, we may well change the world… Anonymous has no centralized infrastructure. We use existing facilities of the Internet, especially social networks, and we are ready to hop on to the next one if this one seems compromised, is under attack, or starts to bore us… We are more than you think. We are more than anybody thinks. We are many. And you are now one of us. Welcome to Anonymous. At the time of this writing, Facebook, Twitter and the IRC appear to host the most active congregations. But this may change at any time. Still, these are probably the best places to get started. Look for terms like "anonymous," "anonops" and other keywords that might be connected to our activities. (Soundcloud recording, 2013)

The reference to boredom hints not only at the characteristic of changeability but also of unpredictability. This reference is one of many across different images, texts, and recording that participates in a rhetoric of evasion. Paradoxically, Anonymous cannot be joined and yet you can be part of it if you want, "Join us if you may in our revolution for the Internet" (Soundcloud recording, 2013). What is the nature of "us" then?

In his seminal book, *The community of those who have nothing in common*, philosopher Alphonso Lingis (1994) writes, "community is usually conceived as constituted by a number of individuals having something in common – a common language, a common conceptual framework – and building some-thing in common: a nation, a polis, an institution" (p. ix). This configuration, for Lingis, is the rational community "that forms in the exchange of informational exchanges abstract entities, idealized signs of idealized referents" (p. 12). Lingis, however, is haunted by the feeling that, "the dying of people with whom we have nothing in common – no racial kinship, no language, no religion, no economic interests –concerns us" (p. x). More specifically, Lingis comes to understand that "what concerns us in another is precisely his or her otherness" (p. x). And so he identifies a paradox:

In the midst of the work of the rational community, there forms the community of those who have noth-ing in common, of those who have nothingness, death, their mortality, in common. But is the death that isolates each one a common death? And can it be identified as nothingness? (p. 13)

In the "self-stylization" (see Irmscher, C. 1992 Masken der Moderne) of Anonymous, the gap between contradictory positions, the seeming nothingness is embraced as a concept of self as infinite non-identity. They are and they are not. Just as the mask highlights the tension between difference and identity, the symbolic meaning is that of a celebration of paradox itself. The trope of masking is, textually and psychologically, a strategy of alternative discursive practice that protects the self as subject who is always already under surveillance. Thus the non-identity of Anonymous becomes a self-affirming way to interact with mainstream culture and its imaginaries. They attempt to reject the binary of presence/absence by means of symbolic inversions, laughter, rule-breaking behaviours, in short, through the carnivalesque. In carnival, "laughter is simultaneously a protest and an acceptance. During Carnival, all social distinctions are suspended... The escape from social personality is symbolized by the wearing of masks" (Howard 1997, para. 3).

The critical strength of secrecy is also used by the Zapatistas in this way, they mask their faces in order to be seen, and in order to be heard, and finally so that they will no longer need the mask. Mystery moves margins toward the centre, so that the "community of those who have nothing in common" and may be commuting on the same bus manage to emerge in the midst of the "work of the rational com-munity." However, of the key differences between groups such as the Zapatistas, who also maintain a strong online presence, and those that call themselves Anonymous, it is paramount to remember that members of Anonymous while maintaining a strong "face" of public benevolence may include police, military, and intelligence officers just as easily as it may include international mafia operatives, and can be more easily infiltrated than the Zapatistas.

Despite the ephemeral, changeable and particularistic manifestations of Anonymous, always threat-ening to disappear and reappear differently elsewhere, there are consistencies that can be remarked on. As Lingis (1994) observes:

A thing is by engendering images of itself: reflections, shadows, and halos. These cannot be separated from the core appearance which would make them possible, for they make what one takes to be the core appearance visible. The surfaces of things are not more real than their facades; the reality that engenders the phantasm is engendered by it. (p. 40)

While Anons are indeed a shadowy presence online, their profuse publications, announcements, and their strategic actions do make them visible in the sense that the "phantasms, lures, forms made of shadows, omens, halos, and reflections make the things visible and are the visibility the things engender" (pp. 41-42). One of these forms is the history of this mobile-tiered assemblage, also fragmented, but coming gradually into view as a narrative of actions.

BACKGROUND

Although it was not their first coordinated action, the group *Anonymous* gained global notoriety by orchestrating a series of online uprisings in support of Wikileaks in 2010. In June 2011, NATO published a report on "Information and Information Security" calling for "Anonymous to be infiltrated and dismantled... In July Anonymous hackers infiltrated NATO" (Coleman, 2012, p. 3). Under the increasing intensity of scrutiny the members of the group have burrowed deeper underground, however, anthropologist Coleman (2012) who has been studying what has often been called a "movement" since its inception and is the foremost expert on this group notes, "the reach of their icons has increased" (p. 3).

For a faceless assortment of people with an absolute requirement for anonymity to emerge from the Internet, a visual identity was required. Both online and offline anonymity was, for many reasons, seen as essential. The choice was the Guy Fawkes mask popularized by the film *V for Vendetta* based on Alan Moore's graphic novel of the same name. This mask is a stylized depiction of Guy Fawkes himself with his pointed black beard and moustache. It is most frequently a stark white face frozen in a smile. How this particular choice was made is connected to the history of a meme, a movie, and the man himself.

In brief, some of the defining characteristics of Anonymous are a changing membership, they are increasingly politicized, and taking illegal actions, and by all appearances are organized in networks. This network structure is one of the keys to Anonymous. The group has gathered many followers. Some are passionate hackers, others merely sympathizers. Some work around the clock, others participate only sporadically. The structures are loose, the exchange sporadic. They communicate through a channel called IRC (Internet Relay Chat) and historically an image board called 4chan, which hosts spaces for dialogue and exchange on a wide variety of topics.

Their signature attacks, which are motivated not by profit or espionage, but rather take the form of political protest and "lulz," which can be roughly understood as laughing at someone's expense, are a trickster or prankster way of registering the fact that they have witnessed something objectionable. As O'Neill (2011) writes, "the people of the Internet use denial of service attacks to show their protest on any attempt to hide the truth from the public" (p. 4).

So, how does masking both enable and constrain new ways for Anonymous to address regimes of representation, spatial imaginaries, borders, and spaces? In this chapter I theorise how they, like their counterparts globally, have become protagonists by making meaningful interventions in chaotic social contexts such as Distributed Denial of Service (DDOS) sit-ins/attacks to overwhelm Websites, and providing tools and support to activists in need of evasive tactics online. In order to do this I examine their messaging and recruitment process as well as the way they reflexively portray their own image/s. In this context, I explore what agency might mean for those who claim to be part of an emergent, nonlinear, and process driven uprising.

Thus, the use of V-masks forms of indirection such as irony and fantasy are used to question and challenge cultural assumptions and court the chaos of the present by facing opposing forces, and the fear of the unknown. Interestingly, "throughout history, masks have appeared in art and literature at times when change was occurring" (Napier, p. xxiii).

TRANSFIGURATIONS: MAN, MOVIE, MEME, AND MASK

In the movie *We are Legion* (2013), the formerly Anonymous interviewees give only a vague suggestion of how using the Guy Fawkes mask taken from the film *V for Vendetta* was appropriate for the real-life appearance of people from the Internet identifying themselves as Anonymous (or Anons). There need not be agreement on how or why this came about. However as I will illustrate, this figure is ironically more significant and evokes a deeper issue around the notion of a control society and surveillance state than one might at first suspect. Thus, some aspects of the historical context are worth exploring and subsequently invoke a certain ethos around the identity of Anonymous.

In this section I outline salient aspects of the story of the face beginning with Guy Fawkes. Though the story is resurrected, redirected, and popularized by the graphic novel in the 1980s, I will focus on the more widely distributed and impactful 2006 movie *V for Vendetta* that was drawn in large part from the graphic novel with significant divergences. Next, I describe the online representation/adaptation: a popular meme emerges called Epic Fail Guy who oddly sets the stage for Anonymous's adoption of the mask. Regardless, there is repeated association with the historical Guy Fawkes in a to-be-seen-as seamless cognitive linking. It is not without a healthy dosage of poetic license as shown below in Figure 3

Figure 3. Posted by the Facebook page: "Anonymous ART of revolution." (6 comments below, shared 54 times and "liked" 158 times) (Screenshot by C. CAMBRE, 2012-12-16. Retrieved from https://www. facebook.com/pages/Anonymous-ART-of-Revolution/362231420471759.)

Anonymous ART of Revolution
The Guy Fawkes mask is a stylised depiction of Guy Fawkes, the best-known member of the Gunpowder Plot, an attempt to blow up the House of Lords in London in 1605.
We have the mask from Guido. Here is when anonymous activitity starts...

where the caption above describing the Gunpowder Plot also adds, "Here is when anonymous activity starts…." While it would be a mistake to think all anonymous activity started at this point, this was a time of pervasive surveillance where the emergence of crypto-Catholicism has been documented. But the image caption seems to indicate that the *idea* of Anons started at this point, in effect it is claiming an origin, a root, even if it is a tenuous and fictional one.

For centuries, the folk verse beginning with "Remember, remember! The fifth of November, the Gunpowder treason and plot" has been chanted to celebrate the failure of a conspiracy by a group of English Catholics to assassinate the Protestant King James I of England. Guy Fawkes himself was caught guarding a woodpile close to barrels filled with explosives as the verse (c. 1870) recalls:

Guy Fawkes and his companions
Did the scheme contrive,
To blow the King and Parliament
All up alive.
Threescore barrels, laid below,
To prove old England's overthrow.
But, by God's providence, him they catch,
With a dark lantern, lighting a match! (Habing, 2006)

That very night of November 5th, 1605, the public was allowed to celebrate the King's survival by lighting bonfires. Observance of the date was legislated in 1606 as a remembrance of thanksgiving for the plot's failure and as an anti-Catholic occasion warning of the dangers of "popery" (Fraser, 2005; Sharpe, 2005). James I was quick to approve of harsh controls on non-conforming English Catholics and in May 1606, Parliament passed the Popish Recusants Act whereby citizens could be forced to take an oath of allegiance denying the Pope's authority over the king.

A rope, a rope, to hang the Pope,
A penn'orth of cheese to choke him,
A pint of beer to wash it down,
And a jolly good fire to burn him. (Habing, 2006)

First known as the Gunpowder Treason Day, it was occasionally called Bonfire Night and was only later to become Guy Fawkes Day and Firework Night. The practice of burning effigies emerged in the early 1600s and included figures of the pope, Catholic bishops, and of course Guy Fawkes himself as political and religious statements. Over time the English observance of the 5th of November became an occasion for riots, and vandalism, as well as all kinds of other excuses for drunken disorder, while the range of subjects for effigies ranged wildly.

Interestingly, under James I, British authorities and religious figures portrayed Catholics as terrorists much as followers of Islam are often demonized today. According to David Cressy (1992), Catholics were plotting to dig tunnels "from Oxford, Rome, Hell, to Westminster, and there to blow up, if possible, the better foundations of your houses, their liberties and privileges" (p. 74).

A display in 1647 at Lincoln's Inn Fields commemorated "God's great mercy in delivering this kingdom from the hellish plots of papists," and included fireballs burning in the water (symbolising a Catholic association with "infernal spirits") and fireboxes, their many rockets suggestive of "popish spirits coming from below" to enact plots against the king. (Sharpe, 2005, p. 92, as cited in Wikipedia Guy Fawkes Day Entry)

What most accounts of the gunpowder treason and plot of 1605 omit is the context of a surveillance society under which this dominant narrative of fear was taking place. The intensification of surveillance should not be seen as a natural occurrence but an intentional project to create particular kinds of citizens obedient to particular visions and agendas. Constant surveillance, writes Michel Foucault (1977) in *Discipline and Punish*, is the central technique of disciplinary power. It is initially directed toward disciplining the body, but takes hold of the mind as well to induce a psychological state of "conscious and permanent visibility" (p. 201). What Foucault clearly understood was the importance of microstructures of domination, such as surveillance, in their role of creating "docile bodies" that is to say, in restricting freedom. Thus he identified:

...a policy of coercions that act on the body, a calculated manipulation of its elements, its gestures, its behaviour. The human body was entering a machinery of power that explores it, breaks it down and rearranges it... Thus, discipline produces subjected and practiced bodies, "docile" bodies. (pp. 138-139)

Surveillance can essentially be understood as an over-arching means of accruing and sifting information. Today, from Facebook to the so-called "war on terror," citizen-subjects or "consumers" are being sold a narrative encouraging them to share more and more personal data ostensibly for their own good, their better security, their health, or even their fun. And yet surveillance regimes are not new, and it benefits us to recall some of the more overt expressions of these regimes in the past, and recognize that while the motives and language are now more covert, the aim remains unchanged and our need to respond is as urgent and as critical as ever. What is at stake in the discourses of subjection is the social scope that they afford, particularly with respect to the links between surveillance and obedience/control, which I illustrate later in this paper are key issues for Anonymous.

In the early 17th century James I articulated a "doctrine of subjection whose key motif is the power of perception" (Davis, 1993, p. 94). The stated ideology is eye-poppingly relevant today, if we look at this treatise of James I:

The duty of subjects is to obey social order and perpetuate its pattern. Obedience penetrates them internally to 'the botome of [their] heartes. It inscribes a bodily subjection whose very organs can be anatomized. As James I warns in the Basilicon, obedience, while an internalized disposition, is also an omnipresent physical sign to be read by 'superyors.'.... let no man thinke that he can escape unpunyshed, that committeth treason, conspiracie, or rebellyon, agaysnte his soveraigne Lord ..., thoughe he commyt the same never so secretlye, either in thought, worde or dede...." (as quoted in Davis, 1993, p. 94)

Knowledge of these circumstances serves to dramatically heighten the daring of Fawkes and the others, as well as reveal the terrible odds against them. Tortured horrifically until he confessed and revealed the identities of some of the other conspirators, Fawkes was publicly hung. He jumped from the scaffold breaking his neck, ensuring he would be dead for the gruesome drawing and quartering that followed: "in the very place which they had planned to demolish in order to hammer home the message of their wickedness" (Britannica History online) and extract obedience from the populace (this was the third assassination attempt on James I). In other words, citizens are *constituted* by obedience and must *be seen* to obey. They must also be visibly transparent in thought, word or deed where the state can see through them to their most secret intentions. The consequences of not doing so were dire. While James I reinforced obedience and order, his warnings against conspiracy assumed an omnipercipient position. Thus both, "rejoicing at a royal procession [for example] reveals and inspires obedience," as does "the frequent publication of accounts of seditious acts" (Davis, 1993, p. 97).

An exemplary and telling contemporary visual parallel to this stagecraft emerged when two events were broadcast together within one week in the late spring of 2011. In the English-speaking world and beyond, both the news of the Royal Wedding, and the assassination of Osama bin Laden were equally unavoidable in their visibility. *The Telegraph*: *Expat Edition* displayed a cover semiotically representing both faces of the doctrine of subjection, that is to say, rejoice in order and stability by assuming your place and value in society through obeying. And the accompanying face of, no matter where you are, or how long it takes, if you disobey or are disloyal through acts of "treason" you will be found out and punished. This kind of obedience forecloses other ways of knowing, and appropriates a subjects' means of departing from compulsory modes of vision, speech and thought (see Figure 4).

Figure 4. Screen shot of The Telegraph front page April 29, 2011 (Publish a credit of: © Telegraph Media Group Limited 2011)

This doctrine of subjection is an undercurrent running through the film *V for Vendetta* as seen throughout by the depicted government's control of media and image-management at the same time as its obsession with surveillance. Linking itself explicitly to the events of 1605, the film opens using flashbacks depicting Guy Fawkes's capture and execution with actress Natalie Portman's voice narrating. Her opening words stress that while a man can fail and die, an idea lives on. She acknowledges the power of the idea, while at the same time underscoring that it is a human being that loves, is loved, and missed. Reinforcing her words, the camera pans the crowd cheering the anticipated execution and from Fawkes's position we see one woman weeping. A close up of her face precedes the hanging so that we, as viewers, take her position understanding that there was a romantic relationship involved, thus humanizing Fawkes. The rest of the film, loaded with rich symbols and inter-textual references, repeatedly plays on the tension between the power of an idea and the moral imperative to preserve one's humanity through love of the other.

The links to Guy Fawkes are made explicit when V first introduces himself in a wordy blizzard of alliteration saying:

Voilà

In view, a humble vaudevillian veteran, cast vicariously as both victim and villain by the vicissitudes of fate.

This visage, no mere veneer of vanity...

Is a vestige of the vox populi, now vacant, vanished

However this valorous visitation of a bygone vexation stands vivified

and has vowed to vanquish these venal and virulent vermin vanguarding vice...and vouchsafing the violently vicious and voracious violation of volition.

Invoking Fawkes through his reference to his visage or mask, V describes him as vivified, or brought back to life through V himself. He then slashes a "V" on a billboard with his sword reminiscent of Zorro's "Z." Later when it appears in a circle, it recalls the anarchist "A." He is thus simultaneously linked to a Robin Hood like figure, a champion of the masses, an anti-hero, a non-figure. An assertion and a negation combined, perhaps into something new. The mark "V" enacts a defacement of (usually) government or institutional propaganda or signage in a sign of the dissenting and disobedient bent of this character's mission. He sighs, and continues, in a darker vein:

The only verdict is vengeance, a vendetta...held as a votive not in vain, for the value and veracity of such shall one day vindicate the vigilant and the virtuous.

A votive is a prayer, or an offering often symbolically in the form of a candle, which is left burning until it is gone. It stands in for V himself. But V suddenly regains his sense of humor referring to his speech as something of a chunky soup of words:

Verily this vichyssoise of verbiage veers most verbose.

So let me simply add that it's my very good honor to meet you and you may call me V.

After her period of imprisonment where V radicalizes her, Natalie Portman's character, Evey, rejects V calling him a "monster" for his uncompromising obsession with revenge. Reciprocally, Evey causes V himself to regain some of his humanity. When she leaves he breaks down, sobbing and angry with himself, ripping off his mask in the darkness.

Set in a dystopic future under a totalitarian regime in England, the man later known as V appears reborn like a phoenix out of the fire of a concentration camp where people had been subjects for medical experiments. V takes his name from the Roman numeral for five on the door where he had been imprisoned. Disfigured beyond recognition he dons a mask resembling Guy Fawkes and takes up his vendetta as well as a mission to overthrow the state and liberate the populace who are subdued, narcotized by omnipresent state-run television shows and under absolute surveillance and control. There are constant curfews, and fear-mongering news items bombarding the populace, while omnipresent cameras and government spies are watching everywhere combined with audio surveillance where people's conversations are recorded and analyzed to measure the pulse of the populace and respond accordingly. Given today's increasing technological powers of surveillance, it is eerie to see how even the computers are shown to be listening devices as revealed when the chief detective puts a sound distortion device in front of his screen in order to speak freely.

In contrast to other films with masked heroes or anti-heroes, V's mask is never removed to reveal his face. This absence of a face creates the possibility that any face can be under that mask and in fact this is something many moments of the film gesture towards. Early in the film V mentions that the man behind the mask is of no consequence, rather it is the idea that matters. This notion is taken up repeatedly in the messaging used by Anonymous.

Where Guy Fawkes failed, V succeeds in spectacularly blowing up the parliament buildings. Significantly it is Evey who pulls the lever, while the police inspector watches the train pull away taking V's body to his as-if Viking funeral pyre. Meanwhile, hordes of people take to the streets not only as witnesses, but also as accomplices. Any one of them could have pulled that lever. We see masks being pulled off at the end revealing faces of characters that had died earlier in the film indicating that in the greater body politic they lived on, the vox populi (voice of the people) referred to by V in his introductory speech has indeed been vivified.

While receiving mixed reviews amongst critics and media pundits, the movie struck a chord with many youth: a chord, perhaps a romanticized one, of revolution. One blogger, Wael Khairy (2012) begins his review of the film by recalling that:

During the revolution Egyptians referenced "V for Vendetta" more frequently than any other work of art. Protestors held up signs that read "Remember, remember the 25 of January." On the Internet, Photoshop was used to alter Pharaoh Tout Ankh Amoun's face into a Fawkes smile.

Sarah Abdel Rahman, an activist who ended up on TIME magazine's cover page during the revolution referred to scenes from the film when I discussed the revolution with her. Guy Fawkes' bumper stickers are stuck on the back windows of dozens of cars driving through Cairo traffic; his mask painted red, white, and black resembling the Egyptian flag. The list goes on and on, there's no doubt about it, in 2011

"V for Vendetta" stirred up as much conversation in Egypt as when it first spread controversy the day it was released here. (The Cinephile Fix, http://cinephilefix.wordpress.com/2012/08/24/film-analysis-v-fo...)

The controversy Khairy (2012) refers to surrounds the question of whether V is a terrorist or freedom fighter. He is called a terrorist in the film, and the actors who discuss the film in the additional clips also refer to him as a terrorist. However, it is the state apparatus that maintains the citizenry in a state of perpetual fear as a policy. And it is worth recalling that the term was made famous, if not actually coined, during the French revolution precisely to describe the character of the state, not of an individual actor. Harper's (2001-2013) entry in the *Online Etymological Dictionary* names 1795 as one of the earliest uses:

1795, in specific sense of "government intimidation during the Reign of Terror in France" (1793-July 1794), from French terrorisme (1798), from Latin terror (see terror). ...General sense of "systematic use of terror as a policy" is first recorded in English 1798. At one time, a word for a certain kind of mass-destruction terrorism was dynamitism (1883); and during World War I frightfulness (translating German Schrecklichkeit) was used in Britain for "deliberate policy of terrorizing enemy non-combatants." (http://www.etymonline.com/index.php?term=terrorism)

Ordinary people have nothing to fear from V, yet he remains, "cast vicariously as both villain and victim."

In its trajectory from concrete to virtual, the man, and movie character are taken up by a meme called Epic Fail Guy (EFG) who essentially failed at everything in a catastrophic (and very funny) way. According to *Encyclopedia Dramatica*'s online entry about EFG, the character was a semi-successful meme drawn as a stick figure. The meme becomes widely popular after the adventure where he pulls a Guy Fawkes mask out of a trash bin: "That f***ing mask is f***ing clownshoes" (http://encyclopediadramatica.se/Epic_Fail_Guy) (see Figures 5 and 6).

While the stick figure takes up Guy Fawkes mask from the movie, the epic fail is referencing and laughing at the misfortune of the actual Guy Fawkes who is caricatured as a chump:

...to whom a bunch of real terrorists said, "Here, Guy, just stand here and mind these barrels" and then ran off chortling to themselves because they knew he'd take the rap despite being completely unimportant in the plot. ...Thus Guy became an Epic Fail that would be remembered for at least 100 years. (online)

The hilarity is partly due to the reversal of a serious, tragic history of a man, whose story is dramatized in a dark theatrical movie character that unexpectedly becomes a goofy ne'er-do-well meme. The fast-spreading status of the meme may also be derived from the fact that it is fun to draw and create adventures for. In this way, the mask came unhinged from its story taking on a new set of primarily comedic meanings and a role in sets of ongoing and expanding jokes and stories in a process of recontextualization (see context collapse Cf. M. Welsch).

Through participant observation over time and reading comments on social media, a diverse range of news reports both online and in print, as well as self-identified Anonymous publications on the Internet, a story comes into view regarding the genesis of an idea. It appears that the on-line community in the /b/ forum on 4chan.org was developing by, essentially, playing in the same playground and learning to distinguish insiders from outsiders by evolving a kind of language of inside jokes. This Website is considered by many as one of the most offensive sites on the Internet. From about 150 thematic forums,

Figure 5. Example image of EFG taken from Encyclopedia Dramatica (Creative Commons, Screenshot by C. CAMBRE, 2012. Retrieved from https://encyclopediadramatica.es/Efg (defunct).)

Figure 6. EFG joke temporarily up on Wikipedia taken from Encyclopedia Dramatica (Creative Commons, Screenshot by C. CAMBRE, 2013. Retrieved from https://encyclopediadramatica.es/Efg (defunct).)

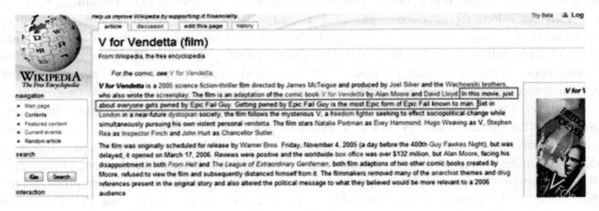

the one called /b/ is truly nasty. It is a non-censored forum full of pornography, racist slurs, and insults of all kinds targeting anyone and everyone. Communication here is cryptically reduced to a number of English swear words and text message abbreviations. What is vile and disturbing to outsiders seems normal for insiders, constituting an essential and valued quality of /b/: not just anyone can handle this play. In the film *We are Legion*, former Anon Gregg Housch remarks that on the /b/ board anything goes, and that part of the implicit goal is to "post something that can never be unseen" and that "posts are there specifically to make people never want to come back to /b/." The type of humor gleefully celebrated on this site gave some people the impression that the majority of people involved were racialized, gendered and from a certain age category. In other words, demographically this was assumed by many to be the domain of young white males. This idea rapidly dissolved in the 2008 emergence from the Internet according to online commentary and interviewees in *We are Legion*.

According to online accounts, regular participants on 4chan.org became increasingly aware of their ability to join together for a common aim mainly through a series of catalyzing exercises in collaborative trolling roughly between 2004 and culminating in 2007 with the exposure of self-professed racist, neo-nazi Hal Turner. The Turner take-down was perhaps the first instance of members referring to themselves publicly as Anonymous when calling his radio show. There was a consciousness of some kind of "we" that was forming, although participant comments also indicate an awareness of the paradoxical formlessness of the form that was embraced. After uncovering his FBI informant status, and the aftermath that led to Turner's jail sentence, unsettling notions of the power that these netizens had in the off-line world, but with material results, became apparent. No longer was this just a game, and there were rumours of an internal division between resistance to becoming involved in more serious endeavours on the part of some, wanting to move beyond the insular games on 4chan.org on the part of others, and a range of positions in between.

The Scientology indoctrination video featuring Tom Cruise was a major turning point (*We are Legion* 2013). Originally meant as an internal document for the sect, it had somehow been leaked or accessed and rapidly spread online as a subject of ridicule far and wide. The Church of Scientology engaged their legal machinery and issued cease and desist notices, had videos rapidly taken down when they were posted and mounted a large scale effort to stop the spread of the video. The result, however, was the opposite. In what is sometimes referred to as the Streisand Effect (the more one tries to contain something, the more it spreads) the video's reproductions reproduced exponentially all over the World Wide Web. Escalating their efforts, the Church of Scientology's "agents" began identifying and persecuting those who would get involved in trolling their phonelines and Websites, or spreading the video. The range of their access to information about individuals and their ability to phyically track them down was perceived as not only an unacceptable assault on personal freedom, but also as a sign of a dangerous level of surveillance.

Members of what was more regularly being referred to as Anonymous decided to take to the streets in an operation called Chanology, to the doorsteps of Scientology buildings around the world. How would this faceless mass appear? How would they know each other? Issuing a series of three preparatory videos beginning with a call to arms, "be very wary of the 10th of February" members urged people on the Internet to join together in physical protest. The common goal spurred this organizing effect and the third video, "code of conduct" urged would-be participants to cover their faces "rule 17." The choice of the Guy Fawkes mask came almost "naturally" according to former Anon Vitale (in *We are Legion*) who explains, "what's the only fucking mask that we all already know or having a fucking joke about?" (*We are Legion*).

And so in 2008, Anonymous members became visible to the world and to each other through a successfully orchestrated protest in major cities around the world from Sydney, Australia to Tel Aviv, Israel. And the Guy Fawkes mask was transfigured once more, this time from a screen drawing of little more than an outline to a material representation, whether mass produced as movie paraphanelia or hand made from cloth or paper cutouts, with a flesh and blood face behind it.

Mask/Face and Identity

Within the collection of images the wide range of modalities used to represent the mask is demonstrated. For example, the very popular use of Gandhi's image modified to show him holding the mask, the imposition of the mask on movie characters, often from *The Matrix*, tattoos, (appearing regularly and in diverse renderings), and graffiti are all popular posts. They appear via multiple modalities and combinations of production techniques such as photo editing as commentary and dramatic irony, or to provide messages through inter-iconicity.

Following the genealogical approach within the indigenous typology of *V for Vendetta*, consistent themes regarding the indestructibility of an idea, and the fiction-to-reality trajectory of the origin myth of Anonymous. This thematic grouping unites notions of community/anonymity, and mask/face identity with direct visual citations from the movie. A typical and often repeated image in this set for example is the screen capture posted by Anonymous ART of revolution figure five where V confronts the Highchancellor's right-hand man Mr. Creedy, who is the last of those against whom V's vendetta is being carried out. Creedy has just emptied all the bullets in his gun into V. This image is reposted at irregular intervals reminding viewers not only of the power of ideas, but also of what they have in common behind the mask. The phrase "ideas are bulletproof" mutates as it is taken up by a multitude of other representations yet recalling this originating filmic moment (see Figure 7).

Among the other images frequently posted is below in figure eight where one of the culminating scenes in the film is reproduced in slightly varying contexts, but always with the main thrust of creating a parallel between the fictional representations of the crowd that emerges finally (see Figure 8).

Figure 7. Posting by Anonymous Art of Revolution (Shared 93 times, liked 326 times, with 11 comments on Facebook) Four-shot subway sequence "ideas are bulletproof." (Screenshot by C. CAMBRE, 2013. Retrieved from https://www.facebook.com/pages/Anonymous-ART-of-Revolution/362231420471759.)

Figure 8. Evolution from fiction to reality (Mash-up Screenshot by C. CAMBRE, 2013. Retrieved from https://www.facebook.com/pages/Anonymous/450296804989549.)

We are anonymous. Many of us like to wear Guy Fawkes masks on demonstrations. Some of us even show them in their profile pictures in social networks. That helps to recognize each other. (Soundcloud recording, 2013)

The often-repeated slogans of having no nationality, revolution, and fighting for agency as actors using the Internet, that is, freedom from surveillance, are interspersed with what can be seen as a telling discontinuity. As the epigraph at the commencement of this paper from an Anonymous twitter user claimed: "*Today I took off my face.*" Whereas, many activist movements have used carnivalistic components as part of a strategy of resistance and embraced masking, others have emphasized the removal or erasure of the human face, or the defacement of the subject. The notion of mask *becoming* face or vice versa is a new element within the discourse of evasion, and may be seen as a move reflecting the utter facelessness of online existence. Unlike other assemblages, this one originated online *first* and materialized through actions within the realm of the Internet, and finally emerged on the street as Lingis (1994) reminds us, "to act is to give form to one's powers" (p. 161). In other words, the actions themselves create subjects who, through the materialization of forces, gain the power to realize themselves as a coordinated entity.

The links between the becoming of the mask or the mask as a virtual face have been observed before. Over a decade ago, as part of the Quebec protests against the Free Trade Area of the Americas, an art collective created 4,000 silk-screened bandanas given away in the streets. They hid the wearer from constant police surveillance, and were some protection against the 6,000 canisters of teargas fired over the course of two days. When donned, the laughing mouth printed on the bandana became that of the wearer (2001, see oneworld.org online, Issue 338). However, the figures below indicate the characteristic of facelessness particular to Anonymous. Figures 9 to 13 show various approaches to the removal of the particularistic aspects of identity by stressing metamorphosis, removal of names, removal of face, and the transgression of difference. All of these images merit further within and across case analysis. For the purposes of this paper they take an illustrative status in order not to reduce the complexity of meanings they embody.

A POLITICS OF MASKING

These tales of old disguisings,

are they not Strange myths of souls that found themselves among

Unwonted folk that spake an hostile tongue (From Masks by Ezra Pound)

In *Anonymity as Culture*, Auerbach (2012) notes that Anonymous favours three cultures that are defined in part by masquerade: those of fandom, trolling/pranking, and role-playing games. The cultures of science-fiction and anime/manga fandom emphasize fan fiction and cosplay. Masquerade is a key part of role-playing games online and offline, from *Dungeons & Dragons* to *World of Warcraft*, etc. Counter to the traditional role of witness as someone actually having a face, and giving an identity to legitimize the event they have witnessed, "the masquerade while demanding that participants take on roles as actors or witnesses, requires that the focus not be on the identities of the enthusiasts themselves" (p. 13).

Figure 9. Posted by Divided ByZero (Screenshot by C. CAMBRE, 2013. Retrieved from https://www. facebook.com/divided.byzero.92?fref=ts.)

Figure 10. Posted by Divided ByZero (Screenshot by C. CAMBRE, 2013. Retrieved from https://www.facebook.com/divided.byzero.92?fref=ts.)

Figure 11. Posted by Occupy Bahrain (Screenshot by C. CAMBRE, 2013. Retrieved from https://www.facebook.com/pages/Occupy-Bahrain/431085300237384.)

Figure 12. Posted by World wide freedom on February 22, 2013 (Screenshot by C. CAMBRE, 2013. Retrieved from https://www.facebook.com/anonpics.)

Figure 13. Posted by Facebook page: the cat photo (Screenshot by C. CAMBRE, November 9, 2012. Retrieved from https://www.facebook.com/AnonymousPortugalInternacional.)

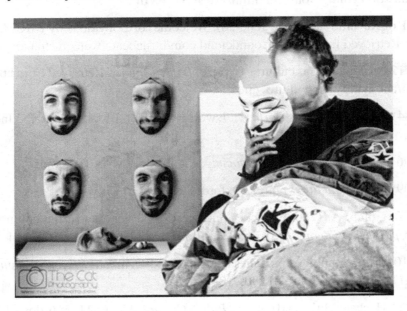

Masks then are required both for the internal online activities of culture of Anonymous as well as for any external manifestation of its members. Of course masks have a long history, they are aligned with the concept of transformation. They are paradoxical because they enable a person to look like what she is not; however, the physical paradox of disguise is complicated by notion of duality. We are also reminded of Bakhtin's description of the folk tradition of using masks to "liberate the world from all that is dark and terrifying" (Bakhtin, 1984, p. 47).

The generative trait of the V-mask, as Deleuzian multiplicity, like the quality of undecideability, ensures resistance to representation because it provides a riddle rather than a clear relationship, it is a non-identity acting as-if an identity, but instead of choosing one or the other it oscillates between them. It rejects dominant "either/or" alternatives. The mask becomes the site where subordination is transformed into resistance through tactical conversions that allow a "dialectical movement of subjectivity that disallows, yes – but at the same time allows – individual expression, style, and personality" (Sandoval, 2000, p. 35). The mask is like "a congealed residue of performance and agency in object-form, through which access to other persons can be attained, and via which their agency can be communicated" (Gell, 1998, p. 68).

The task of the mask and of seeing in relation to the dispersed mechanisms of power in the so called 'societies of control' is to protect and actually provide "…the spaces where politics can even occur, where people can learn and assert a sense of critical agency, embrace the civic obligation to care for the other" (Giroux, 2012, p. 5). In this way, "critical discourses that allow us to think outside of and against the demands of official power" (p. 5) can emerge.

REFERENCES

Anonymous. (n.d.). What is anonymous? Everything you ever wanted to know about the shadowy internet group. *Learn Hacking from Home*. Retrieved from http://learnhackingfromhome.blogspot.in/2013/04/what-is-anonymous-everything-you-ever.html#.UcBEYufFVdI

Anonymous ART of Revolution. (2013, June 26). WelcomeToAnonymous by BIRNABEATZ. *Soundcloud Recording*. Retrieved from https://soundcloud.com/birnabeatz/welcometoanonymous

Auerbach, D. (2012). Anonymity as culture: Treatise. *Triple Canopy*. Retrieved from http://canopycanopypycanopy.com/15/anonymity_as_culture__treatise

Bakhtin, M. (1984). *Rabelais and his world* (H. Iswolsky, Trans.). Bloomington, IN: Indiana University Press.

Castells, M. (1996). *The rise of the network society*. Cambridge, MA: Blackwell.

Castells, M. (2009). *Communication power*. Oxford, UK: Oxford University Press.

Coleman, E. G., & Golub, A. (2008). Hacker practice: Moral genres and the cultural articulation of liberalism. *Anthropological Theory*, 8(3), 255–277. doi:10.1177/1463499608093814

Coleman, G. (2010). Ethnographic approaches to digital media. *Annual Review of Anthropology*, 39(1), 487–505. doi:10.1146/annurev.anthro.012809.104945

Coleman, G. (2011). Hacker politics and publics. *Public Culture*, 23(3), 511–516. doi:10.1215/08992363-1336390

Coleman, G. (2011). Anonymous: From the lulz to collective action. In G. Coleman (Ed.), *Politics in the age of secrecy and transparency cluster. The New Everyday: A Media Commons Project*.

Coleman, G. (2012). Our weirdness is free, the logic of anonymous—Online army, agent of chaos, and seeker of justice. *Triple Canopy, 15.*

Cressy, D. (1992). The fifth of November remembered. In R. Porter (Ed.), *Myths of the English*. Cambridge, UK: Polity Press.

Davis, L. (1993). *Guise and disguise: Rhetoric and characterization in the English renaissance*. Toronto, Canada: University of Toronto Press.

Deleuze, G., & Guattari, F. (1987). *A thousand plateaus: Capitalism and schizophrenia*. Minneapolis, MN: University of Minnesota Press.

Foucault, M. (1970). *The order of things: An archaeology of the human sciences* (A. Sheridan, Trans.). New York, NY: Pantheon.

Foucault, M. (1977). Nietzsche, genealogy, history. D. F. Bouchard (Ed.), Language, counter-memory, practice: Selected essays and interviews. Ithaca, NY: Cornell University Press.

Foucault, M. (1977). *Discipline and punish: The birth of the prison* (A. Sheridan, Trans.). Harmondsworth, UK: Peregrine.

Foucault, M. (1988). The ethic of the care for the self as a practice of freedom. In J. Bernauer & D. Rasmussen (Eds.), *The final Foucault*. Cambridge, MA: MIT Press.

Fraser, A. (2005). The gunpowder plot. London, UK: Phoenix.

Gardner, M. (1990). *More annotated Alice*. New York, NY: Random House.

Gell, A. (1998). *Art and agency: An anthropological theory*. Oxford, UK: Clarendon Press.

Giroux, H. (2012, May 18). *The occupy movement and the politics of educated hope*. Retrieved from http://truth-out.org/news/item/9237-the-occupy-movement-and-

Guy Fawkes Night. (n.d.). Retrieved from http://en.wikipedia.org/wiki/Guy_Fawkes_Night

Habing, B. (2006, November 3). *The fifth of November - English folk verse*. Retrieved from http://www.potw.org/archive/potw405.html

Harper, D. (2001-2013). Terrorism. *The Online Eytmological Dictionary*. Retrieved from http://www.etymonline.com/index.php?term=terrorism

Herber, D. (n.d.). Guy Fawkes: A biography. *Britannia History*. Retrieved from http://www.britannia.com/history/g-fawkes.html

Himanen, P. (2001). *The hacker ethic: And the spirit of the information age*. New York, NY: Random House.

Howard, D. C. (1997). Carnival and pilgrimage. *Essays and Articles on Chaucer*. Retrieved from http://web.archive.org/web/20100507100256/http://lonestar.texas.net/~mseifert/carnival.html

Irmscher, C. (1992). *Masken der moderne: Literarische selbststilisierung bei T. S. Eliot, Ezra Pound, Wallace Stevens und William Carlos Williams* [Modern Masks: The Art of Self-Stylisation in T. S. Eliot, Ezra Pound, Wallace Stevens and William Carlos Williams]. Würzburg, Germany: Könighausen & Neumann.

Juris, J. (2008). *Networking futures: The movements against corporate globalization.* Durham, NC: Duke University Press. doi:10.1215/9780822389170

Kaomea, J. (2000). A curriculum of aloha? Colonialism and tourism in Hawai'i's elementary textbooks. *Curriculum Inquiry, 30*(3), 319–344. doi:10.1111/0362-6784.00168

Lingis, A. (1994). *The community of those who have nothing in common.* Indianapolis, IN: Indiana University Press.

Lovink, G. (2008). *Zero comments: Blogging and critical Internet culture.* New York, NY: Routledge.

Lysloff, R. T. A. (2003). Musical community on the Internet: An online ethnography. *Cultural Anthropology, 18*(2), 233–263. doi:10.1525/can.2003.18.2.233

Mahon, M. (1992). *Foucault's Nietzschean genealogy: Truth, power and the subject.* Albany, NY: State University of New York Press.

Malaby, T. (2009). *Making virtual worlds: Linden lab and second life.* Ithaca, NY: Cornell University Press.

Mitchell, A. (2004). *Carnivalesque: Rabelais and his world.* Retrieved from http://www.csudh.edu/dearhabermas/carnival01bk.htm

O'Neill, G. (2011). Why defending anonymous matters. *Guild Notes, 36*(1), 4.

Quinn Patton, M. (1990). *Qualitative evaluation and research methods* (2nd ed.). Newbury Park, CA: Sage.

Said, E. (1994). *Orientalism.* New York, NY: Vintage Books.

Sandoval, C. (2000). *The methodology of the oppressed.* Minneapolis, MN: University of Minnesota Press.

Senft, T. (2008). *Camgirls: Celebrity and community in the age of social networks.* New York, NY: Peter Lang.

Sharpe, J. A. (2005). *Remember, remember: A cultural history of Guy Fawkes Day.* London, UK: Harvard University Press.

Shohat, E. (1995). The struggle over representation: Casting, coalitions, and the politics of identification. In R. de la Campa, E. A. Kaplan, & M. Sprinkler (Eds.), *Late imperial culture* (pp. 166–178). New York, NY: Verso.

KEY TERMS AND DEFINITIONS

Activism: Activism comes in diverse forms from writing letters, signing petitions, political campaigning, boycotts, street marches, sit-ins, and hunger strikes. Generally, activism is directed at either raising awareness in order to bring a social, economic, environmental or other types of issues to the attention of the general public, and to promote or prevent government action.

Anonymous: An Internet based group, which has adopted the Guy Fawkes Mask as their symbol. Members wear such masks for protests on the streets of cities worldwide or pubic appearance generally. The have been described in various ways and have referred to themselves loosely as "an internet gathering." They gained notoriety after coordinating series of distributed denial-of-service (DDoS) events on government and institutional websites.

Community: A small social unit that contains people or living organisms that share common values or an environment; the word is derived from the Latin term *communitas* (*com* "with/together" and *munus* "gift"). It can refer broadly to fellowship as well as to organized society.

Hacker: Term that emerged in the 1960s through various groups associated with the Massachusetts Institute of Technology (MIT) and refers to one who loves to program in the spirit of playful ingenuity. Excellence as a hacker refers more to the style or process of an activity than to the activity of say programming itself. Hackers are known for exploring limits, creativity, and being dedicated to codes of behavior and ethics determined from within the varied Hacker subcultures. They are often confused with "Crackers" or those who exploit the weaknesses of computer security for an array of purposes.

Identity: Latin word "identity" stands for sameness, continuity, and distinctiveness of things. Giving something a name.

V for Vendetta: Author Alan Moore's graphic novel was written in serial form through comic strips with the final episodes published by 1985. It was adapted in 2006 for a feature film released by Warner Brothers and directed by James McTeigue.

This research was previously published in Educational, Psychological, and Behavioral Considerations in Niche Online Communities edited by Vivek Venkatesh, Jason Wallin, Juan Carlos Castro, and Jason Edward Lewis, pages 297-321, copyright year 2014 by Information Science Reference (an imprint of IGI Global).

Section 4
Web Crawling

Chapter 14
Design of a Least Cost (LC) Vertical Search Engine Based on Domain Specific Hidden Web Crawler

Sudhakar Ranjan
Apeejay Stya University, India

Komal Kumar Bhatia
YMCA University of Science & Technology, India

ABSTRACT

Now days with the advent of internet technologies and ecommerce the need for smart search engine for human life is rising. The traditional search engines are not intelligent as well as smart and thus lead to the rise in searching costs. In this paper, architecture of a vertical search engine based on the domain specific hidden web crawler is proposed. To make a least cost vertical search engine improvement in the following techniques like: searching, indexing, ranking, transaction and query interface are suggested. The domain term analyzer filters the useless information to the maximum extent and finally provides the users with high precision information. Through the experimental result it is shown that the system works on accelerating the access, computation, storage, communication time, increased efficiency and work professionally.

1. INTRODUCTION

The hypertext was introduced in July of 1945 after around 50 years web sites began. As huge amount of information is available on Web and the numbers of web sites are increasing, the quantity of pages are also increasing more rapidly. The information stored over the web is accessible through the internet. Web pages over WWW (World Wide Web) are generally classified into static and dynamic pages. The static / fixed pages fall under category of surface web and dynamic pages fall under hidden web category. As the volume of hidden web is growing exponentially, a lot of time is spending by the user

DOI: 10.4018/978-1-5225-3163-0.ch014

in searching relevant web pages. For accessing, searching and retrieval of the web information a search engine is generally required. The conventional search engines classify and index only static pages. The dynamic pages are not indexed by the conventional search engines. The general purpose search engine does not work effectively for finding the topic of relevant search over the hidden web. This drawback has been removed after the development of the vertical search engine which operates on the principle of finding the topic relevant pages there by leading to the better quality of web search for Hidden Web. The "Hidden Web" or "Invisible Web" contents are currently not a part of conventional search engine. The searching of the hidden web is very difficult due to the two basic reasons. The first issue is size of the content stored in online database and secondly it requires access to the database through restricted search interface so as to extract relevant content. This increases the cost of accessing, searching and retrieval. Hence, there is a need to design and develop a Least Cost Vertical Search Engine for hidden web that can reduce the cost of crawling, accessing and storing along with communication cost for searching of the hidden web contents.

2. RELATED WORK

In Shettar and Bhuptani (2008) the vertical search engine based on domain classifier is built on seven modules: crawler (spider), HTML parse, filter, domain classifier, page ranker, URL db, search interface. In Peshave (2005) the work on structured-data on the web has focused mostly on providing users access to the data. However, the significant value can be obtained from analyzing collections of meta-data on the Web. Desa (2007) describes in detail the basic tasks a search engine performs. An overview of how the whole system of a search engine works is provided. A WebCrawler application is implemented using Java programming language. In Raghavan and Garcia-Molina (2001) a large amount of on-line information resides on the invisible web – web pages generated dynamically from databases and other data sources hidden from current crawlers which retrieve content only from the publicly Indexable Web. Specially, they ignore the tremendous amount of high quality content "hidden" behind search forms, and pages that require authorization or prior registration in large searchable electronic databases.

Zhou, Xiao, Lin, and Zhang (2010) provides a framework for addressing the problem of extracting content from this hidden Web, built a task-specific hidden Web crawler called the Hidden Web Exposer (HiWE), describes the architecture of HiWE. In Huitema and Fizzano (2010) a distributed template-customized vertical crawler which is specially used for crawling Internet forums. The performance of centralized vertical crawler and distributed vertical crawler are compared in the experiment. In Li, Zhaol, and Huang (2010) the focus is on the tasks of crawling and indexing a large amount of highly relevant Web pages, improved HITS algorithm combining link value with topic similarity highlights the difference of links and it assigns different weights to different links. In Bhatia and Sharma (2008), The framework extracts hidden web pages by accrue benefits of its three unique features: 1) automatic downloading of search interfaces to crawl hidden web databases, 2) identification of semantic mappings between search interface elements by using a novel approach called DSIM (Domain-specific Interface Mapper), and 3) the capability to automatic filling of search interfaces. The effectiveness of proposed framework has been evaluated through experiments using real web sites and encouraging preliminary results were obtained.

3. SYSTEM ARCHITECTURE

In this section the proposed architecture of vertical search engine based on domain specific hidden web crawler is provided. The major functions are: Hidden web crawler, Repository, Indexer, Index, Result Merging Rank Calculator, Query Interface, Query Processor, Query Term Generator, Domain Identifier Analyzer, Term Matcher, Query Log, Web Log, Frequency Calculator and Next Query Predictor. In design of a least cost (LC) vertical search engine based on domain specific hidden web crawler through parallel computing reduced the cost. Out of four cost component, the most important is the access cost, storage cost and communication cost. The cost minimization depends on the size and type of application. In the parallel system, the communication cost is minimizing as because many sites are involved for the data transfer. If the data can be completely stored in main memory, then computation cost is reduced. Hidden web crawler and Index Integrator load balancer distributes the hardware and software traffic load. Once the hardware and software load is distributed then systems work efficiently and effectively and also running cost of the access time, memory time, communication time, storage time and computational time is reduced. In indexing segmentation and automatic segmentation techniques are used, the main advantage of automatic segmentation is no maintenance cost and easy to realize, and segmentation gives effective and high precision result. The architecture of Least cost vertical search engine based on the domain specific hidden web shown in Figure 1.Users interact with the proposed least cost vertical search engine through query interface and end users are able to retrieve the desired information. The

Figure 1. Least Cost Vertical Search Engine Architecture

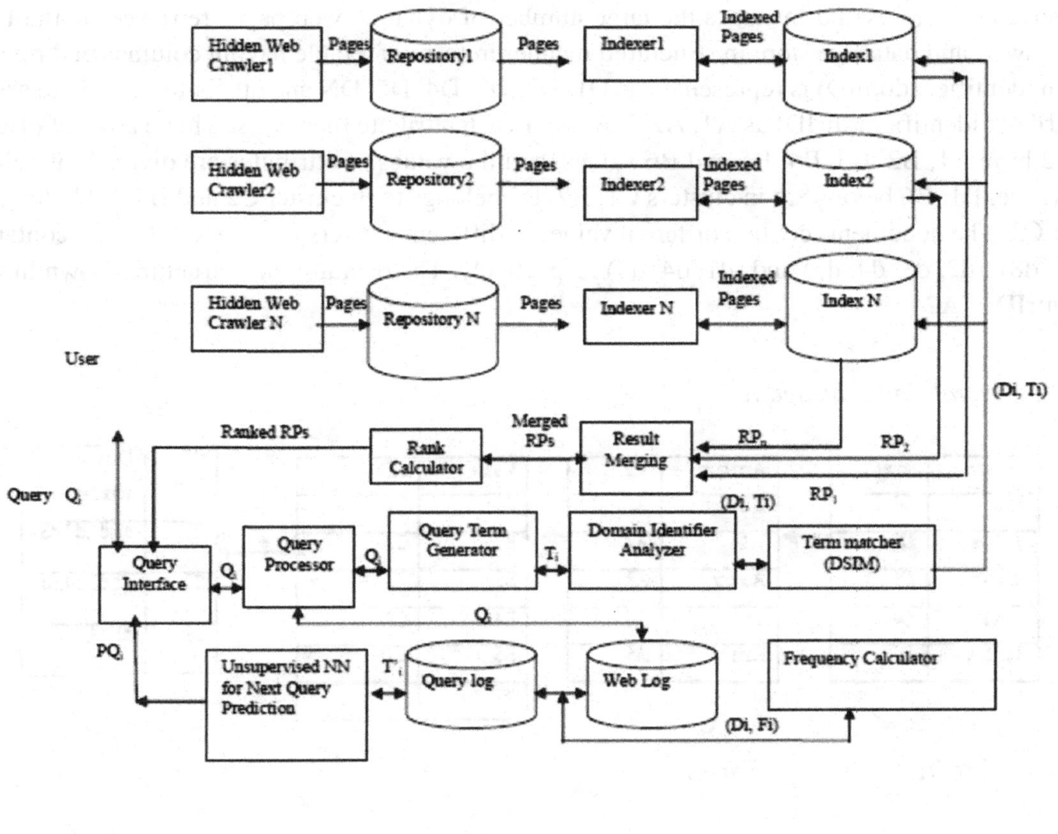

query interface is look and feel similar to the local interface with system. Query interface technique keeps the related documents in the same domain so that searching of documents becomes more efficient in terms of time complexity and hidden web crawler start extracting content from searchable databases and attempts to automate the process of information gathering from Hidden Web sites.

3.1. Hidden Web Crawler

To search access and retrieve the content from hidden web the user need to specify URL and database which involves a lot of time and requests. As per the literature review presented above usually there are 3-5 methods of Domain Specific hidden web crawler searches, however the desired information is processed in the following four phases:

1. Search Interface
2. Domain Specific interface mapping
3. Automatic form filling
4. Response page analysis

3.2. Indexing

Indexing mechanism is the core part of "Design of a least cost (LC) Vertical Search Engine based on DSHWC" system. The attribute value pair based indexing mechanism applied on hidden web documents for a particular domain. The Hidden web crawler uses the page repository to download the web pages. Page repository stores and manages the large number of dynamic web pages retrieved by the Hidden Web Crawler and database store in structured manner in form of a table having columns and rows. The domain identifier (domID) is represented as D1, D2, D3, D4, D5, DN and attributes of D5 are assigned the attribute identifier (attrID) as A1, A2… A5. For each attribute there exist a huge amount of values, like A2 have B1, B2, B3, B4, B5 and B6 values, and the values of attributes are divided into clusters. In this case, B1, B6 belongs to in clusters C1; B2, B5 belongs to in cluster C2 and B3, B4 belongs to in cluster C3. The documents contain different values in different clusters i.e. now C1, C2, C3 contain (d1, d6, d7, d8), (d2, d3, d4, d5) and (d1, d4, d5) respectively. The overall index structure shown in Figure 2 for attrID = A2.

Figure 2. Overall Index Structure

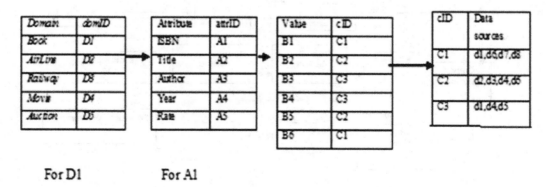

For D1   For A1

The algorithm for index construction and search is given in Figure 3 (a &b)

The advantage of adopting attribute value indexing mechanism is increased search speed, reduced cost, high accuracy and improve qualtity of indexing.

3.3. Query Processing: After the Receiving of a Query From the Query Interface: Query Processing Performs Five Steps to Get the Result

Step 1: Apply Linguistic modules such as Tokenization, Stop-word removal, Lemmatization and Normalization before processing the query

Figure 3. (a) Index construction; (b) Index Search

```
Algorithm index construction ( )

{

Step1: Classify the documents according to the domains.

2: Assign domID to each domain.

3: Identify the attributes of different domains from Unified search interface of that
domain and assign attrID to each attribute in the index structure.

4: Create the clusters of documents depending upon the value of each   attribute.

}
```

```
Algorithm index_search ( )

{

Read a user's query                        // Identify the domain and its domain ID

dom=domain

domID=domain ID                            // Identify the attributes and their values

attr[ ]=attributes

for each attribute in attr[ ]              // retrieve the attribute ID

 attrID[ ]=attribute ID                    // retrieve the value

val[ ]=value

for each attributeID in attrID[ ]          // LOOK UP INDEX

for value in val[ ]                        // retrieve the clusterID

clD[]=cluster ID

for each clD in clD[ ]                     // retrieve the data sources

list_of_ds=data sources

return list_of_ds

}
```

Step 2: Identify the domain from the query after applying step 1 by comparing each keyword with the list of domains.

Step 3: Delete the keyword that helped to identify the domain from the Query.

Step 4: Search the Query in the attribute value based index

Step 5: Represent the result in the form of structure manner

3.4 Ranking

The proposed ranking method is the main objective of this section is to compute the ranking distance (RD). The ranking distance (RD) is measured by the distance between the two tuple records. The pair of two tuple position is represented in the form of Ti and T_j and N is the total number of result records. The formula to compute ranking distance given below:

$$RD = \sum | T_i \text{-} T_j | / N \tag{1}$$

Here RD: Ranking Distance

T_i = i[th] position of tuple, The staring position of T_i is 2, increment in each step by one (T_{i+1}) and reached at Tj_ N;

T_j = j[th] position of tuple, The staring position of Tj is 1, increment in each step by one (Tj_{+1}) and reached at Ti< N;

N = Total number of tuple in table

The R_T is relationship of the given tuple or record as the sum of the number of pair wise transactions (RD) and the score of the TF-IDF. It is calculate by the equation

$$R_T = Score + RD \tag{2}$$

3.4.1. Findings of Proposed Work

The comparison chart between the proposed work and the existing techniques is shown in the table (I & II) for Books domain & Flight domain. According to the comparison table, it can be observed that the search terms "computer science" and "Go Air" were assigned the lowest value of priority in the conventional system of search. However the proposed system rightly assigns the highest value of the priority to the search term on the basis of the fields discussed in the previous sections

Table 1. Comparison chart Flight domain and Book domain

Related work(TF-IDF)						Proposed work	
Flight	**From**	**TO**	**Reuters Collection**	**DF**	**score**	**RD = $\sum | T_i\text{-}T_j | / N$**	**R_T = Score + RD**
All	Delhi	Lucknow	83	83	0	0.98	0.98
Go Air	Delhi	Lucknow	83	3	1.02	0.98	2.00

Table 2. Comparison chart Flight domain and Book domain

	Related work (TF-IDF)				Proposed work	
Term	**Search**	**Reuters Collection**	**DF**	**score**	$RD = \sum |T_i\text{-}T_j| / N$	$RT = Score + RD$
Subject	Computer Science	30	7	0.63	0.85	=0.63+0.85=1.48
Publisher	PHI	30	3	1	0.42	=1+0.42=1.42
Title	Operating System	30	3	1	0.29	=1+0.29=1.29
Author	Andy Tanenbaum	30	2	1.18	0.14	=1.18+0.14=1.32

4. EXPERIMENTAL RESULT

The proposed architecture of Least Cost Vertical Search Engine using DSHWC that takes crawling cost, query execution cost and communication cost into the consideration and makes an attempt to reduce these costs. This is developed on Ubuntu operating system using MySQL and PHP. The experimental result of the proposed architecture shows that there is considerable reduction in the magnitude of communication cost, access cost, storage cost and computation cost, which is shown through the prototype of the software results

4.1. Crawling Cost

The cost of crawling depends upon the size of database and the communication rounds between the crawler and the Web server Figure 4 used for the searching of the books with different parameters like author name, book title, ISBN and Publisher name.

Figure 4. Search form

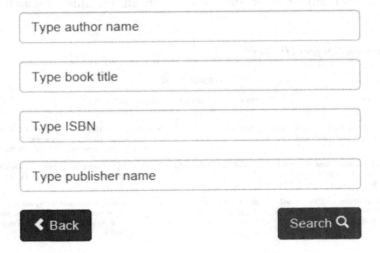

If there are 30 records used in database matching the attribute value "Author Name" and each result page displays the next 20 Records, the total cost to retrieve the entire answer set will be 30/20. In this case two communication rounds are required. Results are based on the type of query generated. For example, if a query is fired about the specific search result like search on subject history and its gives only three records then its takes distinct 3/30 records. This is because each result page can typically hold a fixed number *of* matched records and thus every initiated connection retrieves *at most k* data records. The crawling cost *cost (qi, DB)* of querying the database *DB* with query *qi* is defined as: *cost (qi,DB)=*, where stands for the number of all the records in *DB* matched by *q* num(*qi, DB*) / *k and* num(*qi, DB*) *i* and *k* corresponds to the maximum number of records displayed in each result page from the target Web site. The output is shown in Figure 5.

4.2. Communication Cost

The communication cost refers to the amount spent in transferring the query and its result from server to client site. This is achieved by employing multiple N numbers of crawlers working in parallel for performing the given tasks. Another reason to reduce the communication cost is making use of load balancer. It distributes the hardware and software load in order to obtain good processing speed on application programs. The main advantages are: There is no Synchronization required between crawlers and there is no communication required between crawlers as each crawler works independently. Thus there is no inter-task communication delay. Figure 6 represent the server traffic data.

4.3. Access Cost

The access cost calculation depends upon the three main tasks performed in a system they are searching, reading and writing information that exists in on secondary storage space. The Access Cost find out through the [Running time * Number of processors]. In Figure 7(a & b) represent the value of the task and time taken by the processor to complete the jobs.

According to the query which is shown below out of 30 records match records are only five and its takes only 0.0020 sec through one processor shown in Figure 8. The same can be reduced further when accessed through parallel multiple processors. This also lessens the time for searching.

Figure 5. Result Page on Subject History

Result page

Author's First Name	Author's Last Name	Title	ISBN	Publisher	Subject	Keywords	Buy now
Levi	Tillemann	The Great Race: The Global Quest For The Car Of The Future	1476773491	Simon & Schuster	History	agined. They will drive themselves, won't consume oil, and will come in radical shapes and sizes. But the path to that future is fraught The top contenders	Buy now
Mike	Mueller	The Complete Book Of Corvette - Revised & Updated: Every Model Since 1953 (Complete Book Series)	0760345740	Motorbooks	History	flagship sports car has become a timeless part of American culture and a household name across the	Buy now
A. J.	Baime	Go Like Hell: Ford, Ferrari, And Their Battle For Speed And Glory At Le Mans	0547336055	Mariner Books	History	omobile transportation to the masses was falling behind. Baby boomers were taking to the roads in droves, looking for speed not safety style not comfort	Buy now

Figure 6. Server traffic

Server traffic: These tables show the network traffic statistics of this MySQL server since its startup.

Traffic [1]		ø per hour	Connections		ø per hour	%
Received	103 KiB	67 KiB	max. concurrent connections	1	---	---
Sent	559 KiB	362 KiB	Failed attempts	0	0.00	0.00%
Total	662 KiB	429 KiB	Aborted	0	0.00	0.00%
			Total	138	89.50	100.00%

Query statistics: Since its startup, 1,570 queries have been sent to the server.

Total	ø per hour	ø per minute	ø per second
1,570	1.02 k	16.97	0.28

Query type		ø per hour	%	Query type		ø per hour	%	Query type		ø per hour	%
select	412	267.195	28.77%	show create table	51	33.075	3.56%	show master status	4	2.594	0.28%
set option	324	210.124	22.63%	insert	44	28.535	3.07%	show slave status	4	2.594	0.28%
change db	221	143.326	15.43%	show keys	33	21.402	2.30%	create view	2	1.297	0.14%
stmt prepare	108	70.041	7.54%	show variables	27	17.510	1.89%	show plugins	2	1.297	0.14%
stmt execute	108	70.041	7.54%	show databases	10	6.485	0.70%	show grants	2	1.297	0.14%
stmt close	108	70.041	7.54%	show storage engines	8	5.188	0.56%	show charsets	2	1.297	0.14%
show table status	102	66.150	7.12%	show triggers	8	5.188	0.56%	show collations	2	1.297	0.14%
show fields	80	51.883	5.59%	delete	7	4.540	0.49%	truncate	1	0.649	0.07%
show tables	77	49.937	5.38%	show binlogs	6	3.891	0.42%	show status	1	0.649	0.07%

Figure 7. (a) Time and Task Allocation;(b) Graphical Representation of Task & Time

Task	T1	T2	T3	T4	T5
Time	5	10	15	10	5
Task	T6	T7	T8	T9	T10
Time	8	1	4	2	5

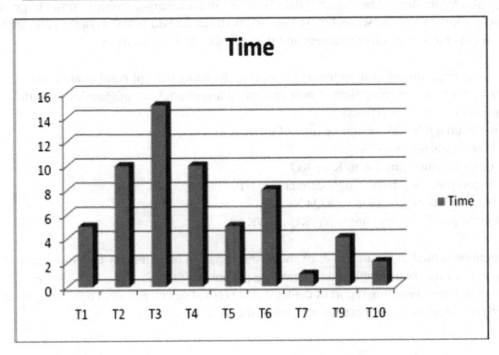

Figure 8. Searching Time

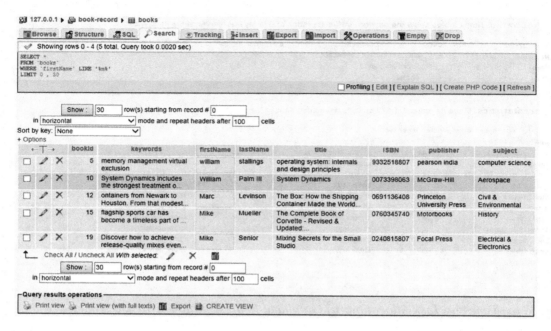

4.4. Storage Cost

This is defined as the cost of storing intermediate relation. It is generated by the execution strategy for the query fired by the user. The valuable data is stored in an arranged fashion in the large scale data management warehouses. The secondary storage index stores the additional storage in the database. The storage cost depends upon two parameters and they are speedup & efficiency.

Speedup = Running time of best sequential algorithm/ Running time of parallel algorithm.
Efficiency= Worst case running time of best sequential algorithm/Cost of Parallel algorithm.
Let the number of jobs = N (Pages)
Let the time to do a job = P (searching time of the pages)
Let there be K extractor to do the job.
Let the time to distribute the job to K be KQ.
The time to complete N jobs by single extractor = NP
The time to complete N jobs by K = KQ+NP/K
Speedup due to parallel processing= NP/KQ+NP/K

The graph presented in Figure 9(a & b) shows the variation of efficiency and speed up with respect to the number of processors employed for crawling purposes.

In Figure 10 shows profiling report of the least cost vertical search engine. The starting time, sending time, query end time and other parameters shown in Figure 10.

Figure 9. (a) Comparison chart; (b) Speedup and Efficiency

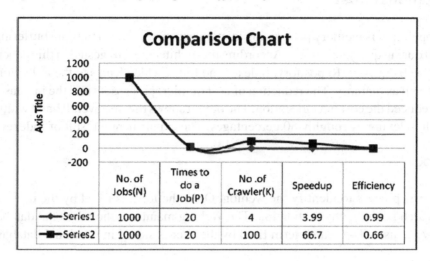

	No. of Jobs(N)	Times to do a Job(P)	No .of Crawler(K)	Speedup	Efficiency
Series1	1000	20	4	3.99	0.99
Series2	1000	20	100	66.7	0.66

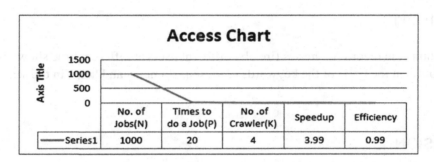

	No. of Jobs(N)	Times to do a Job(P)	No .of Crawler(K)	Speedup	Efficiency
Series1	1000	20	4	3.99	0.99

Figure 10. Profiling

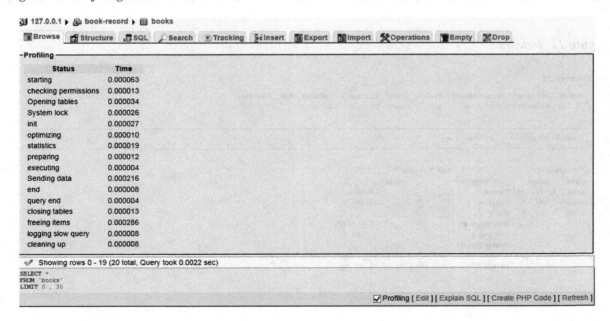

4.5. Computational Cost

The cost of computation is memory performing in memory operations on the data buffering and memory buffered needed during query execution. According the architecture suggested in this paper, since there is N no. of hidden web crawlers, Repository, Indexer and Index which lead s to the reduction in the cost of computation as well as memory. The reduction of cost of microprocessors and the increase in their speed has drastically reduced the cost of workstation. The output shows that the overall band width consumption reduced through indexing by roughly 50 percentages. The experimental result of Indexes shown below.

4.5.1. Buy Log

Logging is the first process to identify the weblog. Once the form is filled by the user for instance the user wants to search flight to any destination. The Weblog maintains the relational database of the queries accessed by the user. The search term fired by the user is stored in relational database as shown in the Figure 12.

4.5.2. Search Log

Search log contains the record of queries fired by different users at different time shown in Figure 13. It stores the database on the basis of the keywords of various domains and helps in the searching or firing the query.

5. CONCLUSION

In this paper, the structure and working of least cost vertical search engine based on domain specific hidden web crawler is discussed as the smart engine. The considerable reduction in costs of various

Figure 11. Indexes

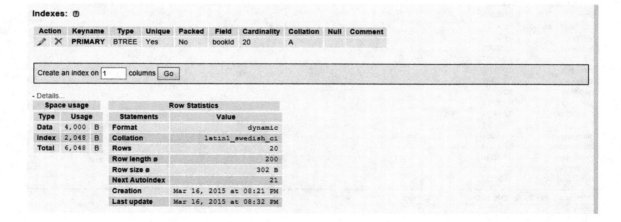

Figure 12. Buy log

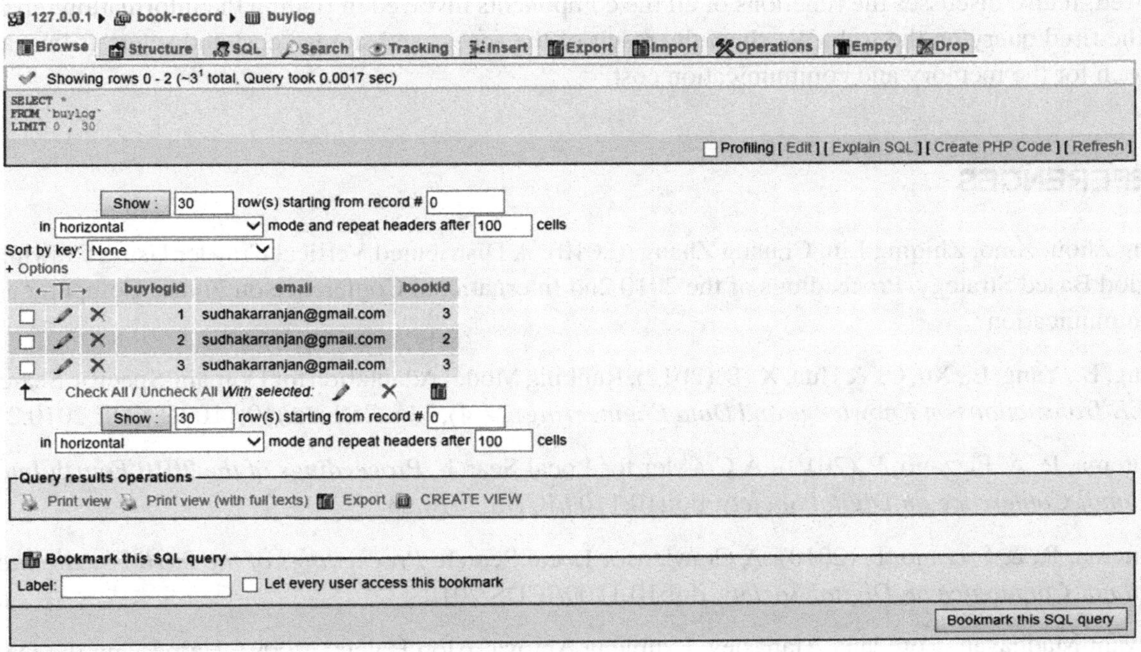

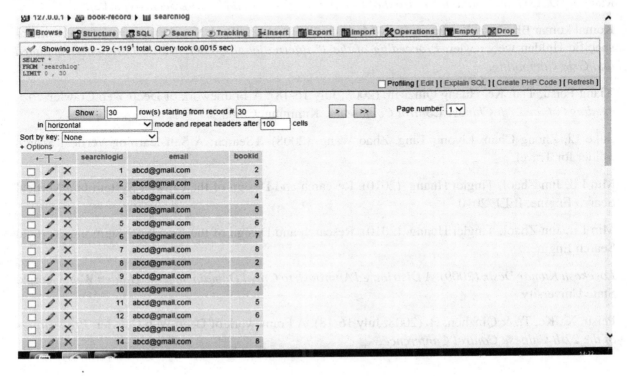

Figure 13. Search log

search fields and increase in the efficiency of the search engine through the use of parallel processors is proved. It also discusses the functions of all the components involved in finding the information related to the fired query on the web. We show the result of the access and storage cost and suggests best approach for the memory and communication cost.

REFERENCES

Bing Zhou, Xiao, Zhiqing Lin, Chuang Zhang. (2010). A Distributed Vertical Crawler Using Crawling-Period Based Strategy. *Proceedings of the 2010 2nd International Conference on Future Computer and Communication.*

Geng, B., Yang, L., Xu, C., & Hua, X.-S. (2012). Ranking Model Adaptation for Domain-Specific Search. *IEEE Transactions on Knowledge and Data Engineering, 24*(4), 745–758. doi:10.1109/TKDE.2010.252

Huitema, P., & Fizzano, P. (2010). A Crawler for Local Search. *Proceedings of the 2010 Fourth International Conference on Digital Society.* doi:10.1109/ICDS.2010.23

Huitema, P., & Fizzano, P. (2010). A Crawler for Local Search. *Proceedings of the 2010 Fourth International Conference on Digital Society.* doi:10.1109/ICDS.2010.23

. Jayant Madhavan, Loredana Afanasiev, Lyublena Antova, Alon Halevy (2009). Harnessing the Deep Web: Present and Future, CIDR perspective

Komal kumar Bhatia, & Shrma A.K. (2008, December). A Frame Work for Domain Specific Interface Mapper (DSIM). *International Journal of Computer Science and Network Security, 8*(12).

Komal kumar Bhatia, A.K. Shrma, Rosy Madaan. (2010). AKSHR: A Novel Framework for a Domain-specific Hidden webcrawler. *Proceeding of the 1ˢᵗ international Conference on Parallel, Distributed and Grid Computing.*

Xiang Peisu, Tian Ke, Huang Qinzhen. (2008, July 16-18). A Framework of Deep Web Crawler. *Proceedings of the 27th Chinese Control Conference,* Kunming, China.

Suke Li, Zhong Chen, Liyong Tang, Zhao Wang. (2008). TSearch: A Self-learning Vertical Search Spider for Travel.

Min Lil, Jun Zhaol, Tinglei Huang. (2010). Research and Design of the Crawler System in a Vertical Search Engine, IEEE 2010

Min Lil, Jun Zhaol, Tinglei Huang. (2010). Research and Design of the Crawler System in a Vertical Search Engine.

Lovekesh Kumar Desa. (2009). A Distributed Approach to Crawl Domain Specific Hidden Web. Georgia State University.

Peisu, X., Ke, T., & Qinzhen, H. (2008, July 16-18). A Framework of Deep Web Crawler. *Proceedings of the 27th Chinese Control Conference.*

Peshave, M. (2007). *How Search Engines Work and a Web Crawler Application*. University of Illinois at Springfield.

Raghavan, S., & Garcia-Molina, H. (2001, September). Crawling the Hidden Web. Proc. of the 27th International conference on very large Databases (VLDB '01).

Ranjan, S., & Bhatia, K.K. (2013). Query interface integrator for domain Specific Hidden web. *International Journal of Computer Engineering and Applications*, 4(1-3).

Ranjan, S., & Bhatia, K. K. (2013, October). Indexing for Vertical Search Engine: Cost Sensitive. *International Journal of Emerging Technology & Advanced Engineering*, 3(10).

Sudhakar Ranjan, Komal Kumar Bhatia (2014, July). Indexing for Domain Specific Hidden Web. *International Journal of Computer Engineering and Applications*, 7(1).

Ranjan, S., & Bhatia, K. K. (2014, July). Web Log for Domain Specific Hidden Web. *International Journal of Computer Engineering and Applications*, 7(1).

Ranjan, S., & Bhatia, K. K. (2014, November). Transaction in Hidden Web. *International Journal of Computer Engineering and Applications*, 8(2).

Rajashree Shettar, Rahul Bhuptani. (2008). A vertical Search Engine –Based On Domain Classifier. *International Journal of Computer Science and Security*, 2(4).

Sri khetwat Saritha, Kishan Dharvath. (2011). Domain and Keyword Specific Data Extraction From Invisible Web Databases. *Proceedings of the 2011 Eighth International Conference on Information Technology*.

von der Weth, C., & Datta, A. (2012). *Multiterm Keyword Search in NoSQL System*. IEEE Computer Society.

Lei Zhang, Yong Peng, Xiangwu Meng, and Jie Guo. (2008). Personalized Domain-specific Search Engine.

Zheng, J., & Nie, Z. (2009). Architecture and Implementation of an Object-level Vertical Search. *Proceedings of the 2009 International Conference on New Trends in Information and Service*.

This research was previously published in the International Journal of Information Retrieval Research (IJIRR), 7(2); edited by Zhongyu (Joan) Lu, pages 19-33, copyright year 2017 by IGI Publishing (an imprint of IGI Global).

Chapter 15
A Novel Architecture for Deep Web Crawler

Dilip Kumar Sharma
Shobhit University, India

A. K. Sharma
YMCA University of Science and Technology, India

ABSTRACT

A traditional crawler picks up a URL, retrieves the corresponding page and extracts various links, adding them to the queue. A deep Web crawler, after adding links to the queue, checks for forms. If forms are present, it processes them and retrieves the required information. Various techniques have been proposed for crawling deep Web information, but much remains undiscovered. In this paper, the authors analyze and compare important deep Web information crawling techniques to find their relative limitations and advantages. To minimize limitations of existing deep Web crawlers, a novel architecture is proposed based on QIIIEP specifications (Sharma & Sharma, 2009). The proposed architecture is cost effective and has features of privatized search and general search for deep Web data hidden behind html forms.

1. INTRODUCTION

Traditional Web crawling techniques have been used to search the contents of the Web that is reachable through the hyperlinks but they ignore the deep Web contents which are hidden because there is no link is available for referring these deep Web contents. The Web contents which are accessible through hyperlinks are termed as surface Web, while the hidden contents hidden behind the html forms are termed as deep Web. Deep Web sources store their contents in searchable databases that produce results dynamically only in response to a direct request (Bergman, 2001). The deep Web is not completely hidden for crawling. Major traditional search engines can be able to search approximately one-third of the data (He, Patel, Zhang, & Chang, 2007) but in order to utilize the full potential of Web, there is a need to concentrate on deep Web contents since they can provide a large amount of useful information. Hence, there is a need to build efficient deep Web crawlers which can efficiently search the deep Web contents. The deep Web pages cannot be searched efficiently through traditional Web crawler and they can be

DOI: 10.4018/978-1-5225-3163-0.ch015

extracted dynamically as a result of a specific search through a dedicated deep Web crawler (Peisu, Ke, & Qinzhen, 2008; Sharma & Sharma, 2010). This paper finds the advantages and limitations of the current deep Web crawlers in searching the deep Web contents. For this purpose an exhaustive analysis of existing deep Web crawler mechanism is done for searching the deep Web contents. In particular, it concentrates on development of novel architecture for deep Web crawler for extracting contents from the portion of the Web that is hidden behind html search interface in large searchable databases with the following points:

- Analysis of different existing algorithms of deep Web crawlers with their advantages and limitations in large scale crawling of deep Web.
- After profound analysis of existing deep Web crawling process, a novel architecture of deep Web crawling based on QIIIEP (query intensive interface information extraction protocol) specification is proposed (Figure 1).

This paper is organized as follows: In section 2, related work is discussed. Section 3 summarizes the architectures of various deep Web crawlers. Section 4 compares the architectures of various deep Web crawlers. The architecture of the proposed deep Web crawler is presented in section 5. Experimental results are discussed in section 6 and finally, a conclusion is presented in section 7.

2. RELATED WORK

Deep Web stores their data behind the html forms. Traditional Web crawler can efficiently crawl the surface Web but they cannot efficiently crawl the deep Web. For crawling the deep Web contents various specialized deep Web crawlers are proposed in the literature but they have limited capabilities in crawling the deep Web. A large volume of deep Web data is remains to be discovered due to the limitations of deep Web crawler. In this section existing deep Web crawlers are analyzed to find their advantages and limitations with particular reference to their capability to crawl the deep Web contents efficiently.

Application/Task Specific Human Assisted Approach

Various crawlers are proposed in literature to crawl the deep Web. One of the deep Web crawler architecture is proposed by Raghavan and Garcia-Molina (2001). In this paper, a task-specific, human-assisted

Figure 1. Mechanism of QIIIEP-based deep web crawler

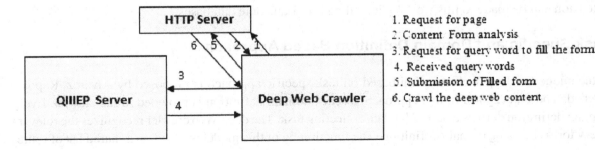

approach is used for crawling the hidden Web. Two basic challenges are associated with deep Web search, i.e. the volume of the hidden Web is very large and there is a need of such type of user friendly crawler which can handle search interfaces efficiently. In this paper a model of task specific human assisted Web crawler is designed and realized in HiWE (hidden Web exposure). The HiWE prototype was built at Stanford and it crawls the dynamic pages. HiWE is designed to automatically process, analyze, and submit forms, using an internal model of forms and form submissions. HiWE uses a layout-based information extraction (LITE) technique to process and extract useful information. The advantages of HiWE architecture is that its application/task specific approach allows the crawler to concentrate on relevant pages only and automatic form filling can be done with the human assisted approach. Limitations of this architecture are that, it is not precise in responding to partially filled forms and it is not able to identify and respond to simple dependency between form elements.

Focused Crawling With Automatic Form Filling Based Approach

A focused crawler architecture is proposed by Luciano Barbosa and Juliana Freire (2005). This paper suggests a strategy which deals with the problem of performing a wide search while avoiding the crawling of irrelevant pages. The best way is to use a focused crawler which only crawl pages relevant to a particular topic. It uses three classifiers to focus its search: Page classifier is which classifies pages, belonging to topics, Form classifier is used to filter out useless forms and Link classifiers is used to identify links that are likely to lead to pages that contain searchable form interfaces in one or more steps. Advantages of this architecture are that only topic specific forms are gathered and unproductive searches are avoided because of application of stopping criteria. A limitation of this architecture is that quality of forms is not ensured since thousands of forms are retrieved at a time. Furthermore scope of improvement in this type of crawler is that focused crawlers can be used for making domain specific crawlers like hidden Web database directory.

Automatic Query Generation for Single Attribute Database Based Approach

A novel technique for downloading textual hidden Web contents is proposed by Ntoulas, Zerfos, and Cho (2005). There are two basic challenges in implementing a hidden Web crawler; firstly the crawler should understand and model a query interface secondly the crawler should generate meaningful queries to issue to the query interface. To address the above mentioned challenges, this paper suggests how a crawler can automatically generate queries so that it can discover and download the hidden Web pages. It mainly focuses on textual databases that support single-attribute keyword queries. An advantage of this technique is that query is generated automatically without any human intervention therefore crawling is efficient and limitation of this technique is that it focuses only on single attribute databases. Further an extension can be made to this work by including multi-attribute databases.

Task Specific and Domain Definition Based Approach

A technique for deep Web crawling based on task-specific approach is proposed by Alvarez, Raposo, Cacheda and Pan (2006). In this approach, a set of domain definition is provided to the crawler. Every domain definition defines a particular data collecting task. The deep Web crawler recognizes the relevant query forms by using domain definition. The functioning of this model is based on a shared list of routes

(URLs). The overall crawling process consists of several sub crawling processes which may run on different machines. Each crawling process selects a route from the route list, analyzes it and downloads the relevant documents. The advantage of this algorithm is that results are very effective against the various real words data collecting tasks. Further scope in this regard is to make this algorithm to be capable of automatically generate new queries from the results of the previous ones.

Focused Crawling Based Approach

A focused crawler named DeepBot for accessing hidden Web content is proposed by Alvarez, Raposo, Pan, Cacheda, Bellas, and Carneiro (2007). In this work an algorithm is developed for developing the DeepBot, which is based on focused crawling for extracting the deep Web contents. Challenges behind the crawling of the deep Web contents can be broadly classified into two parts, i.e., crawling the Hidden Web at server-side and crawling the Hidden Web at client-side. Advantages of this DeepBot crawler are that a form may be used in this crawling but it may have some field that do not correspond to any attribute of the domain, Accuracy of DeepBot crawler is high when more than one associated text are present in the field. The context related to the whole form is also considered in the crawling mechanism and DeepBot is fully compatible with java-script sources. A disadvantage of such type of crawling is that all the attributes of the form should be filled completely and precisely. Problem in crawling arises when one uses sources with session mechanisms. As a future work, modification can be done in the DeepBot crawler so that it can be able to generate new quires in automatic fashion.

Sampling Based Approach

An approach to deep Web crawling by sampling based technique is proposed Lu, Wang, Liang, Chen, and Liu (2008). One of the major challenges while crawling the deep Web is the selection of the queries so that most of the data can be retrieved at a low cost. A general method is proposed, which maximize the coverage of the data source, while minimizing the communication cost. The strategy behind this technique is to minimize the number of queries issued, by maximizing the possibility of the unique returns of each query. An advantage of this technique is that it is a low cost technique that can be used in practical applications and limitation of this algorithm is that the efficiency of the crawler reduces when the sample and pool size is very large. As a future work, modification can be done to lower the overlapping rate so that the maximum Webpages can be downloaded.

Domain Specific Search With Relevancy Based Approach

An architectural framework of a crawler for locating deep Web repositories using learning multi-agent systems is proposed by Akilandeswari and Gopalan (2008). This paper uses multi-agent Web mining system to discover pages from the hidden Web. Multi-agents system is used when there are troubles in storing large amount of data in the database indices. The proposed system has variety of information agents interacting with each other to learn about their environment so that they can retrieve desired information effectively. Advantages of this framework are that crawling through this technique is efficient because the searching is concentrated on a specific domain. The crawling technique of this framework extract the relevant Web forms by using the learning multi-agents and it learns effectively which reduces form retrieval time. Limitation of this framework is that it is not easy to maintain multiple agents. In future, this framework can be extended so that genetic algorithms can be implemented in the crawler to perform a broad search to improve the harvest rate.

Domain-Specific Deep Web Sources Discovery Based Approach

A technique of domain-specific deep Web sources discovery is proposed by Wang, Zuo, Peng, and He (2008). It is difficult to find the right sources and then querying over them online in huge collection of useful databases. Hence, this paper presents a new method by importing focused crawling technology to automatically accomplish deep Web sources discovery. Firstly, Websites are located for domain-specific data sources based on focused crawling. Secondly, it is judged where the Website exists in deep Web query interface. Lastly, judgment is done to find whether the deep Web query interface is relevant to a given topic. Implementation of focused crawling technology facilitates the identification of deep Web query interface located in a specific domain and capturing of relevant pages associated with the topic. This method has dramatically reduces the quantity of pages for the crawler to crawl the deep Web. Advantage of this technique is that fewer numbers of pages need to be crawled since it applies focused crawling along with the relevancy search of the obtained results about the topic. Limitation of this technique is that it does not take into account the semantics, i.e., a particular query result could have several meanings. As a future work this technique can be extended to include semantics while querying.

Input Values for Text Search Inputs Based Approach

A technique for surfacing deep Web contents is proposed by Madhavan, Ko, Kot, Ganapathy, Rasmussen, and Halevy (2008). Surfacing the deep Web is a very complex task because html forms can be associated with different languages and different domains. Further large quantities of forms are associated with text inputs which require the submission of valid input values. For this purpose authors have proposed a technique for choosing input values for text search inputs by which keywords can be accepted. Advantage of this technique is that it can efficiently navigate for searching against various possible input combinations. The limitations as well as future work in this regard can be to modify the technique to deal with forms associated with java script and to analyze the dependency between the values in various inputs of a form in more depth.

Label Value Set (LVS) Table Based Approach

A framework of Deep Web Crawler is proposed by Peisu, Ke, and Qinzhen (2008). The proposed framework processes the actual mechanics of crawling of deep Web. This paper deals with the problem of crawling a subset of the currently uncrawled dynamic Web contents. It concentrates on extracting contents from the portion of the Web that is hidden behind search forms in large searchable databases. This proposed framework presents a model of form with form submission facility. One of important characteristics of this proposed crawler is that it uses Label Value Set (LVS) table. Access and additions to the LVS table is done by LVS manager. The LVS manager also works as an interface for different application specific data sources. Advantage of this deep Web crawler is that it uses the additional modules like LVS table which help the crawler to design the model of frame. If the crawler uses the LVS table than the number of successful form submissions increase. Limitations of this framework are that crawler is unable to extract label (E) and the value of domain (D) in LVS is repeated.

Minimum Executing Pattern (MEP) and Adaptive Query Based Approach

A technique for crawling deep Web contents through query forms is proposed by Liu, Wu, Jiang, Zheng, and Liu (2009). The proposed technique of crawling the deep Web content is based on minimum executing pattern (MEP). The query in this technique is processed by deep Web adaptive query method. Query interface is expended from single text box to MEP set by using deep Web adaptive query method. A MEP, associated with keyword vector is selected for producing optimum local query. Advantages of this technique are that it can handle a different Web forms very effectively and its efficiency is very high compared to non prior knowledge methods. Further it also minimizes the problem of "data islands" to some extent. The limitation of this technique is that it does not produce good results in case of the deep Web sites which have limited size of result set. Further Boolean logic operators, such as AND, OR, NOT, cannot be used in queries which can be a part of the future work.

Iterative Self Organizing Data Analysis (ISODATA) Based Approach

A novel automatic technique for classifying deep Web sources is proposed by Zhao (2010). The classification of deep Web sources is a very critical step for integrating the large scale deep Web data. This proposed technique is based on iterative self organizing data analysis (ISODATA) technique. This technique is based on hierarchical clustering method. Advantage of this technique is that it allows the user to browse the relevant and valuable information. Method for extraction of characteristics in Web pages can be further improved to browse the valuable information.

Continuously Update or Refresh the Hidden Web Repository Based Approach

A framework for incremental hidden Web crawler is proposed by Madaan, Dixit, Sharma, and Bhatia (2010). In a world of rapidly changing information, it is a highly required to maintain and extract the up-to-date information. For this, it is required to verify whether a Web page has been changed or not. The time period between two successive revisits needs to be adjusted based on probability of updating of the Web page. In this paper, architecture is proposed that introduces a technique to continuously update or refresh the hidden Web repository. Advantages of this incremental hidden Web crawler is that information fetched is updated even if Web pages change and limitation of this incremental hidden Web crawler is that efficient indexing technique is required to maintain the Web pages in the repository. In future, a modified architecture of a search engine based on incremental hidden Web crawler using some indexing technique can be designed to index the Web pages that stored in the repository.

Reinforcement Learning Based Approach

An efficient deep Web crawling technique using reinforcement learning is proposed by Jiang, Wu, Feng, Liu, and Zheng (2010). In the reinforcement learning technique, the deep Web crawler works as agent and deep Web database plays a role of environment. The deep Web crawler identifies a query to be submitted into a deep Web database, depending upon Q-value. The advantage of this technique is that deep Web crawler itself decides about a crawling technique to be used by using its own experience. Further, it also permits the use of different characteristics of query keywords. Further scope in this technique is that to develop an open source platform can be developed for deep Web crawling.

After going through analysis of deep Web crawlers, it is concluded that each deep Web crawler has certain limitations with reference to their capabilities of efficient crawling of the deep Web contents. Some of the challenges for efficient deep Web crawling are that a crawler should not overload the Web servers. A deep Web crawler must be robust against hazardous situations. It must be fault tolerant so that its performance degrades gracefully. It should be highly configurable. The download rate of a crawler must be adequate so as to process the harvested data. A crawler must be flexible to enable quick adoption to new publishing technologies and formats used on the Web as they become available. The crawler must include the management tools that enable the quick detection of its failure. The deep Web crawler should have a focused way of crawling the information from the deep Web. They should automatically download the pages from the deep Web so that search engine can index them.

3. SUMMARY OF VARIOUS DEEP WEB CRAWLER ARCHITECTURES

By going through the literature analysis of some of the deep Web crawlers, It is concluded that every crawler have some relative advantages and limitations. A tabular summary is given in Table 1, which summarizes the techniques, advantages and limitations of some of important deep Web crawlers.

4. COMPARISON OF THE VARIOUS DEEP WEB CRAWLER ARCHITECTURES

Based on the literature analysis, a comparison of some of various deep Web crawlers architectures is shown in Table 2 and Table 3. Comparison is done on the basis of some parameters such as technique used, need of user support, reflection of change in Web page, automatic query selection; accuracy of data fetched, database sampling and focused crawling.

5. PROPOSED WORK

By going through literature analysis with their relative comparison with reference to efficient deep Web crawling, it is observed that each deep Web crawler has limitations in efficient crawling of the deep Web. To fulfill this need, a novel architecture for efficient deep Web crawling is proposed with particular reference to QIIIEP specification. Proposed architecture incorporates all the features of existing deep Web crawlers and tries to minimize the limitations of existing deep Web crawlers. Figure 2 shows the architecture of proposed novel deep Web crawler mechanism.

Description of Modules of Proposed Architecture for Deep Web Crawler Mechanism

What follows is a module-wise description of proposed novel architecture of deep Web crawler.

Table 1. Summary of various deep Web crawler architectures

Authors, Year	Technique	Advantages	Limitations
Raghavan et al., 2001	Extraction is application/task specific.	Extraction of irrelevant pages is minimized.	Crawling is not precise due to possibility of missing of some pages.
Barbosa et al., 2005	Focused crawling with automatic form filling.	Crawling is highly relevant, which saves time and resources.	Quality of forms is not ensured and form verification is a complex task.
Ntoulas et al., 2005	Based on automatic query generation form.	Efficient crawling due to crawler generated query.	Does not involve frequently used multi-attribute database.
Alvarez et al., 2006	Task specific approach. A set of domain definition is provided to the crawler. Every domain definition defines a particular data collecting task. The deep Web crawler recognizes the relevant query forms by using domain definition.	Results are very effective against the various real words data collecting task.	Algorithm can be modified to be able to automatically generate new queries from the results of the previous ones.
Alvarez et al., 2007	Focused crawling for extracting deep Web contents	Accuracy is high with the field having more than one associated text. The context of the whole form is used. Fully compatible with java-script sources.	The form should be filled precisely and completely. Difficulty with sources having session mechanism.
Lu et al., 2007	Sampling data from the database.	Low cost, Efficient in practical applications.	Efficiency is less in case of large sample and pool size.
Akilandeswari et al., 2008	Use of multi-agent system on a large database.	Time efficient, fault tolerant and easy handling due to multi-agents.	Cost may be high due to maintenance of multi-agents.
Wang et al., 2008	Focused crawling and results are located in a specific domain.	Crawl fewer numbers of pages due domain specific technique.	Sometimes semantics may be wrong due to crawling of useless pages.
Madhavan et al., 2008	Input values for text search inputs are selected. Identification of inputs for a particular type of values.	It can efficiently navigate for searching against various possible input combinations.	Technique can be modified to deal with forms associated with java script and the dependency between the values in various inputs of a form can be analyzed in more depth.
Peisu et al., 2008	Proposes a model of form. Form submission with four additional modules with LVS table.	Successful form submissions increase with the use of LVS table.	If crawler is unable extract label (E) then the value of domain (D) in LVS is repeated.
Liu et al., 2009	Based on the concept of minimum executable pattern (MEP).	Effective handing of different Web forms. Higher efficiency against non prior knowledge method. Reduces the problem of "data islands".	Results are not good with Websites having limited size of result set. Boolean logic operators (AND,OR,NOT) cannot be used.
Zhao, 2010	Based on iterative self organizing data analysis (ISODATA) technique.	Allows the user to browse the relevant and valuable information.	Extraction method of characteristics in Web pages can be further improved to browse the valuable information.
Madaan et al., 2010	Regularly updates Web repository.	Fetched Web pages are regularly updated.	Indexing of Web page is required.
Jiang et al., 2010	Based on reinforcement learning technique. Deep Web crawler works as agent and deep Web database plays a role of environment. Identify a query to be submitted into a deep Web database, using Q-value.	Deep Web crawler itself decides about a crawling technique to be used by using its own experience. Permits the use of different characteristics of query keywords.	Can be developed as an open source platform for deep Web crawling.

Table 2. Comparison of the various deep Web crawler architectures

Crawling Technique → / Parameter ↓	Crawling the Hidden Web	Searching for Hidden Web Databases	Downloading Textual Hidden Web Contents	Domain Specific Deep Web Sources Discovery	Approach to Deep Web Crawling by Sampling	Framework for Incremental Hidden Web Crawler	Locating Deep Web Repositories Using Multi-Agent Systems
Technique used	Application/ task specific human assisted approach.	Focused crawling with automatic form filling.	Automatic query generation for single attribute database.	Domain specific relevancy based search.	Sampling of data from the database.	Frequent updation of Web repository.	Multi-agent system is helpful in locating deep Web contents.
Need of the user's support	Human interface is needed in form filling.	No human interface is needed in form filling.	User monitors the filling process.	It doesn't require user's help.	Not mentioned.	It doesn't require user's help.	Users monitor the process.
Reflection of Web page changes	It doesn't reflect such a change	No concept involved for dealing with it.	It doesn't reflect such a change.	Such changes are not incorporated	It doesn't reflect such a change.	It keeps refreshing the repository for such changes.	It doesn't reflect such a change.
Automatic query selection	Such feature has not been incorporated	Nothing is mentioned about such a feature.	Query selection is automatic.	Nothing is mentioned about such a feature.	Automated query selection is done.	Nothing is mentioned about such feature.	Nothing is mentioned about such feature.
Accuracy of data fetched	Data fetched can be wrong if the Web pages change.	Data fetched can be wrong if the Web pages change.	Data fetched can be wrong if the Web pages change.	Data fetched can be wrong if the Webpages change.	Data fetched can be wrong if the Web pages change.	Data fetched can be wrong if the Webpages change.	Only correct data is obtained since repository is refreshed at regular time interval.
Database sampling	Such feature is not incorporated.	Such feature is not incorporated.	Such feature is not incorporated.	Such feature is not incorporated.	Large database is sampled into smaller units.	Such feature is not incorporated.	Such feature is not incorporated.
Focused crawling	Focused crawling is not involved although it is task specific.	Focused crawling is the basis of this work.	Nothing is mentioned about focused crawling.	Focused crawling is done.	Nothing is mentioned about such concept.	Nothing is mentioned about it.	Nothing is mentioned about it.

Agent for Authenticated Crawling Module

This module works when the information in a site is hidden behind the authentication form. It stores authentication credentials of every domain in its knowledge base situated at crawler, which is provided by the individual user. At the time of crawling, it automatically authenticates itself on the domain for crawling the hidden Web contents. The crawler extracts and store keywords from contents and makes it available to privatized search service to maintain the privacy issue.

Page Fetcher Module

Page fetcher fetches the pages from the http server and sends them to the page analyzer to check whether it is required appropriate page or not based on the topic of search and the kind of form, the page contains.

Table 3. Comparison of the various deep Web crawler architectures

Crawling Technique → Parameters ↓	A Framework of Deep Web Crawler	Google's Deep Web Crawl	Efficient Deep Web Crawling Using Reinforcement Learning	Crawling Deep Web Contents through Query Forms	Study of Deep Web Sources Classification Technology	A Task-Specific Approach for Crawling the Deep Web
Technique Used	Proposes a model of form with form submission facility with four additional modules with LVS table.	Input values for text search inputs are selected and identification of input for a particular type of values.	Based on reinforcement learning technique. Deep Web crawler works as agent and deep Web database plays a role of environment. Identify a query to be submitted using Q-value.	Minimum executable pattern (MEP) and based adaptive query technique.	Based on iterative self organizing data analysis (ISODATA) technique.	Task specific approach. A set of domain definition is provided to the crawler. Every domain definition defines a particular data collecting task. The deep Web crawler recognizes the relevant query forms by using domain definition.
Need of user's support	Human interaction is not needed for modeling the form.	Human interface is needed in form filling.	Human interaction is required	Need of user support.	No need of user support.	No need of user support.
Reflection of Web page change	No effect of Web page changes in the result.	There is effect of these changes in the result because it is based on the content of the pages.	There is effect of these changes in the result but changes may generate an error.	Yes	Yes	Yes
Automatic query selection	Yes	No	Yes	Yes	-	No
Accuracy of data fetched	Good	Data can be wrong if the Web pages change.	High	Average	-	Average.
Database sampling	No	Yes	Yes	Yes	-	Yes
Focused crawling	Yes	Yes	Yes	Yes	-	It is task based crawling.

Page Analyzer/Parser Module

The page analyzer/parser is used to parse the contents of the Web page. Texts and links are extracted. The extraction of links and text is done on the basis of the concept of page classifier. Form classifier link is used to filter the pages topic wise. It also filters out useless forms and identifies links that are likely to lead to pages that contain searchable form interfaces.

Figure 2. Architecture of proposed deep web crawler mechanism

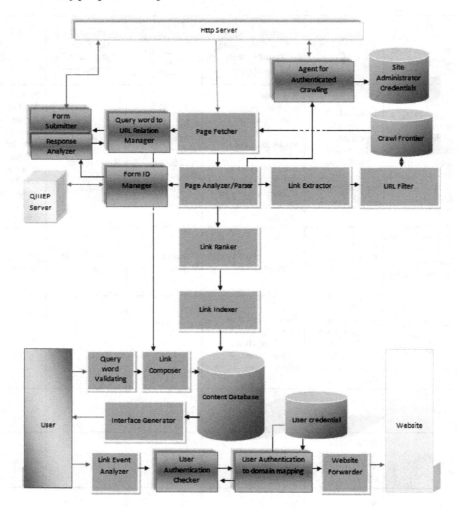

Form ID Generator

This module helps to implement QIIIEP (query intensive interface information extraction protocol) on current architecture of Website. It parses every form of that Web site and merge the form ID with QIIIEP server query word list so that at the time of crawler request the crawler, it identifies the search interface properly for sending the request of keywords to the QIIIEP server.

Form Submitter Module

After filling the form, the form submitter sends again the request to the HTTP server for the further retrieval. This module simply sends the filled form to the http server for further information.

Query Word to URL Relation Manager Module

This module generates meaningful queries to be issued to the query interface. It stores each and every query word associated with specific element of form by creating reference of domain path, so that at the time of link generation, query word can be mapped to provide the contents by sending query word in post request to the domain.

Crawl Frontier

Crawl Frontiers contains all the links which are yet to be fetched from the HTTP server or the links obtained after URL filter. It takes a seed URL to start the procedure and processes that page and retrieves all forms, and adds and rearranges them to the list of URLs. The list of those URLs is called crawl frontier.

Link Extractor Module

Link Extractor extracts the links or the hyper links from the text file for the further retrieval from the HTTP server. The extraction of links is done as per the link identified by the page analyzer/parser that is likely to lead to pages that contain searchable form interfaces in one or more steps. This dramatically reduces the quantity of pages for the crawler to crawl in deep Web. Fewer numbers of pages are needed to be crawled since it applies focused crawling along with searching the relevancy of obtained result to the topic and hence result in limited extraction of relevant links.

Query Intensive Interface Information Extraction Protocol (QIIIEP) Server

QIIIEP (Sharma & Sharma, 2009) is an application-level protocol for semantic otology based query word composition, identification and retrieval systems. It is based on request/response semantics. This specification defines the protocol referred to as QIIIEP 1.0.The QIIIEP server work on this protocol. QIIIEP (Query Intensive Interface Information Extraction Protocol) reduces complexity by using pre-information about the form and its elements from QIIIEP server. The knowledge base is either generated by auto query word extractor or it is provided by site administrator.

Link Ranker Module

This module is responsible for providing the best match query word assignment to the form filling process and reduce the over loading due to less relevant queries to the domain. It is required to rank the link accordingly so the more information is gathered from each link. This is based on link ranking algorithm.

Link Indexer Module

This module plays an important role in the indexing of the generated keywords to the content database. Indexer collects, parses, and stores data to facilitate fast and accurate information retrieval. It maps the keywords to URL for the fast access and retrieval.

Content Database Module

Content Data Base stores all the generated links or keywords in the Content Data Base. When user put any query into the user interface, the index is matched with the corresponding links and information is displayed to the user for further processing.

Searching Agent Module

It provides the searching interface through which user places the query. This involves the searching of keywords and other information stored in the content database which is actually stored in it after the whole process of authenticated crawling.

Link Composer Module

This module takes the reference from the Query word to URL Manager for the form submission.

Interface Generator Module

Interface generator is used to give the view of the contents stored in the content database after the search is completed. For example, the interface generator shows the list of relevant links indexed and ranked by link ranker module and link indexer module respectively.

Link Event Analyzer

Link event analyzer analyzes the link which is activated by the user so that it could forward the request to display the page on the requested URL.

User Authentication to Domain Mapping Module

This module of crawler is responsible for mapping the login credentials provided by users to the crawler with the information provider domain. The main benefit of using this mapper is to overcome the hindrance of information retrieval between result link and information. The crawler uses the mapping information to allow the specific person to receive information contents directly from the domain by automatic login procedure and eliminate the step of separate login for user.

Working Steps of Proposed Architecture for Deep Web Crawler Mechanism

The steps proposed are:

1. Crawler request to the Web server to fetch a page.
2. The second step has three parts:
   a. After the page is fetched it is being analyzed and parsed for the relevant contents (links and text).
   b. The page is sent to the query word to URL relation manager.

     c.   If the authentication of administrator credentials is required then the links are sent to the agent for authenticated crawling.

3.   After being analyzed by the page analyzer/parser, links are selected and filtered out.

4.   Filtered URLs sent to crawl frontier, which again chooses a link and sends it to the page fetcher.

5.   Now, crawler analyzes the form to identify the search interface. The form must include the form id.

6.   Then the form id is used to send the request to query word to the QIIIEP (query intensive interface information extraction protocol) server, where the extraction takes place to correlate the form fields.

7.   Now, the server replies to the crawler about each entry to that form.

8.   Crawler sends the filled form by placing the received query words to the HTTP server.

9.   Crawler crawl the contents generated by that query word.

10.   Finally fetched pages are ranked, indexed and stored in the search engines database.

User interacts with user interface through the following steps:

1.   User enters the query about search.

2.   The query words validation takes place and link composer fetches the link from the data base according to the query word.

3.   Now links are searched from the content database.

4.   The content is then provided to the user with the help of interface generator.

5.   The link, i.e. chosen by the user, diverts the user for user authentication through domain mapper so that the user can retrieve those authenticated contents without explicit login.

6.   Query word, submitted to URL relation manager use the post and get request to generate the specific page.

7.   The link opens the Website in a browser.

The algorithm for the simple Web crawler is given below:

Input initial URL = seed.

1.   Maintain a queue Q={u}.

2.   While(Q!=NULL).

3.   Pop a element from Q.(using FIFO).

4.   Process that URL and fetch all the relevant URL's.

5.   Assign an unique index for each page visited.

6.   For each relevant URL's fetched (URL1,URL2,URL3…..).

7.   If(URL1 is not indexed && URL1 does not belong to Q).

8.   Add URL1 to Q.

9.   end.

The algorithm for deep Web data extraction is given below:

1.   Extract Web page by using initial seed URL or crawl frontier.

2.   Analyze for contents and form.

3. Extract query URL from page and store in crawl frontier after applying filter.
4. If page content form.
5. Request query word for all the elements in form from QIIIEP server.
6. Submit and extract the deep Web contents.
7. Manage query word to URL relation.
8. Rank and index the page and store in content database.
9. Go to step 1.

The algorithm for search and result link generator is given below:

1. User input in the form of query.
2. If this is a valid query then goto step3.
3. Search the content database as follows:
    a. Efficient query is generated.
    b. Check the indexed words and the corresponding links.
    c. IF query words match then.

Select the appropriate links and go to step 4.
else:
goto interface generator & display keywords did not match & stop.

4. If found then Interface generator will display the results.
5. Link event analyzer will take user authentication to domain mapping if site want login.
6. If user's credential found authenticated on Website and open specific page by using query word to URL relation manager.

else:
Display login form of that Web site.

7. If Web site does not want login.
8. Just open the deep Web content by using query word to URL relation manager.

The code for parser, downloader and link repository module is given in Box 1.

Features of the Theoretically Justified Proposed Architecture

These features are given below:

1. This proposed architecture crawl the deep Web if the administrator of that site follows the framework of QIIIEP based on focused crawling.
2. It definitely removes the complex task of query interface identification and values allotment as the huge majority of deep Web query interfaces on the Web are html forms.
3. The program tries to classify deep Web query interface according to different users.
4. Dynamic discovery of deep Web sources are done according to the user's query.

Box 1. Link repository module

```
void Crawler_book_1() throws IOException,MalformedURLException
 {
        try
        {
      Class.forName("sun.jdbc.odbc.JdbcOdbcDriver");
      Connection con=DriverManager.getConnection("jdbc:odbc:Web");
      Statement stmt=con.createStatement();
      ResultSet rs=stmt.executeQuery("select id from book");
       while(rs.next())
       {
           count=Integer.parseInt(rs.getString(1));
       }
       try{
{
        urlc =new URL(seedurl);
       pageInput = new InputStreamReader(urlc.openStream());
        source = new BufferedReader(pageInput);
}
       }catch(NullPointerException e){}
while ((sourceLine = source.readLine()) != null)
       {
           content += sourceLine ;
       }
tag = Pattern.compile("href=\"(.*?)\"",Pattern.DOTALL);
        mtag = tag.matcher(content);
       while (mtag.find())
       {
           content = mtag.group(1);
           if(content.startsWith("http:"))
           {
               if(!(content.endsWith(".css")||content.endsWith(".xml")))
               {
                   // System.out.println(""+content);
                   dsp=""+content;
         ta.append(dsp+"\n");repaint();
                   if(!ar.contains(content))
                   {
                     ar.add(content);
                   }
               }
           }
       }
```

continued on following page

Box 1. Continued

```
            ai=ar.iterator();
            while(ai.hasNext())
            { content1=null;
                runner.sleep(100);
                System.out.println(ai.hasNext());
                 o=ai.next();
              urls=new URL(""+o);
              pageInput1 = new InputStreamReader(urls.openStream());
         ta.append(dsp+"\n");repaint();
                source1 = new BufferedReader(pageInput1);
         dsp="link";
         ta.append(dsp+"\n");repaint();
         while ((sourceLine = source1.readLine()) != null)
         {
            (!(content1.contains("under construction")||content1.contains("cannot
be displayed ")||content1.contains("not available")))
                 content1 += sourceLine ;
          }
         tag1= Pattern.compile("<form(.*?)</form>",Pattern.DOTALL);
         mtag1 = tag1.matcher(content1);
        dsp="The Forms Link Are:....."+mtag1.find();
         ta.append(dsp+"\n");repaint();
         while ((mtag1.find()))
         {
             content1 = mtag1.group(0);
             dsp=""+content1;
         ta.append(dsp+"\n");repaint();
             tag2= Pattern.compile("book",Pattern.DOTALL);
             mtag2 = tag2.matcher(content1);
             tag3= Pattern.compile("author",Pattern.DOTALL);
             mtag3 = tag3.matcher(content1);
              tag4= Pattern.compile("title",Pattern.DOTALL);
             mtag4 = tag4.matcher(content1);
              tag5= Pattern.compile("isbn",Pattern.DOTALL);
             mtag5 = tag5.matcher(content1);
            if(mtag2.find()||mtag3.find()||mtag4.find()||mtag5.find())
             {
                 dsp="Both r found";
         ta.append(dsp+"\n");repaint();
             tag6= Pattern.compile("action=\"(.*?)\"",Pattern.DOTALL);
             mtag6 = tag6.matcher(content1);
              System.out.println("tag6"+mtag6.find());
```

continued on following page

Box 1. Continued

```
        if(!(mtag6.group(1).contains("http")))
        {
            //System.out.println("www found");
            dsp="www found";
    ta.append(dsp+"\n");repaint();
            content1=mtag6.replaceAll("action="+o+mtag6.group(1));
        }
    try
    {
      count++;
      qry="insert into book values('"+count+"','"+o+"')";
            stmt.executeUpdate(qry);
```

5. Provide input i.e. auto of filling the form of search queries.
6. Auto form ID generation and auto query extraction modules are used by QIIIEP server to extend its knowledge.
7. Privatized search plus general domain search are the two features which are based on the overall protocol.
8. Authenticated crawling is provided for privatized search.
9. Forms are classified with various levels depending on the administrator.
10. Different domains will have their content links and indexes in different databases.
11. Implicit authentication takes place when registered user clicks on a link at domain site.
12. The final content page opened after link is clicked which was crawled by post or get request.
13. Only the meta data of private area is stored so there is no privacy issue for crawling authenticated private content.
14. There is a huge list of query word generated through cross-site user query submission module but the ranking algorithm choose most appropriate query word for specific query interface to reduce the bandwidth wastage.

Limitations of Existing Deep Web Crawlers Improved Through Proposed Architecture

Limitations that are improved by the proposed architecture follow:

1. Crawling is precise and the chances of missing of pages are less. As we are using multithreaded downloading techniques so multiple threads run simultaneously which eliminate the chances of page miss. URL filter module makes the crawling very precise, eliminating the duplicate links.
2. It involves multi-attribute database accessing.
3. Form verification can be done very easily with the help of our form manager which extracts different domains attribute accordingly.

4. The form filling can be done very precisely and the user needs not to fill the complete form.
5. Extraction method that is improved by query word extraction module.
6. Useless pages if crawled cannot affect the semantics.
7. Time and cost is less due to the use of multithreaded downloading technique and automatic form filling by the QIIIEP server.
8. Forms with searchable interfaces are provided directly to the users.
9. Web page forwarding technique that is used while forwarding by submitting the form has no chances of error at all. If the action part is not start with = "http://" then we have attached the relative link part to the Web site, so if any relative link comes then it is attached with the Web site and is forwarded to related page.

6. EXPERIMENTAL RESULTS

The experiment has conducted on a machine having Intel Core 2 Duo T5870 @ 2.0 GHz with 2 GB of RAM. This machine was running with Windows 7 OS. Tests are performed using WAMP server equipped with php v. 5.2.6 and mysql v. 5.0.51b., Microsoft Visual Basic 2008.net 3.5 and Net beans IDE. All of the tests were performed on Firefox 3.5.4. All tests were performed multiple times to minimize measurement errors. Results of the various modules are shown in Table 4.

Certain performance metric are defined and calculated to judge the overall performance of the deep Web crawler. Objectives of the performance metric are given below.

1. Analytical data based on the number of sites visited which reflects the reach of the crawler.
2. Assessment of the different forms which show the ratio of relevant forms processed.
3. Calculation of the performance ratio to check the overall efficiency of the deep Web crawler.

Performance Metrics are calculated as follows. The various performance criteria are taken to measure the overall efficiency of proposed deep Web crawler architecture and its results are as follows.

Table 4. Results of the various modules

Modules	Results
1. Page Fetcher	The downloaded html content
2. Page Analyzer	Selected pages which contain forms.
3. Form Id Manager	A list of Search Interfaces (forms).
4. QIIIEP SERVER	Provide query word to the forms wherever possible and give result to response analyzer.
5. Form Submitter	Send the filled form to the Http server.
6. Link Extractor	A list of extracted links those are relevant.
7. Link Ranker Module	A list of ranked links.
8. Link Composer Module	Composed list of links by using query word to URL relation manager.
9. Interface Generator	Shows the list of relevant links ranked by rank module & link indexer.
10.Link Filter	Fresh links are shown.

Deep Web crawler is implemented based on QIIIEP specification and the corresponding results are analyzed. Three different test domains are used to judge the precision of retrieved contents. Table 5 shows the form identification statistics and Table 6 shows the query words and content extraction statistic.

The graph shown in Figure 3 is plotted between received query words and successful content extraction at different domain. It can be concluded from the graph that contents extraction are close to query

Table 5. Form identification statistics

Domain	Query Forms	Context Identification
Auto	5	5
Book	8	8
Job	12	12

Table 6. Query words and content extraction statistics

Domain	Form ID	Query Words Received	Successful Content Extraction
Auto	55c64ad2fDd6a6ef4388b33c54123890	34	30
Book	eOcftfd062a28403d966261Obe421eOe	56	42
Job	67c76add7110dbe02Obb401a4672565f	131	96

Figure 3. Comparison of success with number of query words at different domain

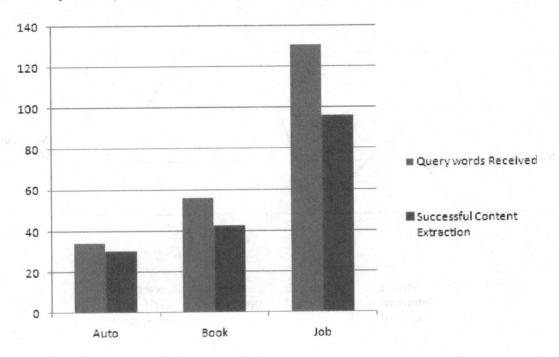

words received at a satisfactory level for all three domains. The successful content extraction means relevant page have more than five query words and minimum length of content is four hundred words.

Table 7 shows the default values for some of the parameters that are used for experiments.

As indicated in Table 7, the crawler encountered 41 forms during crawling of the 12 sites, of which 2 were ignored, because form id manager do not found any associated id corresponding to the sites.

Figure 4 shows the number of links generated for a particular query word search and the overall count of pages indexed with given query words.

The graph shows the number of pages in result for the specific query word. It depends upon the total number of crawled pages. For overall 1508 stored pages the results have good ratio.

Table 7. Parameters and values statistics

Parameter	Default Value
No. of sites visited	12
No. of links stored	1508
No. of forms encountered	41

Figure 4. Graph showing number of links generated for a particular query words search

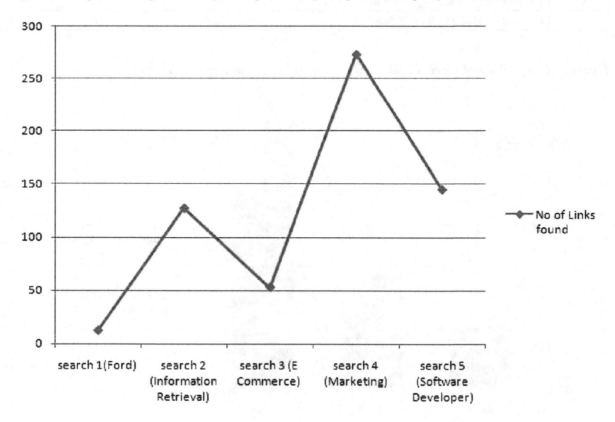

Harvest Ratio

To evaluate the performance of the proposed architecture, the "harvest ratio" is adopted as the performance metrics, which is the ratio of relevant Web pages downloaded among all the downloaded Web pages. Here relevant downloaded pages are those which have at least five times repeated query word in overall content. It is defined as follows:

HR= (RWPD/AWPD)*100

where HR= harvest ratio, RWPD= relevant Web pages downloaded and AWPD= all Web pages downloaded.

Table 8 depicts the domains and its relevant Web pages downloaded and all Web pages downloaded statistic.

The harvest ratio for different domain is shown in Table 9.

The result shows very good harvest ratio when considering a focused domain approach which reflects that proposed architecture is significantly improved compared to existing approach. Figures 5 and 6 show screen snapshots from the implementation of the hidden Web crawler system.

Summary of the Results of Proposed Architecture

The features of proposed architecture are improved from the features of the existing crawlers as proposed architecture deals with the overall strategy of hidden query interfaces including the features of both privatized search and general search for the deep Web data that is hidden html forms. Every solution is taken into consideration to make the crawler as efficient as possible including all the features of the existing Web crawlers. Proposed architecture tries to minimize the overall cost and time that are relevant to the deep Web searching. However at some points, time and space complexity are compromised with performance but overall results are as per expectation. Proposed architecture performs better compared to other existing crawlers as reflected from performance metric. For example, the performance of the proposed architecture is better and satisfactory with reference to number of links crawled. Cost of the

Table 8. Domains and statistics for the relevant Web pages downloaded and all Web pages downloaded

Domain	Job	Book	Auto
RWPD	629	377	93
AWPD	795	531	182

Table 9. Domains and harvest ratio statistics

Domain	Harvest Ratio
Job	79.11%
Book	77.99 %
Auto	51.09 %

Figure 5. Snapshot graphical user interface of hidden web crawler

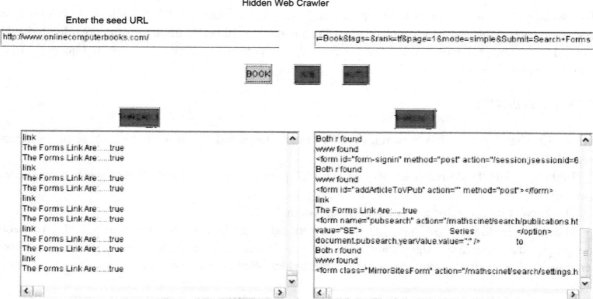

Figure 6. Snapshot of database for hidden web crawler

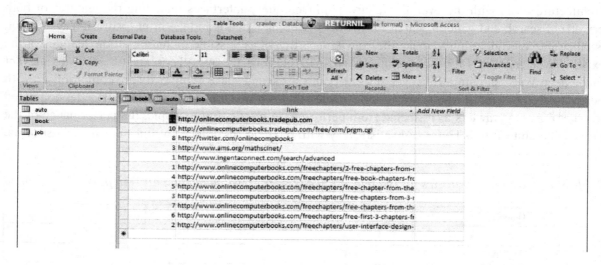

deep Web search also reduces through this crawler due to searching with domain specific formula. Initial seed set of links is such that the number of relevant search interfaces and forms are quite effective. Pre determination of the domain context provide effective results with more than 40% effective links with forms extraction on every loop while generating links for the databases. At last performance metric are calculated after the implementing and integrating all the modules and necessary modifications are done to improve the model.

7. CONCLUSION

Deep Web information has a very large volume compared to surface Web and the quantity of deep Web content depends upon underlying domain and crawling mechanism. Extraction of deep Web information can be highly fruitful for a general user or a specific user. Traditional Web crawlers have limitations in crawling the deep Web information so some of the Web crawlers are specially designed for crawling the deep Web information yet a very large amount of deep Web information is yet to be explored due to inefficient crawling of the deep Web. In literature survey, analysis of some of the important deep Web crawlers is done to find their advantages and limitations. A comparative analysis of deep Web crawlers is also done on the basis of various parameters and it is concluded that a new architecture for deep Web crawler is required for efficient searching of the deep Web information by minimizing the limitations of the existing deep Web crawlers as well as incorporating the strengths of the existing deep Web crawlers. The architecture should be compatible to crawl existing deep Web with nominal modification with ongoing infrastructure based on QIIIEP specification. A novel architecture for deep Web crawler is proposed which possesses the all the features of existing deep Web crawlers but tries to minimize limitations of existing deep Web crawlers. Experiments results reflect that it is efficient both for privatized as well as general search for the deep Web information, which is hidden behind the html forms. The proposed architecture is cost and time effective as search process depends on query interface crawling the contents with ranking of most appropriate keyword against the context of domain.

REFERENCES

Akilandeswari, J., & Gopalan, N. P. (2008). An Architectural Framework of a Crawler for Locating Deep Web Repositories Using Learning Multi-Agent Systems. In *Proceedings of the 2008 3rd International Conference on Internet & Web Applications and Services* (pp. 558-562).

Alvarez, M., Raposo, J., Cacheda, F., & Pan, A. (2006). *A Task-specific Approach for Crawling the Deep Web.* Retrieved from http://www.engineeringletters.com/issues_v13/issue_2/EL_13_2_19.pdf

Alvarez, M., Raposo, J., Pan, A., Cacheda, F., Bellas, F., & Carneiro, V. (2007). A Focused Crawler for Accessing Hidden Web Content. In *Proceedings of DEECS2007* (pp. 18–25). San Diego, CA: DeepBot.

Barbosa, L., & Freire, J. (2005). Searching for Hidden-Web Databases. In. *Proceedings of WebDB, 05*, 1–6.

Bergman, M. K. (2001). The Deep Web: Surfacing Hidden Value. *Journal of Electronic Publishing, 7*(1). Retrieved from http://www.press.umich.edu/jep/07-01/bergman.html. doi:10.3998/3336451.0007.104

He, B., Patel, M., Zhang, Z., & Chang, K. C. (2007). Accessing the deep Web. *Communications of the ACM, 50*(5), 94–101. doi:10.1145/1230819.1241670

Jiang, L., Wu, Z., Feng, Q., Liu, J., & Zheng, Q. (2010). Efficient Deep Web Crawling Using Reinforcement Learning. In Advances in Knowledge Discovery and Data Mining (LNCS 6118, pp. 428-439).

Liu, J., Wu, Z., Jiang, L., Zheng, Q., & Liu, X. (2009). Crawling Deep Web Content through Query Forms. In *Proceedings of the 5th International Conference on Web Information Systems and Technologies*, Lisbon, Portugal (pp. 634-642).

Lu, J., Wang, Y., Liang, J., Chen, J., & Liu, J. (2008). An Approach to Deep Web Crawling by Sampling. In *Proceedings of the IEEE/WIC/ACM Web Intelligence Conference*, Sydney, NSW, Australia (pp. 718-724).

Madaan, R., Dixit, A., Sharma, A. K., & Bhatia, K. K. (2010). A Framework for Incremental Hidden Web Crawler. *International Journal on Computer Science and Engineering*, 2(3), 753–758.

Madhavan, J., Ko, D., Kot, L., Ganapathy, V., Rasmussen, A., & Halevy, A. (2008). Google's Deep-Web Crawl. In. *Proceedings of VLDB, 2008*, 1241–1252.

Ntoulas, A., Zerfos, P., & Cho, J. (2005). Downloading Textual Hidden Web Content through Keyword Queries. In *Proceedings of JCDL* (pp. 101-109).

Peisu, X., Ke, T., & Qinzhen, H. (2008). A Framework of Deep Web Crawler. In *Proceedings of the 27th Chinese Control Conference*, Kunming, China.

Raghavan, S., & Garcia-Molina, H. (2001). Crawling the hidden Web. In *Proceedings of the 27th International Conference on Very Large Data Bases,* Rome, Italy.

Sharma, D. K., & Sharma, A. K. (2009). Query Intensive Interface Information Extraction Protocol for Deep Web. In *Proceedings of the IEEE International Conference on Intelligent Agent & Multi-Agent Systems* (pp. 1-5).

Sharma, D. K., & Sharma, A. K. (2010). Deep Web Information Retrieval Process: A Technical Survey. *International Journal of Information Technology and Web Engineering*, 5(1), 1–21. doi:10.4018/jitwe.2010010101

Wang, Y., Zuo, W., Peng, T., & He, F. (2008). Domain-Specific Deep Web Sources Discovery. In *Proceedings of the Fourth International Conference on Natural Computation*.

Zhao, H. (2010). Study of Deep Web Query Interface Determining Technology. In *Proceedings of CESCE 2010* (Vol. 1, pp. 546-548).

This work was previously published in the International Journal of Information Technology and Web Engineering (IJITWE), Volume 6, Issue 1, edited by Ghazi I. Alkhatib and Ernesto Damiani, pp. 25-48, copyright 2011 by IGI Publishing (an imprint of IGI Global).

Chapter 16
Search Engine:
A Backbone for Information Extraction in ICT Scenario

Dilip Kumar Sharma
Shobhit University, India

A. K. Sharma
YMCA University of Science and Technology, India

ABSTRACT

ICT plays a vital role in human development through information extraction and includes computer networks and telecommunication networks. One of the important modules of ICT is computer networks, which are the backbone of the World Wide Web (WWW). Search engines are computer programs that browse and extract information from the WWW in a systematic and automatic manner. This paper examines the three main components of search engines: Extractor, a web crawler which starts with a URL; Analyzer, an indexer that processes words on the web page and stores the resulting index in a database; and Interface Generator, a query handler that understands the need and preferences of the user. This paper concentrates on the information available on the surface web through general web pages and the hidden information behind the query interface, called deep web. This paper emphasizes the Extraction of relevant information to generate the preferred content for the user as the first result of his or her search query. This paper discusses the aspect of deep web with analysis of a few existing deep web search engines.

INTRODUCTION

Information and communication technology have tremendous potential for social impact, human development and improving the lives of people they serve Through ICT peoples are able to communicate in better way and can access relevant information. It also helps in developing collaborative and research skills. People can gain confidence and avail opportunities on their potential. Information and communication technology provides appropriate hardware, software and networking services to the search engine. To

DOI: 10.4018/978-1-5225-3163-0.ch016

find out relevant pages instantaneously from billions of web pages available on the internet is a complex task. So, information extraction in web scenario is must to provide the relevant search to the user at the very first instant. An effective search engine is the necessity of today's information era. Search engine is a software program that searches for web sites that exist on the World Wide Web. Search engines search through its personal databases of information in order to provide the relevant information. A web crawler is an automated program that starts with a set of URLs called seeds and stores all the URL links associated with downloaded web page in a table called crawl frontier. The extractor sends all these information attached to the textual raw data to the analyzer. The analyzer then takes the entire HTML code of the downloaded web page and analyzes the code, keeping the relevant data and rejecting the rest. Some composing techniques are applied to link containing the similar types of information from the database to generate the relevant query results. Information and communication technology can be related to information extraction in web context or in search engine in a variety of ways (Anderson & Weert, 2002; Kundu & Sarangi, 2004). Traditional web crawling techniques have been used to search the contents of the web that is reachable through the hyperlinks but they ignore the deep web contents which are hidden because there is no link is available for referring these deep web contents. The web contents which are accessible through hyperlinks are termed as surface web while the hidden contents hidden behind the html forms are termed as deep web. Deep web sources store their contents in searchable databases that produce results dynamically only in response to a direct request (Bergman, 2001) (Sharma & Sharma, 2011). Figure 1 shows the benefits of information extraction using ICT in human development in context of search engine.

ANALYSIS OF APPLICATION AREA OF ICT

Some of the area in which ICT plays a significant role in their development is analyzed below.

Figure 1. Benefits of information extraction using ICT in human development in context of search engine

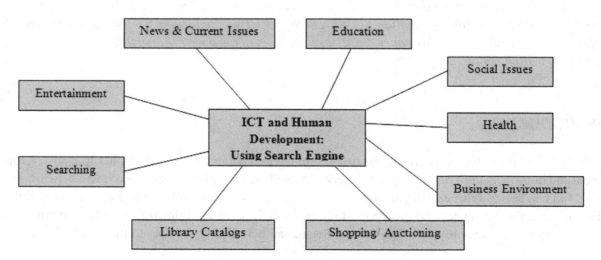

ICT in Education

In 1999 an analysis was done to find out the use of computer in schools. In that analysis it was found that a large number of students were sound enough to use the computers without taking help from school. The analysis also reveals that male and female students have different area of interest regarding the use of computer. A complete frame work can be divided into five modules.

Resource: It corresponds to a range of sources to access information.
Tutorial: It helps to acquire new knowledge along with feedback.
Exploration and Control: It investigates and provides the situations.
Support: It facilitates in communicating and providing the information to users.
Link: It facilities the interactive information exchange between individuals and groups.

Analysis of ICT evolution reveals that four specific approaches should be applied to adoption and use of ICT in educational organization. These four approaches are evolvement, application, hybridization and transformation (Hyper History, 2010; Anderson & Weert, 2002).

The deep web provides for a wide range of educational resources which varies from a student searching for an ideal school based on key personal requirements to an administrator looking for fund-raising resources. The key resources include directories and locators, general education resources, statistics resources etc.

ICT in Business

ICT is also useful in business environment. It underpins the achievement of current business and it offers government with a proficient communications. At the same time, ICT adds value to the processes of learning in the organization and management of learning institutions. The Internet is a driving force for large development and innovation in both developed and developing countries. The following competencies are gaining importance with reference to ICT:

- Decision-making
- Expert advice
- Control on dynamic situations
- Collaborative working
- Seamless communicating

Technological developments lead to changes in work and changes in the organization of work, and required competencies are therefore changing (Kundu & Sarangi, 2004).

ICT in Human Resource Development

ICT can be applied in rationalization and transformation of human resource development. ICT facilitates managers and employees to have direct accessibility to resources. Human resource development with ICT is termed as eHRDM. The public service commission (PSC) is an autonomous body for recruitment of human resource for government jobs. The Various steps in recruitment and selection process of PSC are to receive demands of human resource from government offices, verification of the given information, advertisement through media, receiving and sorting the applications, screening of applications, conduct pre-selection process, conduct interview process and final appointment.

Over the years, whole recruitment and selection process of PSC is in a typical paper based system. Recently, PSC has introduced the recruitment and selection database system which invites online job applications for the advertized jobs. The recruitment and selection (R&S) process developed by ICT personnel has objectives to find out the duplicity and redundancy in the R&S system, develop and maintain the system at par with the organization, which has successfully employed the ICT based R&S system, documentation of benchmark standard with recommendation, establishment of system implementation committee with technical personnel, implementation of the system, to conduct the workshops related to the system organization, formation of rollout process and establishment of monitoring and evaluation system.

Guidelines required for successful establishment of ICT based system for R&S are to establish LAN, MAN and WAN, procurement of leased line, increase the band width of system to facilitate the efficient data transmission. The requirements for system hardware and software for ICT based R&S system are to develop the system database server, backup server, windows based server and SQL based server, development of antivirus and firewall software, endorsement of physical access and control, connecting PCs website through World Wide Web, 24/7 browsing of advertisement by easy submission of online application and tracking of the job application (Wachira, 2010).

ICT in Social Issues

Planners, policy makers and researchers hold highly polarized and equivocal views on the diffusion of Information Communication and Technology (ICT). The role of search engine is significant in promoting objectives such as poverty alleviation, universal education, and reduction in mortality and health hazards, sustainable development and bridging the socio-economic divides in the world. It leads us with many online social work search that are providing number of free services to the social work and related professions.

ICT in Job Information

ICT can be used in job information extraction. It can therefore enhance human development. User can utilize a search engine for extracting job related data hidden behind the search forms and can identify the job according to their requirement. This makes the job searching easier and thereby increasing the number of online job seeker and net users. Therefore, it is beneficial for both common people and Internet service providers. It helps us to provide the different and desired web pages related desired year of job and attaining the job according to their demand.

ICT in Shopping and Auctioning

ICT can also be useful in terms of web context in online shopping and online bidding. There are various shopping and auction sites such as amazon.com, ebay.com etc. that utilize the concept of ICT to support human development. User is required to enter the prerequisites on the website form and submit it online. The search engine then produces the list of items related to the user's query. It helps us in determining the current market trends by leading us to give the idea about the price raised and price fall for the smooth flow of business.

ICT in Database Related Information Extraction

Information from the database can also be extracted with the help of Web crawler that uses ICT. Tremendous amount of data remain hidden behind the database which can be explored using various programs which illustrates the use of ICT in database information extraction.

ICT in E Commerce/Banking

ICT plays a vital role in e commerce as well as e banking that has a better transparent system in which users can trade efficiently and can participate globally. Security is prime concern in this matter and requires further improvement. It helps to provide many E commerce development solutions to give the company many supports that are needed to run the day to day business (Kumar & Sareen, 2009).

ICT and Environment

The impact of ICT on environment has made tremendous changes like paperless offices and global society for environmental protection. ICT companies are working more upon green technologies and promoting biodiversity and preservation to reduce the impact of their own activities. It helps in optimizing many of the environmental health safety jobs and to use this employment by various workers.

In spite of the high-quality and authoritative information it provides, Deep web offers some excellent resources focusing on entertainment that are as useful as its serious counterparts. These entertainment resources such as movies, music, amusements, live performances, and other activities people do mostly for fun and pleasure.

ICT in Health

ICT has increased the access to information and has therefore increased the effectiveness of health care services by promoting the expansion of health and social services. It provides many links related to the health field showing numerous numbers of diseases and their related researches as well as their therapies concerned to it. The deep web avails a vast amount of authoritative information, offered by reputed health care organizations. Unlike the surface web resources that can even mislead the users, the deep web resources promises to provide the exceptionally high quality information on diseases, medical procedures, pharmaceutical drugs, nutrition, clinical trials, or other healthcare related issues.

Figure 2. Distribution of web sites on content types (Bergman, 2001)

Content Types	Topic Databases	General Search	Messaging / Chatting	Jobs Search	Calculators	White / Yellow Pages	Library	Portals	Classified	Shopping	Publications	Internal Sites
Percentage	54%	1%	1%	1%	2%	2%	2%	3%	5%	5%	11%	13%

ICT in E Government

The use of ICT in governance is increasing to deliver its services to the citizens at the location of their connivance in an efficient and transparent manner. Electronic governance is the application of ICT. Through the ICT, government can exchange information and services, communicate transactions between Government and citizen (G2C), Government and business (G2B). Therefore, being a service provider, Government should motivate their employees for delivering services through ICT (Sharma et al., 2007). Governments today are putting more and more information on the every day. Most of the portals to government information are covered by the surface web materials. The outstanding government Deep Web resources provide for sites that offer "general" type of information, directly from government entities themselves. These resources are useful for searcher who relies solely on the general purpose search engine.

ICT in Other Fields

ICT can be used in online messaging and chatting. In general, web portals, classifieds, publications etc. use ICT. All of these areas use the concept of Information extraction based on form values. The Deep Web delivers many resources that meet all the important criteria required by the people who conduct legal research on the web by providing the correct, authoritative, and easy to access material in a timely manner. Real-time information is probably the "purest" type of Deep Web data, and it's not likely that general-purpose search engines will ever in their indices. Real-time information is almost always stored in databases that are constantly updated in real or near-real time. In some cases, such as stock quotes or airline flight arrival information, each update obliterates the previous data record. Even if a search engine could somehow crawl and index this information, it would be like isolating a single frame from a feature length movie. In other cases, real-time data is preserved, but the key point is that it is archived data in raw form, which a searcher cannot easily manipulate.

Figure 2 shows the distribution of websites based on content type. In order to utilize the full potential of web, there is a need to concentrate on web content so that it can prove to be a great source of information i.e., information extraction should be done in the context of web which leads to utilization of Information Communication and Technology.

Deep web information are useful in education, business environment, human resources development, social issues, job information, shopping, in e-commerce/banking, database related information extraction, health, e-government, and other field such as messaging & chatting because the database can publish the result through direct query. Deep web sites post their result as dynamic web pages in real–time. These dynamic web pages have a distinct uniform resource locator address that permits them to be recovered again later. But in surface web pages, web pages are static and linked to other pages. Static pages do not have a unique URL address and therefore are not allowed to access information again later. Deep web sites also tend to improve the quality of search because it does not provides a long list of hits instead a right list. It means, it provides relevant information for each query. Through Deep web sites users can choose authoritative sites, but it is advisory to be careful about the selection of searchable sites. Users can make their own determination about the quality.

SEARCH ENGINE: A BACKBONE FOR INFORMATION VISUALIZATION

Search engine is a tool to gain information to the search of a specific collection; this may be a library, the internet, or have a personal collection. Search engine plays a vital role in extraction of information from World Wide Web. A search engine consists of web crawler whose function is to download web pages from the internet and store them into the database? The list of URLs is stored in the database queue, from where a scheduler selects URLs. These URLs are then downloaded by a multi-threaded downloader. Once downloaded, the text and meta data is stored in the database storage.

Need of Search Engine

The size of the World Wide Web is drastically increasing. Therefore, it is necessary to find out the required information in lesser time. Web crawlers are used to take all the links from the visited pages by the search engine and indexing is done in order to arrange them according to their preferences. Crawlers are used to carry out the maintenance by checking the links and HTML code. It is used to test web pages and links for valid syntax and structure. A Search engine should be able to search the information in World Wide Web in different formats from different sources. Search engine combines all the modules required for a particular application. Examples are online discovery, compliance of financial regulatory services, pharmaceutical research, counter measure for terrorisms sells prediction and customer support etc.

Working of the Search Engine

Figure 3 shows the working of a typical search engine. A crawler uses the HTTP network protocol in order to browse the internet which allows it to download or upload data from and to it. The crawler browses this URL and downloads the associated web page. It then looks for hyperlinks in the downloaded page. The URLs attached to these hyperlinks are then added to the queue. First of all, the crawler crawls over the http server through the search engine in which the crawl frontier, contains the links to be crawled. After the Links are extracted, they are parsed for further processing. After indexing, all the links are saved into the Content Database after applying ranking on them. Whenever the user enters the query in the search engine, it first checks the link from the Content Database and shows the corresponding results to the user. After that user does the event on the given link, the corresponding to which relevant pages are shown to the user from the web. A search engine consist of three major modules i.e. extractor, analyzer and indexer and interface generator (Brin & Page, 1998). Algorithm of these modules is given below.

Extractor

The Extractor is a Page Fetcher which fetches the web pages from the internet. A link extractor takes out a web address from a server reply to play it back as well as the dynamic parameters of the web address (Craven, 2003; Kaplan, Iida, & Tokunaga, 2009). The algorithm of the extractor is as follows:

- Extract the URL from the crawl frontier table which has not been parsed till now.
- Send HTTP GET request for that particular URL to the server.
- Download the URL's related page for further parsing procedure.

Figure 3. Working of a typical search engine

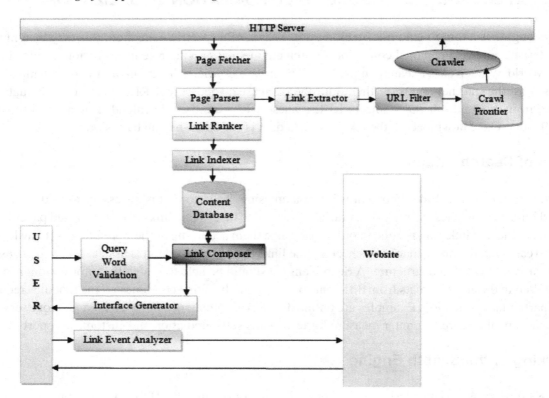

- Call the analyzer module to parse this URL.
- Repeat the steps from step1 until all the URL of crawl frontier are been parsed.

Analyzer and Indexer

Analyzer is an indexer that processes words of the web page and stores the resulting index in a database. The algorithm of the analyzer is as follows:

- Receive the downloaded URL's HTML code string.
- Check for internal links, and if present, convert them into external links.
- For each external hyperlink present in the HTML code, do:
- Extract the URL attached to the hyperlink if not already present in the crawl frontier table else skip.
- If this URL is unwanted (.gif,.jpg,.css,.xml,.doc,.pdf,.mp3 etc), then skip.
- Else, insert this URL in the crawl frontier table.
- Extract other information attached to the downloaded web page from its HTML string, like title, meta description etc.
- If two of the strings are same then decide their precedence on the basis of HTTPs labelled.
- Save all this information in the data table in the database.

- For each search word in the array, do:
- Search the number of occurrences of the word in the database table data.
- Arrange the search results in decreasing order of number of 'hits'.
- Stop

Utility of Search Engine

These algorithms describe the procedure about how the URLs are been parsed and fetched from the web and how actually the crawler works by getting collected with all of the URLs from the web. They also describe the way the parsing should be done after fetching the HTML page related to that corresponding URL. Since the crawler is intended for getting the information depending upon the query fired, so these algorithms also describes that how query is processed and the related information to that of the query is displayed to the user. The main part of search engine is web crawler which is used for collecting and storing the information in database.

Interface Generator

Interface generator is a query handler that understands the need and preferences of the user.
   The algorithm for the composer is as follows:

- The query that is to be searched is been entered.
- The query is been filtered by stemming process by removing white space, special characters, symbols etc from the user's search query.
- If search query is empty, then return, else continue.
- Break the search query into individual search words and store them into an array.
- Club together the search results of individual search words and again arrange them.
- Display the results on the output screen for the user.
- Stop.

TYPES OF WEB CRAWLERS

The following are the general types of web crawlers.

Simple Crawler

Developed by Brian Pinkerton in 1994, is a, single-process information crawler which was initially made for his desktop. Later, it was extended on to the internet. It had a simple structure, and hence had limitations of being slow and having limited efficiency.

Parallel Crawler

Initially given by Junghoo Cho in 2002, this approach relied on parallelizing the crawling process, which was done by multi-threading. It had faster downloading and was less time consuming but required more bandwidth and computational power for parallel processing. It parallelizes the crawling process and uses the multithreading that reduces the downloading time. For example, Google Bot employs parallel, single-threaded processes (Yadav, Sharma, & Gupta, 2008).

Focused Web Crawler

This concept was given by Manczer in 1998, refined by Soumen et al. (1999). They focused on specific topics and get the relevant result. They are also called as topical crawler. They do not carry out the unnecessary task by downloading all the information from the web instead it download only the relevant one associated with those of the predefined topics and ignores the rest. This is advantageous for time saving factor. They are limited in its field. Examples: Healthline, Codase etc.(Chakrabarti, Berg, & Dom, 1999).

Distributed Web Crawler

Distributed web crawling is a distributed computing technique whereby Internet search engines employ many computers to index the Internet via web crawling. It uses distributed computing and reduces the overload on server. It also divides the works into different sub servers. Their main focus is on distributing the computational resources and the bandwidth to the different computers and the networks. Examples: YaCy: P2P web search engine with distributed crawling (Boldi, Codenott, Santini, & Vigna, 2004).

Deep Web Crawler

ICT provides various tools and one among them is deep web or web wrappers. But to have an access on these tools developer requires deep knowledge as web wrappers are site specific solutions that have dependencies with web structure and also, web a wrapper requires constant maintenance in order to support new changes on the web sites they are accessing. The deep web / hidden web refer to World Wide Web content that is not part of the surface Web, which is not indexed by surface web search engines. In Deep web, Pages are not indexed by search engine. It mainly requires registration and signing up. Example- Yahoo Subscriptions, LexiBot etc (Sharma & Sharma, 2010; Bergman, 2001). Table 1 shows a summary of the different types of web crawlers.

Issue of Network Interoperability in ICT

ICT is built upon numerous computers and telecom networks. For efficient communication on a global basis, all networks should be compatible to each other or some type of interface should be provided between networks. The main reasons to cope up with inter platform and architecture compatibility that enables the seamless information extraction. So research should be done in the direction of network cooperation and international standards should be made that can facilitate the cooperation among the diverse platforms (Acevedo, 2009).

Table 2 (Bergman, 2001) illustrates that Deep web searching would be useful for development work because it create dynamic content, response to a direct query and gave relevant information for market and all other domain. It more secure for professional contents, Government reports, strategy statements, research/sell reports, operational papers.

Table 1. Summary of different types of web crawlers

Name	Description	Advantage	Limitation
Simple crawler	Single process information, iteratively download the web pages and follow the breadth first traversal.	Simple structure, indexing process is straight forward.	Slow and limited efficiency.
Parallel crawler	Process is parallelized and indexing is done through identifying a keyword to make the search more relevant.	Faster downloading, less time consumption.	More bandwidth, more computational power.
Focused Web crawler	Downloaded web pages related to predefined topic or domain.	Relevant downloading, provide relevant results, reduces number of retrieving pages thereby regulating the visiting pages and analyses is more deep so as to define high quality pages.	Limited in field. Pre decided resource extraction.
Distributed Web crawler	Distributed computing technique and interact in peer to peer fashion.	Reduces overload on server, division of work in sub servers.	More computational power. Complex to manage.
Hidden/Deep crawler	Dynamic generation of web pages.	Access huge amount of online data.	More resource and processing needed

Table 2. Surface web vs. deep web

Surface Web	Deep Web
1. Surface web page is static and linked to other pages. 2. They are not narrower with deeper content. 3. Total quality content of the Surface web is less. 4. Surface web is not relevant for every information need and for others domain. 5. The surface web does not publish the result through direct query. As search engines look through links, they are unable to access certain type of web pages These pages never enter the system and, therefore, are never indexed. 6. Surface web make static HTML pages that are less likely to be from professional content suppliers. 7. The Surface Web, crawled by popular search engines running today, contains only a fraction of the overall unstructured content available on-line today. 8. The surface web is the "general web" and is what one can find using general web search engines. It is also what one see in almost all subject directories.	1. Deep web page is dynamic content served up in real time from a database in response to a direct query. 2. Deep Web sites ought to be narrower with deeper content. 3. Total quality content of the Deep Web is thousand times much greater than Surface web. 4. Deep Web content is highly pertinent to every information need and other domain. 5. The Deep Web search is the content that resides in searchable databases, the results from which can only be discovered by a direct query. Without this direct query, one would not be able to reach the results. 6. Professional contents suppliers typically have the kind of database-based sites that are more secure in deep web. 7. The Deep Web contains all the "unknown or hidden", unstructured content that the surface web failed to provide to its users. 8. The Deep web is the "hidden web" and is what one cannot find using the normal search engine for this they need the Deep web crawlers to get the information fetched.

ANALYSIS OF SOME OF IMPORTANT DEEP WEB SEARCH ENGINES

Complete Planet (www.completeplanet.com)

Complete Planet is an invisible web portal with fast service, relevant results and an easy to use interface. Complete Planet searches over more than 7000 database and search engines. Complete planet's advanced search is pretty standard. It provides the option to search by title, keyword, description, date etc. Every database is extremely alert in character. While surfing the web, user can click on the links that are provided by the search engine, to reach the individual high value databases. It is easy to use, simple and broadens the search.

IncyWincy (www.incywincy.com)

IncyWincy is an invisible Web search engine and it behaves as a meta-search engine by tapping into other search engines and filtering the results by searching the web, directory, forms, and images. It discovers search engines when spidering the web. It features a unique search engine relevancy algorithm. It provides user listings, premium keyword purchase, and custom website spidering. Information may change quickly and become unavailable or may become the part of the visible web.

Scirus (www.scirus.com)

It contains the latest search engine technology and searches over 410 million- specific web pages that enable the user to quickly pinpoint the scientific, scholarly, technical and medical data on the web. It has a wide range of special features to help to get the scientific information which are needed. It can find specific conference, abstracts and patents. It helps to refine, customize and save the searches. Scirus is a search engine mainly made for science subjects. It concentrates simply on pages containing technical content.

DeepDyve (www.deepdyve.com)

DeepDyve is the largest online rental service for scientific, technical and medical research with over 30 million articles from thousands of authoritative journals. It makes research easy and affordable. It can copy entire sentences, paragraphs and even complete articles against the specific query. It also finds related information for every article by clicking the "More like this" button on search result page. Their search is not restricted to keywords or literals. It can search by simply pasting the whole of the article into the search bar. Some of the articles in the DeepDyve are "open access" and are marked as "free" for any user to read.

Biznar (www.biznar.com)

Biznar is a free, publicly available deep web search engine that uses advanced "federated search technology" to return high quality results against the search query in real time. It accelerates search by returning the most relevant results from over 60 authoritative business collections to one easily navigable page. It is very effective search engine created especially for those professional businesses that need to get access to specific information for their works. This system is a federated search which means that by using this tool one can look the information not from only one source but from many databases at the same time (Price & Sherman, 2001; Basu, 2010).

COMPARATIVE ANALYSIS OF DIFFERENT SEARCH ENGINES

After analyzing the different types of search engines, it is concluded that surface web search engine results in large number of surface web results, whereas deep web search engine extracts the hidden web data. Table 3 and Table 4 shows query words versus results counts for surface web search engines and deep web search engines respectively.

Figure 4 and Figure 5 reflects the graph between the results obtained against query words for the different search engines.

Deep web search engines shows small number of results as they are not so efficient as compared to surface web search engines due to less advancement in the field of deep web search.

Table 3. Query words vs. Results counts for surface web search engines

Query words	Surface Web Search Engine			
	Google Search	**Yahoo Search**	**Bing Search**	**AOL Search**
Mobile computing	9,980,000	311,000,000	11,00,000	12,400,000
Electronic commerce	8,400,000	2,290,000	3,85,00,000	9,350,000
Digital signal processing	9,850,000	1,590,000	31,00,000	1,370,000
Compiler	15,200,000	965,000	1,68,00,000	4,820,000
Soft computing	3,110,000	1,510,000	1,39,00,000	2,690,000
Medical	465,000,000	57,100,000	38,60,00,000	136,000,000
Research	708,000,000	88,800,000	50,40,00,000	273,000,000
Numerology	38,20,000	7,190,000	31,70,000	1,380,000

Table 4. Query words vs. results counts for deep web search engines

Query words	Deep Web Search Engine				
	Scirus	**deepdyve**	**biznar**	**IncyWincy**	**complete planet.com**
Mobile computing	1,794,169	4,232,459	2,781	114,154	177
Electronic commerce	1,096,216	3,446,266	2,969	1,18,746	238
Digital signal processing	18,88,306	7,953,655	1,446	46,248	73
Compiler	18,88,306	2,261,880	1,523	1,09,087	85
Soft computing	5,95,501	39,72,039	1,496	20,206	33
Medical	32,669	37,71,574	3,400	39,15,116	4,767
Research	9,55,84,523	44,19,671	3,495	53,21,514	5,000
Numerology	16,233	211,515,718	933	15,018	40

Figure 4. Variations of results counts vs. query words for surface web search engines

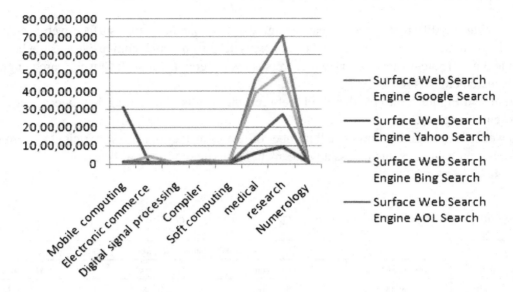

Figure 5. Variations of results counts vs. query words for deep web search engines

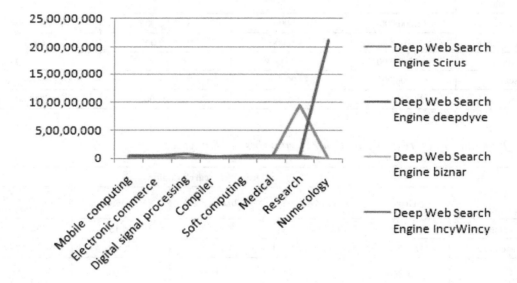

CONCLUSION

This paper highlights the role of information extraction in human development. Information extraction is facilitated by ICT. Search engine plays a vital role in information extraction from World Wide Web. An important module of the search engine is a web crawler. Web crawler can result in desired information extraction from www. A lot of important information is hidden behind the deep web. Normal web crawlers are not capable of effective crawling of the deep web. For effective crawling of the deep web, a specialized web crawler is required, which is known as deep web crawler. Finally, this paper also presents the analysis of some of the important deep web crawlers to find out their role in the information extraction from www. One of the two important areas of application of ICT i.e. education and human resource development are discussed in details. ICT can be applied in the education field very effectively. Educational organizations are the main contributors in the field ICT revolution. Use of ICT brings out the new teaching methods with the use of new gadgets. ICT becomes the common source of information in present knowledge age. ICT enables the commons users to access the relevant information at one click at their home. ICT improves the resource functioning of human resource development management practice by making the system cost effective by minimizing the cost by providing the resources to the people without a traditional paper work system. ICT makes information omnipresent without the limitations of time, place and availability. ICT minimizes the cost of the system by providing the information to various users from one source in less time. Using ICT human's resource development service can be improved by redefining the responsibilities of the employees through a improved strategic orientation of human resource development.

ACKNOWLEDGMENT

All the companies/products/services names are used for identification purposes.

REFERENCES

Acevedo, M. (2009). Network cooperation: Development cooperation in the network society. *International Journal of Information Communication Technologies and Human Development, 1*(1). doi:10.4018/jicthd.2009010101

Anderson, J., & Weert, T. V. (Eds.). (2002). *Information and communication technology in education.* Paris, France: UNESCO.

Basu, S. (2010). *Search engines to explore the invisible Web.* Retrieved from http://www.makeuseof.com/tag/10-search-engines-explore-deep-invisible-web/

Bergman, M. K. (2001). The deep web: Surfacing hidden value. *Journal of Electronic Publishing, 7*(1). doi:10.3998/3336451.0007.104

Boldi, P., Codenott, B., Santini, M., & Vigna, S. (2004). UbiCrawler: A scalable fully distributed web crawler. *Software, Practice & Experience, 34*(8), 721–726. doi:10.1002/spe.587

Brin, S., & Page, L. (1998, April 14-18). The anatomy of a large-scale hyper textual web search engine. In *Proceedings of the Seventh International World-Wide Web Conference*, Brisbane, Australia.

Chakrabarti, S., Berg, M., & Dom, B. (1999). Focused crawling: A new approach to topic-specific web resource discovery. In *Proceedings of the Eighth International Conference on World Wide Web* (pp. 1623-1640).

Craven, T. C. (2003). Html tags as extractor cues for web page. *Journal of Information Science, 6*, 1–12.

Hyper History. (2010). *History education and information communication technologies (ICT)*. Retrieved from www.hyperhistory.org/images/assets/pdf/ict.pdf

Kaplan, D., Iida, R., & Tokunaga, T. (2009). Automatic extraction of citation contexts for research paper summarization: a co reference-chain based approach. In *Proceedings of the Workshop on Text and Citation Analysis for Scholarly Digital Libraries* (pp. 88-95).

Kumar, M., & Sareen, M. (2009). Building trust in e-commerce through web interface. *International Journal of Information Communication Technologies and Human Development*, *1*(1). doi:10.4018/jicthd.2009092205

Kundu, A., & Sarangi, N. (2004). *ICT and human development: Towards building a composite index for Asia*. Amsterdam, The Netherlands: Elsevier.

Price, G., & Sherman, C. (2001). *The invisible web: Uncovering information sources search engines can't see*. Medford, NJ: CyberAge Books.

Sharma, D. K., & Sharma, A. K. (2010). Deep Web information retrieval process: A technical survey. *International Journal of Information Technology and Web Engineering*, *5*(1), 1–21. doi:10.4018/jitwe.2010010101

Sharma, D. K., & Sharma, A. K. (2011). A Novel Architecture for Deep Web Crawler. *International Journal of Information Technology and Web Engineering*, *6*(1), 25–48. doi:. doi:10.4018/jitwe.2011010103

Sharma, D. K., Varshneya, G., & Upadhyay, A. K. (2007). AJAX in development of web-based architecture for implementation of e-governance. *International Journal of Electronic Government Research*, *3*(3), 40–53. doi:10.4018/jegr.2007070103

Wachira, F. N. (2010). *Improving the management of human resources in the public service through application of information and communication technologies (ICTs)*. Paper presented at the APSHRMnet Workshop, Cotonou, Benin.

Yadav, D., Sharma, A. K., & Gupta, J. P. (2008). Parallel crawler architecture and web page change detection techniques. *WSEAS Transactions on Computers*, *7*(7), 929–941.

This work was previously published in the International Journal of Information Communication Technologies and Human Development, Volume 3, Issue 2, edited by Susheel Chhabra and Hakikur Rahman, pp. 38-51, copyright 2011 by IGI Publishing (an imprint of IGI Global).

Index

A

Activism 317
Al Qaeda 18-19, 22, 24-28, 31
ambivalent sexism 1, 4-6, 9-11
analyzer 68-70, 319, 321, 342-343, 345-346, 359-360, 365-366
anonymity 3, 29, 44, 51-52, 58, 248, 256-257, 262, 287-288, 293, 295, 297, 299, 309, 311
Anonymous 25, 52, 248, 253, 256-257, 261, 290-302, 305-306, 308-311, 313, 317

B

Backstop 287
botnet 55, 62

C

claimed responsibility 22, 28
Client Side Hidden Web 112
content mining 230, 232, 240, 253, 260, 287
coordinated attacks 24-25, 31-32
Crackers 52, 54-55, 57-58, 62, 317
crawler 65-68, 70, 72-77, 79-81, 85, 88, 100, 103, 105, 108-109, 129-130, 232, 319-322, 325-326, 330, 334-340, 342, 344-347, 352-357, 359-360, 363, 365, 367-368, 372-373
crawling systems 84, 109, 112
cyberbullying 38, 40-41, 45-46, 49
cybercrime 51-58
Cybernetics 288
cyber-physical confluence 255, 283-284, 288
Cyberpsychological 49

D

Dark Triad 1, 4-6, 9-11
Data Crawl 263, 288

E

eLearning 37-40, 46, 48, 50
electronic profiling 255-256, 283-284
encryption 22, 29, 248, 257, 283, 288
End-User Development 197
extractor 71, 73, 202, 207-208, 210, 213-214, 220, 345, 359-360, 365

F

Fraud analysis 244, 249, 253
Frequency Calculator 321

G

geolocation 265, 271, 288
Global Web 84-85, 87, 99, 105-106, 112

D (column 2)

data extraction 125, 127-129, 175-176, 183, 191, 194, 199-213, 216, 219-222, 226, 228, 237, 253, 270-271, 280-281, 283, 285, 347
DDoS Attacks 62
Deep/Hidden/Invisible Web, Deep Net, Undernet 65-68, 73, 79-81, 85-87, 102, 104-105, 109, 112, 114-120, 123-127, 129-131, 133, 138, 143, 175-180, 185-186, 191, 194-195, 197-199, 202, 211, 213, 219, 221, 237-238, 247-248, 253, 255, 285, 288, 319-322, 330, 334-340, 342, 344-347, 351-353, 356-357, 359-361, 363-364, 368-373
Demeanor 38, 50
digital technologies 18, 20, 26-27, 29, 293
DOM tree 89, 188, 200, 207, 210-211, 219, 221, 226
Domain Specific Hidden Web Crawler (DSHWC) 319, 321-322, 330
domain term analyzer 319
Doxing 261, 288
Doxing Attack 288
Dumpster Diving 57, 63

GSP algorithm 241, 253

H

hacker 30, 52-58, 317
Hashtag 265, 267, 288
Hidden Data 84, 112
hidden web crawler 65-68, 73, 81, 319-322, 330, 336, 339, 355-356
Homeland Security 27, 31
Hyper Text Markup Language 200, 226

I

I2P 248, 253
ICT 359-364, 368, 372-373
indexing 70, 80, 99, 114-115, 117, 219, 319-323, 330, 339, 345, 365
Inference Exposure 288
information retrieval 114, 116, 127-128, 179, 202, 216, 226, 228, 230, 345-346
Information Science 138-139, 141-142
intellectual property 138-139, 142-143, 166, 175
Interface Generator 346, 348, 359, 365, 367

L

literature review 53-54, 66, 322

M

Macro 288
Maltego Radium™ 255, 267, 270-271, 273-274, 278, 280, 288-289
mashup 192-194, 198-199, 213
Massive Open Online Course (MOOC) 288

N

Narrowcasting 27, 288
network analysis 245, 258-260, 285
Network Footprint 288
Network Overview 255, 263, 271
networking sites 20, 288
NodeXL™ 255, 263, 271

O

OAI-PMH 128
ODeL 38-40, 46, 48, 50
online disinhibition 45-47, 50

online presence 23-24, 26, 30, 298
ontology 70, 115, 121-122, 124, 131
Open-Source Intelligence (OSINT) 255, 288
Optimal Query Generation 65
Overfitting a Model 288

P

Page Rank 240, 253
patent 141-142, 144-171
Personally Identifiable Information (PII) 261, 281-282, 288
pledged allegiance 30-31
political communication 20, 26
potential recruits 20, 27
precision 92, 120, 216-217, 226, 235, 242, 278, 319, 321, 353
problematique 37, 39-40, 43, 45-48, 50
proclivity 1, 4-5, 7-12
produsers 175-176, 179-180, 194-195, 198
Profiling 255-256, 283-284, 288, 328-329
pseudonymity 257, 288
public health 138-141, 171

Q

QIIIEP 334, 340, 344-345, 353, 357
query ranking 80

R

random ranking 65, 75-76, 78-79
Ransomware 57, 63
recall 120, 216-217, 226, 242, 302
repository 65-66, 70, 73, 75, 84, 117, 121, 176, 199, 216, 219, 321-322, 330, 339, 348
reserve 243-244, 257, 288
Resilience 226
response analysis 65, 67, 124, 133
revenge porn 1-5, 7-12

S

sadism 1, 4-11
schema mapping 119-120, 131
search engines 70, 84-87, 89, 92, 97-99, 101, 108-109, 112, 127-133, 175-178, 182, 195, 197-198, 202, 204, 211, 230-231, 233-234, 237, 247-248, 253, 261, 263, 288, 319-320, 334, 359-360, 364, 368-372
Server Side Hidden Web 102, 112

Server-Side Template 208, 226
social media 3-4, 6, 18-19, 22-25, 27-32, 42, 212, 245, 259, 263, 265, 285, 288, 291, 293-294, 306
Social Media Platform 288
social network 42, 212, 244-245, 258-263, 271, 273, 285, 288
Social Network Analysis (SNA) 245, 258-260, 285
Sociotechnical System (STS) 289
Sousveillance 281, 289
Spanish Web 85, 112
SRU 127
Structure Mining 230, 235, 240, 259, 289
subordinate influential factors 39, 43-47, 50
superordinate influential factors 39, 43, 45-47, 50
Supervised 207-208, 226, 237
surface web 65, 114-115, 126, 130-132, 176-177, 198, 202, 285, 288-289, 319, 334-335, 357, 359-360, 363-364, 368, 371-372

T

terrorist groups 18-19, 23, 29
terrorist organizations 18, 21, 23-28
Traceability 257, 289
traditional media 23, 25-28
Triàngulation 289

U

Underfitting a Model 289
unique identifier 177, 194, 289
Unlinkability 257, 289
unsupervised 68, 206-208, 210, 226, 237
Use Case 194, 289

V

Vendetta 299-300, 304-306, 309, 317

W

web 2.0 139, 205, 212, 219
Web characterization 86
Web Content Mining 230, 240, 253
Web crawlers 65, 86, 114-115, 126, 176-177, 230, 237, 246, 330, 334-335, 340, 351, 355, 357, 365, 367-368, 372-373
Web Log 236, 242, 321
Web source 177, 179, 198
Web Wrapper 207, 209, 226
Weighted Page Content Rank Algorithm (WPCR) 240, 253
wolf attacks 20-21, 23
wrapper 179-180, 198, 207-209, 211, 213-214, 219, 226, 368
www 2, 38, 65-66, 84, 86, 182, 199-200, 221, 226, 256, 263-266, 280, 284-285, 288, 291-292, 300, 306, 309-313, 319, 359, 369-370, 372-373

X

XGMML 239, 253

Z

Z39.50 127-128

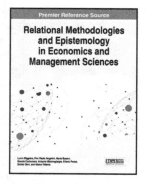

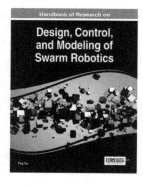

Stay Current on the Latest Emerging Research Developments

Become an IGI Global Reviewer for Authored Book Projects

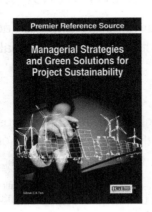

The overall success of an authored book project is dependent on quality and timely reviews.

In this competitive age of scholarly publishing, constructive and timely feedback significantly decreases the turnaround time of manuscripts from submission to acceptance, allowing the publication and discovery of progressive research at a much more expeditious rate. Several IGI Global authored book projects are currently seeking highly qualified experts in the field to fill vacancies on their respective editorial review boards:

Applications may be sent to:
development@igi-global.com

Applicants must have a doctorate (or an equivalent degree) as well as publishing and reviewing experience. Reviewers are asked to write reviews in a timely, collegial, and constructive manner. All reviewers will begin their role on an ad-hoc basis for a period of one year, and upon successful completion of this term can be considered for full editorial review board status, with the potential for a subsequent promotion to Associate Editor.

If you have a colleague that may be interested in this opportunity, we encourage you to share this information with them.

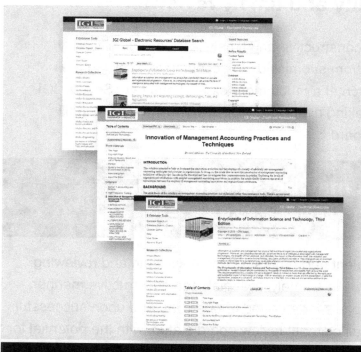

Printed in the United States
By Bookmasters